Our Blessed Rebel Queen

Contemporary Approaches to Film and Media Series

A complete listing of the books in this series can
be found online at wsupress.wayne.edu.

GENERAL EDITOR

Barry Keith Grant
Brock University

Our Blessed Rebel Queen

Essays on Carrie Fisher and Princess Leia

Edited by Linda Mizejewski
and Tanya D. Zuk

WAYNE STATE UNIVERSITY PRESS
DETROIT

ISBN (paperback): 978-0-8143-4686-0
ISBN (hardcover): 978-0-8143-4685-3
ISBN (ebook): 978-0-8143-4687-7

Library of Congress Control Number: 2021935718

On cover: *Our Heavenly Mother*, illustration by Lindsay van Ekelenburg
(www.lindsayvanek.com). Cover design by Brad Norr.

Wayne State University Press rests on Waawiyaataanong, also referred to as Detroit, the
ancestral and contemporary homeland of the Three Fires Confederacy. These sovereign
lands were granted by the Ojibwe, Odawa, Potawatomi, and Wyandot nations, in
1807, through the Treaty of Detroit. Wayne State University Press affirms Indigenous
sovereignty and honors all tribes with a connection to Detroit. With our Native
neighbors, the press works to advance educational equity and promote a better future
for the earth and all people.

Wayne State University Press
Leonard N. Simons Building
4809 Woodward Avenue
Detroit, Michigan 48201-1309

Visit us online at wsupress.wayne.edu

This anthology is dedicated to the memory of
Carrie Fisher in all her guises: writer, mental health advocate,
comedian, feminist activist, Princess Leia, and Space Mom.

It is also dedicated to the fans and community her presence
inspired to keep fighting to flip off the world another day.

Contents

Illustrations

Acknowledgments

The editors are deeply grateful to the people and institutions that supported and enabled this anthology. We're most of all thankful to the essay writers for their brilliance, enthusiasm, and commitment to the extra labor involved in an interdisciplinary project. They responded to our many requests and directions with unfailing good humor, and their astute insights about Carrie Fisher/Princess Leia drive this collection.

We are also much indebted to the thorough and generous external readers who made invaluable suggestions about each of the essays and deserve credit for many improvements in the final stages of the manuscript.

One of the highlights of this project has been our good fortune to work with artist Lindsay van Ekelenburg, whose widely circulated fan-tribute drawing, *Blessed Rebel Queen*, is the source of our book title and appears in our introduction. Elaborating on the same theme, Van Ekelenburg designed *Our Heavenly Queen* as our cover illustration. We're deeply grateful for her ability to capture our vision for this anthology.

We're also grateful to the Galactic Fempire and Bun Squad fan groups for their support of this anthology through inspiration, images, and enthusiasm for *Star Wars*, feminism, and friendship. We especially want to acknowledge *Looking for Leia* creator Annalise Ophelian, whose work complements that of this collection and who supported this anthology through the use of images and materials.

We thank the staff of the online media commons project *In Media Res*, which hosted a Carrie Fisher theme week in 2017. Tanya's contribution to that project became the seed of this anthology. That seed of an idea further developed at the annual Society for Media and Cinema Studies conference in 2018, which hosted a Carrie Fisher panel whose participants coalesced into an anthology team over lunch.

At Wayne State University Press, Marie Sweetman embraced our project from the beginning and propelled it forward, offering good advice and careful attention to detail. We're thankful to Marie and her team for their help and guidance on many levels. We're also grateful to be part of the Contemporary

Approaches to Film and Media series and for the support of series editor Barry Grant.

Funding from the College of Arts and Sciences of the Ohio State University covered research and artwork costs, and we much appreciate this institutional assistance. We extend our thanks to Professor and Chair Shannon Winnubst and to Lynaya Elliott of the Department of Women's, Gender, and Sexuality Department for their facilitation of this funding and for their excitement about this project. We also thank Maghan Jackson at Ohio State for her excellent work as our research assistant.

Tanya would also like to thank Dr. Lisa Armistead, associate provost for graduate programs at Georgia State University. The support of the university during Tanya's year as a provost fellow has allowed her to take on editing this anthology while working on her dissertation full-time. The freedom to pursue writing and research has been and will always be invaluable.

Linda extends a special thank you to friends and colleagues for their empathy, humor, and moral support throughout this project. Her thanks also goes to her sisters and brothers, who continue the family tradition of unqualified support for whatever projects any of us takes on. And at home, George Bauman made it possible to live and write during the pandemic with sanity and humor.

Finally, Tanya is extraordinarily grateful for her family, friends, and collegiate community in their support of this project and her. Their support and compassion in stressful days is much appreciated. She would like to thank her students, who dealt with delayed grades and her general absent-mindedness, especially as deadlines grew near. Of course, at the end of the day, Tanya must thank her wife, Thia Zuk, who always seems to know when to bring the glitter to make the dark days a little brighter, just like Carrie.

Carrie On

An Introduction

Linda Mizejewski and Tanya D. Zuk

> I *liked* being Princess Leia. Or Princess Leia's being me. Over time I thought we'd melded into one. I don't think you could think of Leia without my lurking in that thought somewhere. And I'm not talking masturbation. So Princess Leia are us.
>
> Carrie Fisher, *The Princess Diarist*

The death of Leia Organa in *Star Wars Episode IX: The Rise of Skywalker* (2019) was an emotional farewell not just for the beloved character but also for Carrie Fisher, the star who had embodied her for more than forty years. The double meaning of Leia's death was all the more moving because the film was released on December 20, a week before the third anniversary of Fisher's death by cardiac arrest on December 27, 2016. Leia's peaceful death scene—a self-sacrifice that channeled all her strength to the redemption of her errant son—provided fans of both Leia and Fisher with a touching closure. Although the character was widely known as Princess Leia, she had been promoted in the final *Star Wars* films to General Organa, military and spiritual leader of the resistance forces against the evil empire. And Leia's final act of heroism takes place within a film that powerfully vindicates the feminism of both the character and the actress. The closing shots reveal that the title refers not to Luke, the series' putative hero, but to the fearless heroine Rey (Daisy Ridley), who identifies herself as the triumphant youngest Skywalker.

Fisher's uncanny appearance in *The Rise of Skywalker* three years after her death was possible through the use of outtake footage from *Star Wars*

Episode VII: The Force Awakens (2015). This virtual performance of a "real" but constructed Carrie Fisher encapsulates how she and the character had "melded into one," as she says in *The Princess Diarist*. Later in that memoir she asks, "What would I be if I weren't Princess Leia?"[1] It's not a rhetorical question. Few stars are so closely conjoined to a singular film or television character, not even stars who have created an iconic role. Harrison Ford will forever be Leia's *Star Wars* compatriot Han Solo, but he is as much Indiana Jones and multiple other adventure and action heroes as well. The same is true of Jennifer Lawrence's Katniss Everdeen, Audrey Hepburn's Holly Golightly, or Julie Andrews's Mary Poppins. These characters are identified as specific stars, but these stars have multiple other fictional identities. Carrie Fisher, though, thrives in the popular imagination exclusively as Princess Leia, and this anthology embraces, amplifies, and challenges this phenomenon by not only exploring her *Star Wars* iconicity but also her writing, her comedy, and her mental health advocacy. In answer to her question, "What would I be?," we offer Fisher's many voices, performances, and personas, all of which merit our attention as cultural scholars and fans. And while this anthology focuses on Fisher's stardom rather than her *Star Wars* character Leia, the essays often engage with the multiple interfaces between Fisher's most famous character and her other creative work.

After Fisher's death in 2016, the editors of this anthology were among those who felt personally touched by her loss. We are from two generations of feminists and Fisher fans. Linda Mizejewski was in graduate school aligning herself with nascent feminist literary scholarship when the first film in the series, *Star Wars Episode IV: A New Hope*, appeared in 1977, shocking her with a smart-aleck heroine whose story was neither rom-com nor melodrama—the stories that had generated Hollywood's strongest female characters until then. She and Fisher grew into middle age together, so Linda richly appreciated Fisher's wry midlife perspectives on Princess Leia in the memoirs Fisher began publishing in 2008. By that time, Linda had moved into feminist media and comedy studies, making Fisher's comic writing and performances especially exciting for in-depth study. In contrast, Tanya Zuk was born into a world in which Princess Leia and other feminist action heroines already ruled. As a very young *Star Wars* fan, she had the childhood nickname of Ewok after the creatures she resembled from *Star Wars Episode VI: Return of the Jedi* (1983). She lost touch with *Star Wars* during the prequel years, and it was Carrie Fisher's autobiographical work that brought her back to the fandom. As an academic focused on fan/reception studies and self-representation, she found Fisher's first memoir, *Wishful Drinking* (2008), especially compelling because Carrie expounds on her relationship with her fans as well as with Leia and the *Star Wars* franchise.

The feminist perspective of this anthology honors Fisher's lifelong politics and her star image as cinema's first blockbuster action heroine. She marched for the Equal Rights Amendment in the 1980s and spoke on behalf of women's causes in interviews throughout her life. Fisher's biographer Sheila Welland comments that "if second-wave feminism had a science-fiction stand-in, it was the Princess Leia created by Carrie Fisher," and she dedicates her biography to feminists "everywhere" as well as to all those struggling with mental illness—that is, to the two causes with which Fisher was most associated.[2] In the topics covered in this anthology, we likewise acknowledge these strands of Fisher's activism as important elements of her stardom.

Feminist media scholarship has had surprisingly little to say about Carrie Fisher's stardom, even though the enormity of public mourning for her death said volumes about her cultural significance. In fact, with a few notable exceptions, there has been little academic work focused on Fisher or Leia prior to and since her death.[3] We see this anthology as an early foray into animated conversations that will continue to bring together scholars and fans. Covering key aspects of Carrie Fisher's work, celebrity, and cultural impact, these essays represent a variety of academic fields and methodologies, demonstrating that Fisher's impact is felt in disciplines as far afield as film studies, sociology, comedy studies, celebrity studies, marketing research, health communication, and fan studies. The work gathered here interrogates issues around Carrie Fisher's work as writer, performer, and advocate as well as her impact on audiences, culture, and industry.

This anthology also represents the shift in stardom studies from a focus on the production of stars to a focus on star interactions with fans and technologies. For decades, stardom studies has been influenced by Richard Dyer's theory of the star as a cluster of images and discourses produced by star texts and performances as well as by promotion and publicity materials, reviews, and popular journalism. Although Dyer also explored the interaction of the star image with fan communities, he posited fan interactions as secondary to the industrial machineries constructing the star image, which in turn both reflected and created cultural ideologies and fantasies. Andrew

Kemp-Wilcox's essay in this anthology argues that Dyer's star methodology is a "top-down model of signification" that better explains stars of the Hollywood studio era, such as Fisher's mother Debbie Reynolds, than a star like Fisher who is thoroughly enmeshed in interactive communities and technologies. Most of the essays in this collection focus on these interfaces: the conflicting claims made by fans, consumers, and industrial producers of Fisher's Princess Leia image, and the impact of Fisher's image and persona on feminist politics and mental-health advocacy.

Our anthology title, *Our Blessed Rebel Queen*, and the cover art represent this focus on fan interaction, too. *Blessed Rebel Queen* is the title of a watercolor drawing by Canadian artist Lindsay van Ekelenburg, which went viral in 2017 after she posted it as a tribute piece on her Facebook page: a mash-up of Madonna-and-Child religious imagery, art nouveau organic style, and fan knowledge about Fisher's persona and private life, encapsulated by her irreverent middle-finger salute and her fugly, beloved dog Gary.[4] This representation also honors Fisher's feminist fan base by depicting her as a middle-aged spiritual icon, revered rather than glamorized. In Van Ekelenburg's commentary on this piece, included as Appendix 1 of this anthology, she writes about the inspirational impact of Fisher as a star who spoke candidly about her mental illness, which is the theme of the final two essays in this anthology and a major factor in Fisher's fandom. *Blessed Rebel Queen* is a personally meaningful icon, Van Ekelenburg remarks, because it shows Fisher "flipping the bird as a reminder to my demons that they are not in control and they can shut up and take a back seat." The artist carries this sentiment and imagery into *Our Heavenly Mother*, the watercolor she created for this book's cover art.

In addition, this anthology reflects the growing convergence of stardom studies and celebrity studies. At one time, the difference between "star" and "celebrity" was a distinction between performers made famous in film and performers made famous by television, the latter deemed a less prestigious venue partially because its performers were considered more accessible and "ordinary." While stars were famous for their extraordinary talent in acting roles, celebrities were famous for their everyday lives. But the tension between "ordinary" and "extraordinary" has long fueled the dynamics of stardom, and the star/celebrity distinction has been further eroded by the multiple media and industrial platforms that make contemporary stars accessible.[5] Fans of Carrie Fisher had access to an "everyday" star through

Fig. 1.1. *Blessed Rebel Queen* by Lindsay van Ekelenburg was a viral sensation in 2017 when it was created and shared as a tribute to Carrie Fisher.

her Twitter postings, talk-show chats, and appearances at Comic Con, but fans could also have Fisher in their own everyday lives through her Princess Leia image in *Star Wars* merchandise—an image she legally signed away to George Lucas at the age of nineteen, well before anyone could have guessed its commercial value or ideological and emotional charge.

Rebel in a Family of Stars

Carrie Fisher's stardom is exceptional not only because her acting career was bound up with a single fictional character but also because of the mythic nature of her family background and her defiance of that legacy. Brought up in the very heart of the Hollywood studio system, she was neither glamorous nor tried to be. She was brilliant, a writing prodigy in love with language and gifted at comedy. And unlike female stars who are bullied by tabloid stories of their failures and addictions, Fisher took charge of her own narrative, writing it as both fiction and memoir. She was renowned for her wit and humor, so we can hear her droll comments in talk-show clips and in interviews describing her unique personal saga. We also have access to extraordinary film footage of Fisher in the documentary *Bright Lights: A Different Kind of Hollywood Love Story* (2016), released just before her death, which includes film clips from her younger days and also from the last years of her life, showing a middle-aged woman without her makeup, plodding around her funky home sneaking Coca-Colas against the advice of her worried assistants, light years away from princess-hood.

Carrie Fisher's public life began on covers of movie magazines when she was a toddler, first as a prop for the perfect Hollywood family and then for its dramatic breakup. Her mother, Debbie Reynolds, had become an overnight sensation at the age of nineteen in *Singin' in the Rain* (1952), exactly as Fisher would do at almost the same age in *Star Wars* twenty-five years later. The popularity of the name "Debbie" peaked in the mid-1950s when a generation of white parents was bedazzled by Reynolds's wholesome charm. After Reynolds married popular crooner Eddie Fisher in 1955, MGM manufactured and sold them as America's Sweethearts. As Carrie Fisher puts it, they were the "Brad Pitt and Jennifer Aniston of the late '50s, only slightly more so—because they actually managed to procreate."[6] She was born in 1956, and her brother Todd was born two years later. But the idyllic family image was destroyed by a scandal that remains one of Hollywood's most

salacious stories. In 1959 Eddie Fisher left his family for the recently widowed Elizabeth Taylor, who was the 1950s quintessence of sultry sex appeal.
The tabloids glorified every sordid, melodramatic detail—a married young
singer seduced by a fabulous femme fatale, leaving America's girl next door
abandoned with two small children.

In her memoirs and in interviews, Fisher describes being raised in
the spotlight by a larger-than-life movie-star mother and growing up in a
house with a projection room for MGM screenings. The house-party guests
included Hollywood's A-list, which, through marriages and divorces over
the decades, became her own extended family. In *Wishful Drinking*, Fisher
locates herself by drawing a celebrity family tree that includes some of the
twentieth century's most iconic pop-culture figures, from Debbie Reynolds
to Paul Simon to Richard Burton as well as someone identified simply as
"Miss Louisiana." Fisher presents the chart as a joke about being the product of "Hollywood inbreeding" and about figuring out if her daughter's
relationship to Elizabeth Taylor's grandson would be incestuous.[7] But it's
also startling visual evidence of how deeply Carrie Fisher was embedded in
mainstream Hollywood culture.

Fisher often commented about her alienation from this glamorous culture and her refuge in books and writing. When she was eleven, she started
copying lines from Somerset Maugham's *Of Human Bondage* into her diary.
"My family called me 'the bookworm' and they didn't say it in a nice way," she
told a journalist. "I fell in love with words." She felt especially keenly her difference from her ebullient, picture-perfect mother: "I'm different [from her]
in a lot of ways. I was always very bookish, sort of an intellectual. I thought too
much, and I was way too hard on myself."[8] Nor was it only her mother who
embodied the female-star ideal. Her stepmother, after all, was the sex symbol
Elizabeth Taylor. Fisher tells us that as a very young girl, she realized that she
wasn't going to be glamorous and she'd better be smart and funny instead.[9]
You can glimpse this dynamic in a touching scene in *Bright Lights* that shows
Fisher taking care of her father in the last months of his life. At eighty-two, the
famous crooner can barely speak and can't hear well either. He once swallowed
his hearing aids, Fisher tells us in voice-over, because he mistook them for his
morning pills, so "we had to shout into his stomach and ass." Fisher comments
that becoming his parent, taking care of him, was a way to connect and to
reconcile after his years of neglect. "Was I always funny?" she asks him. "I
used to be funny for you because I thought if I was really funny you'd want to

be around me all the time." He nods and whispers yes, she was always funny. "I wanted to be your best girl," she says. "I think I'm funnier than Elizabeth Taylor. Anyway, that's always been a goal."

This is both absurdly comical—a life goal of being funnier than Elizabeth Taylor—and heartbreaking. At the same time, it's a defiant mode of identification with the funny voice that competes against the fabulous image. In her first novel, *Postcards from the Edge* (1987), Fisher describes her alter ego as someone who "identified herself in her voice. She was as close as she ever got to being whoever she was when she was talking. . . . She wasn't what she looked like, she was what she sounded like."[10] This assertion flies in the face of celebrity culture, where what a woman looks like *is* her primary identification and also her narrative, her casting possibilities, her likelihood of being the heroine of the story. So "funnier than Elizabeth Taylor" isn't a one-liner but a rewrite, a scenario in which voice triumphs over image. Fisher's voice is her superpower in all her manifestations, beginning with Princess Leia. We first heard and loved that low-pitched, brazen voice talking back to Darth Vader in the first *Star Wars* and camping up her lines to Jabba the Hutt in *Return of the Jedi*. Later we heard her snappy comebacks in comedy films and in dozens of television guest-star roles. Fisher's comic voice and keen wit also animate her four novels, three memoirs, two screenplays, and the many Hollywood scripts for which she wrote lines. And in her later years, she also became a powerful voice on behalf of the treatment of mental illness.

Carrie Fisher had a lovely singing voice, too, which figures in her entrance into show business. She refused her mother's entreaties, when she was young, to get professional training, part of her decades-long resistance to being movie-star Debbie Reynolds's movie-star daughter. The *Bright Lights* documentary includes several scenes in which we hear Carrie sing, including a scene from one of her mother's cabaret acts when Fisher was a miserable teenager, dutifully performing and then slouching shyly off stage. She suffered severe stage fright throughout her lifetime, her brother Todd reports, so that even after decades of successful performances, she went into a panic before going onstage, "always so frightened that she wouldn't be as funny or as powerful a singer or as charismatic as she was sure audiences expected her to be," though once she was onstage, "her terror would transform into pure joy."[11] Fisher's stage fright suggests that the cliché "born entertainer" is too glib to describe her, but she was the daughter of singers and performers, and the background noise of her entire life was the sound of films and stage shows being planned, made, discussed, reviewed, panned, celebrated. As a teenager, Fisher was coerced into her mother's nightclub acts and the 1973 Broadway revival of *Irene* in which her mother starred, but by the time she was seventeen, she went into film auditions entirely of her own volition. She won a small part as a promiscuous teenager in the comedy *Shampoo* (1975) and afterward got professional training at the Central School of Speech and Drama in London for eighteen months, dropping out when she got the part in *Star Wars* that transformed her narrative from rebellious star-of-the-child to a princess leading a rebellion.

Icon and Image

"George Lucas ruined my life. And I mean that in the nicest possible way," Fisher remarked about being cast as Leia in the first *Star Wars* film and continuing her role in *The Empire Strikes Back* (1980) and *The Return of the Jedi*.[12] Her accounts of her Lucasfilm experiences range from comic absurdity to feminist outrage and poignant confessional. The story she repeated most often on talk shows and in interviews was Lucas's deadpan instruction to her, while making the first film, that she couldn't wear a bra under her white Leia princess dress because, he said, "there's no underwear in space." Fisher reports that he said this "like he had been to space and looked around and he didn't see any bras or panties or briefs anywhere." Lucas later told her, again in all seriousness, that weightlessness would cause her body to expand so that tight clothing like a bra would be fatally constrictive. "Now I think that this would make a fantastic obit," Fisher comments in *Wishful Drinking*, "so I tell my younger friends that no matter how I go, I want it reported that I drowned in moonlight, strangled by my own bra."[13]

This commentary captures Fisher's gift for funny, lyrical writing and her use of humor to resist casual Hollywood sexism and expose its absurdities. Along the same lines, Fisher reports she was sent to a "fat farm" where she failed to lose the ten pounds Lucas had demanded for *Star Wars*, though by *Return of the Jedi*, she was metallic-bikini-ready for the notorious scene in which she's held captive by Jabba the Hutt.

This iconic image is one of the most problematic moments in the *Star Wars* franchise: the enslaved Leia, in chains and wearing a gold bikini, perches in front of Jabba the Hutt, an extraordinarily large, wormlike alien who has captured and sexually desires her. Fisher often joked about meeting middle-aged men decades later who confessed that as adolescents, they spent time with this image of her daily. Unlike the widely circulated poster image, the film scene itself restores Leia's agency with gratifying feminist vengeance. Leia slips out of Jabba's control and chokes him with the chain that had held her in place; her face contorts with effort, his tongue lolls out of his mouth, Jabba groans in death agony, and Leia groans in triumph and relief. She uses the trappings of sexist oppression—Jabba's own chain—to free herself and redeem her character with self-determination and strength. But there's no denying that the captive-in-bikini poster image is more widely known than the ensuing scene of revenge and escape.

Carrie Fisher was outspoken about the misogyny of the gold bikini and the slave motif of this scene. Note that Jabba and George Lucas are ambiguously positioned as objects of her revenge wish in a 2016 interview on NPR's *Fresh Air*:

> It wasn't my choice. When [director George Lucas] showed me the outfit, I thought he was kidding, and it made me very nervous. . . . What redeems it is I get to kill him [Jabba], which was so enjoyable. . . . I really relished that because I hated wearing that outfit and sitting there rigid straight, and I couldn't wait to kill him.[14]

The infamous slave costume also figured largely in Fisher's advice to younger costar Daisy Ridley, who plays the heroine Rey in *The Force Awakens*. In a joint interview with Ridley for *Interview Magazine*, Fisher told her: "You should fight for your outfit. Don't be a slave like I was. You keep fighting against that slave outfit."[15] The fight she references is the battle against the male gaze in Hollywood cinema, a concept that Laura Mulvey named in 1975, just two years before the first *Star Wars* appeared. The influence of second-wave feminism showed up not only in film criticism around that time but also in the cinematic depiction of action heroines, first with Pam Grier's Blaxploitation films and then with Princess Leia and Sigourney Weaver's Ripley (*Alien*, 1978). Mulvey's critique remains robust despite its limitations regarding race and sexualities because it pinpoints the ongoing power dynamic in which women function as decor, fetish object, or prize within male narratives.[16] Leia's battle with Jabba serves as a metaphor for that ongoing struggle.

The power of Leia's image is evident in feminist fan movements that have taken up Fisher's protests about the bikini and rechristened the "slave outfit" as the "Hutt-killer" or "Hutt-slayer" costume, arguing that the only proper use of the outfit is to kill the patriarchy. Fan groups like Galactic Fempire, an all-women Facebook community, have created patches, pins, and T-shirts around Leia as Hutt Killer, and Women's Marches have featured papier-mâché Jabbas with their tongues lolling out. At the 2017 Women's Marches, Hutt-Killer Leia killed Trump-Jabba in protest posters that photoshopped Jabba wearing President Donald Trump's toupee or his trademark MAGA (Make America Great Again) cap that had become a symbol of antifeminist sentiment through its inference that in a better time, women and minorities knew their place.

Another strand of Leia feminism comes from cosplay or costume play at fan conventions, like the gender-bent or gender-flipped couple cosplay of Leia and Han, where men dress as Prince Leia and women dress as Lady Han.[17] However, the Bearded Leia movement, which began in 2014 by Julz a.k.a. "BeardedLeia," crossplaying (crossdressing + cosplay) Leia in the "hutt-killer" outfit with a full beard is the most well known. The fan movement around Bearded Leias, particularly Hutt-Killer Leias, is attached to political activism around issues such as gender disparity and sexual consent. Activist movements associated with the Bearded Leias are "Cosplay for All," and "Cosplay Is Not Consent," which focus on educating convention-goers about respecting boundaries within the convention space, particularly in regards to photography, costuming, touching, and sexual assault at these events.[18] Emma Pett has observed that crossplay is a political act that "for some extends beyond the performative, becoming a subversive act that challenges heteronormative forms of sexual harassment within the public sphere."[19] Feminist fans believe Fisher would approve of this movement, given her political leanings and her adversarial relationship with Leia's costuming. As Leia she brought feminists hope, and as the "Hutt Slayer" she brought us a focus for rebellion.

The appeal of Fisher's Princess Leia for the marginalized is eloquently demonstrated in Annalise Ophelian's 2019 docuseries *Looking for Leia* (YouTube), a tribute to the women and nonbinary fans who find in the *Star Wars* saga a way to project and express their racial and queer identities. Given the relative lack of diversity in the first decades of the saga, cultural critic Tracy Deonn explains in *Looking for Leia* that these fans enter a fictional world and reimagine it, she says, "finding a crack in the story and getting themselves into it like water, and then like ice [they] expand, and then live in that world." Bárbara Lazcano, a nonprofit development director, speaks of the impact Leia had when she was a child in Mexico and saw a heroine she could emulate. "I could be part of a group of people fighting for social justice," she says, "which is what I saw in Leia, growing up." Many of the fans in the documentary engage in cosplay, so the film abounds in dynamic images of Leia embodied by older women, large women, queers, and women of all races. Puerto Rican photographer Rhynna Santos works to create some of these images. "How is it to love something that you don't see your-self in?" she asks, and explains that she captures images of women of color in Princess Leia costumes as a way to see her heroine through her own eyes.

Fisher clearly understood the galvanizing power of Leia's image. In the last decade of her life, she began the practice of "anointing," "baptizing," or "knighting" fans at conventions with handfuls of glitter as an expression of affection. Many fans have written blog posts and tweets about being "glitter-bombed" this way. Amy Ratcliffe, author of the blog *Geek with Curves*, recounts her experience in line for an autograph:

> I watched Carrie Fisher apply gold eyeliner and glitter to several peo-ple. She told one lady she was drawing a hawk on her forehead and Carrie serenaded her while she applied it. She told a little girl the

Fig. 1.2. Featuring Leia cosplayers of all ages and several ethnicities, this still from *Looking for Leia*, directed by Annalise Ophelian, highlights the wide reach of the char-acter (2019; What Do We Want Pictures).

glitter would keep her safe and sprinkled generous amounts into her hair. By adopting this glitter blessing tradition, Fisher turned what would be a fleeting moment with her while she signed her name into an unforgettable and fabulous occasion.[20]

Another fan writes, "It was her way of making the world sparkle and shine even when it felt dark. It made her feel better, and she wanted to share that with others."[21] Fisher described these interactions as "more than fun. It's joyous."[22] At conventions this often meant longer lines for autographs but better stories as fans walked around the con space wearing proof that they "ran into Carrie too."[23] Fisher was the "Alderaan Glitter Bomber"[24] bringing a little more sparkle to life at conventions. The Glitter for Carrie campaign has become an annual tribute on May the Fourth ("May the Fourth Be With You") where fans wear glitter to remember Fisher.

For many fans, as artist Van Ekelenburg suggests, the most significant aspect of Fisher's stardom was her candor about her lifelong struggles with mental illness and addiction and her advocacy on behalf of both conditions. In a 2000 interview with Diane Sawyer on *Primetime* (ABC), Fisher publicly announced that she had been diagnosed with bipolar disorder when she was in her twenties and had been dealing with manic-depressive episodes ever since. The announcement was a turning point and the beginning of Fisher's new role as advocate and activist. In the last fourteen years of her life, she increasingly became a public voice for bipolar disorder as part of a larger effort to lessen the stigma of mental illness and to increase public funding for facilities and care. The Leia persona inflected this dimension of her stardom, too, as she became a voice of support for her fellow sufferers. Fans began to refer to Fisher/Leia as "Space Mom" and created memes using images of Fisher/Leia incorporating words of encouragement regarding self-care, medication compliance, and resistance to stigma. Our favorite of these is of General Organa with her arms crossed and the text "Take your pills. Do self-care. Live to flip off the world another day. Make Space Mom Proud." After her death, fans also honored Carrie's mental health advocacy through hashtag campaigns including #CarrieOn(Forever), #KeepCalmAndCarrieOn, and #GlitterForCarrie. As a *New York Times* article put it, her death "triggered a wave of affection on social media and elsewhere, from both fans and fellow bipolar travelers, whose emotional language she knew and enriched."[25]

Actress, Writer, and Humorist

The superhero status of Princess Leia has tended to eclipse Fisher's larger professional career as an actress, celebrity, writer, and comedian. As documented in Appendix 2 of this anthology, her acting career encompassed scores of film and television roles; she also performed voice work that included a recurring role on *The Family Guy* (2005–) and made dozens of appearances on talk shows, specials, award shows, and in documentaries. Her comic timing landed her supporting roles in key films such as *The Blues Brothers* (1980) and in the high-profile comedies *Hannah and Her Sisters* (1986) and *When Harry Met Sally* (1989), the latter of which is widely considered the launch of the rom-com's resurgence in popular culture. Her casting as the witty best friend rather than the romantic heroine suggests that Fisher's star persona in the wake of her *Star Wars* roles was already pitched toward comedy rather than glamour, as seen in her cameo roles over the next two decades. This reputation eventually landed her a spot in the 2005 compendium film *The Aristocrats*, in which dozens of comedians ad lib their versions of an infamous dirty joke. Certainly, her most self-reflexive comic cameo was her Emmy-nominated 2007 spot on *30 Rock* ("Rosemary's Baby") in which she played a satirical version of herself, a delusional, alcoholic comedy writer still fiercely attached to her feminist ideals.[26] Fisher's final television role was likewise tinged with autobiographical overtones. On the British sitcom *Catastrophe* (2015–19), she won critical acclaim as the brash mother of leading man Rob (Rob Delaney) in scripts about his addiction issues; the cross-generational family melodrama was especially resonant given Delaney's own well-known addiction and recovery. Fisher's role on the show was a creative one, too, because she was the only cast member who was allowed to improvise her lines.[27]

Creativity was in fact central to Fisher's identity. She was a good actress and entertaining performer, but her gift, her genius, was sharp comic writing. From the time she was twelve years old, writing had been a way to deal with the surreal nature of her life as Debbie Reynolds's daughter, Fisher reported: "That was therapeutic for me in those days. I wrote things to get out of feeling them, and onto paper. So, writing in a way saved me, kept me company."[28] She began to write for publication when the *Star Wars* franchise was behind her in the 1980s, confiding to a friend that "she'd stopped thinking of herself as an actress who writes and started thinking of herself as a writer who acts."[29] Her pungent writing skills are evident not only in her books but also in her uncredited work as a script doctor, punching up the dialogue in films such as *Hook* (1991), *Sister Act* (1992), *Last Action Hero* (1993), and *Coyote Ugly* (2000). Fisher wrote two screenplays as well. She adapted her first novel, *Postcards from the Edge* (1987), into a 1990 film of the same name starring Meryl Streep and Shirley MacLaine, and she wrote *These Old Broads* (2001), a campy made-for-television comedy starring Debbie Reynolds, Shirley MacLaine, Joan Collins, and Elizabeth Taylor as the title's grand old women. Fisher also contributed to the dialogue of *Star Wars Episode VIII: The Last Jedi* (2017). Director Rian Johnson reports that her funniest and most emotional lines were her own, including her quip about having changed her infamous hairdo, delivered when she meets up with her long-lost brother Luke Skywalker.[30]

Fisher wrote her first novel, *Postcards from the Edge*, after surviving a drug overdose in 1985, thinly fictionalizing her experiences in rehab and her relationship with an over-the-top celebrity mother. Her writing was always humorous, no matter how dark the topic. "I dream jokes in my sleep, and I make things funny that are not," she admitted.[31] The "not funny" things she covered in her next three novels include divorce, single motherhood, the death of a friend with AIDS, addiction, and institutionalization in a psychiatric ward. But these crises are always staged in the comic-absurdist context of celebrity culture, with an eye toward Hollywood's stock superficial treatments of sorrow and disaster. Her 1980s marriage and divorce from songwriter Paul Simon is the basis of *Surrender the Pink* (1990), in which the Fisher heroine writes a soap opera featuring dreadful dialogue about marriage and divorce from a famous writer. In *Delusions of Grandma* (1994) the main character is a script doctor hired to develop movie characters who are compelling but not so compelling that all their problems can't be solved within a two-hour screening time. Fisher's final novel, *The Best Awful* (2004) fictionalizes her late 1990s relapse into drug use—"the best awful"—after her divorce from a man who left her for another man and includes Fisher's rendition of a horrific psychotic breakdown. The heroine's commentary about her breakdown is irreverent but never coy about the seriousness of her mental illness and her grim prognosis: "She only hoped she had some better days remaining and she hadn't used up her coupon for good times once and for all."[32] The "better days" in *The Best Awful* are about recovery and advocacy for mental health research. The heroine's big comeback moment, far from being a glamorous reentry into show business, is her speech at a fundraiser for research on bipolar disorder, reflecting Fisher's own new role as an advocate following her disclosure on *Primetime*.

In her final writing projects, Fisher dropped her fictional avatars and told her life story more directly through autobiography, beginning with a one-woman comedy stage play, *Wishful Drinking*, which became the basis of her 2008 memoir of the same name. She followed this with her memoir *Shockaholic* (2011), about memories reconstructed after electroshock therapy for her depression. These first two memoirs are origin stories, chronicling her Hollywood parentage and coming to terms with a world-famous mother and an absent father. The centrality of her family in these books aligns them with the child-of-the-star memoir, "blurring the lines between biography and autobiography," as Mary R. Desjardins puts it, in revealing the life of the famous parent and the experience of growing up as the star's child. Fisher's memoirs differ in that Fisher is as famous as her star parents, but *Wishful Drinking* and *Shockaholic* share the subgenre's fascination with the family romance: the stories and fantasies that explore, explain, and develop our sense of origin and our sense of self.[33] In *Wishful Drinking*, the dreadful details of the family scandals are recounted in the punchy anecdotes and funny one-liners of stand-up comedy, but in *Shockaholic*, Fisher's family stories draw on comedy in its broadest sense—as the celebration of inclusion and renewal and the acceptance of loss as part of a larger picture of regeneration.

Fisher's final memoir, *The Princess Diarist* (2016), which appeared just weeks before her death, is composed mostly of diaries Fisher had kept at the age of nineteen during the filming of the first *Star Wars* movie. Rediscovering these diaries, she told friends they were an "incredible archaeological find," an unfiltered record of a young woman who did not yet know she suffered from bipolar disorder, who was at the mercy of her moods and beginning to realize that writing, rather than acting, would be crucial for her self-survival.[34] This memoir also reveals the details of Fisher's first serious love affair: her involvement with Harrison Ford, married and fourteen years older, during the filming of the first *Star Wars* movie. The diaries disclose a heartbreaking story of unrequited love for a man who was emotionally inaccessible despite her best efforts to make him laugh and pay attention, uncannily repeating Fisher's experience with her own father: "I thought if I was really funny you'd want to be around me all the time." And finally, for fans convinced that the "real" Carrie Fisher is Princess Leia, this last memoir

Fig. 1.3. Her one-woman show *Wishful Drinking* (2008–10) highlights all the aspects of Carrie's career: writer, actress, comedian, advocate, and activist. Image by Shannon Kringen is licensed with CC BY 2.0.

offers a dazzling argument about why that is both true and not. Fisher writes that her "real" life is unimaginable without her fictional avatar to whom she was been devoted: "Answering questions about her, defending her, fed up with being mistaken for her . . . but then wondering who I'd be without her, finding out how proud I am of her, making sure I'm careful not to do anything that might reflect badly on her or that she might disapprove of."[35]

"Drowned in Moonlight"

The *Bright Lights* documentary about Carrie Fisher and Debbie Reynolds was released in 2016 just a few months before their deaths. Fisher, her mother, and her brother had given consent to this film so long as it would not be a "puff piece" about the stardom of Reynolds and Fisher and would focus instead on the family's relationships.[36] The film's subtitle, *A Different Kind of Hollywood Love Story*, is about the mother-daughter bond that defined the final years of these actresses, when they lived in adjacent houses and were devoted to each other's needs. *Bright Lights* frankly portrays the vulnerabilities of both women, Reynolds struggling to maintain her glamorous image with nightclub appearances for elderly crowds and Fisher struggling with her mood disorders. At one point, deep into depression, she recites T. S. Eliot's "Love Song of J. Alfred Prufrock" while watching Barbra Streisand in *Funny Girl* (1968) on TV, encapsulating Fisher's erudition as well as her attunement to comedy in the face of despair. The final scene of *Bright Lights* shows Fisher, her mother, and her brother breaking into an impromptu song, "There's No Business, Like Show Business," during a Christmas celebration in the living room, attesting to the family identity and resilience. *Bright Lights* begins with shots of the opulent home in which the Fisher children had grown up, so the modesty of their final homes is striking; the bright lights of the last scene are ordinary Christmas tree lights rather than the lights of a marquee, and the setting is home instead of a public screening or spectacle. *Bright Lights* is an especially poignant picture of Fisher's domestic life with her mother given that Debbie Reynolds's death followed barely twenty-four hours after her daughter's. She collapsed while planning Fisher's funeral, not long after changing her own burial plans and telling her son, "I want to be with Carrie."[37]

In the final year of her life, Fisher had contended with her worsening bipolar disorder, the declining health of her mother, and legal battles that ensued after the overdose death of a young actress who had lived with Fisher for a time. So family members said they were not surprised when, following her death, the autopsy revealed she had been using a number of opiates and other addictive substances which may have contributed to her cardiac arrest.[38] As Fisher recounts in *Wishful Drinking*, her problems with drug addiction and mental illness were sinuously intertwined. Substance abuse, she writes, had been her way of treating manic depression, "putting the monster in the box."[39] After her death, her daughter, Billie Lourd, issued a statement emphasizing Fisher's commitment to mental health and addiction issues: "I know my Mom; she'd want her death to encourage people to be open about their struggles. Seek help, fight for government funding for mental health programs."[40] At the time of her death, Fisher was still filming episodes of *Catastrophe* and taping episodes as a character voice on *Family Guy*. But as Fisher had predicted in *Wishful Drinking*, reports of her death were overwhelmingly imbued with images of Princess Leia and headlines like, "Goodnight Princess," "Beloved Princess," "She Was a Force," "May the force be with you, Carrie," "Goodbye, Princess Leia," "Child of Hollywood and 'Star Wars' Royalty, Dies at 60,"—used by tabloids and legitimate media outlets alike, including the *New York Post*, the *Daily Record*, the *Sun*, *CNN*, *ABC*, and the *New York Times*.[41] Yet the media spectacle around Fisher's death seems fitting to her persona, much like the use of a giant Prozac-pill-shaped urn to hold her ashes.

Tanya happened to be at Disney World for Christmas when news of Carrie Fisher's death broke on December 27, 2016. She and her wife decided to go to Hollywood Studios the next day, thinking there would be some sort of tribute to Fisher because so many people hoped for something to mark her passing. They were waiting for *Star Wars: A Galactic Spectacular* at Hollywood Studios to start when the news broke of Debbie Reynold's death, and you could see the information pass through the waiting crowd like a ripple on a lake as people checked their phones. We were a public mourning the loss of people we knew only through the silver screen but who meant the world to us in that moment. There was no special tribute to Fisher that day except for the one the audience made when those with light sabers gave Princess Leia a Jedi salute when her moment appeared in the show. It was a surreal experience being at "the happiest place on earth" in such a somber crowd.

Dimensions of Fisher's Stardom

The relationship between Carrie Fisher and Princess Leia/General Organa is the through-line of these essays, summarized by Fisher's comment that "Princess Leia are us." The dynamics and discourses of fans also undergird many of these essays. The first section, "Leia/Carrie," focuses on Fisher's embodiment of Leia in the *Star Wars* saga as a site of contested consumption and meaning. Jennifer M. Fogel, in "Who Owns Carrie Fisher? A Complicated Embodiment of Manufactured Commodity and Avatar of Resistance," analyzes the commodification of Fisher's image as Leia, the gendered consumption of those images, and Fisher's complex responses to the uses of her likeness. Gendered fan practices are further explored in Philipp Dominik Keidl's essay "Gatekeeping the Past: Fandom and the Gendered Cultural Memory of *Star Wars*," which reveals how, despite feminist interventions, fan discourses about Leia have been dominated by masculinist and often antifeminist perspectives, influencing *Star Wars* histories and Leia's place

Fig. 1.4. One of the many shrines created by fans on Carrie's death. This one is at her star on Hollywood's Walk of Fame with Rey, Kylo Ren, and R2-D2 cosplayers in vigil. Image by Justin Sewell is licensed with CC BY 2.0.

within collective memories of the franchise. Moving to another aspect of fan investment in Princess Leia, Andrew Kemp-Wilcox's "Harvesting the Celebrity Interface: Carrie Fisher, Virtual Performance, and Software Stars" explores the impact of digital technologies that have created both anxieties about authenticity and opportunities for creative fan-star interactions. These technologies, Kemp-Wilcox argues, have created "software celebrity," a new kind of stardom that includes opposition to studio-created star imagery. The final essay in this section elaborates on the topic of creative fan interaction; Tanya D. Zuk's "'Carrie Fisher Sent Me': Gendered Political Protest, *Star Wars*, and the Women's March," explores the cultural and political impact of Carrie Fisher/Leia Organa through the use of their memetic images in the Women's March protest posters.

The second section, "Carrie/Leia," foregrounds Fisher's work as a writer, feminist, and advocate, illustrating that this work is often inflected by the Leia persona. Linda Mizejewski's essay, "Comedy From the Edge: Carrie Fisher's Autobiographical Writing," demonstrates Fisher's use of comedy as a strategy to resist the cultural narratives of melodrama and tragic female stardom in telling her own story. In the following essay, "Postcards from the Valley of the Broads: Carrie Fisher, Jacqueline Susann, and Feminist Camp Authorship," Ken Feil explores Fisher's lesser-known work as a screenplay writer, focusing on her 1990 film adaptation of her 1987 novel *Postcards from the Edge* and her screenplay for the 2001 television comedy *These Old Broads*. Like Mizejewski, Feil is attentive to Fisher's use of camp to critique and distance herself from celebrity culture. Fisher's treatment of aging actresses in *These Old Broads* illustrates her insights on the aging process in Hollywood, where glamorous female stars are expected to be flash-frozen in their lithe twenty-something bodies. Fisher's funny and animated responses to this sexism are the focus of Kristen Anderson Wagner's essay "'My body hasn't aged as well as I have. Blow us': Carrie Fisher and the Unruly Aging Actress," which also compares Fisher's responses to aging with that of Debbie Reynolds, her movie-star mother who refused to grow old. The final two essays of this anthology highlight the influence of Fisher as an advocate for mental health awareness and addiction. Cynthia Hoffner and Sejung Park, in their essay "'Stay afraid, but do it anyway': Carrie Fisher's Mental Health Advocacy," describe Fisher's role as a mental health advocate through her own self-disclosure of bipolar disorder. Hoffner and Park examine the reduction of social and self-stigma created by celebrity disclosure and the parasocial relationships fans develop with celebrities like Fisher, who use humor and candor to address their own struggles with mental health. Slade Kinnecott demonstrates the impact of such a relationship in her essay "Threshold Guardian to Space Mom: Here, But For the Sake of Carrie, Go I," which interweaves intimate readings of Fisher's work with self-reflection about her own struggles. We conclude with this essay because it powerfully reveals the meanings of Carrie Fisher/Princess Leia/General Organa as inspiration and champion.

Fisher's significance as a star clearly goes much further and deeper than *Star Wars*. Though we've brought many of her contributions, creative and cultural, to the fore in this anthology, there is still much yet to be explored and critiqued, including her work as a script doctor, the myriad contingents of her fan community, and the issues experienced by people of color cosplaying as Leia to start. We also hope this anthology contributes to the conversations Carrie herself started with her fans through her performance of Leia, her presence at conventions, her mental health advocacy, and her own writing. These essays reflect the nuances of her celebrity as well as the complexities of her fandom.

Carrie Fisher was an actress, an advocate, an activist, a comedian, and "Space Mom." Princess Leia was a senator, a general, a rebel, and the "Hutt Slayer." Both were heroes to us and to her many fans.

Notes

1 Carrie Fisher, *The Princess Diarist* (New York: Blue Rider Press, 2016), 5, 244–45.

2 Sheila Weller, *Carrie Fisher: A Life on the Edge* (New York: Farrar Straus, 2019), 5 and dedication page.

3 The exceptions include Paul Booth, "Disney's Princess Leia," in *Disney's Star Wars: Forces of Production, Promotion, and Reception*, ed. William Proctor and Richard McCulloch (Iowa City: University of Iowa Press, 2019), 179–91; Douglas Brode and Leah Deyneka, *Sex, Politics, and Religion in Star Wars: An Anthology* (Lanham, MD: Scarecrow Press, 2012); Carolyn Cocca, *Superwomen: Gender, Power, and Representation* (New York: Bloomsbury Academic, 2016); Stephen Fry, *The Secret Life of a Manic Depressive, Part 1* (New York: Films Media Group, 2011); Catherine Grant, "Videographic Star Studies and the 'Late Voice': Carrie Fisher, John Hurt, and Jeanne Moreau,"

academic blog, *In Media Res*, August 15, 2017; Hilde Van den Bulck, " 'She Died of a Mother's Broken Heart': Media and Audiences' Framing of Health Narratives of Heart-Related Celebrity Deaths," *International Journal of Communication* 11 (January 2017): 4965–87; Christine Widmayer, "The Feminist Strikes Back: Performative Mourning in the Twitter Response to Carrie Fisher's Death," *New Directions in Folklore* 15, no. 1/2 (2017): 50–76.

4 See Andrew Kemp-Wilcox's discussion of the middle finger salute in his essay in this anthology.

5 Suzanne Leonard and Diane Negra trace the relationship between stardom and celebrity, the development of celebrity culture, and the accompanying development of scholarship on these phenomena in "Stardom and Celebrity," in *The Craft of Criticism*, ed. Mary Celeste Kearney and Michael Kackman (New York: Routledge, 2018), 219–30.

6 Carrie Fisher, *Wishful Drinking* (New York: Simon & Schuster, 2008), 3.

7 Fisher, *Wishful Drinking*, 35–37, 163.

8 The information about *Of Human Bondage* can be found in Paul Slansky, "Carrie Fisher: A Quick Study," *Esquire*, May 1985, 120–22. Fisher spoke about being a bookworm in an interview with Irene Lacher, "Princess Carrie Books," *Los Angeles Times*, September 7, 1990. Her comments about her mother can be found in Jeanne Wolf, "Carrie Fisher," *Redbook*, March 2001.

9 Fisher, *Wishful Drinking*, 50.

10 Carrie Fisher, *Postcards from the Edge* (New York: Simon & Schuster, 1987), 172.

11 Todd Fisher, *My Girls: A Lifetime with Carrie and Debbie* (New York: Harper Collins, 2018), 59.

12 Fisher, *Wishful Drinking*, 79.

13 Fisher, *Wishful Drinking*, 88.

14 "Carrie Fisher Opens Up about 'Star Wars,' The Gold Bikini, and Her On-Set Affair," NPR.org, accessed April 2, 2017,www.npr.org/2016/11/28/503580112/carrie-fisher-opens-up-about-star-wars-the-gold-bikini-and-her-on-set-affair.

15 Jacob Bryant, "Carrie Fisher's 'Star Wars' Advice to Daisy Ridley: 'Don't Be a Slave Like I Was,' " *Variety* (blog), October 30, 2015, http://variety.com/2015/film/news/star-wars-carrie-fisher-daisy-ridley-sexist-costumes-1201630611/.

16 Laura Mulvey, "Visual Pleasure and Narrative Cinema," *Screen* 16 (1975): 6–18. Also see bell hooks's critique of Mulvey's limitations regarding race,

"The Oppositional Gaze," in *Black Looks: Race and Representation* (Boston: South End, 1992), 115–31, and Judith's Mayne's reconsideration of the racial, sexual, and cultural differences involved in spectatorship, *Cinema and Spectatorship* (London: Routledge, 1993): 53–102.

17 Julz, "Bearded Leia: Crossplaying Like a Boss," Nonprofit, Cosplay For All, July 16, 2015, http://cosplayforall.com/bearded-leia-crossplaying-like-a -boss/. Cosplay is a portmanteau of costume and play and is a common practice at fan conventions where people dress and act like their favorite characters. Crossplay is when someone dresses as a character of a gender different from their own.

18 Tara Edwards, "Cosplay Is Not Consent," *Geeks*, 2015, https://geeks.media/ cosplay-is-not-consent.

19 Emma Pett, "Crossplay, Gender Fluidity, and Star Wars Fandom | In Media Res," academic blog, *In Media Res*, September 12, 2018, http:// mediacommons.org/imr/content/crossplay-gender-fluidity-star-wars -fandom.

20 Amy Ratcliffe, "Getting Blessed with Glitter by Carrie Fisher," March 17, 2015, www.geekwithcurves.com/2015/03/getting-blessed-with-glitter-by -carrie.html.

21 Imgur, "For Carrie," Imgur, accessed June 13, 2019, https://imgur.com/ gallery/k82sK.

22 Ratcliffe, "Getting Blessed with Glitter by Carrie Fisher."

23 Stubby the Rocket, "Carrie Fisher Would Cover You in Glitter If She Thought You Were Having a Bad Day," Tor.com, May 4, 2017, www.tor .com/2017/05/04/carrie-fisher-glitter/.

24 Randall A. Golden, "The Alderaanian Glitter Bomber Strikes!" *Midlife Crisis Crossover!* (blog), March 15, 2015, https://midlifecrisiscrossover.com/ 2015/03/14/the-alderaanian-glitter-bomber-strikes/. Princess Leia was of the planet Alderaan, and this fan conflates Leia and Carrie in his interaction at a convention.

25 Benedict Carey, "Carrie Fisher Put Pen and Voice in Service of 'Bipolar Pride,' " *New York Times*, December 28, 2016.

26 See Linda Mizejewski's discussion of this episode in "Feminism, Postfeminism, Liz Lemonism: Comedy and Gender Politics on 30 Rock," *Genders* 55 (2012).

27 See "Rob Delaney: 'I Revered Carrie Fisher Until I Met Her, Then I Loved Her,' " *The Guardian*, December 28, 2016, and Hanh Nguyen, " 'Catastrophe':

Rob Delaney and Sharon Horgan on Depicting a Type of Alcoholism Rarely Seen on TV," *IndieWire* May 5, 2017.

28 Spencer Kornhaber, "Carrie Fisher's Perfect Final Farewell on Catastrophe," *Atlantic*, May 2, 2017.

29 Weller, *Carrie Fisher: A Life on the Edge*, 191.

30 Zack Sharf, "'Star Wars: The Last Jedi': Carrie Fisher Is Responsible for Writing These Emotional Final Leia Lines," *Indiewire*, December 16, 2017. Also see Emma Stefansky, "Of Course Carrie Fisher Wrote Her Best 'Last Jedi' Lines," *Vanity Fair*, December 23, 2017.

31 Leslie Bennetts, "Carrie On Baggage," *Vanity Fair*, November 2009, 120.

32 Carrie Fisher, *The Best Awful* (New York: Simon & Schuster, 2004), 208.

33 Mary R. Desjardins, "Dietrich Dearest: Family Memoir and the Fantasy of Origins," in *Dietrich Icon*, ed. Gerd Gemünden and Mary R. Desjardins (Durham, NC: Duke University Press, 2007), 314–15. Desjardins finds Marianne Hirsch's description of the family romance especially useful as a way to think of the discursive nature of family relationships given the stories and fantasies about these relationships circulating in culture. See Marianne Hirsch, *The Mother-Daughter Plot: Narrative, Psychoanalysis, Feminism* (Bloomington: Indiana University Press, 1989), cited in Desjardins, "Dietrich Dearest." 316.

34 Weller, *Carrie Fisher: A Life on the Edge*, 328.

35 Fisher, *Princess Diarest*, 243–44.

36 Todd Fisher, *My Girls*, 337.

37 Weller, *Carrie Fisher: A Life on the Edge*, 349.

38 Weller, *Carrie Fisher: A Life on the Edge*, 327–43, 355–56.

39 Fisher, *Wishful Drinking*, 117.

40 Scott Stump, "Billie Lourd Speaks Out on Addiction after Autopsy Says Carrie Fisher Had Cocaine in System," *USA Today*, June 19, 2017.

41 "Goodnight Princess," *The Sun*, December 28, 2016; "Beloved Princess," *Daily News*, December 28, 2016; "She Was a Force," *New York Post*, December 28, 2016, www.alamy.com/stock-photo-front-pages-and-headlines-of-the-new-york-tabloid-newspapers-on-wednesday-130658717.html; "May the Force Be with You, Carrie," *Daily Record*, December 28, 2016; "Goodbye, Princess Leia," News, CNN, December 27, 2016; Dave Itzkoff, "Carrie Fisher, Child of Hollywood and 'Star Wars' Royalty, Dies at 60," *New York Times*, December 27, 2016, sec. Movies, www.nytimes.com/2016/12/27/movies/carrie-fisher-dead-star-wars-princess-leia.html.

I

✳ ◆ ✳ ◆ ✳

Leia/Carrie

Who Owns Carrie Fisher?

A COMPLICATED EMBODIMENT OF MANUFACTURED

COMMODITY AND AVATAR OF RESISTANCE

Jennifer M. Fogel

In her bawdy 2005 American Film Institute roast of *Star Wars* director George Lucas, Carrie Fisher sarcastically lamented Lucas's complete appropriation of her likeness in perpetuity. In what would soon become a comedic calling card for the remainder of her life, Fisher caustically announced that among "George's many possessions, he owns my *likeness*, so that every time I look in the mirror I have to send him a couple of bucks!"[1] Fisher's image as Princess Leia has been commodified to the point that—as she herself told *Newsweek* in 2011—it eclipses any other persona the actress and novelist had fought to create.[2] The *Star Wars* franchise not only triggered a new investment in film licensing for various merchandise, but in its forty-plus-year history it has also spurred a long-lasting trend of fan collectability. Running parallel to the franchise's success and reinvention, Fisher—a collector of kitsch, memorabilia, and fan-made gifts—was able to navigate eccentric and grotesque seizures of her image through humor and a biting wit.

But what does it mean when your likeness is no longer your own? When it becomes a paradox of reverie and parody? On the one hand, Fisher remains a pin-up girl for male fanboys, and on the other, the embodiment of a feminist icon. While her Princess Leia persona is a highly contested catalog of hyperfeminized attributes (e.g., the inexhaustible discussion of Leia's hair and the "golden metal bikini") that have leeched into the gendered marketing of *Star Wars* products for forty years, General Leia—Fisher's contemporary incarnation within the franchise—was met with a misogynistic disparagement of the actress's aged physique. The lambasting of a sci-fi sex symbol for "getting older" is a toxic reminder that Fisher's image has been annexed and commodified by a largely nostalgic (male) fandom.

In a day and age where celebrity is both a cultural fashion and an economic consumer trade, the complicated reification of Fisher's image—both as Princess Leia and as herself—has largely defined generations of *Star Wars* fandom. But who owns Carrie Fisher? The character she embodied long ago in a galaxy far, far away may be a cultural icon, but Fisher, for all intents and purposes, brought Princess Leia to life, thoroughly promoted—if at times unwillingly—and sustained audience interest in the character, and managed to imbue the beloved princess with an authenticity unparalleled even within the expanded *Star Wars* universe. Carrie Fisher was a successful novelist and script doctor beyond her sci-fi roots, but her celebrity status was coauthored by a burgeoning use of movie tie-in merchandise and the fans that consumed these cultural commodities. The conflation of Carrie Fisher and Princess Leia only intensifies the maddening entanglement of fans' imagined cultural ownership of Fisher's likeness (as Leia, of course) in the form of collectibles and licensed merchandise put forth by the marketing agents that financially *own* her "likeness." All this being a lamentable consequence of Fisher "blithely sign[ing] away any and all merchandising rights relating to [her] image and otherwise" before the premiere of the first *Star Wars* film in 1977.[3]

This chapter draws extensively from two of Carrie Fisher's autobiographies—*Wishful Drinking* (2008) and *The Princess Diarist* (2016)—and numerous interviews with the actress about her iconic role. Always full of acerbic wit and a brazen ease with truth-telling, Fisher's writing avails both fans and academics with a sophisticated and fascinating reverie of her bumpy road to and with fame. Underscoring each biting truism and (sometimes) scandalous memory is a complex rumination on what her celebrity means for herself and to her adoring fans. This chapter first examines the ways in which Carrie Fisher's character served as both goddess and warrior for a burgeoning fandom but whose likeness was appropriated to sell hyperfeminized products to these same fans. Next, a discussion of Fisher's complicated love-hate relationship with her iconic character, particularly the body shaming she endured by both George Lucas and the fandom. Lastly, the chapter contemplates how an emboldened Women's March in January 2017 wrested control of Fisher's image away from corporate owners after her unexpected death and finally redeemed this warrior princess in a way her portrayer would be proud of.

Fan Consumption of the Commodified Image

As the story is so often told, George Lucas saw past the Hollywood machine and with cunning foresight not only negotiated the sequel rights to one of the most successful film serials in history but also 100 percent of the merchandising rights.[4] Now one of the highest-grossing films of all time, most of the success of this megafranchise is due to the massive amount of merchandise the films produced, selling more than $100 million worth of toys within a year after *Star Wars: A New Hope*'s 1977 release.[5] To date, *Star Wars* licensed toys and merchandise sales have earned $12 billion for the franchise—nearly triple the box office revenue from the original and prequel trilogy films combined.[6] Referring to this groundbreaking explosion of movie tie-in products, Carrie Fisher wrote in *The Princess Diarist* (2016), the film "leaked out of the theater, poured off the screen, [and] affected a lot of people so deeply that they required endless talismans and artifacts to stay connected to it."[7] As paratextual materials, the action figures, novelizations, comics, clothing, and such, all became essential in facilitating enjoyment, loyalty, and later, nostalgia within the *Star Wars* fan base.

Carrie Fisher herself recounts in *Wishful Drinking* the litany of products to bear her likeness:

> George Lucas was the man who made me into a little doll! And it barely even hurt. A little doll that one of my exes could stick pins into whenever he was annoyed with me. . . . He also made me into a shampoo bottle where people could twist off my head and pour liquid out of my neck. . . . And there was a soap that read, "Lather up with Leia and you'll feel like a Princess yourself." . . . But the thing I've been made into that has really enhanced the quality of my life? I'm a PEZ dispenser.[8]

Importantly, these products were not simply tokens of a popular film character but invoked the now-infamous visage of Princess Leia styled by creator George Lucas. As noted by Fisher in *The Princess Diarist*, the cinnamon bun hairstyle she grudgingly complied with for fear of being sacked from *A New Hope*, "would impact how everyone—every filmgoing human—would envision me for the rest of my life."[9] She also admits, she "definitely would have argued against that insane hair (although the hair was, in its own modest way, a big part of that noise)."[10]

Of course, the hotly debated skimpy metal bikini slave outfit she wears in *Return of the Jedi* (1983) often overshadows Princess Leia's initial iconic look and otherwise reserved fashion. Whether the bikini was Lucas's "cynical nod" to "his growing nerd culture fan base,"[11] a crude objectification of the heroine, or an ironic and empowered spin on the damsel in distress trope—Leia does use the elements of her enslavement to kill her captor[12]—the controversial outfit is now a commodified cultural artifact symbolic for both modern-day cosplaying and constructed Princess Leia as a (nostalgic) sci-fi sex symbol. Herein lies the rub; at the same time that Lucas was successfully leveraging the toyetic nature of his *Star Wars* films and commodifying the likeness of each of his actors, the fan base became a highly gender constrictive landscape overseen by the twin suns of toy marketers and merchandising agents.

Despite featuring a smart and sassy princess as one of its lead characters, within the geek kingdom that *Star Wars* has become there is an oft-refused and marginalized fandom of women, as detailed by Philipp Dominik Keidl in the following essay in this anthology. The realms of science fiction and fantasy have traditionally, though wrongly, been assumed to

Fig. 2.1. A representation of the litany of collectibles bearing Carrie Fisher's likeness can be seen in Mary's ever-growing "Leia Land."

belong to the male fan domain. Scholars detail how fandom is often highly pigeonholed into very gendered aspects of fan creativity and practices of fan consumption.[13] While women may be "fans" of *Star Wars*, they are not its target market: "This is not to say that female fans have not been a power in the consumption of *Star Wars* merchandise, just that more toys are produced with male consumers in mind."[14]

As of late, critics and scholars alike have taken to task the undeniably gendered impetus of Lucasfilm (and now, Disney), its texts and supplementary merchandise, and the more general dismissal of women favoring sci-fi and fantasy. This marginalization was solidified early in the countless television ads hawking toys for the original trilogy that rarely featured any little girls playing with Leia action figures (or even dolls) and emphasized the franchise as a "boy thing,"[15] combined with the few hyperfeminized products that were available for girls and women including Princess Leia bubble bath, dolls, costumes, wigs, and, perhaps the most egregious, a Slave Leia perfume from 1983 that was "reissued" for fans anew at the 2010 *Star Wars* Celebration festival.

According to journalist Peter Beech, "The sci-fi genre is designed, it seems, for feminist ideas, offering us the chance to imagine a place free of gender-stereotyping and sexism."[16] In fact, audiences for sci-fi/fantasy films and television series have nearly achieved gender parity.[17] And yet, in his work on fandom, Joseph Reagle addresses how "geekdom" is on the one hand diverse and accepting and yet on the other offers a double bind for women, often accusing them of "being too geeky and not geeky enough."[18] Hence, the overarching problem is that while female fans debate if Leia's "slave" outfit in *Return of the Jedi* is objectifying or empowering—or why this iteration of Princess Leia is currently the most *available* form of *her* action figure—the marketing agents behind *Star Wars'* lineup of consumer products prior to and following the release of *The Last Jedi* of 2017 continue to "vastly underestimate the interest girls would have in the movies and related merchandise, and how toy buying has changed in the . . . years since the first *Star Wars* film was released."[19] Even as General Leia (and thus, Carrie Fisher) gave way to new heroine Rey (Daisy Ridley) in *The Force Awakens* in 2015, both characters were largely missing from toy shelves in favor of a line of CoverGirl cosmetics, jewelry at Kay Jewelers, kitchen goods, and a women's clothing line from Rock & Republic for Kohl's.[20]

Amid this tangled weaving of fan consumption, marketing, and gender, Carrie Fisher's star turn as Princess Leia has become both cultural icon and commodified image. Despite being born into celebrity as the daughter of two famous individuals (i.e., actress Debbie Reynolds and crooner Eddie Fisher), with *Star Wars*, Fisher was launched into a category beyond the traditional turn for an actress. She became the "simultaneous embodiment of media construction, audience construction, and the real, living and breathing human being."[21] It was a plight she admits in *The Princess Diarist*: she was wholly unprepared. But it was not the piles of fan mail, promotional interviews, or merchandise spreading her likeness across the globe that fazed her. It was the continual conflation and misappropriation of Carrie Fisher (actress) with that of Princess Leia (fictional character) by the fans writ large that contributed to a lifelong love-hate relationship with her iconic figure.

Will the Real Princess Leia Please Stand Up?

In his seminal work on celebrity, *Heavenly Bodies: Film Stars and Society*, film scholar Richard Dyer argues that fans obsessively search the star persona for the real and the authentic. Carrie Fisher's star persona consisted of a complex hodgepodge of manufactured appearances, paratextual commodities, and the screen image of Princess Leia. The "star image," as noted by Dyer, is merely part of the Hollywood machine that both exploits the actress's labor and yet, at the same time, divorces her *self* from the star persona.[22] Celebrity scholar P. David Marshall goes further, explaining that "as an audience we are drawn to deconstruct the star, and in that process . . . we are compelled to debate the nature of the star's public and private selves."[23] Whereas most star images become further authenticated through the exploration of the *real* private self, Fisher's off-screen foibles were repressed in favor of her "image's popular currency."[24] Hence, Carrie Fisher is no longer the actress but the fictional icon she portrayed. Fans presume that this loss of autonomy is a reasonable trade-off for celebrity status, but it certainly constrained Fisher's off-screen life and work as an actor.

Both Dyer and Marshall examine the celebrity as commodity, one that "enters into the very lexicon of a culture, its personality instantiated and immortalized into caricature."[25] Dyer writes, "Stars appear before us in media texts . . . but unlike other forms of representation, stars do not only exist in media texts."[26] In most cases, celebrities are simply used to market goods to the masses; their selective endorsement is a sign of the presumed caliber of the product and a way to leverage both celebrity status and personal taste. As Marshall notes, stars possess both cultural and economic capital.[27] Unlike the young celebrities of today that can control the ways in which they leverage their star image—whether through social activism or commercial practices—Fisher's image was fundamentally manufactured from the onset within a film franchise with a central impetus of commodification, which would later lead to its own cultural capital. Thus, Carrie Fisher becomes merely the body through which fans can assert their imagined ownership of and nostalgic participation in one of the biggest fan franchises of all time. But where does that leave Carrie Fisher who now uncomfortably navigates the conflation of her private self with the public persona that has been manufactured for her? Or worse, that the caricature of that persona—one now thoroughly and forever commodified—eclipses and dictates her life as an actor? For Carrie Fisher, celebrity was a perplexing duality of symbolic figure and corporate brand that left little separation for a private self or control of her likeness.

Although legally the presumption is that the celebrity has a "right to publicity," availing them recognition of the commercial value of their persona ranging from a signature to mannerism to frequently used phrases,[28] Carrie Fisher's likeness (as Princess Leia in all iterations) is currently owned by Disney. The corporate appropriation of Fisher's likeness has become increasingly problematic because not only is it constitutive of a global cultural commodity, but also its endless reproduction has forced her to lose any "autonomy from the objects that circulate in her likeness."[29] Furthermore, the visage of Princess Leia (as played by Fisher) has become part of our cultural heritage, and as legal anthropologist Rosemary Coombe argues, the "conditions that give her image its meaning, resonance, and authority" are generated from the imagined ownership of a passionate fan base spanning multiple generations that have shelled out money for merchandise and collectibles, stood in line waiting for autographs and selfies at conventions, and, more generally, affirmed the character's iconic status through reverie and parody.[30] As noted by film scholar Jason Scott, "the fans themselves have . . . contributed to *Star Wars*, not simply as consumers but participating in creating and producing the *Star Wars* culture."[31] He continues, "This is epitomized in the complementary ways *Star Wars* characters continue to be used, by both Lucas and the fans, as heroes and villains, mythic archetypes, icons, identities and objects of affection."[32] As a consequence, the reification of Princess Leia as cultural commodity and Fisher's celebrity status as a by-product, forms a paradoxical situation for the actress when meeting fans whereby they often fuse the two identities. Carrie Fisher, too, struggled to ascertain the configuration of her own identity: "This *Star Wars* fame meant that Princess Leia was famous and not Carrie Fisher. I just happened to look like her."[33]

As Fisher comments in the passage from *The Princess Diarist* quoted in this anthology's introduction, she "*liked* being Princess Leia. Or Princess Leia's being me. Over time I thought that we'd melded into one."[34] And in an interview with *Newsweek*, she admitted, "Princess Leia so eclipses any other identity that I've ever had."[35] Carrie Fisher had all but disappeared into the creation of this meaningful cultural figure, but her custodianship was rife with personal insecurities and shaped by both corporate brand management and fan adoration. From the onset, Fisher was asked to conform to the lithe figure George Lucas had envisioned for his cinematic princess by not only losing ten pounds after she was cast in the role but also foregoing a brassiere in favor of gaffer's tape to bind her breasts to her body.[36] The iconic hairstyle and, later, ambiguously objectified costume were both celebrated and considered crudely, though unexpectedly, masturbatory by the actress—as she equivocally expressed: "I had endless issues with my appearance in *Star Wars*. . . . What I saw in the mirror is not apparently what many teenage boys saw."[37] Even though Fisher expressed surprise at her sex symbol status, she rationalized, "I think boys may have been attracted to my accessibility. . . . I wasn't conventionally beautiful and sexy, and as such was less likely to put them down or think I was too good for them."[38] As the physical embodiment of the sassy heroine and the sexy sci-fi princess, Fisher was tasked with the unyielding management of the emotional fan attachment to this cultural icon, which would later become a burden in the face of fan incredulity when she failed to conform to this heavily commodified image later in life.

While Carrie Fisher wrestled with her own insecurities surrounding her appearance, she also had to make peace with her oft-conflated though extremely humbling appropriation as nostalgic talisman within the fan base. The pseudointimacy fashioned by various comic con and sci-fi convention appearances not only bred further fan connection and kinship to Fisher as object but was also an emblematic fusion of Fisher's love-hate relationship with the character. Celebrities often cite eccentric fans mistakenly fusing their public personas with their private selves, but this incongruous internalized impression of a personal connection to a character was perpetuated on Carrie Fisher tenfold. Whether as former sexual object, feminist heroine, or figure of childhood nostalgia, the actress felt these appearances bordered on prostitution—a "celebrity lap dance," she called it; and yet, at the same time, "incredibly sweet and mystifying."[39] Sentimental remembrances and personal affected responses to *Star Wars* dogged each of her appearances, and she was often pressured to render herself as Princess Leia and not Carrie Fisher: "Initially it was very weird to me, because they're saying you and it's Leia but to them it's you and Leia. Over the years, they both get mixed up."[40]

Moreover, Fisher noted, "[Fans] also frequently want you to write a piece of dialogue, and that is how I first came to understand who they thought Leia was."[41] Further problematizing this conflation was the disappointment and resentment Fisher earned when she unsuccessfully tried to distinguish herself from the character she once played:

> I wish I'd understood the kind of contract I signed by wearing [the metal bikini], insinuating I would and will always remain somewhere in the erotic ballpark appearance-wise, enabling fans to remain connected to their younger, yearning selves—longing to be with me without having to realize that we're both long past all of this in any urgent sense, and accepting it as a memory rather than an ongoing reality.[42]

As explained by journalist Chris Taylor in his book *How Star Wars Conquered the Universe*, Fisher was cognizant early on that her acting "career had stalled outside of this caricature."[43] Despite a successful writing career outside of the *Star Wars* universe, forty years on, Carrie Fisher was still a mere caricature—the real-life embodiment of a cultural text—and ultimately forced to placate fans and give in to the misappropriation of her identity.

Still, despite Fisher's acerbic attitude toward constantly wrestling with her celebrity status and the products that bore her likeness, she remained grateful to be irrevocably tied to one of the biggest media franchises in the world. In *The Princess Diarist* she writes:

> It turns out that it/she matters to me. Leia. Unfortunately. . . . But as it happens, I've spent the lion's share of my life, . . . being as much myself as Princess Leia. Answering questions about her, defending her, fed up with being mistaken for her, overshadowed by her, struggling

with my resentment of her, . . . wishing she'd finally just go away and leave me to be myself alone, but then wondering who I'd be with-out her, . . . feeling honored to be her representative here on earth, her caretaker, . . . doing what I can to be worthy of the gig, and then feeling beyond ridiculous and wishing that it would just fade away, leaving me to be who I was all those years ago.[44]

But while Fisher is certainly protective of the avatar she embodied all those years ago and recognizes the cultural significance of Princess Leia to fans, the lack of distinction between Carrie Fisher and Princess Leia was never more apparent than when she returned to her infamous role in *The Force Awakens* of 2015 and faced intense scrutiny over having failed to remain frozen in time and desecrating her image with age.[45]

When Princess Leia Failed the Ideal Beauty Test

While fans were ecstatic when it was revealed that the "old" *Star Wars* cast would reprise their roles in *The Force Awakens*, Carrie Fisher spoke candidly with *Good Housekeeping* (UK) that her return was dependent on losing over thirty-five pounds, which Fisher said was the equivalent of asking her to "get younger."[46] The film's producers were not the only ones to take Fisher to task for not "aging well" or "letting herself go," as Kristen Anderson Wagner recounts in her essay in this anthology. The fan giddiness over seeing the "ageless" Harrison Ford enter the Millennium Falcon in the first trailer was tempered by the unflattering response to Fisher's own minute presence in it and later during the subsequent press tour.

Despite the fact that Fisher did lose the weight as asked, some (male) fans took to social media to completely scrutinize and attack her looks. The biggest culprit was *New York Post* critic Kyle Smith, who rudely chastised Fisher for rebuking Hollywood's image-conscious nature, saying that she should just be grateful to simply still have a job—one that, of course, was dependent on her looks in the first place. Smith nastily writes:

No one would know the name Carrie Fisher if it weren't for her ability to leverage her looks. George Lucas only cast her in the first place because she was young, slim and cute at the time. . . . Fisher made millions off being pretty. Far from being bitter about this, she and other actresses who profited nicely from their looks should be grateful they had a turn at the top.[47]

Aging has long been recognized as a negative aspect of celebrity careers, one exacerbated by the ecology associated with maintaining one's star status and the preternatural condition of a particular image transfixed on screen.[48] Body image, an ideal beauty standard, and ageism have raised concern and outrage among a number of (young *and* old) actresses within Hollywood. Add to that the rising volume of female fan voices excoriating the toxic sexism rampant within popular (and geek) culture, and the "trouble with Fisher as Leia" is even more cause for distress.

While the debate surrounding Princess Leia has vacillated from feminist role model to sexually objectified damsel, the release of *The Force Awakens* renewed the heroine paradox—"heroines are unlike other women in their agentic characteristics but [must also be] 'quintessentially feminine.'"[49] *The Force Awakens* highlighted Leia's role as wife, mother, and now, General of the Rebel Alliance. *Salon* writer Mary Elizabeth Williams saw this "new" Princess Leia as a call to action and praised *The Force Awakens* for giving a "grown woman . . . permission to look like a grown woman."[50] But most male fans did not see it that way.

Fisher herself understood some of the rancor. Prior to *The Force Awakens* casting announcement, Fisher was ready to move on from the character that had overshadowed her life and that she no longer physically embodied:

> Here we are enacting our very own Dorian Gray configuration. You: smooth, certain, and straight-backed, forever condemned to the vast, enviable prison of intergalactic adventure. Me: struggling more and more with post-galactic stress disorder, bearing your scars, graying your eternally dark, ridiculous hair. You always act the heroine; I snort the stuff in the feeble attempt to dim the glare of your intense, intergalactic antics. You take the glory; I give way to age. . . . Though you are condemned to reenact the same seven hours of adventures over a span of now almost four rowdy decades, at least you look good fighting evil. I look lived in.[51]

And yet, that attitude changed once she recommitted to the character. Fisher responded to the haters with the infamous "Blow us" tweet[52] discussed at length by Kristen Anderson Wagner later in this volume.[53] Ever the vociferous humorist, Fisher also wrestled with how to deal, once more, with the commodified image of her likeness—one petrified in sci-fi history:

> [It was] a scornful reminder of just how old you're getting and how fat you've gotten—not only a reminder of what you once were but also of what you no longer are and never will be again. And, as if that wasn't enough, some stranger *owns* this horrific image and is free to do whatever with it in private or with his friends.[54]

In his book *Celebrity*, sociologist Chris Rojek comments on the ways in which the aging celebrity parallels that of the fan base growing up: "celebrities function not only as objects of desire but as objects of nostalgia that can be further commodified by the market."[55] Moreover, media scholar Kirsty Fairclough argues that "in an increasingly individualistic culture, a woman's outward appearance represents her entire selfhood."[56] Therefore, it was not surprising that Carrie Fisher became vilified for aging by a fan base encumbered by a nostalgic image of her likeness, but she did feel a bit demoralized by the quick descent into online harassment. Fisher mockingly asked, "Why did all these men find it so easy to be in love with me then and so complex to be in love with me now?"[57]

And it was not just Fisher who faced such online ridicule; Daisy Ridley (who plays a very benignly—if not practically—costumed Rey) was also body-shamed with regard to her "lack of curves," with critics writing that she was not a "real woman" and instead was "setting unrealistic expectations for young girls."[58] Hence, the criticism of Ridley is evidence that the double standard surrounding Carrie Fisher—and by extension Princess Leia—was not simply about "aging well" but also a general paradox when it comes to the expectations of our on-screen heroines, particularly since none of their male counterparts meet with this same scrutiny.

A Woman's Place Is in the Resistance

The paratexts created to help hype the return of the beloved *Star Wars* franchise have greatly perpetuated the sexist hierarchies in the *Star Wars* fan community. The constant regaling of journalists that *The Force Awakens* broke boundaries and was "not just for boys anymore" merely drives the marginalization of female fans—as if they, too, need to be rescued by the corporate bigwigs who deign to recognize them as a viable demographic. But why is this still a thing? Why are young girls and women still made to feel like they don't belong in geek culture, made fun of for wanting to cosplay their favorite characters or bring a *Star Wars* lunchbox to school? And how does Carrie Fisher's commodified image further highlight and codify a burgeoning resistance to this patriarchal corporate power?

In the same way that popular culture heroines are relegated to buxom costumes, hyperfeminized, and rarely made the hero of their own journey, female fans are forced to navigate the gendered tensions that exist in fandom that highlight its male exclusivity. This gendered hierarchy has been constructed over time by social, economic, and political institutions that leech into popular culture. Hence, it is unsurprising that after her unexpected death in December 2016, Carrie Fisher's cult status as sci-fi heroine was reimagined as feminist hero of numerous contemporary causes, including the Women's March. The various eulogies that accompanied Fisher's death, particularly those written by female fans, expressed a deep-seated understanding of not only the preeminence of the character of Princess Leia but also the personal affliction that Fisher bore as the embodiment of this heroine.

Even prior to Fisher's death, attempts at refurbishing the character of Princess Leia for modern times were underway. In *Elle*, Glynnis Macnicol wrote a rousing defense of Leia as feminist icon, one idolized for her accessibility and take-charge attitude amid a clearly masculine hero's journey narrative.[59] With regard to the merchandise, the postfeminist twenty-first century envisioned Leia as a "self-rescuing princess" on t-shirts and witnessed the rise of Leia-moms—"female fans who grew up with the original series and [were] now strong, smart, powerful role models in their own right."[60] In a study of *Star Wars* fans, Jason Davis and Larry Pakowski noted one fan said, "I like a smart-ass woman who can shoot a gun, negotiate treaties, pose undercover as a bounty hunter, have two guys fighting over her, and still have awesome hair."[61] And in her remembrance of Carrie Fisher for the *Baltimore Sun*, Meredith Woerner spoke devotedly of Princess Leia: "Leia proved that you don't have to choose between being the damsel in distress and the hero; you can be both. You could be the princess and the rebel, the peacemaker and the general."[62]

The adoration for Princess Leia was matched with personal admiration for Carrie Fisher. NBC News correspondent Adam Howard noted that

Fisher was herself a feminist icon: "[Fisher] defiantly marched to the beat of her own drum, especially off-screen, where her blunt-spoken, no-nonsense persona made her a distinct voice in Hollywood, particularly when it came to issues of sexism and ageism."[63] Quoted in Howard's article, filmmaker Naomi McDougall Jones memorialized Fisher's brash persona and willingness to embrace her messy *real* life: Fisher took "the sex-symbol image off the pedestal and flipp[ed] it on its head."[64] Aside from noting her indelible connection to Princess Leia—something Fisher omnisciently predicted with regard to her eventual death—some eulogized Carrie Fisher as advocate for political causes that were not necessarily de rigueur for celebrities, particularly as an outspoken advocate for issues of mental health and substance abuse. Prior to her death, Fisher was also a candid challenger to President Donald Trump, his policies, and his venomous use of social media. For all intents and purposes, this overwhelming grief for a newly lost feminist icon and adoration for a feisty arbiter of celebrity and social causes emboldened female fans once more to use Fisher's image as cultural icon; this time not as nostalgic talisman, but as warrior princess.

In the wake of the sexist undertones of a contentious election, Donald Trump's misogynistic statements and likely future policies caused a rebellion of mostly female protesters to challenge his nascent presidency by demonstrating in full force the day after his presidential inauguration in January 2017. The Women's March advocated for increased legislation regarding women's rights—particularly, reproductive rights—as well as health care and immigration reform. It became a global demonstration composed of nearly five million people. But as described by Tanya D. Zuk in her essay in this anthology, it was the surprising appearance of images of Princess Leia (and therefore Carrie Fisher) that captured the attention of many. Despite the fact that a number of celebrity activists promoted and heavily participated in the marches, it was the visage of Carrie Fisher that led to a convergence of pop culture history with feminist rebellion. Fisher's death inspired Mississippi designer Hayley Gilmore to fashion the graphic of "a faded, red image of Leia clutching her blaster and staring down the camera loomed behind the slogan 'A Woman's Place is in the Resistance'"[65] (see figure 5.1). Gilmore admired that Fisher was "very vocal about what's been going on recently with the election. She's honest. To me that's important. To be open and honest and transparent about what's going on right now. She's become an icon."[66]

Similarly, Los Angeles–based artist Vanessa Witter also found her Carrie Fisher–inspired poster "We Are the Resistance" taken up by demonstrators—some of whom, among the sea of pink "pussyhats"— dressed up as Princess Leia in cities all over the world. Witter's black-and-white image of a stoic Leia in a white dress and twin hair buns brazenly looking forward, hands at the back of her neck with "we are the resistance" emboldened in red and white underneath feels like a woman on the verge. A woman (and princess) ready to assert herself against the tyranny of galactic patriarchy.

A personal interview with Witter further examined the fusion of the Fisher-as-Leia conundrum. Asked if it was Carrie Fisher or Princess Leia

Fig. 2.2. The image of Carrie Fisher taken up by demonstrators at the 2017 Women's March.

who sparked the creative impulse, Witter thoughtfully reasoned that Fisher was the ultimate catalyst for the poster:

> [Fisher] had just recently died and we were all grieving her sudden loss and reflecting on her life. . . . Her personal life was a dichotomy of strength and vulnerability, which we can all relate to on some level, and so many women were feeling both of those things very acutely in the wake of the 2016 election. So while the image on my poster is Princess Leia—leader of the rebellion and feminist heroine—it carries the cultural and emotional weight that it did because of Fisher.[67]

Carrie Fisher—as Princess Leia—became a recognizable avatar of the Women's March, converting the cultural cachet of the iconic figure from commodity to an embodiment of "feminine power and leadership" and materializing a new "symbol of hope" for more than just fans, but women in general.[68] The generational impact of Princess Leia combined with Carrie Fisher's own spirited activism now would be forever linked to a renewed wave of feminist protest and solidified the movement.

It is likely that the protesters who took part in the global Women's March did not fully understand the magnitude of co-opting the image of Carrie Fisher as Princess Leia for their handmade signs and t-shirts. They probably were not aware that this gesture of mobilizing their grief in a constructive manner would signify more than a cult appreciation for a cultural text. This was not only a sign (both literally and figuratively) of a feminist rebellion for women's rights, it was also a chance to wrest control of Carrie Fisher's likeness away from the corporate overlords who had commodified her image for years to sell licensed merchandise. Gilmore did allude to some legal issues she faced with copyright infringement from Lucasfilm/Disney in an interview with the *New York Observer*;[69] however, fan practices have continually walked a fine line in repurposing corporate-owned intellectual property.[70] Fisher's influence on multiple generations of women was making itself known, not through the economics of merchandise but through a recasting of the twenty-first century as the heroine's journey. Princess Leia's pertinent role in a *real* revolution for human rights was highlighted.

The story of Carrie Fisher may seem convoluted to many and was certainly humorously censured by the actress herself. But despite her autobiographies continually alluding to the problematic nature of her personal

Fig. 2.3. The generational magnitude of recasting Fisher for the feminist rebellion.

celebrity—one rife with an accoutrement of licensed products bearing her image—Fisher deserves to be remembered for more than a passing resemblance to a character she once embodied. As she would tell fans at signings:

> I'll sign it Princess Leia. But you do know I'm not *actually* her, right? I might resemble this character that doesn't really exist offscreen and in human form—well, maybe I don't resemble her quite as much as I *used* to, but for a while there I looked almost *exactly* like her.[71]

Carrie Fisher's memorialization through the Women's March is an enduring symbol of resonance with female fans and Fisher's own legacy of activism—both for herself and others. Does this finally answer the question of "Who owns Carrie Fisher?" Likely not. Even though the original intention of the imagery used for the march was merely to craft a tribute to the pop culture heroine, it has, in the interim, become commodified once more with unauthorized permissions by third parties now selling the artwork for profit online.[72] But the signification of Fisher's facetious meditation on her celebrity status and commodification in her autobiographies, combined with fans' own mediation of her image for either purposes of nostalgia or activism, is a testament to the ways in which a celebrity becomes a custodian of our cultural heritage and *not* the conglomerations that leverage them for economic value. As Carrie Fisher understood, "I would never not be Princess Leia. I had no idea how profoundly true that was and how long forever was."[73]

Notes

1 Carrie Fisher, *Wishful Drinking* (New York: Simon & Schuster, 2008), 87.

2 Ramin Setoodeh, "Carrie Fisher on How George Lucas Stole Her Identity," *Newsweek*, last modified December 27, 2016, www.newsweek.com/carrie -fisher-george-lucas-star-wars-archive-interview-67321.

3 Carrie Fisher, *The Princess Diarist* (New York: Blue Rider Press, 2016), 194–95.

4 Mike Fleming Jr., "*Star Wars* Legacy II: An Architect of Hollywood's Greatest Deal Recalls How George Lucas Won Sequel Rights," *Deadline.com*, last modified December 18, 2015, http://deadline.com/2015/12/star-wars -franchise-george-lucas-historic-rights-deal-tom-pollock-1201669419/.

5 Brian Warner, "How One Brilliant Decision in 1973 Made George Lucas a Multi-Billionaire Today," *Celebrity Net Worth*, last modified December 14, 2015, www.celebritynetworth.com/articles/entertainment-articles/how -one-genius-decision-made-george-lucas-a-billionaire/.

6 Jamal Andress, "The Empire Strikes It Rich: How 'Star Wars' Built a Franchise Dynasty," *Newsy.com*, last modified December 11, 2017, www.newsy .com/stories/how-much-is-star-wars-actually-worth/.

7 Fisher, *Princess Diarist*, 194.

8 Fisher, *Wishful Drinking*, 86–87.

9 Fisher, *Princess Diarist*, 34. In *Wishful Drinking*, Fisher even jokes that the picture used of her in an abnormal psychology textbook on a chapter regarding bipolar disorder was of Princess Leia with the infamous hairstyle.

10 Fisher, *Princess Diarist*, 194.

11 Glynnis Macnicol, "In Defense of Princess Leia and 'Star Wars' Feminism," *Elle*, last modified August 14, 2015, www.elle.com/culture/career-politics/ a29876/in-defense-of-princess-leia-and-star-wars-feminism/.

12 Diana Dominguez, "Feminism and the Force: Empowerment and Disillusionment in a Galaxy, Far, Far Away," in *Culture, Identities, and Technology in the Star Wars Films: Essays on the Two Trilogies*, ed Carol Silvio and Tony M. Vinci (Jefferson, NC: McFarland, 2007), 109–33.

13 Camille Bacon-Smith, *Enterprising Women: Television Fandom and the Creation of Popular Myth* (Philadelphia: University of Pennsylvania Press, 1992); Henry Jenkins, *Textual Poachers: Television Fans and Participatory Culture* (New York: Routledge, 1992); and for fan consumption, Will Brooker, *Using the Force: Creativity, Community, and Star Wars Fans* (New York: Continuum, 2002).

14 Erika Travis, "From Bikinis to Blasters: The Role of Gender in the Star Wars Community," in *Fan Phenomena: Star Wars*, ed. Mika Elovaara (Bristol: Intellect, 2013), 54.

15 Jennifer M. Fogel, "The Force Is Now Female: The Gendered Marketing of Star Wars," in *Beyond Princess Culture: Gender and Children's Marketing*, ed. Katherine Foss (New York: Peter Lang, 2019).

16 Peter Beech, "Sci fi—It's Not Just for Boys," *The Guardian*, last modified May 16, 2009, www.theguardian.com/commentisfree/2009/may/16/ science-fiction-men-women.

17 Victoria McNally, "Why 2016 Is the Year We Need to Stop Pretending Women Aren't Geeks," *MTV.com*, last modified December 22, 2015, www .mtv.com/news/2683640/geek-media-numbers-breakdown/.

18 Joseph Reagle, "Geek Policing: Fake Geek Girls and Contested Attention," *International Journal of Communication* 9 (2015): 2866.

19 Kathleen Day, "Looking for Leia? May the Force Be with You," *Washington Post*, last modified March 15, 1997, www.washingtonpost.com/wp-dyn/ articles/A99038-1997Mar15.html.

20 See Suzanne Scott, "#Wheresrey?: Toys, Spoilers, and the Gender Politics of Franchise Paratexts," *Critical Studies in Media Communication* 34, no. 2 (2017), for further discussion.

21 P. David Marshall, *Celebrity and Power: Fame in Contemporary Culture* (Minneapolis: University of Minnesota Press, 1997), xi.

22 Richard Dyer, *Heavenly Bodies: Film Stars and Society* (London: British Film Institute/Macmillan Education, 1986).

23 Marshall, *Celebrity and Power*, 18.

24 Richard Dyer, "*A Star Is Born* and the Construction of Authenticity," in *Stardom: Industry of Desire*, ed. Christine Gledhill (London: Routledge, 1991), 136.

25 Marshall, *Celebrity and Power*, 58.

26 Dyer, "*A Star Is Born* and the Construction of Authenticity," 135.

27 Marshall, *Celebrity and Power*.

28 Rosemary Coombe, "The Celebrity Image and Cultural Identity: Publicity Rights and the Subaltern Politics of Gender," *Discourse* 14, no. 3 (1992): 59–88.

29 Coombe, "Celebrity Image and Cultural Identity," 66.

30 Coombe, "Celebrity Image and Cultural Identity," 66.

31 Jason Scott, "*Star Wars* as a Character-Oriented Franchise," in *Fan Phenomena: Star Wars*, ed. Mika Elovaara (Bristol: Intellect, 2013), 11.

32 Scott, "*Star Wars* as a Character-Oriented Franchise," 11.

33 Fisher, *Princess Diarist*, 192.

34 Fisher, *Princess Diarist*, 5.

35 Setoodeh, "Carrie Fisher on How George Lucas Stole Her Identity."

36 Fisher, *Princess Diarist*. In *Wishful Drinking*, Fisher recounts the story of George Lucas explaining to her why *the character* can't wear a bra in space during *A New Hope*. After making this story a part of her one-woman comedic show, Lucas would later offer Fisher a full technological accounting of why "you can't wear your brassiere in other galaxies" (Fisher, *Wishful Drinking*, 88).

37 Fisher, *Princess Diarist*, 38.

38 Fisher, *Princess Diarist*, 193.

39 Fisher, *Princess Diarist*, 211–13.

40 Meredith Woerner, "Carrie Fisher Thinks Slave Leia Bikini Haters Are Asinine," *Lost Angeles Times*, last modified December 17, 2015, www .latimes.com/entertainment/herocomplex/la-et-hc-star-wars-carrie-fisher -20151216-story.html.

41 Fisher, *Princess Diarist*, 226–27.

42 Fisher, *Princess Diarist*, 228.

43 Chris Taylor, *How Star Wars Conquered the Universe* (New York: Basic Books, 2014), 247.

44 Fisher, *Princess Diarist*, 243–44.

45 Fisher, *Princess Diarist*.

46 Ben Child, "Carrie Fisher: I Felt Pressured to Lose Weight for *Star Wars: The Force Awakens*," *The Guardian*, last modified December 1, 2015, www.theguardian.com/culture/2015/dec/01/carrie-fisher-weight-loss-star-wars-the-force-awakens.

47 Kyle Smith, "If Carrie Fisher Doesn't Like Being Judged on Looks, She Should Quit Acting," *New York Post*, December 30, 2015, http://nypost.com/2015/12/30/if-carrie-fisher-doesnt-like-being-judged-on-looks-she-should-quit-acting/.

48 Barbara L. Marshall and Momin Rahman, "Celebrity, Ageing, and the Construction of 'Third Age' Identities," *International Journal of Cultural Studies* 18, no. 6 (2014): 577–93.

49 Suzy D'Enbeau and Patrice M. Buzzanell, "The Erotic Heroine and the Politics of Gender at Work: A Feminist Reading of *Mad Men*'s Joan Harris," in *Heroines of Film and Television: Portrayals in Popular Culture*, ed. Norma Jones, Maja Bajac-Carter, and Bob Batchelor. (Lanham, MD: Rowman and Littlefield, 2014), 3.

50 Mary Elizabeth Williams, "*Star Wars* Lets Princess Leia Age Realistically: Is This an Alternate Hollywood Universe?" *Salon*, Last modified October 20, 2015, https://www.salon.com/2015/10/20/star_wars_lets_princess_leia_age_realistically_is_this_an_alternate_hollywood_universe.

51 Carrie Fisher, "Character Study: Carrie Fisher Bids Farewell to Princess Leia," *BulletMedia*, last modified January 4, 2013, http://bullettmedia.com/article/character-study-carrie-fisher-makes-peace-with-princess-leia/ (URL inactive).

52 Carrie Fisher, Twitter/@carrieffisher: "Please stop debating about whetherOR not [I]aged well.unfortunately it hurts all3 of my feelings.My BODY hasnt aged as well as I have.Blow us," December 28, 2015.

53 Sarah Seltzer, "Carrie Fisher Slams Critics of Her Appearance in 'The Force Awakens,'" *Flavorwire*, last modified December 30, 2015, http://flavorwire.com/553819/carrie-fisher-slams-critics-of-her-appearance-in-the-force-awakens.

54 Fisher, *Princess Diarist*, 200.

55 Chris Rojek, *Celebrity* (London: Reaktion Books, 2001), 189.

56 Kirsty Fairclough, "Nothing Less Than Perfect: Female Celebrity, Ageing, and Hyper-scrutiny in the Gossip Industry," in *Gender, Race and Class in the Media*, ed. Gail Dines, Jean M. Humez, Bill Yousman, and Lori Bindig Yousman (London: Sage, 2017), 265.

57 Fisher, *Princess Diarist*, 38.

58 Jennifer Pearson, " 'I will not apologize for how I look': *Star Wars* Star Daisy Ridley Hits Back at Body Shamer Who Ridiculed Her Online for Not Having Curves Like a 'Real Woman,' " *Daily Mail*, last modified March 9, 2016, www.dailymail.co.uk/tvshowbiz/article-3484676/Daisy-Ridley-hits-body -shamers-complained-s-skinny.html.

59 Macnicol, "In Defense of Princess Leia and 'Star Wars' Feminism."

60 Taylor, *How Star Wars Conquered the Universe*, 49, 55.

61 Jason Davis and Larry Pakowski, "The Influence of The Force," in *Fan Phenomena: Star Wars*, ed. Mika Elovaara (Bristol: Intellect, 2013), 99–100.

62 Meredith Woerner, "Remembering Carrie Fisher: Actress, Writer, Icon," *Baltimore Sun*, last modified December 27, 2016, www.baltimoresun.com/ sdhoy-remembering-carrie-fisher-actress-writer-icon-20161229-story .html.

63 Adam Howard, "Carrie Fisher Was a Feminist Force to Be Reckoned With," *NBC News*, last modified December 27, 2016, www.nbcnews.com/news/us -news/carrie-fisher-was-feminist-force-be-reckoned-n700531.

64 Howard, "Carrie Fisher Was."

65 Joanna Robinson, "How Carrie Fisher Became the Surprising Face of the Rebellion against Trump," *Vanity Fair*, last modified January 23, 2017, www .vanityfair.com/style/2017/01/carrie-fisher-todd-fisher-womens-march -donald-trump.

66 Robinson, "How Carrie Fisher Became the Surprising Face."

67 Vanessa Witter, email message to author, September 19, 2020.

68 Esther Zuckerman, " 'The Nerds Are Also Here': Talking With the Women Who Marched With Princess Leia," *AV Club*, last modified January 24, 2017, https://film.avclub.com/the-nerds-are-also-here-talking-to-the -women-who-mar-1798256791.

69 Matthew Corkins, "Princess Leia Poster: Legal Issues Won't Keep This Artist Out of the Rebellion," *New York Observer*, last modified February 17, 2017, https://observer.com/2017/02/princess-leia-poster-legal-issues-wont -keep-this-artist-out-of-the-rebellion.

70 Scott, "*Star Wars* as a Character-Oriented Franchise."

71 Fisher, *Princess Diarist*, 213.

72 Matthew Corkins, "Princess Leia Poster: Legal Issues Won't Keep This Artist Out of the Rebellion," *New York Observer*, last modified February 17, 2017, https://observer.com/2017/02/princess-leia-poster-legal-issues-wont

-keep-this-artist-out-of-the-rebellion. Even Witter's "rebellious" art eventually became commodified as for-profit entities appropriated the image for a variety of merchandise. Eventually Witter, too, began to sell screen prints on Etsy to reclaim some control over her art, but she donates a percentage of the sales to progressive causes (Vanessa Witter, email message to author, September 19, 2020).

73 Fisher, *Princess Diarist*, 31.

Gatekeeping the Past

FANDOM AND THE GENDERED CULTURAL MEMORY OF *STAR WARS*

Philipp Dominik Keidl

Upon Carrie Fisher's sudden death in 2016, and the subsequent public events of light saber vigils or gatherings at conventions, fans shared celebratory tributes and obituaries in the form of tweets, blog posts, videos, and podcasts.[1] Commemorations like these point to Fisher's legacy among and beyond *Star Wars* fans, particularly accentuating the impact she had on female fans who expressed their admiration for the actress and the character of Leia perceptibly after her death. They celebrate Fisher's achievements as an artist, feminist activist, and mental health advocate throughout her life. Among these tributes, however, are also examples that reiterate misogynist and sexist ideas of how *Star Wars* actresses and the characters they portray should be represented. Possibly the crudest examples are so-called fap-tributes or jerk-off challenges, featuring images of Fisher in and out of her role as Leia.[2] Demonstrably reinforcing hypermasculine notions about the *Star Wars* franchise, the videos demonstrate the readiness of male fans to ridicule Fisher's rejection and critique of her sexist depiction and reception since the 1970s.[3] And even examples in which some male fans try to paint a more nuanced image of Fisher and her impact in the role of Leia reveal a certain degree of disinterest and obliviousness toward her concerns. Together, these obituaries and tributes illustrate the struggles, and in some cases outright refusal, of many men to articulate more complex personal connections and meanings to Fisher other than her being a sex symbol, mother figure, or just the female lead in their favorite movie.[4]

These Carrie Fisher and Leia tributes are characteristic of a wide range of male-centric engagements with the past that position *Star Wars* and its fandom in relation to normative notions of gender and sexuality. Belonging to a movement within the *Star Wars* fandom that opposes representational parity and diversity in the fictional universe of the franchise, such male-centric fan memories and fan histories contribute to marginalizing, degrading, and excluding characters and fans that challenge such heteronormative philosophies. Whereas works such as the "De-Feminized Fanedit (aka The Chauvinist Cut)" of Rian Johnson's *The Last Jedi* (2017) try to take ownership of the *Star Wars* storyworld by erasing nearly all scenes with the female cast, male fans use nonfiction projects to control the commemoration of *Star Wars*.[5] As self-proclaimed gatekeepers of the past, their histories draw a picture of *Star Wars* and its "genuine" fan base as being predominantly male (as well as white, middle-class, straight, and cis), assigning an interpretative sovereignty of the franchise to men. In turn, women's fandom is presented as ephemeral or fake next to sexist and objectifying descriptions of female actresses, characters, and fangirls themselves. If women are addressed in more detail, they are portrayed as destructive for the franchise and its fan community. This is especially true regarding Kathleen Kennedy, current president of Lucasfilm, who is targeted as the cause for a decreasing interest in the franchise. Illustrated with demeaning depictions of her in Leia's metal bikini from *Return of the Jedi* (directed by Richard Marquand, 1983), such arguments degrade the worth and role of her and other women for the franchise and the fandom to that of sex objects readily available for men's consumption.[6]

Besides Fisher herself, feminist and queer fan activists have challenged and corrected such misconceptions by producing their own inclusive histories. They demonstrate that the franchise's female characters are more than hypersexualized cue givers and illustrate that *Star Wars* fandom has always been a more diverse group than many male fans would like to acknowledge.[7] A prominent example is Annalise Ophelian's documentary series *Looking for Leia*, which premiered in 2019 and explores the underrepresented history of female, nonbinary, and BIPOC *Star Wars* fans. As she explains, the perception that *Star Wars* fandom is predominantly driven by men persists not because men have been more active but because they have "been the most visible or the loudest or the most prominent."[8] Crucially, male fans could also achieve this advantageous visibility because "Star Wars' own official histories . . . erase[d] and marginalize[d] women's stories."[9] Even though several women have written books about the history of *Star Wars* for Lucasfilm, or curated successful museum exhibitions, Lucasfilm has elevated none of them to the same popularity and prominence as the company's former in-house historians J. W. Rinzler and Stephen J. Sansweet. In addition, many fan histories are constructed around or dedicated to action figures and the practice of collecting, thereby drawing from an industry that itself acts as a gatekeeper by limiting access to the franchise with their gender coding of action figures as "toys for boys."[10] Considering these discriminatory alliances, feminist and queer fan activists are up against four decades of *Star Wars* history-making and gatekeeping from a male point of view that keep the male gendering of the franchise and its fan community alive to the present day.

This chapter analyses how male fans have been acting as self-proclaimed "gatekeepers of the past" in order to claim ownership over the interpretative control of the franchise. By putting Fisher's death and the resulting tributes and homages into the context of these fan practices and discourses, this chapter has three interrelated goals. *First*, it determines the importance of history-making as a fan practice. The first section argues that fan-made histories ultimately shape what and how the past of *Star Wars* and its fan community is communicated within and beyond their respective fan communities. As is the case in all fan communities and practices, the creation and dissemination of knowledge about the past is highly hierarchized, giving women in the works discussed here little to no voice, resulting in a distorted view on female fandom. *Second*, it highlights the importance of action

Fig. 3.1. Several generations of *Star Wars* fans coming together in *Looking for Leia* (2019), directed by Annalise Ophelian.

figures and other merchandise in fan-made *Star Wars* histories. Since many fans reached for toys when they produced their Fisher and Leia tributes, the second section shows that *Star Wars* and its toys are not only gendered by toy design, branding, and retail but also by the nonfiction stories that fans tell with and about these toys. *Third*, Fisher and Leia homages help us understand how fans try to establish and position a collective memory of the actress and the character that leaves little space for questioning the dynamics undergirding the hypermasculine gendering of the franchise. Thus, the third section's analysis of action figure memorials demonstrates how some fans continue to strengthen such gender divides rather than to challenge them and how such dynamics functioned as a template when fans remembered Fisher/Leia and positioned the actress and the character into a male-centric history of *Star Wars*.

The Gender of Fan-Made Histories and Cultural Memory

Fans' obituaries and tributes to Fisher should be understood as a form of history-making. By engaging the past in different ways, they evoke a collective memory of the *Star Wars* fan community that is consumable for old fans and future fans alike. In their homages, fans cover information about the production history of the films, address Fisher's contribution to them, and also discuss the franchise's cultural impact. On a more personal level, they recall memories of watching scenes with Leia, seeing and meeting Fisher at conventions, or they show their Princess Leia merchandise collections, review the latest toy and collectible releases, and put them into context with previous lines. The presentation of this information and these memories differs in style and form, depending on the medium they use. While fans primarily work with spoken word, sound effects, and music in their podcasts, blogs include old and more recent pictures of Fisher in her roles, on the set, or at publicity events. Videos often feature moving images such as film scenes or interview snippets, and they also contain music and sound effects from the *Star Wars* films as well as from other sources. Some videos featuring toys use them in storylines to pay tribute to the actress, recreate scenes, or document the customization of figures, while other fans dedicate their toy reviews, unpacking videos, or "collections tours" to Fisher but do not address her death directly in much detail in the clips themselves.[11] In any case, by exploring the history of *Star Wars*, its merchandise, and its fan

Fig. 3.2. Here's a photo of Mary's ever-growing "Leia Land" (2020), an example of a female-driven *Star Wars* collection. Mary is a member of the Galactic Fempire, a social group devoted to feminist *Star Wars* fandom.

community, fans' tributes and obituaries engage with *Star Wars* history on both micro- and macrolevels.

In their popular uses of the past and the introduction of their own perspectives and individual voices, fan-made histories are part of a "participatory historical culture" in which knowledge about the past is formed and communicated outside academia and educational institutions.[12] Rather than dismissing such activities as amateurish or unprofessional, public historians like David Thelen argue that we take more seriously how "people can reshape the civic forum to better hear their voices and meet their needs . . . by using the past on their own terms."[13] Similarly, Raphael Samuel maintains that history is a "social form of knowledge; the work, in any given instance, of a thousand different hands," and not the prerogative of academic historians.[14] However, although public history leans toward the political left, the use of the past can be progressive and reactionary, empowering and discouraging, diverse and homogenous, striving for connection with others or pushing for exclusions. In the case of the works discussed in this chapter, the notion of "participatory historical culture" is applied to the work of male fans who seek for exclusion rather than inclusion and for reinforcing gendered hierarchies rather than breaking them down by producing and disseminating memories of *Star Wars* and its fan community.

The concept of "participatory historical culture" refers to various practices located outside academic structures and also often norms, ranging from the production of media by amateurs to conversations of the past over dinner. Despite this inclusive definition of history-making as a common cultural practice, the form and format of how people engage with the past matters as it ultimately results in new forms of institutionalization and hierarchization. Jan Assmann's differentiation between communicative memory and cultural memory is helpful to think about different hierarchies and forms of manifestations in this "participatorily historical culture" as well as the endurance of the knowledge and narratives produced. Whereas *communicative memory* is social and informally shared in personal interactions in everyday life by nonspecialists, *cultural memory* represents a form of institutionalization that is formalized and communicated by specialists and exists in disembodied form and does not rely on personal interactions.[15] And while there are "no specialists in informal, communicative memory," the "participation of a group in cultural memory is always highly differentiated" and therefore shows an "inherent tendency to elitism" as it "is never strictly egalitarian."[16] In the case of fan-made histories about *Star Wars*, and echoing Ophelian's remarks, male fans have been visibly, loudly, and prominently positioning themselves as specialists through the avid production of media. Supported by what Suzanne Scott calls the "convergence culture industry," discursively framing men as their primary target group, male fans could thereby forcefully shape the institutionalization and formalization of their version of the franchise's cultural memory in which women are either diminished, objectified, or, at best, play a supporting role.[17]

The difference between communicative and cultural memory points to the problems female fans have when attempting to gain visibility and recognition. On the one hand, women are often outnumbered by men in many projects. For instance, by December 2018, out of twenty-eight episodes of the podcast *My Star Wars Story*, only three interviews were with women.[18] On the other hand, while many male fans have gained public visibility through the production of museum exhibitions and print media, female fans often share their own memories and knowledge about the past through other or less formalized channels. Thus, they are in danger of being and remaining less visible, despite their contemporary vocal criticism and hashtag activism efforts on social media and emerging projects focusing on their experiences. For example, female fans expressed their discontent after J. J. Abrams explained that "*Star Wars* was . . . always a boys' thing and a movie that dads take their sons to" and expressed his hopes that even "though that's still very much the case, [he] was really hoping that [*The Force Awakens*] could be a movie that mothers can take their daughters to as well."[19] While tweets may challenge the masculine grip on the franchise, the attention they get is relatively short-lived in comparison to the institutionalized and formalized communication channels that male fans have built and that privilege their own memories. What I want to point to here is not that there are no female *Star Wars* fans, or that they do not have a bigger presence in other pockets of the fan community, but rather that they are rarely given space by male fans in their take on the franchise's cultural memory.

Consider the following three key themes that illustrate male-gendered biases in fans' history-making, all of which can be exemplified through fan autobiographies. *First*, fan autobiographies often feature more or less explicit references to Fisher's sex appeal in her role as Leia. They contribute to reducing the only female lead character in the first trilogy to a sex symbol for pubescent boys. Reflecting about the lasting appeal of the franchise for a twelve-year-old boy in *Collect all 21!: Memoirs of a Star Wars Geek*, John Booth comes to the conclusion that "lightsabers and spaceships and stormtroopers remained fun ideas, and if you're going to put Princess Leia in a metal bikini: Again perfect age for it."[20] In another section, he recalls how being "twelve and getting a signed picture of Princess Leia in the Jabba's Palace Slave Girl outfit" was "cool," while telling his parents what was actually in the envelope was "squirmy."[21] Tony Pacitti pushes the heterosexist objectification of Fisher and Leia even further by providing a more detailed description of Fisher's body in *My Best Friend Is a Wookie: A Memoir* when he recalls how he "memorized every inch of Carrie Fisher's illustrated body on the covers of *Star Wars* and *Jedi*—her boobs lifted to kingdom come on the former and the obvious, sultry pose in her metal slave bikini on the latter."[22] Moreover, the objectification of Fisher is propelled by homophobic descriptions, such as Pacitti's anecdote about a gay schoolmate whom he "would have socked [if he] didn't think it would have looked like [he] was hitting a girl, and [he] was certainly brought up better than to hit a woman, regardless of any amount of stubble that may be showing from under her rouge."[23] While Pacitti retells "one boy's journey to find his place in the galaxy," his memories clearly exclude non-gender-conforming boys from the galaxy far, far away.[24] A pattern also evident in other projects in which gay men, if they address their sexual identity and voice their perspectives at all, usually do so in an asexual manner. They join straight fans in celebrating Leia as a heroine but do not express any memories of sexual desire for the male cast.[25]

The *second* narrative trope is not directed toward Fisher but to female fans, whose fandom male authors recall as ephemeral and less likely to last into adulthood, unlike their own experiences. Consider the following quotes from Gib van Ert's autobiography *A Long Time Ago: Growing Up with and out of Star Wars*: "I was ecstatic. My sister was also very pleased, but looking back and considering how her interests developed in later years I think she liked these [Kenner *Star Wars*] toys mainly because her big brother liked them, and she liked him."[26] His account of his sister's passion for *Star Wars* implies that it was not due to her own interest in the franchise but rather because of her brother. A "sort-of-fannish" follower rather than a true fan. The idea of fangirls is something that he also questions in regard to his children and their likeliness to become fans. According to him, the birth of his son was "more consequential, from a *Star Wars* perspective . . . for [he], and much of the rest of the world, still consider *Star Wars* to be chiefly a boy's interest."[27] And even though he immediately acknowledges that "this is demonstrably wrong in specific cases" and hopes that his daughter will like *Star Wars*, his comments clearly indicate how the gendered notions of fandom are projected from one generation onto another.[28] This is also possible because, in some cases, fangirls are mentioned but their fandom is never explored in as much detail as the fan identities of the authors or their male friends. For instance, in Booth's anecdote about a girl in one of his middle school classes who'd picked Fisher as a celebrity she admired, we never learn about the motivations behind her choice. The main point of the short chapter seems to be the simple equation that boys like Harrison Ford and girls like Carrie Fisher, period.[29] Such a gender-biased evaluation stands for the predicament that a gap of diversity in *Star Wars* history has left: as long as fans do not include a more diverse set of voices more rigorously into the history of *Star Wars*, they will remain the rather vague and unspecific "specific cases" to which Van Ert refers.[30]

igrewupstarwars.com
Photos and Memories of Everyone who grew up with Star Wars

Vader and the rest of the lineup 1982

By Tom Berges   December 8, 2015   In Photo   No Comments

A Motley Crew indeed! Vader (Jake) and the rest of the Halloween lineup in 1982.

Fig. 3.3. "Jake is Vader" but who is Leia in this Halloween photo? One of many examples in which female *Star Wars* fans are present but nevertheless remain unacknowledged. (Screenshot recreated from *I Grew Up Star Wars* with permission. Original family photo "Church Halloween Festival" [1982] by Jake Stevens.)

The *third* narrative trope is that of the "fake geek girl" who knows allegedly little to nothing about *Star Wars* and therefore cannot compete with male fans when it comes to fundamental comprehension of the franchise. Pacitti describes one female fan who challenges his authority as a "bandwagoner"—"and girl no less"—who dares to challenge him and attempts as "a neophyte to sound like she knew what she was up to when she undeniably did not."[31] His ideas about female fans is either that they do not know what they are talking about or that they identify as *Star Wars* fans for the wrong reasons—an unreasonable "swooning over the dashing Han Solo"—while his passion for Leia is grounded in, and evidence for, a long-standing fandom.[32] Such descriptions are in line with Suzanne Scott's observation that "fan culture has expanded so dramatically, but women continue to be framed as an invasive and unwelcome presence."[33] Through such autobiographical accounts, the idea of the fake geek girl actually becomes a seemingly historically grounded identity that continues to devalue fangirls in the present.

For Scott, narrow, exclusive, and highly gendered visions of fan identity are the result of the "convergence culture industry" that privileges fan boys and therefore supports the promulgation of "misogynist boundary-policing practices within fan culture."[34] Interestingly, Lucasfilm has shown efforts to hire more women on its staff who produce and promote works on the franchise's history, in addition to hiring Kennedy as president of Lucasfilm in 2012. In December 2018, eleven out of the twenty-three contributors listed on StarWars.com were female. Moreover, Laela French from the Lucasfilm Archives has curated exhibitions, and Carol Titelman, Deborah Call, and Trisha Biggar, among others, have written *Star Wars* publications.[35] In this regard, Lucasfilm-sponsored histories have a more diverse authorship than the predominantly male history community working independently from the company. But just as the diversification of the film's cast does not necessarily translate into the production of merchandise for female characters, the parity in authorship admittedly does not necessarily result in more attention to fangirls or a correction of the masculine heterosexist branding of such histories. And as was already mentioned in the introduction, the most prominent *Star Wars* historians who have produced their histories with the support of Lucasfilm continue to be men.

There is a crucial difference between fan fiction and fan-made histories. At least in its mainstream iteration, fan-made histories are less likely to actively challenge conventions of gender as well as sexuality, race, ethnicity, class, or age. In contrast, through the combination of reality and fiction, fanfic "makes *unreal* events and characters . . . *real*; makes *absent* events and characters *present*; and brings *past* or *dead* events and characters into the *now*" so that the "archive of history now contains cultural forms that hybridize science fiction and global crises and interweave popular entertainment genres and public protests."[36] Although such debates may happen more visibly in communicative practices, they are less present in the existing fan-made *Star Wars* histories that are formalized and institutionalized across media by men. Megen de Bruin-Molé argues that "it is not *Star Wars*' representation of women or its own feminist agenda that matters most, but rather how these representations and aims are continually negotiated and reinterpreted by fans, creators, licensees, and feminists around the world."[37] Fan-produced histories are evidence of fans' masculine-driven (re)negotiation and reinterpretation of *Star Wars*, reproducing existing discriminatory gender discourses rather than challenging them. This male-centered cultural memory continues to frame an alleged lack of fangirls as a historical continuity rather than to expose it as an artificial construct and form of gender policing of the past, therefore also enabling male fans to claim ownership over the interpretation of female characters. As the next section will show, action figures and fan-made histories of action figures play an important role in anchoring and expanding such themes and tropes.

Action Figures and Their Historization as Toys for Boys

Action figures are highly gendered toys, which were invented and designed as a masculine counterpart to fashion dolls for girls and directly targeted at the market for toys for boys.[38] Considering the overwhelming success of Kenner and Hasbro *Star Wars* action figures, this particular toy genre has also contributed to the gendering of *Star Wars* fandom. To the present day, male action figures outnumber figures dedicated to female characters. Pointing to the gendered business infrastructure of media franchises, Kathleen Kennedy admitted that, if she is "sitting in a meeting about toys, it's predominantly men."[39] And as another insider report revealed, these men often believe that if "you put a [female character] in a boy's toy, boys will not buy it."[40] While there have been Leia action figures from the first moment, there are considerably fewer iterations of her, or any of the other few female characters, than for some of the male characters:

> Kenner/Hasbro made forty-four Leia figures between 1978 and 2012. Compare this to Luke Skywalker, the most frequently reproduced figure, who had eighty-nine versions in the same period. Including Leia, Hasbro has released ninety-five different female characters in total from across the franchise, many of which have multiple versions and releases (Padmé comes in twenty-six varieties).[41]

The reluctance to produce female action figures became evident once more with the lack of Rey toys when *The Force Awakens* was released and Disney's limited production of Leia toys in the face of expanding "pink franchising" practices.[42] Their absence signifies the rigidness with which media conglomerates and toy producers stick to their gendered imaginations of their audiences as predominantly male.[43]

Bearing in mind the storytelling agency of action figures as "authoring tools" and their paratextual capacity to strengthen or weaken established meanings, the lack of female action figures ultimately restricts the *Star Wars* stories that can be told.[44] In addition, the disproportional number of female action figures limits imaginations of who can tell *Star Wars* stories or be a fan in the first instance.[45] Given the prominence of action figures in *Star Wars* histories, some of the causalities can be reformulated as follows: it not only matters how many female action figures are produced or how they are gendered through design and branding, but also how their feminist agendas are negotiated and interpreted—if not denied in some examples—in stories fans tell about them in regard to their cultural and production histories. If the lack of female action figures does restrict what *Star Wars* stories can be told and who can tell them, the lack of fangirls and female voices in fan-made histories of *Star Wars* further strengthens gendered notions of fan identities and attempts to erase accounts of female fandom spanning from the 1970s to the present day. It is therefore necessary to examine how (female) action figures are positioned in fans' discourses about the past.

Looking at action figures from this perspective reveals that even though Leia action figures and other female-themed merchandise are discussed in every collectible guide, authors seldom include accounts of actually playing with these toys that would establish deeper connections between owner and character/toy. On the one hand, male fans put less emphasis on their recollections of playing with action figures of Leia as they do with characters such as Luke, Chewbacca, Han Solo, Darth Vader, or Boba Fett. Most of the time, Leia runs as a poor second or appears as the love interest in need of rescue. To put it differently, even though Leia as an action figure is a toy for boys, her gender nevertheless seemingly restricts her appeal for boys.[46] On the other hand, girls who might have identified or played in more creative ways with the action figure are rarely included in these histories and therefore cannot present alternative play stories. As such, the Leia action figures' "first life" as toys finds less attention than their "second life" as collectibles in fan-made histories. There, instead of a leading role in playground recollections, Leia stars in stories about acquisition, restoration, trade, and exhibition. *Star Wars* fans and collectors pay attention to her due to their goals to build a complete collection or their connoisseurship about the material culture of the franchise as a whole and less because they connect childhood memories with her comparable to those they have with male characters and toys.

Consider the article "Princess Leia Organa Life Size Action Figure" in *The Star Wars Collectors Archive*, which demonstrates male fans' confusion about a toy that is branded as an action figure (and therefore "for boys") but comes with hairstyle demonstrations and beauty accessories rather than guns (and therefore reads for them as such "for girls"):

> [the toy] straddled the precarious divide that exists between "action figure" and . . . umm, girly toy. On the one hand, it was part of an action figure line, and its box referred to it as such. On the other hand, the company's advertising and the doll's play features made it clear that it was geared towards young girls. . . . Trust me, no self-respecting guy kid wanted this thing. Shoot, instead of the film shots and cool action scenes featured on some of the other 12″ figure boxes, what do we get on the reverse of the Leia package? Hair style demonstrations, for crissakes! . . . She didn't even come with a weapon, the first sign that a toy might be coming up a little bit short in the masculinity department.[47]

The quote shows the perception that intersections between gendered play themes and toys is impossible, going as far as to claim that boys' playing with these toys would result in a loss of self-respect as well as respect from their peers. Only as a collector did the author learn to appreciate the figure and "the kitschiness of the hairdo paraphernalia."[48] These dynamics are interesting, as the author as well as other fans have shown awareness about the aggressive gendered branding of the toys, arguing that "Kenner's tendency to market its products to boys" implied that *Star Wars* "was not a suitable enthusiasm for a girl."[49] Interestingly, however, the article does not include opinions about the toy from people who have actually played with it—be it from a girl or a boy—but rather implies that since no self-respecting boy would have ever played with her nobody ultimately did. As a result, the toy's worth is established through its status as a collectible, which in its perceived obscurity is closer to some of the more obscure merchandise on the market rather than everyday toys. If "merchandise can help fans establish their legitimacy within particular communities while also functioning as a status symbol that reinforces hierarchies and differences within that community," this Leia action figure as a collectible and not as a toy creates hierarchies among *Star Wars* merchandise (past mass-market toy versus present rare collectible), its use (playing versus collecting and displaying), as well as among fans' interactions with them (player versus collector; or girl/effeminate boy versus man).[50]

The blog *I Grew Up Star Wars* not only shows similar patterns in neglecting research on fangirls' perspectives but also exhibits how outright documentations of girls expressing their fandom are relegated. *I Grew Up Star Wars* features images of fans playing with their *Star Wars* toys and also with the fans dressed up as their favorite characters. Often taken at Christmas, birthdays, or on Halloween, the blog photos give intimate insights into fans' private lives. The vast majority of the images are of boys in the 1970s and 1980s, while women and girls are mostly present as (nameless) grandmothers, mothers, sisters, or friends who, at first sight, are showing little or no interest in *Star Wars*. In some instances, the pictures document clear gender roles with girls holding dolls and plush cats while the boys are depicted with toys from the franchise.[51] However, even if we may attribute this to the documentation of specific interests in sibling dynamics, in other instances, images show girls dressed up as a *Star Wars* character yet they still do not get mentioned in the image's captions. For instance, one image description reads: "A Motley Crew indeed! Vader (Jake) and the rest of the Halloween lineup in 1982," completely ignoring that there is a girl dressed up as Princess Leia in the picture.[52] Granted, nobody remembers all their acquaintances from their childhood by name, and yet it is interesting to see how the blog leans toward documenting how it was to grow up with *Star Wars* for boys and not for girls. Only a few images capture shared fandom for *Star Wars*, such as an example of a man's recollection of his "first Halloween with [his] sister after [they] saw a *New Hope* at the drive-in" that shows her in a Leia and him in a Han Solo costume.[53] Still, considering the overall few images of female fans on the blog, they can be seen more as a reinforcement than deconstruction to the perception that female fandom is possible "in specific cases" but not the norm, or that grown-up women are less likely to bother posting pictures of themselves because their fandom has long vanished and is of no meaning to them in the present.

The absence or marginalization of female fandom fuels contemporary fan rejections of Lucasfilm's goal to diversify the storyline, cast, and fan community of *Star Wars*. Especially since the release of *The Last Jedi*, some male fans have visibly expressed their discontent online and often in openly toxic manners. One strategy has been to use action figures to visualize the lack of interest in the new trilogy, which some male fans criticized for being allegedly too female and diverse. While some fans removed female characters in the abovementioned "de-feminized" edits of *The Last Jedi* to imagine *Star Wars* without women, other fans use action figures with the opposite strategy: rather than making female characters invisible, they produce footage of large numbers of unsold female action figures in retail stores. In these YouTube videos, fans use the footage of merchandise-filled shelves and special offers as evidence that girls do not care about *Star Wars* products as well as that boys still do not want to play with female-themed action figures. Even worse, some fans argue, Lucasfilm is putting off the core *Star Wars* fan base so much that they have stopped buying merchandise altogether. In turn, the Marvel franchise is presented as a successful counterexample, completely ignoring the criticism fans have voiced about the lack of female figures in their action figure lines.

In addition, the sexist and heterosexist character of *Star Wars* fandom is further exemplified by references to the supposedly unattractive appearance of the female characters of the more recent films, also referencing Carrie Fisher's aging. Because the female cast is allegedly purposefully styled so unattractively, it supposedly further puts male consumers off to watch the films or buy the action figures.[54] Fans use the notion of "Bolshevik marketing" to describe Disney's strategies and align this marketing with democratic socialism, which they perceive to be anything but democratic. According to some fans, Lucasfilm under Disney tries with their Bolshevik marketing to tell audiences what they ought to want without respecting their actual interest and demographic makeup, thereby mirroring for them communist politics. Thus, Lucasfilm's goals to become more diverse, and diversity politics in general, are equated to restrictions of free will in the sense that boys and girls are forced to play with female action figures when none of them really wants to[55]—an argument supported with footage of boys cheering full of joy when they receive their *Star Wars* gifts, reinforcing the lack of documentation about girls showing the same interest.[56]

These fan arguments have an important temporal and spatial dimension that genders *Star Wars* fandom and its merchandise. In terms of temporality, they present collectors as individuals who are as much *Star Wars* fans as adults as when they were children. Their endurance and continuing interest are in stark contrast to the comparably small number of similar visible female fan collectors turned historians who could correct their masculine bias. Moreover, in addition to the small number of female fans included in these media, women are often cast as uncomprehending girlfriends and wives. Anecdotes about women forcing their partners to get rid of their collections instead of showing support add to such gendered stereotypes.[57] In terms of space, such media show an interesting dynamic between images of retail spaces filled with *Star Wars* merchandise as an example of the lack of female fandom and images of merchandise-filled cabinets in fans' homes as evidence of the commitment of fans to the franchise. Women are rhetorically and visually framed as anti-consumer, while men are the true and big consumers of merchandise and collectibles. These videos send a message to Lucasfilm that their more progressive representational strategies misunderstand the alleged core of *Star Wars* audiences (men) and imagine a nonexistent audience (women). Hence, their argument is that Lucasfilm should focus on the men who have been with the franchise all along and have therefore been responsible for its success in the first place rather than waste talent, resources, and fan patience to diversify fan communities.

Fan-made histories and the mediation of action figures as boy toys are crucial in understanding Carrie Fisher and Leia tributes and obituaries produced by action figures collectors and with action figures. The next section will show how notions of Fisher and Leia as a sex symbol found their ways into these homages. They also exemplify some of the consequences that stem from the exclusion of female perspectives and experiences that would allow such a perspective as well as how they keep gendered fan discourses afloat that police who is part of *Star Wars* fan history and what fan histories are told.

Action Figure Memorials

Carrie Fisher had made it a habit to joke about her ubiquitous presence as merchandise, commenting about it in interviews, at award shows, and in her autobiographies. In *The Princess Diarist*, she recalls how she emerged from her "three-week-long ECT treatment to discover that [she was] not only this Princess Leia creature but also several-sized dolls, various T-shirts and posters, some cleansing items, and a bunch of other merchandise."[58] And in *Wishful Drinking*, she portrays George Lucas as "the man who made [her] into a little doll! . . . A little doll that one of my exes could stick pins into whenever he was annoyed with me."[59] Given the vast number of *Star Wars* products and the collecting subculture, it was no surprise that many fans reached for some of these objects to honor the actress and the character of Princess Leia. Obituaries produced with action figures or by action figure fans and collectors are particularly interesting as they not only demonstrate the gendered dynamics discussed in the previous two sections but also show how these dynamics served as a template in commemorating Fisher/Leia and writing the actress and the character into a highly gendered cultural memory of *Star Wars*.

Following the idea that boys do not play with female action figures, Princess Leia toys generally feature as collectibles rather than toys in these tributes and obituaries. Videos such as "Carrie Fisher 'Princess Leia' Toy Tribute" present images of Leia action figures in their packaging intercut with images and clips from the first trilogy, while images of boys playing with the toys are missing. The toys are staged in front of a white background, directing the attention to their sculptural qualities and how they capture the movie characters rather than moments of actual play and closer insights into personal identifications with the character.[60] Even in cases where fans recall Leia's impact as an action heroine and how they were attracted by her agency, this does not result in a closer description of how this might have translated into actual play.[61] This is not to say that there is a right and wrong way to pay tribute to Leia or Fisher, but if we consider the lack of memories of actual play with Leia toys, such tributes would have been a chance to fill this gap rather than to leave it open or actually extend it by making Leia toys primarily collectibles. If collecting *Star Wars* action figures is about "accumulating human and social significance as each object comes to be in the possession of an individual with their own story to tell and their own reasons for buying and collecting," these tributes mark their producers, and give them significance, as *Star Wars* collectors rather than specific Leia fans.[62] For lack of documentation otherwise, they manifest the idea that men may collect female action figures but that boys cannot be bothered to play with them.

The status of Leia action figures as collectibles rather than toys is also marked by speculation about the potential and actual spike of value of Leia merchandise after Fisher's death.[63] For instance, one comment on the website for the "Hot Toy Princess Leia" figure reads as follows: "I've been collecting the SW figures for a while, holding off on the Leia. I ordered when I heard her health had taken a turn. Now it's sold out. People really loved her. RIP."[64] Not only does the quote imply a previous disinterest in the character, but this particular commentator also measures Leia's popularity by sales numbers instead of personal value. Fisher had predicted this development in her autobiographies, foreseeing that objects with her signature might become more valuable and therefore making her death at least "worth something to some people."[65] Some fans criticized such speculations, providing consultation on how to handle the current spike in prices, but also urging collectors to not forget to "appreciate Carrie Fisher for who she was . . . an actress with a beautiful voice, a ferociously funny writer, and someone whose films have left us with fantastic memories for almost four decades now."[66] Still, through the immediate trading of Leia merchandise, some male fans and collectors presented themselves as rationally following the economic logics of collecting rather than engaging in overly emotional statements. The toys were a catalyst for telling nostalgic stories about one's childhood, but they also capitalized on one's previous investment as a collector in Leia action figures as a commodity.

Generally, many tributes included reflections on Fisher's life and career, covering widely publicized episodes in her life. Fans addressed her childhood growing up as Hollywood royalty, her growing stardom with *Star Wars*, her work as an author and script doctor, and her struggle with drugs and depression that came with her rise to fame. Some of these biographical episodes had even been translated into toys. A fan-made collectible action figure of Fisher's comfort dog Gary, the French bulldog with the floppy tongue who accompanied Fisher in her later years everywhere and therefore became a constant presence at *Star Wars* conventions and promotion tours, had been produced and traded before her death, and images of it circulated widely after she passed away.[67] Crucially, however, these tributes often lack reference to the issues Fisher had with the franchise itself, including her life as a commodity and as a sex symbol. As a matter of fact, in many cases, masculine-driven fan-made tributes and obituaries overlook or downplay Fisher's criticism of *Star Wars*, thereby writing them out of the franchise's histories as well as her biography, thus keeping the franchise free from the blame of sexism and mindless consumption. Indeed, by using action figures in the form of unpacking, reviewing, and customizing them, these tributes celebrate consumer and commodity culture as criticized by Fisher rather than distance themselves from it.

Consider Fisher's thorny relationship to her metal bikini costume from *Return of the Jedi*. Later in life, Fisher primarily used the bikini to lampoon her past status as a sex symbol and the bluntness with which fans occasionally shared their sexual fantasies about her—with her. While Fisher's jokes about it generated laughter, her autobiographies also document how much she scorned being "a fantasy that geeky teenage boys across the globe jerked off to . . . with some frequency."[68] As was the case with her prediction about future financial speculations with her signature, Fisher anticipated that the metal bikini image would be used to announce her death.[69] Indeed, being memorialized for or with this scene was something she did not approve of, and she was considerably upset when the Madame Tussauds Wax Museum chose the metal bikini for her outfit instead of the iconic white dress, while all other cast members wore their regular costumes. Despite Fisher's outspoken criticism of the costume, which in some instances fans construed as affirmation, the metal bikini featured prominently in many tributes, for example in the form of fan-made custom action figures that led to comments such as "She looks sex!"[70]

But the male gaze on Fisher and Leia action figures was also present beyond the bikini, such as in videos showing a custom gown with a larger cleavage, resembling her look on the original *A New Hope* poster that accentuated her legs and bosom.[71] These collectible toys materialize and make fans' sexual desires tangible. And even in instances in which fans acknowledged her resistance to being a sex symbol, they claimed ownership of her and their sexual fantasies, stressing them as undisputable facts that cannot be denied retroactively.[72] Such stories neatly fall in line with numerous videos produced also before her death that sexualized her through action figures, including footage of male fans licking the boxes that contained the toy in the bikini and introduction of the video explaining that jerking off to slave Leia was a rite of passage to manhood.[73] In one podcast, a fan recalls how he was sure that he was straight, despite him not having been grossed out by gay men, because he was into Fisher. He concludes that a lot of boys knew they were heterosexual because they were into her and that guys are unconsciously looking for Leia in their partners.[74] In other words, such remarks do not break with the objectification of Fisher and Leia but transform the actress into a "fannish" Kinsey scale to confirm boys' heterosexuality.

Fisher's criticism of *Star Wars* and its fan community became tangible in the sexual analogies she used to describe her role and submission to the promotion circuit Lucasfilm has established in the last forty years. In *The Princess Diarist*, she spends a whole chapter explaining how she felt like a lap dancer when she was promoting *Star Wars*, comparing the signing of autographs to sex work, to which she agreed due to financial problems. As she explains, signing autographs is

> lap dancing without cash being placed in any underwear, and there's no pole. [. . .] It is certainly a higher form of prostitution: the exchange of a signature for money, as opposed to a dance or a grind. Instead of stripping off clothes, the celebrity removes the distance created by film or stage. Both traffic in intimacy. [. . .] To be sure, it is "selling out," which comes with feelings of embarrassment and shame. But if you're selling for high enough numbers, the duration of that humiliation has a more fleeting quality [. . .] over time I have managed to rejigger my definition of dignity to the point where it comfortably includes lap dancing.[75]

The analogy of the lap dance is an imaginative way to make readers understand how she was able to bluntly criticize Madam Tussauds for their choice of costume for her wax figure and nevertheless choose to include a picture of her visit to the museum with her posing next to the display in her book.[76] It might be this double-edgedness that has led some fans to read

Fisher's presence at conventions as a sign of unconditional appreciation for the impact *Star Wars* had on her life and career in terms of fame and wealth. One fan argues in his podcast that her presence at conventions "was real, . . . she wanted to be there; she embraced it, it was not just a job, it was not just making money; she really embraced the whole fandom and the whole *Star Wars* community," while two other fans interpret in their podcast her presence at conventions as a tribute to the fans who "gave her a decent living" and an indication that she "[gave] it back to the fans."[77] However, these proclamations show ignorance of her reluctance and emotional distance to her presence at such events by implementing an image of an actress full of gratitude and sympathy, with the latter proclamation also claiming ownership over Fisher by putting her in debt to the fan community. No doubt, Fisher was aware of how much *Star Wars* had affected her life for the good, but such claims nevertheless disrespect Fisher and her critical opinions about the franchise and its fan community. If some fans mourned that the Rebellion had lost its most important female and feminist agent, many tributes and obituaries by male fans took the teeth out of Fisher's witty refusals to conform to misogynistic dynamics and gendered stereotypes in franchise logics.

Accordingly, these tributes need to be read within longer heterosexist discourses on *Star Wars* history, including the gendering of action figures, and contemporary debates of the franchise and its fandom. Drawing on sociologist Anthony Giddens, Rebecca Williams deploys the idea of "ontological security" to theorize what happens when an object of fandom ceases to exist or fandom itself ends, such as through the cancellation of a franchise, the death of a celebrity, or a scandal that makes a person or show unsupportable.[78] Ontological security refers to "the confidence that most human beings have in the continuity of their self-identity and in the constancy of the surrounding social and material environments of action."[79] Fisher's death fell at a time when the ontological security of male fans seemed to be in distress. On the one hand, Lucasfilm's attempts to make the franchise more diverse resulted in the creation of more female characters in leading and supporting roles in the *Star Wars* storyworld than in any of the trilogies before. In addition, in the eyes of many fans, *The Last Jedi* transformed Luke from a hero into a bitter old man, not doing justice to his heroic character as he was presented in the first trilogy. Fisher's death therefore left many fans with questions about what would happen in the third episode, now that the actress is dead, and her appearances had been fairly short. In other words, the *Star Wars* storyworld was going through several changes with an unknown outcome in terms of content and its impact on the fandom of many individuals. On the other hand, critical voices about hypermasculine franchise branding practices and sexist depictions of women have become louder from within and from outside fan communities, challenging the hegemony of men by celebrating the feminist agency of Fisher and Leia. Male fans who use and reinforce narrative tropes of Fisher and Leia as sex objects, collectibles, and accomplices in the fan circuit serve to counteract the feminist interventions that occurred with Fisher's death, and function as a protection of these fans' ontological security as the primary audience for *Star Wars*. Their homages and tributes draw a picture of Fisher that seamlessly connects to four decades of male-centric and heterosexist history-making among fans. They add another historical piece to the framework that holds together their ontological security as fans and men.

Conclusion

This is not to say that there are no female perspectives on *Star Wars* history. Fisher's death has encouraged many fangirls to look back at their fandom and the *Star Wars* franchise, and Annalise Ophelian's crowdfunded seven-part documentary series has pushed the boundaries of male-centric *Star Wars* histories.[80] But as long as projects like *Looking for Leia* remain the exception rather than the norm in terms of widely publicized projects on *Star Wars* history that give voice to how women have practiced their fandom over the last forty years, the cultural memory of the *Star Wars* franchise remains dominated by men. As this chapter has argued, those fan historians who have established themselves as gatekeepers of the franchise's past have been predominantly men, whose heterosexist perspectives of the franchise have been primarily sidelining the perspectives of fan girls and minority voices. Action figures have played an important role in this process, since the highly gendered toys have been the primary subject of many *Star Wars* histories or have functioned as a narrative device to structure autobiographical accounts. The result has been a male-dominated and hetero-centric fan-made history of *Star Wars* that functions as a buffer for recent fan activism that challenges the continuing gendering of the franchise and its audience as male. While women may regularly step forward to proclaim their past and present fandom, the gendered, institutionalized, and formalized cultural memory of *Star Wars* continues to frame them as the exception rather than the norm. The lack of documentation about female fandom therefore becomes a discursive tool of heterosexist protectivism that surfaced yet again after the passing of Carrie Fisher. Although Fisher's death has resulted in many publicly feminist interventions, and even if hypermasculine comments on the actress and the character of Leia might have been not as visible, her death has also served for others to brand *Star Wars* history as masculine and hetero-centric. As such, examining what stories fans tell about the franchise and its material culture—and not only representational gender parity on screen and among paratexts—affords an examination of the strategies that keep gender divides and tensions in fandom a contemporary phenomenon rather than one of the past.

Notes

This work was supported by the European Regional Development Fund and the Mobilitas Pluss programme [MOBJD349].

1   For examples of public gatherings, see BigFatPanda, "Carrie Fisher—Debbie Reynolds—Lightsaber Tribute Vigil-Disney's Hollywood Studios—Fan Event," YouTube video, 3:01, January 14, 2017, www.youtube.com/watch ?v=BfVPur_ZIB0; Inside the Magic, "Carrie Fisher Tribute at Star Wars Celebration 2017 with George Lucas, Daughter Billie Lourd," YouTube video, 8:13, April 13, 2017, www.youtube.com/watch?v=9wHtkH4K0_A.

2   For example, see StarWarsFapTributes, "Carrie Fisher—Sexy Fap Tribute #1," YouTube video, 2:06, March 27, 2019, www.youtube.com/watch ?v=yI6aUHsK9Yo; rocky joncen, "HD Carrie Fisher Jerk Off Challenge," YouTube video, 52:02, March 11, 2017, www.youtube.com/watch?v= 5LPTY0o8kDw&t=266s; Hot Celebrities, "Carrie Fisher | Star Wars | Princess Leia | Sexy Tribute |," YouTube video, 5:35, December 9, 2018, www .youtube.com/watch?v=tL1KiZbX5fo&t=74s.

3   Most notably in her autobiographies: Carrie Fisher, *Wishful Drinking* (New York: Simon & Schuster, 2008), Kindle; Carrie Fisher, *Shockaholic* (New York City: Simon & Schuster, 2011), Kindle; Carrie Fisher, *The Princess Diarist* (Boston: Blue Rider Press, 2016), Kindle. Fisher adapted *Wishful Drinking* into a stage show in 2008, which premiered as a documentary film on HBO in 2010.

4 For a discussion of Leia as a mother figure, see "Boushh, Bor Gullet and Bros: The SWCA Podcast Episode 79," *The Star Wars Collectors Archive Podcast* (podcast audio), January 8, 2017, https://podcasts.apple.com/us/podcast/boushh-bor-gullet-and-bros-the-swca-podcast-episode-79/id359016334?i=1000379714724.

5 "The Last Jedi: De-Feminized Fanedit (aka The Chauvinist Cut)," Archive .org video, 46:22, January 14, 2018, https://archive.org/details/thepiratebay-19660049_201809.

6 For example, see the website Disney Star Wars Is Dumb: https://disneystarwarsisdumb.wordpress.com/.

7 For Fisher tributes, see the website Rebel Princes: A Carrie Fisher Tribute (http://carrie-fisher.net/), or tributes published on The Mary Sue, such as: Maddy Myers, "In Memoriam: We Already Miss Carrie Fisher So Much," *The Mary Sue*, December 27, 2016, www.themarysue.com/carrie-fisher-in-memoriam/. In addition to these examples, female-driven projects include the podcasts *Scavenger's Hoard* (www.youtube .com/channel/UCa9hEU3oW1zb4hgv-IrwKnQ); *Rebel Grrrl* (https://makingstarwars.net/category/podcasts/rebelgrrrl/); *Lattes with Leia* (http://coffeewithkenobi.com/lattes-with-leia-featuring-amy-ratcliffe -and-dr-andrea-latemendi-join-the-coffee-with-kenobi-family/); *Fangirls Going Rogue* (http://fangirlsgoingrogue.com/); *Geeky Bubble* (https://thewookieegunner.com/) as well as the blogs and sites *FANgirl* (http://fangirlblog.com) and *Women of Star Wars* (https://womenofstarwars .tumblr.com/). The podcast *Sapphic Skywalkers* focuses on female characters and LGBTQ representation in *Star Wars* (https://podcasts.apple.com/us/podcast/sapphic-skywalkers/id1185696012).

8 "Looking for Leia: I Didn't Know That Other Women Did This," *WePresent*, accessed September 13, 2020, https://wepresent.wetransfer.com/story/looking-for-leia/.

9 Rebecca Harrison, "I Know Because It's Me," *Contingent Magazine*, December 8, 2019, https://contingentmagazine.org/2019/12/08/i-know-because-its-me/.

10 Suzanne Scott, "#Wheresrey?: Toys, Spoilers, and the Gender Politics of Franchise Paratexts," *Critical Studies in Media Communication* 34, no. 2 (2017): 138–47.

11 For select examples, see Geek Flix, "HOT TOYS TALK episode 33—An Unboxing Special #6 (Carrie Fisher Tribute)," YouTube video, March 3,

2017, www.youtube.com/watch?v=wKR4zSUpFnY&t=125s; Star Wars Explained, "In Memory of Carrie Fisher," YouTube video, 7:06, December 28, 2016, www.youtube.com/watch?v=faL4v162-q0; treksf, "Princess Carrie Fisher Tribute," YouTube video, 2:26, December 27, 2016, www .youtube.com/watch?v=kCTg425JCuM, Master Hutt, "'Jabba's Pet' Slave Leia Tribute," YouTube video, 7.28, June 19, 2019, www.youtube.com/ watch?v=FNUiuM-giv4&t=101s; AhsokaTanoRox, "Tribute | Carrie Fisher as Princess Leia," YouTube video, 4:54, December 28, 2016, www.youtube .com/watch?v=k7WsUzMaZVk, soundofsimon, "Paul Simon—Hearts and Bones (Carrie Fisher Tribute)," YouTube video, 5:47, February 19, 2017, www.youtube.com/watch?v=XbQ-mHhOu8E; KenOhwee, "Carrie Fisher Tribute Video—1956–2016," YouTube video, 1:31, December 28, 2016, www .youtube.com/watch?v=ZFc7eVByQpw&t=3s; The reb-jedi Show, "Vader vs Leia (Star Wars Action Figure Stop Motion)," YouTube video, 0:32, February 24, 2017, www.youtube.com/watch?v=Q4yymUPcUJE; ADDOITALL-DAY, "Hot Toys 1/6 Scale TLJ Leia Organa Review and Tribute," YouTube video, 10:27, January 13, 2019, www.youtube.com/watch?v=AtEH7A_ -CMg&t=263s; RetroBlasting, "Carrie Fisher Tribute—Requiem for the Princess—RetroBlasting Special Presentation," YouTube video, 3:00, December 27, 2016, www.youtube.com/watch?v=pDr_KFEOOJo&t=103s; Stigma Customs Collectibles, "WIP! Original Star Wars Black Series Slave Leia Conversion. My Tribute to Carrie Fisher," YouTube video, 13:17, February 7, 2019, www.youtube.com/watch?v=iIgqYqwQdWM; MrPacDan, "My Toy Tribute to Carrie Fisher," YouTube video, 1:11, December 27, 2016, www .youtube.com/watch?v=7oHIPfBSjuc&t=1s; Darth Tuba, "Darthtuba's Star Wars Unboxing Show 19 Carrie Fisher Tribute and Force Awakens Smugglers Bounty," YouTube video, 9:15, December 29, 2016, www.youtube.com/ watch?v=IMffxCHS3uE&t=214s; "Boushh, Bor Gullet and Bros: The SWCA Podcast Episode 79," The Star Wars Collectors Archive Podcast (podcast), January 8, 2017, https://podcasts.apple.com/us/podcast/boushh-bor-gullet -and-bros-the-swca-podcast-episode-79/id359016334?i=1000379714724; "JotW—Carrie Fisher Tribute & Bloodline Recap," TumblingSaber—A Star Wars Podcast (podcast audio), December 29, 2016, https://tumblingsaber .podbean.com/e/jotw-carrie-fisher-tribute-bloodline-recap; "Episode 41: So Long Princess," Toy Run: The Star Wars Action Figure Cast (podcast audio), January 6, 2017, https://open.spotify.com/episode/3ekqPzPnuj5yltAJBmxvP8 ?si=uV0GVJRxRHiAALoireLYWg; "The Sandcrawler #13: A New Year and Goodbye to a Princess," *A Star Wars Collector's Show* (podcast audio), January 8, 2017, https://sandcrawlerpodcast.libsyn.com/page/4/size/25; "Episode 41: So Long Princess," *Toy Run: The Star Wars Action Figure Cast* (podcast audio), January 6, 2017, https://open.spotify.com/episode/3ekqPzPnuj5yltAJBmxvP8?si=uV0GVJRxRHiAALoireLYWg; "The Star Wars Collector Podcast #13: Remembering Royalty," *The Star Wars Collector* (podcast audio), December 30, 2016, www.thestarwarscollector.com/?m=201612.

12 For an introduction to the idea of "participatory historical culture," see Roy Rosenzweig and David Thelen, *The Presence of the Past: Popular Uses of History in American Life* (New York: Columbia University Press, 1998), 190. Also see Hilda Kean, Introduction to *The Public History Reader*, ed. Hilda Kean and Paul Martin (New York: Routledge, 2013).

13 Rosenzweig and Thelen, *Presence of the Past*, 192.

14 Raphael Samuel, *Theatres of Memory* (London: Verso, 1996), 8.

15 Jan Assmann, "Communicative and Cultural Memory," in *Cultural Memory Studies: An International and Interdisciplinary Handbook*, ed. Astrid Erll, Ansgar Nünning, and Sara B. Young (Berlin: de Gruyter, 2008), 110–11.

16 Assmann, "Communicative and Cultural Memory," 114.

17 See Suzanne Scott, *Fake Geek Girls: Fandom, Gender, and the Convergence Industry* (New York: New York University Press, 2019).

18 *My Star Wars Story* (blog), accessed August 29, 2018, http://mystarwarsstory.com/.

19 J. J. Abrams quoted in Suzanne Scott, "#Wheresrey?: Toys, Spoilers, and the Gender Politics of Franchise Paratexts," *Critical Studies in Media Communication* 34, no. 2 (2017): 141–42.

20 John Booth, *Collect All 21!: Memoirs of a Star Wars Geek—The First 30 Years* (Milton: Lightning Source UK, 2008), no pages.

21 Booth, *Collect All 21!*

22 Tony Pacitti, *My Best Friend Is a Wookie: A Memoir* (Avon, MA: Adams Media, 2010), 40.

23 Pacitti, *My Best Friend Is a Wookie*, 151.

24 See Pacitti's cover page.

25 For example, see "JotW—Carrie Fisher Tribute and Bloodline Recap," *TumblingSaber—A Star Wars Podcast* (podcast audio), December 29, 2016, https://tumblingsaber.podbean.com/e/jotw-carrie-fisher-tribute-bloodline-recap.

26　Gib van Ert, *A Long Time Ago: Growing Up with and out of Star Wars* (Lexington: Soi-disant Press, 2013), 20.

27　Van Ert, *A Long Time Ago*, 132.

28　Van Ert, *A Long Time Ago*, 132.

29　Booth, *Collect All 21!*

30　Van Ert, *A Long Time Ago*, 132.

31　Pacitti, *My Best Friend Is a Wookie*, 83.

32　Pacitti, *My Best Friend Is a Wookie*, 82.

33　Scott, *Fake Geek Girls*, 31.

34　Scott, *Fake Geek Girls*, 21.

35　For examples, see Carol Titelman, *The Art of Return of the Jedi* (New York: Ballantine, 1983); Deborah Call, *The Art of Star Wars: The Empire Strikes Back* (New York: Del Rey, 1994); Trisha Biggar, *Dressing a Galaxy: The Costumes of Star Wars* (New York: Insight Editions, 2005).

36　Abigail De Kosnik, "Memory, Archive, and History in Political Fan Fiction," in *Fandom: Identities and Communities in a Mediated World*, 2nd ed., ed. Jonathan Gray, Cornel Sandvoss, and C. Lee Harrington (New York: New York University Press, 2017), 277 and 282.

37　Megen de Bruin-Molé, "Space Bitches, Witches, and Kick-Ass Princesses: Star Wars and Popular Feminism," in *Star Wars and the History of Transmedia Storytelling*, ed. Sean Guynes and Dan Hassler-Forest (Amsterdam: Amsterdam University Press, 2017), 240.

38　Sharon M. Scott, *Toys and American Culture: An Encyclopedia* (Santa Barbara, CA: Greenwood, 2010), 2–6. Also see Scott, "#Wheresrey?"; Megen de Bruin-Molé, " 'Does It Come with a Spear?' Commodity Activism, Plastic Representation, and Transmedia Story Strategies in Disney's Star Wars: Forces of Destiny," *Film Criticism* 42, no. 2 (2018); Jason Bainbridge, "Fully Articulated: The Rise of the Action Figure and the Changing Face of 'Children's' Entertainment," *Continuum: Journal of Media and Cultural Studies* 24, no. 6 (2010): 829–42.

39　Kathleen Kennedy cited in Scott, "#Wheresrey?," 141.

40　Gottlieb cited in Scott, "#Wheresrey?," 143.

41　Bruin-Molé, "Space Bitches, Witches, and Kick-Ass Princesses," 236n43.

42　Paul Booth, "Disney's Princess Leia," in *Disney's Star Wars: Forces of Production, Promotion, and Reception*, ed. William Proctor and Richard McCulloch (Iowa City: University of Iowa Press, 2019), 179–91; Lorna Jowett, "Rey, Mary Sue, and Phasma Too: Feminism and Fan Responses to *The Force*

Awakens Merchandise," in *Disney's Star Wars: Forces of Production, Promotion, and Reception*, ed. William Proctor and Richard McCulloch (Iowa City: University of Iowa Press, 2019), 192–205.

43 Derek Johnson, "'May the Force Be with Katie': Pink Media Franchising and the Postfeminist Politics of HerUniverse," *Feminist Media Studies* 14, no. 6 (2014), 895–911.

44 Henry Jenkins, Foreword to *The Routledge Companion to Transmedia Studies*, ed. Matthew Freeman and Renira Rampazzo Gambarato (New York: Routledge, 2019), xxvi; Jonathan Gray, *Show Sold Separately: Promos, Spoilers, and other Media Paratexts* (New York: New York University Press, 2010), 175–87; Scott, "#Wheresrey?," 141.

45 Scott, "#Wheresrey?," 141.

46 One notable exception is the tribute episode of the podcast *Toy Run* in which the hosts review their Leia figures and also share brief memories of play and "playtime" with these figures, albeit the hosts also quickly return to reviewing the design and material characteristics of the toys. See "Episode 41: So Long Princess," *Toy Run: The Star Wars Action Figure Cast* (podcast audio), January 6, 2017, https://open.spotify.com/episode/3ekqPzPnuj5yltAJBmxvP8?si=uV0GVJRxRHiAALoireLYWg.

47 Ron Salvatore, "Princess Leia Organa Large Size Action Figure," *The Star Wars Collectors Archive* (blog), http://theswca.com/index.php?action=disp_item&item_id=39543.

48 Salvatore, "Princess Leia Organa Large Size Action Figure."

49 Van Ert, *A Long Time Ago*, 66.

50 Avi Santo, "Fans and Merchandise," in *The Routledge Companion to Media Fandom*, ed. Melissa A. Click and Suzanne Scott (New York: Routledge, 2018), 331.

51 For example, see two pictures of the siblings Karl and Amy: "Karl and Amy Share a Moment—1983," *I Grew Up Star Wars* (blog), accessed October 23, 2019, http://igrewupstarwars.com/karl-and-amy-share-a-moment-1983/; "Karl and Amy Enjoy Christmas 1983," *I Grew Up Star Wars* (blog), accessed October 23, 2019, http://igrewupstarwars.com/karl-and-amy-enjoy-christmas-1983/.

52 "Vader and the Rest of the Lineup," *I Grew Up Star Wars* (blog), accessed October 23, 2019, http://igrewupstarwars.com/vader-and-the-rest-of-the-lineup-1982/.

53 "Matt Takes Aim at Star Wars Fun! 1978," *I Grew Up Star Wars* (blog), accessed October 23, 2019, http://igrewupstarwars.com/matt-takes-aim-at-star-wars-fun-1978/.

54 WorldClassBullshitters, "Who Buys Star Wars Toys? No One . . . ," YouTube video, 15:23, January 15, 2018, www.youtube.com/watch?v=RFqsiuPxfn8; WorldClassBullshitters, "The $1 Star Wars Toys," YouTube Video, 12:17, January 21, 2018, www.youtube.com/watch?v=JcHBUqpxOMg; WorldClassBullshitters, "The New Star Wars Toys Are Practically Free," YouTube Video, 12:51, April 18, 2018, www.youtube.com/watch?v= S5nbbU7dHuM; WorldClassBullshitters, "The Cheapest Star Wars Toys Ever," YouTube Video, 10:46, April 25, 2018, www.youtube.com/watch?v= sMcZZrRlFhA; WorldClassBullshitters, "Star Wars Toys and Hasbro Layoffs," YouTube video, 16:22, Ocotber 20, 2018, www.youtube.com/watch ?v=zdf5WQdBSIg; Geek+Gamers, "Star Wars—Nobody Wants Toys from The Last Jedi," YouTube video, 6:52, February 6, 2018, www.youtube.com/ watch?v=P5Rbvow-03Y&t=53s.

55 David Stewart, "Star Wars Toys Don't Sell—Bolshevik Marketing and Marketing in Reverse," YouTube video, 16: 28, January 29, 2018, www .youtube.com/watch?v=8Zd6ljuRikY&t=5s; David Stewart, "'Bolshevik Marketing'—The Rhetoric of Ideas," YouTube video, 5:03, February 4, 2018, www.youtube.com/watch?v=be4VNXKVKUA&t=2s.

56 Drunk 3PO, "Star Wars Toys Not Selling. No One Is buying," YouTube video, 8:50, January 14, 2019, www.youtube.com/watch?v=Ex7ojOsCfk4.

57 For instance, in tours through the fan-run museum Stars of the Galaxy, fan curator Thomas Manglitz introduces displays that were donated to the museum because the owners' partners did not want to have them in their apartments anymore: GROBI.TV, "Wir waren wieder in der Filmfigurenausstellung in Mönchengladbach," YouTube video, 12:27, December 30, 2015, www.youtube.com/watch?v=UySJSMqjz48 &t=1s.

58 Fisher, *Princess Diarist*, Kindle.

59 Fisher, *Wishful Drinking*, Kindle.

60 The Unbox Boys, "Carrie Fisher 'Princess Leia' Toy Tribute," YouTube video, 1:15, December 23, 2016, www.youtube.com/watch?v=lYd9O3IjeTQ.

61 Shaken Not Nerd, "Remembering Carrie Fisher-Princess Leia Hot Toy Review," YouTube video, 9:57, January 10, 2017, www.youtube.com/watch ?v=awxYOYREjC8&t=132s.

62 Lincoln Geraghty, *Cult Collectors: Nostalgia, Fandom, and Collecting Popular Culture* (New York: Routledge, 2014), 121.

63 For example, see Shaken Not Nerd, 2017; "Remembering Carrie Fisher-Princess Leia Hot Toy Review," Geek Flix, "HOT TOYS TALK" episode 33.

64 Robert D., December 31, 2016, Comment on "Princess Leia," *Sideshow.com*, www.sideshow.com/collectibles/star-wars-princess-leia-hot-toys-902490.

65 Fisher, *Princess Diarist*, Kindle.

66 Ron Ruelle, "Life, Death, and the Price of Princess Leia Action Figures," *hobbybd.com* (blog), December 30, 2016, https://blog.hobbydb.com/2016/12/30/life-death-and-the-price-of-princess-leia-action-figures/.

67 "Carrie Fisher's Dog Gary Makes an Awesome Action Figure," *Revenge of the 5th* (blog), December 12, 2015, www.revengeofthe5th.net/2015/12/carrie-fishers-dog-gary-makes-awesome.html.

68 Fisher, *Wishful Drinking*, Kindle.

69 Fisher, *Shockaholic*, Kindle.

70 Stigma Customs Collectibles, "WIP!."

71 Myke Dela Paz, "6″ Custom Star Wars the Black Series Princess Leia Action Figures," YouTube video, 0:50, February 22, 2017, www.youtube.com/watch?v=S9PRHBl1BR4.

72 "JotW—Carrie Fisher Tribute and Bloodline Recap," *Tumbling Saber—A Star Wars Podcast* (podcast audio), December 29, 2016, https://tumblingsaber.podbean.com/e/jotw-carrie-fisher-tribute-bloodline-recap; "The Star Wars Collector Podcast #13: Remembering Royalty," *The Star Wars Collector* (podcast audio), December 30, 2016, www.thestarwarscollector.com/?m=201612.

73 For example. see Glenn Webb, "Star Wars Black Series 2 Princess Leia 6 Inch Action Figure Review," YouTube video, November 11, 2013, 3:11, www.youtube.com/watch?v=a6xh5iCcBUo&t=26s.

74 "Episode 163—Carrie Fisher Remembered," *Now, This Is Podcasting!* (podcast audio), December 29, 2016, www.podbean.com/media/share/dir-9hsdm-3354e7a?utm_campaign=w_share_ep&utm_medium=dlink&utm_source=w_share. The podcast is dedicated not specifically to action figures but covers all aspects of the franchise.

75 Fisher, *Princess Diarist*, Kindle.

76 Fisher, *Princess Diarist*, Kindle.

77 "The Sandcrawler #13: A New Year and Goodbye to a Princess," *A Star Wars Collector's Show* (podcast audio), January 8, 2017, https://sandcrawlerpodcast.libsyn.com/page/4/size/25; "Episode 41: So Long Princess," *Toy Run: The Star Wars Action Figure Cast* (podcast), January 6, 2017, https://open.spotify.com/episode/3ekqPzPnuj5yltAJBmxvP8?si=uV0GVJRxRHiAALoireLYWg.

78 Rebecca Williams, "Introduction: Starting at the End," in *Everybody Hurts: Transitions, Endings, and Resurrections in Fan Cultures*, ed. Rebecca Williams (Iowa City: University of Iowa Press, 2018), 1–16.

79 Williams, "Introduction: Starting at the End," 5.

80 More information on the documentary series can be found on the project's website: www.lookingforleia.com.

Harvesting the Celebrity Interface

CARRIE FISHER, VIRTUAL PERFORMANCE, AND SOFTWARE STARS

Andrew Kemp-Wilcox

When Carrie Fisher unexpectedly passed away on December 27, 2016, the shock was felt not only by her family and many fans but no doubt also by the studio executives and creative teams at Disney and Lucasfilm who had developed significant, public plans for her character, General Leia Organa, in future installments of the *Star Wars* media franchise.[1] "We pretty much started over," confessed franchise producer Kathleen Kennedy, responding to reports that Fisher's role in the upcoming *Episode IX*—the film that would eventually become *The Rise of Skywalker* (2019)—was meant to be as substantial as the role of Mark Hamill's Luke Skywalker in the previous installment, *The Last Jedi* (2017).[2] What Fisher's death meant for her character and her role in the films became a much-discussed subject on social media, where rumors about the then-unreleased *Jedi* and its inevitable sequel flourished, and one repeated rumor suggested that Fisher would still appear in *Episode IX*, albeit not in the flesh, but via digital special effects. The drumbeat of this rumor spread across social media loud enough to draw a direct response from Lucasfilm. In a January 13, 2017, post on StarWars.com titled "A Statement Regarding New Rumors," the studio explained:

> We don't normally respond to fan or press speculation, but there is a rumor circulating that we would like to address. We want to assure our fans that Lucasfilm has no plans to digitally recreate Carrie Fisher's performance as Princess or General Leia Organa. Carrie Fisher was, is, and always will be a part of the Lucasfilm family. She was our

princess, our general, and more importantly, our friend. We are still hurting from her loss. We cherish her memory and legacy as Princess Leia, and will always strive to honor everything she gave to *Star Wars*.[3]

The statement was surprising for two reasons. The first is the unusual decision by a corporate studio to intervene in a fan discussion about an early, ongoing creative process for a film (*Episode IX*) three years before its intended release. The second is that on the same day Lucasfilm asserted their firm opposition to digitally recreating Fisher as Leia, a *Star Wars* fan could visit a movie theater anywhere in the world to watch the studio do exactly that. *Rogue One: A Star Wars Story* was released in North America on December 10, 2016, featuring a rousing final moment in which plans for the original Death Star superweapon are handed off to Princess Leia, digitally recreated to depict Fisher in her appearance from the opening moments of the 1977 film, stitching the newest *Star Wars* film directly to the original via digital trickery. The Lucasfilm statement dismissing the rumors doesn't explicitly take a position on the digital re-creation process or its role in the studio's films, but nevertheless it implies an unseemly element in the technology, an element that would not be appropriate for a member of the "Lucasfilm family," or to use their chosen term for Fisher, a friend. The January statement is a clear departure from Lucasfilm's December position, which released *Rogue One* not only with that brief digital re-creation of Fisher but also with a significant supporting role for Grand Moff Tarkin, "played" once again, virtually, by the late Peter Cushing. Fans were able to envision, and therefore reject, a future virtual version of Fisher because the studio had already deployed the prototype.

After decades of studio investment in virtual performance technology, Fisher's passing exposed a gap between the capitalist interest in the technology and the ethical issues underlying it. But why did the re-creation of Fisher provoke this reaction and not, say, Cushing's? One explanation is that Fisher's sudden passing sparked a "too soon" reaction from the public, but this seems inadequate and only raises more questions. The phrase "too soon" is most often applied to jokes made at the expense of the deceased, an act perceived as disrespectful. Are virtual re-creations *inherently* disrespectful to the dead? Do they mock? If so, why tolerate them at all, for any performer? How is a virtual performer any different from the typical flood of celebrity images that follows in popular media after death?[4] One might

Fig. 4.1. Princess Leia as she appears in the final moments of *Rogue One* (2016, Lucas-film Ltd.). A digital version of Fisher is overlaid onto Ingvild Deila's performance.

argue that posthumous depictions of Fisher are acceptable only insofar as they are respectful, but we are left once again to question what about virtual performance fails to meet the criteria. Complicating the issue further is the simple fact that reanimating deceased celebrities was not only the first, but is likely to date the most common application of the technology, but the very notion of resurrecting Fisher via digital technology was met with enough concern that Lucasfilm issued their strong rejection.

These questions about fan rejection of a virtual Carrie Fisher are the central concern of this essay. The first half will survey the brief history of virtual performance, its past applications, and the studio investment in its future as a tool of studio control. This section includes an extended discussion of Ari Folman's 2013 film *The Congress*, which anticipates and satirizes a new frontier of virtual celebrity and explores the developing relationship between celebrity identity and a software future. The second half will focus on Fisher and her relationship, facilitated and mediated by software applications, with her fans and industry-created images. In this section, I will examine the intersection between Richard Dyer's traditional theories of stardom and two variants of what I call *software celebrity*: the virtual performance technology as deployed in *Rogue One* and the reconfiguration of stardom and celebrity made possible by interaction with software applications like social media. The goal is to explore software celebrity as a new kind of virtual interface, one negotiated by both Carrie Fisher and her fans, which has refashioned her celebrity image in a manner that has made her image difficult, if not impossible, to reconcile with studio control. This chapter is not concerned with what the future will hold for virtual performance or for Fisher's digital double. Lucasfilm is part of the Disney empire, and all that stands in the way of Fisher's virtual redeployment in the *Star Wars* films is the financial incentive to proceed. Instead, this essay will catalog the ongoing anxiety surrounding this new technology, unpack the corporate interest in its perfection, and explore how software celebrity alters the signification process for stardom away from the top-down studio-to-public model in favor of a more dispersed and diverse bottom-up method of signification.

A Brief History of Virtual Performance

Before approaching Carrie Fisher and software celebrity, it's necessary to take a moment to define *virtual performance*, which is a term broad enough to cover many different types of technology and performance that are beyond the scope of this chapter. Briefly sketched, virtual performance refers to the use of software applications and digital effects to create a new, simulated performance of an actor or celebrity personality, often re-created without the presence or input from the target performer. The temptation exists to define creations such as these as *simulacral*, to emphasize the missing referent behind the newly created celebrity signification, but since this may confuse the issue of stardom, which, itself, is concerned with the relationship between the referent and its signifiers, I will set that question aside for another time. We will also put aside predigital examples that appeared to anticipate the coming technology, such as the skillful editing of archival footage in films like *Zelig* (1983) or *Dead Men Don't Wear Plaid* (1982), or traditional makeup effects like those intended to turn Raymond Massey into Boris Karloff in *Arsenic and Old Lace* (1944), or the plain dishonesty of the "Fake Shemp" tactic used in films as diverse as *Plan 9 from Outer Space* (1959), the cycle of "Bruceploitation" films in the 1970s and 1980s, or *Back to the Future Part II* (1989), which so egregiously used makeup and trick photography to fake the presence of actor Crispin Glover that the result was a lawsuit.[5]

Software and digital effects manipulation simplify and make accessible the replication of celebrity performance. Celebrities are, in fact, an ideal subject for virtual performance because of the volume of potential data that accumulate each time the star is seen or heard in public. Although examples of digitally created humans can be found at least as early as 1981,[6] one of the earliest examples of digital star re-creation was *Rendez-vous in Montreal*, an animated short film that premiered for three thousand people at the Engineering Institute of Canada in 1987 that resurrected Humphrey Bogart and Marilyn Monroe as a demonstration of digital technology's photoreal potential.[7] The process, which involved mapping and digitizing busts of the two stars, was groundbreaking but resulted in models far too rigid to be believable. While digital modeling went through cycles of improvement, content creators gravitated toward compositing, turning first to archival footage and using software to blend it seamlessly with new footage. Instead of a plastic, awkward model of Bogart, the actor's real likeness could be composited alongside Elton John, James Cagney, and Louis Armstrong to sell Diet Coke in 1991.[8] John Wayne likewise sold Coors Light alongside R. Lee Ermey the following year, and Fred Astaire ditched Ginger Rogers for a Dirt Devil vacuum in an infamous 1997 spot.[9]

Digital technology's powers of resurrection had their first emergency "field test" after the passing of Brandon Lee in 1993 during the filming of his dark superhero film, *The Crow*. Lee's death from an on-set accident required producers, alongside other analog techniques, to digitally map images of Lee's face onto body doubles for a few key scenes. Similar technology brought celebrities like John Lennon and Lyndon Johnson into contact with Forrest Gump in 1994, and Laurence Olivier was digitally resurrected to star as the villain in the 2001 adventure film *Sky Captain and the World of Tomorrow*.

The late 1990s and early 2000s were a boom period for virtual performers, many of whom were entirely original characters created through a combination of on-set performance work and computer software, including characters like *The Phantom Menace*'s controversial comic relief character Jar Jar Binks (1999), or Aki, the allegedly photoreal protagonist of the computer animated film *Final Fantasy: The Spirits Within* (2001). Over the first two decades of this century, virtual performance proliferated in everything from superhero films to ape epics to Middle-Earth. But resurrection remains the medium's most tantalizing promise: a surprise hologram of Tupac Shakur stunned a Coachella crowd in 2012 and led to speculation about a posthumous tour, while performers like Oliver Reed (*Gladiator*, 2000), Paul Walker (*Furious 7*, 2015), and Nancy Marchand (*The Sopranos*, 2001) all had their final performances digitally manufactured to close their characters' arcs and salvage productions in process.

Strangled by Her Bra

Carrie Fisher's personal struggles with Lucasfilm concerning the uses of her Princess Leia character are well-established and heavily analyzed, both in media and elsewhere in this anthology. But it remains important to empha-size that her relationship with her most famous role began when Fisher signed away her likeness while only nineteen years old, with no conception of what that likeness was worth. "The mistake was I signed away my likeness for free," Fisher told Newsweek in 2011. "In those days, there was no such thing as a 'likeness,' which is a funny thing to say coming from the family that I came from."[10] Much of Fisher's post-Leia career—and especially her public performances after her famous *Primetime* interview with Diane Saw-yer in which she revealed her struggles with mental illness—was directed toward establishing herself as an entity separate from her most famous role, even if she knew she'd never fully eclipse it. "I tell my younger friends that one day they'll be at a bar playing pool and they'll look up at the television set and there will be a picture of Princess Leia with two dates underneath, and they'll say 'aww—she said that would happen.' And then they'll go back to playing pool."[11]

Richard Dyer's well-known work on stars positions them as construc-tions made of signifiers, images that denote particular notions, ideology, and social and cultural hegemony. In other words, "stars," as we know them, are not real people, but the fact that the star image *refers* to a real person is part of what gives the star their power. "Stars are, like characters in stories, representations of people," Dyer writes, a statement that reminds us that the star herself can never be fully accounted for in the images, interviews, and public appearances that define star existence.[12] Dyer demands that we analyze Fisher's stardom the way we might analyze a character in a fictional work, as composites that refer to a larger existence obscured by the gaps in what we see. The audience perceives Fisher as an autonomous, interesting, rounded character based on the limited glimpses offered by various indus-trial modes (from films to journalistic pieces to published work and so on). When the camera cuts, the star becomes invisible, and audiences extrapo-late what happens in the gap based on the information they have. Thus, the popular character becomes part of our image of the star: "Stars . . . collapse the distinction between the actor's authenticity and the authentication of the character s/he is playing."[13] This would appear to set up a binary reveal, an approachable solution as to whether the star either (a) is like the character portrayed, or (b) is not like the character portrayed. For Dyer, however, the distance of the star's personality from the characters portrayed is simply another sign that constructs the image of the star. Therefore, Fisher's struggle with her stardom and her inability to separate herself entirely from Leia becomes a signifier of her own star character. As if stuck in the mud, the harder Fisher divests from her role, the more tightly she is wound up in her own collection of signs.

Fisher told several variations of a story in which she arrived on set for the filming of *Star Wars* in her white gown costume, only to be immediately informed by Lucas that she would have to discard her bra, because, as Lucas explained, there's no underwear in space. The director's explanation supposedly involved zero gravity and the dangers of loose cords strangling an unlucky astronaut. Fisher closed her story by saying "no matter how I go, I want it reported that I drowned in moonlight, strangled by my own bra."[14] The story may be read as a tidy summation of the Fisher-as-star construction: defiant and disobedient, but still inextricably tethered to the role she chose to accept and that cost her control of her image, at nineteen years of age.

It's important, then, to think of the digital performance of Princess Leia in the context of the teenage girl who gave away her likeness. For *Rogue One*, the Fisher (and Cushing) roles were performed on set by actors (Ingvild Deila and Guy Henry, respectively) whose faces were mapped and scanned during shooting. Using digital software, their faces were then swapped with digital maps of Cushing and Fisher's faces, smoothed out and aligned, often frame-by-frame, by technical artists at Industrial Light & Magic.[15] Decades after Fisher signed away her famous face for free, digital re-creation broke that face down into its component data and displaced both the face and, potentially, its star significations.

The Congress and "Demonic" Annexation

The potential for virtual performance to displace signification is only one small element contributing to the anxiety that has followed and surrounded virtual performance since very near its invention, seen at least as far back as Fred Astaire's dance with a household appliance. But the commercial's legacy extends further, into the legislative arena. Although the use of Astaire's likeness had been approved by Astaire's daughter, the star's widow objected.

The California senate eventually passed the so-called Astaire Bill in 1999 to provide families more rights to deceased celebrity likenesses, or, more accurately, limit the avenues along which studios could claim fair use.[16] More recently, director Francis Lawrence refused to use software to finish the late Philip Seymour Hoffman's role in *The Hunger Games: Mockingjay Part II* (2015).[17] A planned Tupac-like hologram of the musician Prince was removed from the 2018 Super Bowl halftime show in the wake of fan protests.[18] Before his death, Prince was on the record about his distaste for virtual performance on what are, essentially, moral grounds:

> That's the most demonic thing imaginable. Everything is as it is, and it should be. If I was meant to jam with Duke Ellington, we would have lived in the same age. That whole virtual reality thing . . . it really is demonic. And I am not a demon. Also, what they did with that Beatles song ["Free As a Bird"], manipulating John Lennon's voice to have him singing from across the grave . . . that'll never happen to me. To prevent that kind of thing from happening is another reason why I want artistic control.[19]

The reaction to Prince's planned hologram and the fan concern of a virtual Carrie Fisher in *Episode IX* share superficial similarities in that the content creators were forced to react publicly to a very vocal fan reaction. The Prince hologram was pulled out of a highly choreographed and produced musical spectacle; Lucasfilm issued their statement, and then added unused footage of Fisher from *The Last Jedi* to build her role in *The Rise of Skywalker*. But while Prince called virtual performance "demonic," Fisher's opinions on her virtual stand-in weren't as clearly established. Lucasfilm executive John Knoll claimed to have received word that Fisher "loved" her digital re-creation.[20] Just a few days before her death, however, Fisher posted a link on her Twitter account to an article from *The Independent* on *Rogue One*. The article, titled "*Rogue One*'s CGI Princess Leia: The Sands of Time Are So Cruel You Can't Even Do Motion Capture for Your Younger Self," briefly describes the difficulties that arise when older actors attempt to recreate their younger selves via motion capture, pinning the blame on an older actor's body language.[21] Fisher accompanied her tweet of the article with a comment (composed, in her style, heavily in emojis) that translates to: "The sands of time, so cruel they should be arrested and sent to a cardiac beach? Get CGI, perspective, and deal with it."[22] Her comment suggests, at the least, ambivalence over the digital future of performance, although without further commentary or more direct quotes, we can only hazard a guess.

One concern with virtual performance, as is clear in both the Prince and Carrie Fisher cases, is that the technology is advancing faster than its ethical questions can be addressed. As Mark Andrejevic has explained, information and digital data are accumulating at an incredible, difficult-to-comprehend rate.[23] Every performance in every film, television show, video game, YouTube clip, news piece—literally *anything* that intersects with software—passively and automatically adds to the virtual archive for that performer, and just like any kind of resource, this glut (to use Andrejevic's term) of data appears poised to devalue the primacy and scarcity of a celebrity's finite talents, skills, or likeness, potentially diluting or destroying the performer's potential for commercial, or even cultural, exploitation of his or her own status as either a celebrity or, taken to an extreme, as a lived being in the world.

The entertainment industry is in the earliest stages of this technology. New software tools and streamlined databases seem certain to one day make this process astonishingly easy. Can we foresee an industry in which the actor's value as a performer is entirely front-loaded to their youth, and exhausted within a few years of work, just enough to stock an archive so that the actor's likeness may be used in perpetuity in any role, genre, title, position, or scenario the studio prefers? This "demonic" annexation of the flesh seems uncomfortably near. Digital effects technician Darren Hendler of Digital Domain emphasizes the comprehensive nature of today's scanning process: "We have a digital archive menu . . . you can archive how your face works and every single expression you make, full body scans. You can archive your voice and the way your voice sounds. You can archive different wardrobes and scans of wardrobes that you may wear."[24] Erin Winick writes that the keepers of the *Star Wars* franchise are already now actively using this process to scan all the lead actors into software, just in case. "Actors and movie studios are buckling down and preparing for an inevitable future when using scanning technology to preserve 3-D digital replicas of performers is routine. Just because your star is inconveniently dead doesn't mean your generation-spanning blockbuster franchise can't continue to rake in the dough."[25]

Implied in that assessment is the fact that the studio would benefit from this arrangement much more than the performers, who would typically be in a position to negotiate based on the demand in the marketplace and the performer's own interest or lack thereof in the material. If, in some future, a digital performer is forced to compete not just with comparable performers drawn to the project, but any number of performers, living or dead, who exist within a studio data bank, then the concept of the performer as a unique, finite, and discrete attraction will fade and a collapse of the commercial value of talent will follow. A future nineteen-year-old in Fisher's position might find that her likeness is just as valueless as Fisher's was in 1977, sold for pennies in a market weighted toward an army of digital scabs and exploited for extravagant sums when she proves a marketable commodity.

There are, however, deeper and more concerning stakes for the ethics of digital performance beyond the impact on an actor's market. Ari Folman's 2013 film *The Congress* provides a set of useful metaphors for exploring the tension between human anxiety of the digital future and Hollywood's financial incentive to control stars' images. The film, based loosely on Stanislaw Lem's novella *The Futurological Congress* (1971), stars Robin Wright as a version of herself, an aging actor whose devotion to her family came at a cost to her career opportunities. To the public in the film, Wright is still beloved as Princess Buttercup, the character she played in *The Princess Bride* (1987), but as she has aged, and as she has withdrawn from the public eye for other, personal reasons, Wright finds difficulty staying afloat in the entertainment economy, much as Fisher did as she aged beyond Leia. In the film, the digital future has arrived ahead of schedule, and Wright is asked by a demanding studio executive (Danny Huston) to sign her final contract. In exchange for a one-time cash payment, Wright will be digitally scanned and placed into a computer for the studio to use however it chooses. "We . . . want to scan you. All of you, your body, your face, your emotion, your laughter, your tears, your climaxing, your happiness, your depressions, your fears, your longings. We want to sample you, we want to preserve you, we want all this thing called Robin Wright."[26] The notion of Wright, the person, as an ownable, consumable commodity-thing weaves throughout the film. After consenting to the scan, ten years pass in Wright's life, ten years in which she has not been allowed to act or perform, those tasks having been conceded contractually to her virtual double who now stars in a series of science-fiction action films, the kind that Wright, the human character, explicitly dislikes. To renew her likeness contract, Wright travels to the studio, which has inexplicably become a hedonistic zone of 2-D animation. Technology has advanced to allow hallucinogenic drugs to create this animated reality within which the studio employees and guests must consent to exist. In the confines of the zone, a person can hallucinate themselves into whatever they want to be, or whoever, including endless copies of Robin Wright, the science-fiction software star.

Once inside the zone and under the influence of the hallucinogen, Wright is given the terms of her contract renewal. In the future, she will not only be a film star but also a consumable product. Customers will be able to eat and drink her essence and transform into whichever form of her they like. Wright consents but later protests the studio's use of the technology in front of an audience, just as an armed revolt overtakes the zone. Wright is injured and falls into a coma in the animated world. When she awakens, she discovers that the hallucinogenic technology has, as intended, spread beyond the confines of the studio and overtaken the world. Every person now manufactures and dwells within their private custom reality, and the few who choose a "real" life live in squalor in an increasingly abandoned flesh and blood world.

The Congress synthesizes fresh anxieties over the digital commodification of the human body with the familiar, public, and ableist alarms surrounding virtual reality and its power to disrupt or destroy the biological ideal of the human body, prominent in 1990s cyberpunk films like *The Lawnmower Man* (1992), *Strange Days* (1995), and many others. But what is more interesting, at least for this essay's purpose, is the film's relationship with the ethical gaps perforating virtual celebrity. Robin Wright is a clever choice for the lead role, but the part could just as easily fit Carrie Fisher, or any of the vast number of actors, overwhelmingly female, who have seen their market value drop as the "sands of time" work against their image. In the film, Wright is told that her physical, mid-forties body is not what the studio desires. Instead, the preferred Wright is Buttercup or *Forrest Gump*'s (1994) Jenny. The age in which Wright's virtual re-creation will appear, in perpetuity, is factored into her contract. The film punctuates this new reality by depicting Wright confronting her own, younger image in a *Bride* poster. (One could swap Fisher for Wright and Leia for Buttercup without as much as a ripple on the premise.) If the future of entertainment belongs to the virtual actors, it is the female star who will face the first wave of obsolescence.

Female stars may likely face the most troubling applications of becoming commodity-things. In *The Congress*, Wright is dismayed to find that

Fig. 4.2. Robin Wright appraises the version of her that will become a commodity-thing in *The Congress* (2013, Pandora Filmproduktion).

her virtual replacement can be deployed to films that Wright, the person, would never have approved, including, it is implied, pornography, antici-pating the recent emergence of deepfakes that use software to map the faces of popular stars onto the bodies of adult film actors.[27] Given the ongoing popularity of images like Princess Leia in her metal "slave girl" costume, one can assume it's only a matter of time before Fisher makes her deepfake pornography debut. In her memoir, *Wishful Drinking*, Fisher laments the endless products, from candy dispensers to shampoo bottles, that have displayed her likeness, a by-product of her having lost the rights to her own face in her contract. The punchline of the list is an "$800 sex doll that you can put in your cornfield to chase away crows," and an anatomically accurate sculpture that prompted Fisher to complain that George Lucas may own her face, but not the rights to her "lagoon of mystery."[28] But in the virtual future that *The Congress* warns against, there is no piece of the star that is off limits or unowned. It's all scanned, all cataloged and archived, with the human body providing only a range of complex data points to be applied via filter, a software application used at the touch of a button, alongside others for color correcting or image stabilization—a total software solution for this "thing" called Robin Wright, or Carrie Fisher. We cannot yet ingest our stars, but that's a problem conceivably solved with just more data.

Software Celebrity and #SpaceMom's Finger

Richard Dyer's writing on stars understandably focuses much attention on stars from the classical era of Hollywood and into the 1950s and 1960s, when stardom itself may have been at or near peak economic and cultural value. But how does Dyer's theory function in this new age of virtual resurrection and participatory culture? Considering the evolving role of software on the star image, I believe Dyer's important and convincing work is no longer entirely sufficient. To provide one relevant example, Dyer writes of stars as primarily constructions of studio production, with relatively minor influence on the star image arising from consumption. Dyer writes that it is "clear . . . that the audience's role in shaping the star phenomenon is very limited," and he leaves four categories of star/audience relations (emotional affinity, self-identification, imitation, and projection) to a weaker, subordinate role in the star image.[29] Dyer's account is a top-down model of signification, heavily reliant on the unchallenged power of the studio to manufacture images, and written before inventions like Twitter and other software tools of participatory culture shifted the conversation on, and the lived reality of, image construction.

Software celebrity is the term I use here for the contemporary intersection between stars and software applications. The term develops from the work of Lev Manovich, who has proposed that existing media theory is in need of revision by way of software theory, since there is no corner of the media landscape untouched by software, which comes with its own ontological affordances that enhance, or in some cases, supersede the affordances of legacy media.[30] Software celebrity is too broad for us to fully apprehend it in this chapter because, if we follow Manovich, literally any method by which software intersects with the star image would fall under the banner of software celebrity, including software focused on production, postproduction, social media, blogging, digital photos, web browsers, email, and "other types of software applications whose primary focus is accessing media content,"[31] which would of course include Twitter, Facebook, Instagram, Reddit, and any of the other near-infinite numbers of applications that seem to rise and fall within the boundaries of a media cycle. Manovich intends to expose the dramatic, unseen influence of software on nearly every facet of contemporary media, which would of course include industry output, but which also applies to fan engagement with and consumption of star images via software application. Software celebrity is an expansive concept that has implications for any intersection point between software and stars.

For the purposes of this argument, I have developed and focused on two general types of software celebrity, from among many other types made possible by software: the first, *virtual performance*, we have already addressed and will return to in short order. The other is *harvested celebrity*, the kind that Carrie Fisher made a hallmark of her late life and career via social media engagement with fans and followers. I chose the word *harvested* as a workaround to avoid terms like "participatory" or "convergence," terms Henry Jenkins coined to define a cultural activity of sharing and collaboration, using media platforms like Twitter as a means to an ends.[32] Following Jenkins's theories, those fans who engaged with and followed Fisher on social media were often made to feel as if they were collaborating with Fisher on a live feed of her life: commenting, tagging, retweeting, conversing. Jenkins doesn't believe that applications like Twitter are intrinsically participatory but rather exist as platforms that facilitate the natural drive for creative participation that has always existed in communities, and in fact helps to form communities.[33]

There is much to appreciate in Jenkins's models, but we must be careful not to simply frame Fisher's direct engagement with fans through an unproblematic lens of content producers and content consumers using digital technology to forge new relationships and avenues for consumer activism. Jenkins too often overlooks or downplays the ways in which consumer participation is turned against the consumer and weaponized by the content creators, disrupting the perceived closeness between the two sides. In many cases, participation is, in fact, an *illusion* of participation fostered and encouraged by the media industries. Is the volume of fan engagement with Fisher over Twitter authentic and open, as a reading of Jenkins might support? Or is it simply a new kind of separated construction, mediated by the boundaries of the software within which it occurs?

Consider, for a moment, Carrie Fisher's middle finger. At the time of this writing, three anniversaries have passed since Fisher's death. On the first anniversary, social media (Twitter, especially) lit up with a specialized hashtag, #CarrieOnForever. In a *Salon* article, Gabriel Bell wrote of the remembrance that "some praised Fisher for her fierce feminism and the way she helped recast what a princess or a woman in a big-budget action film could be. Others remembered her defiance, her humor, her openness with her substance abuse and mental-health issues, or her refusal to grow old gracefully as our society often demands women do."[34] To that list we might also add perseverance, as indicated by the hashtag itself, a call to power through difficulties the way Fisher publicly did with her mental illness. The hashtag returned on the second anniversary, posted among others by Ontario artist Lindsay van Ekelenburg, whose piece titled *Blessed Rebel Queen* has become a popular meme to share among Fisher's fans; it's the source of the title of this anthology and is included in the introduction. The piece depicts Fisher in the image of a saint, holding her dog, Gary, and flashing her middle finger, and is as clear and concentrated an image of Fisher's persona in the eyes of her fans as any other, owing largely to that finger. Fisher's habit of giving the middle finger—so prevalent that images of her flashing the finger have been assembled into collages—has come to stand in for her traits of defiance and perseverance. In her post, Van Ekelenburg uses her own image of Fisher's finger as an inspirational tool. "The last few months have been challenging to get through, and many days I would like to give up. But then I look up at the portrait I painted with her knowing look, and I know she's giving the finger to all my demons. May she continue to do the same for you."[35]

Fisher's finger is a sign in the Dyer sense, one that represents in miniature what Fisher represents to her fans overall: defiance in the face of struggle, against mental illness, celebrity commodification, addiction, and more.

The bulk of Fisher's embrace of software celebrity advanced that theme, from her quirky use of emoji lettering that gave many of her tweets the appearance of ransom notes to her advice columns that openly targeted young readers experiencing emotional traumas (a concern of Fisher's that helped to earn her the nickname "SpaceMom" among fans). Fisher only published three columns before her passing, but the final was addressed to a young reader diagnosed, like Fisher, with bipolar disorder. "We have been given a challenging illness, and there is no other option than to meet those challenges," writes Fisher.[36] "Think of it as an opportunity to be heroic—not 'I survived living in Mosul during an attack' heroic, but an emotional survival."[37]

Fisher's middle finger demonstrates how sign creation occurs in a participatory culture—through fan harvesting. In the Dyer model, signification is top-down, originating from the industry and adopted by consumers. But Fisher's brand of software celebrity was produced in a channel and a stream of vast numbers of potential signifiers that were narrowed and selected by Fisher's fans. Fisher didn't act in the top-down role of the studio, curating images and submitting them to the public with calculation to aid in star signification. The finger was not *Fisher's* image, nor did it originate from Lucasfilm or any other studio. Instead, the digital archiving affordance of social media allowed for images of her middle finger to accumulate and sit passively among her many other potential signifiers. It was Fisher's fans who harvested from the archive, choosing the image of Fisher's finger to signify Fisher herself because it contained those traits with which they chose to identify her—toughness, hardheadedness, resoluteness in the face of struggle. In other words, Fisher's finger is a signifier created from the bottom up. Fan-driven, bottom-up signification is made simple and facilitated by the digital affordances of software. Archiving, searching, malleability, and mediation all make it possible to simply and easily harvest images of Fisher giving the finger, repackage them, and share them among fans, creating a new signification that becomes available and acceptable for canonization in pieces like Van Ekelenburg's *Blessed Rebel Queen*. Software makes it possible for fans to harvest and select the traits that they choose to associate with the star, resulting in a new software model of star signification.

Software Stars as Interfaces

If Dyer's top-down model of celebrity signification means never fully experiencing the star—the human being who never transcends beyond being the real person *behind* the star image—the bottom-up model of Fisher's brand of software celebrity should likewise not be mistaken for "true" engagement with the star, who still remains out of reach, permanently, behind the system of signs identified and harvested by fans. Although readers may believe that they are truly experiencing the "real" Carrie Fisher, it should be uncontroversial to claim that social media remains a composite, and that the star is impossibly mediated behind layers of technology. The human being named Carrie Fisher lived beyond the software, her life only gestured to by the assemblage of columns, photos, tweets, and video available on software platforms. This means that, beyond Manovich, software celebrity also needs to engage with theories of interface.

In *The Interface Effect*, Alexander Galloway argues it's misleading to think of human interactions with software without considering the importance of the interface itself, the mediator of the experience between the user and the code, just as the software image of the star, either virtual performance created in software or the assemblage of signs harvested from the star's interactions with software tools, is a boundary between the viewer and the star herself.[38] Therefore, we should think of both types of software celebrity discussed here as *software interfaces*, and convincing ones at that. Many viewers didn't realize that they were looking at virtual stars at all when they viewed *Rogue One*, just as many people who engage with stars on social media may not intuitively understand the distance that actually separates them from the object of their attention. The aim of the interface is to elide its contributions.

Thinking of software celebrity as an interface in the Galloway sense grants us access to finally apprehending the intense emotions of Fisher's fans generated by the idea of a virtual Princess Leia. Galloway frames his discussion of software interfaces by acknowledging the desire of the viewer to reduce the interface and arrive much closer to the object (in this case, the performer) beyond, noting that "a desire to be brought near—such a desire is most certainly at the very base of human life."[39] Galloway goes on to explain a fundamental difference of the computer as a media tool from legacy media like the cinema:

Maybe this is why we do not cry at websites like we cry at the movies. Maybe it is why there is no "faciality" with the computer, why there is no concept of a celebrity star system (except ourselves), no characters or story (except our own), no notion of recognition or reversal, as Aristotle said of poetry. If the movie screen always directs toward, the computer screen always directs away.[40]

We may take exception with some of Galloway's language. The computer and computer software have proven quite adept at star creation, in certain areas (Twitch streamers and TikTok stars, among others, have cultivated significant audiences and financial rewards), and it's not unknown for the content of a website to bring a person to tears. But Galloway's point is that the interface deflects, that it hides the real world behind a shroud, making the "real" invisible to some extent, leaving ourselves, the users, the most visible person in our online experience. For Galloway, this is a troubling construction because interfaces are not accidents. They are designed, planned, streamlined, and erased. They have histories and agendas that they often work to make invisible, leaving the user wandering in an illusion of independence and autonomy. If Manovich is right that everything is now software, Galloway suggests a problem with this development.

Galloway includes four types of signification regimes (ideological, ethical, poetic, and truth), but we will concern ourselves only with the first two regimes, separated by their aesthetics.[41] The first, ideological, has what Galloway calls a coherent aesthetic, meaning that the interface was built and designed to be invisible and to create an illusion of reduced difference between the user and the material. "The gravity of the coherent aesthetic tends toward the center of the work of art. It is a process of centering, of gradual coalescing."[42] The coherent aesthetic dissolves and erases the coherent politics of the interface, a clear and unconfused political agenda. Our concept of the virtual performer, the digital star that Carrie Fisher and Peter Cushing became in *Rogue One*, or that Robin Wright was forced to accept in *The Congress*, contains an aesthetic so coherent that it vanishes into the real, for some people today, and for all people eventually should the studios achieve their goals. The more coherent the aesthetic of the virtual performer, the better that performer will hide the coherent politics of the same, which is a politics of control. The virtual performer is a protection against death, against aging, against the free will of the "difficult" performer who wants to wear her underwear, even in space, or against the rise of salaries that comes with stardom, and any other biological or legal convenience standing in the way of capitalizing the maximum profit from the image of the star. The ideology of the virtual performer is, as *The Congress* makes clear, total ingestion.

Twitter, on the other hand, along with other social media platforms, is far less dedicated to seamlessness and invisibility. Twitter contains many kinds of windows and text blocks, displays words from countless speakers, and can be quite overwhelming for the unfamiliar. The politics of Twitter are coherent in that they promote a politics of access, but they do so through an incoherent aesthetic, which for Galloway means "tending to unravel neat masses into their unkempt, incontinent elements."[43] This definition isn't meant as a value judgment, just a statement of the image's centering or decentering power. Galloway refers to these interfaces as Brechtian, and the term seems appropriate in summarizing the cumulative, assembled effect of experiencing a star's life via their stream of posts and content.[44] For Galloway, Twitter's coherent politics of access merges with its incoherent, decentering aesthetic to create an ethical construction, which, again, is not meant as a Manichaean binary between good or bad, but rather a means of identifying the central political regime that remains in place no matter the disruption or realignment of the various aesthetic elements. The aesthetics of control present in the case of the virtual performer lose their power if the aesthetic loses coherence, for example, if the photoreal Carrie Fisher were replaced by a 2-D cartoon version, like in *The Congress*'s second half, which forced the fictional studio in that film to absorb the entire world into the 2-D aesthetic, to make all of reality as malleable as the image, in order to retain its power. But the aesthetics of access promoted by Twitter remains the same no matter how incoherent the aesthetic becomes, granting a path to Fisher's own incoherent aesthetic—her Twitter feed—and the harvested star politics of defiance.

Conclusion

Returning, at last, to the case of the virtual Leia, and the strong reaction from her fans that forced the unusual, direct, and pointed abdication of at least some portion of Lucasfilm's capitalist control over Fisher's image—a control they have maintained in some sense or another since she signed it away at roughly the same time she abandoned her bra to space—we can see by combining the star significations of Dyer with the software theories of Galloway and Manovich that a disruption has occurred in Carrie Fisher's star image. Fisher's politics of defiance have been inextricable from her star image for decades, present first in the character of Princess Leia, and then through Fisher's own admission of mental illness and drive for independence from the studio system—but these are all top-down images. Even Fisher's own public confessions and assertions were managed and mediated through a news industry, a publishing industry, and a film industry with their own interests in capitalizing on Fisher's stardom. But software celebrity allowed a bottom-up harvest of Fisher's traits that fans found most appealing. #SpaceMom and Fisher's middle finger are no more comprehensive an image of Fisher's life than her best-selling memoir or her early career in the public eye, but they were constructed and adopted by fans responding to Fisher's own politics of openness, access, and defiance. They became signifiers for a *separate* star image, one informed by the top-down stardom sparked by Princess Leia, but independent of it and able to develop within the interface between Fisher's fans and Fisher's content releases, beyond industry management. Lucasfilm's virtual Leia is an *ideological* construct of control, centered and (near) invisible, but software celebrity has allowed an *ethical*, decentered version of Carrie Fisher to eclipse the original. Fisher's software stardom makes her suddenly incompatible with her original studio image. We can theorize, then, that this disruption of her star image drove, in large part, the fan backlash against her virtual replacement, even after Fisher herself reportedly approved the likeness. With Fisher's defiance decentered, it has thus been repurposed and redistributed among fan channels. This "thing" called Carrie Fisher can no longer be scanned and ingested, even if that is the eventual fate of Princess Leia in future *Star Wars* films, because it has been dispersed and incorporated among those who embrace her images of defiance. The studio version of Fisher can only be a puppet, speaking for a politics of control, while *Blessed Rebel Queen* speaks for the fans who constructed her, who seek to #CarrieOn, and who are raising their middle fingers in solidarity.

Notes

1 Stefan Kyriazis, "Star Wars: Carrie Fisher's Death 'TOTALLY Changed Episode 9' WHAT Was the Original Plot?," *Express*, May 5, 2017, www.express.co.uk/entertainment/films/800801/Star-Wars-8-Carrie-Fisher-death-Episode-9-Leia-plan-Lucasfilm-Kathleen-Kennedy.

2 Anthony Breznican, "Kathleen Kennedy Says *Star Wars: Episode IX* 'Started Over' after Carrie Fisher's Death," *Entertainment Weekly*, April 14, 2017, https://ew.com/movies/2017/04/14/kathleen-kennedy-episode-ix-carrie -fisher-death/.

3 "A Statement Regarding New Rumors," StarWars.com, www.starwars.com/ news/a-statement-regarding-new-rumors.

4 Rachael Krishna, "11 Heartbreaking Cartoons in Memory of Carrie Fisher," *BuzzFeedNews*, December 28, 2016, www.buzzfeednews.com/ article/krishrach/11-heartbreaking-cartoons-in-memory-of-carrie-fisher.

5 Eriq Gardner, " 'Back to the Future II' from a Legal Perspective: Unintentionally Visionary," *Hollywood Reporter*, October 21, 2015, www.hollywoodreporter .com/thr-esq/back-future-ii-a-legal-833705.

6 For the film *Looker*, directed by Michael Crichton.

7 Daniel Thalmann and Nadia Magenat Thalmann, *Rendez-vous in Montreal*, filmed in 1987, YouTube video, 5:50, published August 5, 2015, www .youtube.com/watch?v=vuvvv7Bie4U.

8 Ryan Parker, "R. Lee Ermey and John Wayne Shared Screen Time Together— Kind of," *Hollywood Reporter*, April 15, 2018, www.hollywoodreporter .com/heat-vision/r-lee-ermey-john-wayne-shared-screen-time-together -kind-1102876.

9 Kelli Marshall, "Fred Astaire for Dirt Devil," *Critical Commons*, accessed December 12, 2018, www.criticalcommons.org/Members/kellimarshall/ clips/Astaire_DirtDevil2.mp4/view.

10 Carrie Fisher, "Carrie Fisher on How George Lucas Stole Her Identity," *Newsweek*, December 27, 2016, www.newsweek.com/carrie-fisher-george -lucas-star-wars-archive-interview-67321.

11 Carrie Fisher, *Wishful Drinking* (New York: Simon & Schuster, 2008), 86.

12 Richard Dyer, *Stars* (London: Palgrave Macmillan, 1998), 20.

13 Dyer, *Stars*, 21.

14 Fisher, *Wishful Drinking*, 88.

15 Trent Moore, "Here's What Rogue One's Princess Leia Looked Like without the CGI," *Syfy Wire*, April 3, 2017, www.syfy.com/syfywire/heres-what -rogue-ones-princess-leia-looked-without-cgi.

16 Rhett H Laurens, "Year of the Living Dead: California Breathes New Life into Celebrity Publicity Rights," *Hastings Communications and Entertainment Law Journal* 24, no. 1 (2001): 109.

17 Maane Khatchatourian, " 'Hunger Games: Mockingjay' Director Didn't Use CGI for Philip Seymour Hoffman Scenes," *Variety*, November 15, 2014, https://variety.com/2014/film/news/hunger-games-mockingjay-director-didnt-use-cgi-for-philip-seymour-hoffman-scenes-1201357509/.

18 Opheli Garcia Lawler, "There Will Not Be a Prince Hologram at the Super Bowl," *Fader*, February 4, 2018, www.thefader.com/2018/02/04/there-will-not-be-a-prince-hologram-at-the-super-bowl.

19 Prince, "Prince 1998 Guitar World Interview," *Music Interview Archive*, accessed December 7, 2018, https://sites.google.com/site/themusicinterviewarchive/prince/prince-1998-guitar-world-interview.

20 Michael Rothman and Clayton Sandell, "Carrie Fisher's Reaction to Her Latest 'Star Wars' Cameo," *ABC News*, January 5, 2017, https://abcnews.go.com/Entertainment/carrie-fishers-reaction-latest-star-wars-cameo/story?id=44571752.

21 "Rogue One's CGI Princess Leia: The sands of time are so cruel you can't even do motion capture for your younger self," *The Independent*, December 19, 2016, www.independent.co.uk/arts-entertainment/films/news/rogue-one-cgi-princess-leia-organa-actress-carrie-fisher-ingvild-deila-motion-capture-new-star-wars-a7484161.html.

22 Carrie Fisher, Twitter post, December 21, 2016, 9:11 a.m., https://twitter.com/carrieffisher/status/811620111752663040.

23 Mark Andrejevic, *Infoglut: How Too Much Information Is Changing the Way We Think and Know* (New York: Routledge, 2013).

24 Laura Sydell, "In the Future Movie Stars May Be Performing Even after They're Dead," *NPR*, March 5, 2018, www.npr.org/sections/alltechconsidered/2018/03/05/590238807/in-the-future-movie-stars-may-be-performing-even-after-their-dead.

25 Erin Winick, "Actors Are Digitally Preserving Themselves to Continue Their Careers beyond the Grave," *MIT Technology Review*, October 16. 2018, www.technologyreview.com/s/612291/actors-are-digitally-preserving-themselves-to-continue-their-careers-beyond-the-grave/.

26 Ari Folman, *The Congress*, film, directed by Ari Folman, Drafthouse Films: Austin, Texas, 2013.

27 Drew Harwell, "Fake-Porn Videos Are Being Weaponized to Harass and Humiliate Women: 'Everybody Is a Potential Target,' " *Washington Post*, December 30, 2018, www.washingtonpost.com/technology/2018/12/

30/fake-porn-videos-are-being-weaponized-harass-humiliate-women -everybody-is-potential-target/?utm_term=.3dd39bfa3737.

28 Fisher, *Wishful Drinking*, 87.

29 Dyer, *Stars*, 18.

30 Lev Manovich, *Software Takes Command* (New York: Bloomsbury, 2013).

31 Manovich, *Software Takes Command*, 2.

32 Henry Jenkins, "Defining Participatory Culture," in *Participatory Culture in a Networked Era* (Cambridge: Polity Press, 2016), 1–31.

33 Jenkins, "Defining Participatory Culture."

34 Gabriel Bell, "A Year after Carrie Fisher's Death, #CarrieOnForever Unites a Grieving Galaxy," *Salon*, December 27, 2017, www.salon.com/2017/12/27/carrieonforever-hashtag-carrie-fisher-death/.

35 Lindsay van Ekelenburg, Twitter post, December 27, 2018, 1:41 p.m., https://twitter.com/LindsayvanekArt/status/1078405595911340038.

36 Carrie Fisher, "Ask Carrie Fisher: I'm Bipolar—How Do You Feel at Peace with Mental Illness?," *The Guardian*, November 30, 2016, www.theguardian .com/lifeandstyle/2016/nov/30/carrie-fisher-advice-column-mental -illness-bipolar-disorder.

37 This quote is also referenced by Hoffner and Park later in this anthology, specifically discussing Fisher's mental health advice and advocacy.

38 Alexander Galloway, *The Interface Effect* (Cambridge: Polity Press, 2012).

39 Galloway, *Interface Effect*, 10.

40 Galloway, *Interface Effect*, 12.

41 Galloway, *Interface Effect*, 51.

42 Galloway, *Interface Effect*, 46.

43 Galloway, *Interface Effect*, 46.

44 Galloway, *Interface Effect*, 48.

"Carrie Fisher Sent Me"

Gendered Political Protest, *Star Wars*, and the Women's March

Tanya D. Zuk

In a Galaxy Close to Home

On Saturday, January 21, 2017, the day after the inauguration of Donald Trump as president of the United States, the Women's March on Washington became the single largest protest in the history of the country. The March filled the Washington Mall and surrounding streets with over 500,000 people, with coordinated sister marches in 676 cities across all fifty states (and additional territories).[1] The Women's March originally intended to address women's rights and to protest Trump's political rhetoric against women, but it quickly branched out to address issues of civil rights, racial inequality, LGBTQ rights, immigration, health care reform, and environmental issues. This national protest became international as sister marches were organized in 137 countries around the world, including two research stations in Antarctica, and cities in Kenya, the United Kingdom, and Hong Kong. The March is estimated to have 3.5 to 4.6 million participants worldwide.[2] The large numbers and transnational scope of the protest are due in part to the variety of causes it addressed and the collective reaction to the political rhetoric used during Trump's presidential campaign.

In fact, many of the iconic images presented during the Women's March are in direct response to the rhetoric Trump employed during his campaign for office. One of the most notable icons from the march are the ubiquitous "pink pussy hats"; these knitted hats with cat ears in every shade of pink were seen all over the United States and speckle every protest photo. The hats are in reaction to Trump stating in a 2005 interview that he could do anything to women, even "grab them by the pussy."[3] Many of the posters at the marches reacted to the comment, with taglines like "Not This Pussy," "This Pussy Grabs Back," and "This Pussy's Got Claws," calling Trump and the larger rape culture in the United States to task.

Strikingly, many of the protesters in the March on Washington and sister sites used images from entertainment media, films, and television to create their protest posters. These are images and phrases we more often associate with fandom and fun—not politics and protest. Signs appeared featuring various popular texts including *Game of Thrones*, *Black Mirror*, *Harry Potter*, *Star Trek*, *Mean Girls*, *Spiderman*, and *Supergirl*. However, the most prolific image from a media fandom appearing in the Women's March is that of Princess Leia of the *Star Wars* franchise, with variations of the tagline "A women's place is in the Resistance."

This chapter examines the relationship between media fandom, memes, and political protest through a case study of *Star Wars* protest posters, particularly those using images of Princess Leia, at the Women's March on Washington and its anniversary march in 2018. Protesters use signs featuring iconic media fandoms, like *Star Wars*, because these popular icons are easily digestible and transformable memes, providing quick context for political speech and protest within a community. The choice of *Star Wars* and Princess Leia is in part due to the franchise's association with rebellion and resistance and the passing of Carrie Fisher a month after the presidential election. Thus, we can see protest posters as an extension of the fannish text's values and as a tribute to a fallen hero. Further, this study shows one of the many ways in which fans, and audiences more generally, incorporate ideology from the imaginary worlds of popular media into their lived experiences, ethics, and politics. The use of popular culture memes as political protest then becomes a form of proselytization that is accessible to anyone and for any ideological position.

The Theoretical Cantina: Fandom, Memes, Protest

Before we look specifically at the protest posters from the Women's March, we must first understand the context from which they came, namely, media fandom, and in this case *Star Wars* fandom, as well as the function of memes and their place within protest. Henry Jenkins describes fandom as the "social structures and cultural practices created by the most passionately engaged consumers of mass media properties."[4] Further, fandom's structures are informal, and its practices vary, but the passionate and invested nature of the participants is steadfast, regardless of the text. Though individual fans have a variety of levels of investment, the group as a whole is active, *Star Wars* fans being some of the most devoted.

Star Wars fans and fandom are as diverse and widespread as its properties. Originally a film trilogy starting in 1977 with the film *A New Hope*, then *The Empire Strikes Back* (1980), and *Return of the Jedi* (1983), the media franchise quickly grew. It now includes prequel and sequel film trilogies, several TV shows including *The Clone Wars*, and *The Mandalorian*, and hundreds of books contributing to the expanded universe. The *Star Wars* fandom is well known for various practices including cosplay (costume play) with well-established organizations like the 501st Legion; fan fiction with over 50,000 stories available online at Archive of Our Own and FanFiction.net, and fan videos, including an official competition, as well as the almost nine million videos on YouTube. All of this thereby makes the *Star Wars* franchise and its fandom one of the largest communities and texts in popular media.

There is a long history of media fandoms being engaged in charitable endeavors. This combination of fan practices and civic engagement is called fan activism.[5] The *Star Wars* fandom, in particular, has several fan organizations, including the previously mentioned 501st Legion as well as the Jedi Assembly, Rebel Legion, and Dark Side Alliance. These groups cosplay as Stormtroopers, Rebellion fighters, Jedi, Sith, and other characters from the films for charitable causes, raising hundreds of thousands of dollars annually. In their article "Fandom Meets Activism," Melissa Brough and Sangita Shresthova argue that "fan-driven civic participation, fueled by affective engagement in content worlds, offers overt examples of such linkages and how storytelling and other fan practices may scaffold mobilization for real-world action."[6] That is to say, participatory cultures like fandom provide a training ground for skills used in activism like networking, remixing, criticism, and organization. Additionally, fans incorporate not only the ideology and culture of fandom into their activism and protests but also the underlying themes and ideology of their particular media texts. Fans embody the ideology embedded in the media texts they are invested in and incorporate those messages into their civic participation by means of charitable good works, creative critique, and political protest.

For example, according to Danielle Hart, the *Ms. Marvel* fandom in their protests against the Muslim immigration bans positions resistance as active citizenship.[7] I would argue that *Star Wars* has long since held this position internally within the text, as George Lucas has stated in interviews that the original trilogy was his statement against the Vietnam War, and more recently *Rogue One* writer Chris Weitz has confirmed the newest trilogy as being antifascist.[8] The Women's Marches are the first major protests in which *Star Wars* iconography was actively and widely used in material posters. However, these images have been circulating online as part of fan activism as digital memes for some time.

One of the ways in which fans can be active creatively as well as politically in their fan activism is through the use of visual and verbal memes. Evolutionary biologist Richard Dawkins created the term meme, a combination of "gene" and "mimesis" to capture the viruslike transmission and mutation of cultural ideas and artifacts. There are three primary attributes of memes that are particularly relevant to the discussion of protest and fandom. According to Limor Shifman, memes (1) use grassroots propagation from individuals to larger society, (2) are easily reproduced through mimicry (imitation) and remix (variation), and (3) are diffused through voluntary competition and selective sharing.[9] Memes create a formula of image and text that create a cultural shortcut, which is easily manipulated to allow for a range of political messages to be incorporated, disseminated, and understood.

Memes provide space for dissent and community building among minority groups. According to Kevin Howley, in his article on memes and politics, "memes enable and encourage non-traditional actors to 'speak back' to political authorities in surprising, and surprisingly eloquent ways."[10] Further, the formulaic nature of memes and their propagative properties are useful in creating a cultural performance that can quickly adapt to changing ideologies. Thus, memes are both "meaning-making and disciplining tools in the boundary work of collectives."[11] As new variations of memes are created and contribute toward the collective voice of the community, they are either shared and included in the larger protest changing the ideology or pushed aside and dropped from the collective as being too far astray from the community's core values.

Memes as individual units are concentrated messages of cultural critique, and when viewed collectively, especially in public spaces, memes can be powerful political tools. The ability of memes to be individual and collective as well as cross both the "public and private sphere, not as sporadic entities, but as monstrously sized groups of texts and images" make them the tool of choice in political and civil protest.[12] Memes have been implemented through protest signs, chants, and songs long before the age of the internet. Further, the use of memes alone is not enough to create a protest event or movement, for we often see memes used as criticism, satire, and political speech without contributing to a particular campaign or protest event.

Therefore, memes must be embedded in a concerted effort in "reclaiming space" and in the case of feminist protest, of public space by women—space often described as dangerous or inhospitable to women.[13] The incorporation of entertainment media as a fundamental element of protest memes reclaims not only the physical public space occupied during the protest but also the cultural space the meme relies on to create its meaning. Thus, the protesters at the Women's March are reclaiming the physical space they occupied during the protest as well as the cultural space of *Star Wars*—by connecting the real-life political issues to the fictional ideologies of the Resistance/Rebellion through the creation of memes featuring Princess Leia and other female characters from *Star Wars*.

March against the "Evil Empire": Phrasal Template, Ideology, and Irony

The Women's March on Washington was not intended as a fan activism event; it was not organized with media fandom, much less specifically *Star Wars* in mind. Instead, it was envisioned as an intersectional feminist critique via traditional political protest to a new political regime.[14] Nevertheless, protesters incorporated media fandom into their activism by merging iconic media imagery with political speech creating memetic protest posters. These posters rely on the underlying ideology associated explicitly and implicitly with the *Star Wars* franchise—that the power of resistance is through hope and love.

One of the most prolific fan-inspired political memes at the Women's March was of Princess Leia of *Star Wars*. With countless variations, the root meme is an image created by Hayley Gilmore of Mississippi titled *Resist*. Gilmore made the image file available for free on her website as a

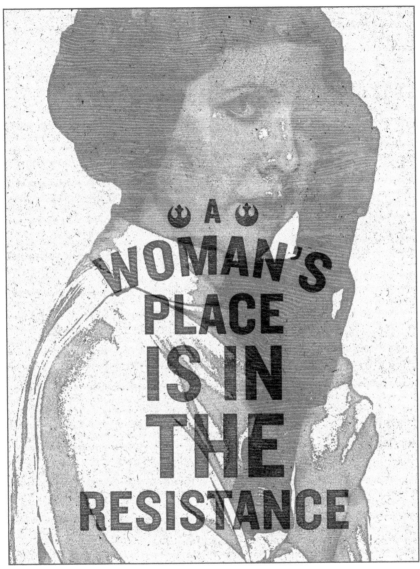

Fig. 5.1. Iconic protest poster *Resist* (2017) by Hayley Gilmore from the 2017 Women's March on Washington.

hi-resolution PDF for friends attending the March. The meme went viral and crashed the site, prompting a transfer to a larger server at Dropbox that could handle the demand for downloads.[15] Created as a tribute to Carrie Fisher, Gilmore manipulated a promotional shot from *A New Hope* remixing commercial media by adding digital layers. The image is of a faded and textured gun-wielding Leia in monotone red on a white speckled background, overlaid with the slogan "A woman's place is in the Resistance" in a transparent blue-black san-serif font.

Beyond the powerful image of Princess Leia defiantly looking into the camera, gun in hand, is the slogan, which is playing with a familiar phrasal template: "A woman's place is in the kitchen/home." This phrase has historical roots as far back as ancient Greece with the playwright Aeschylus, but more substantial ties lie with the Victorians where the exact phrasing was popularized in magazines.[16] The original phrase is often used as a misogynist put-down to women, especially women attempting to leave behind domestic work (usually as wife, mother, or maid). Feminist activists have long since subverted this phrase by replacing the ending with ". . . the House and the Senate," and later with Hillary Clinton's run for the presidency, "the Oval." Here we see what William Loew described as "language system-internal irony" or a type of irony created by breaking the pattern of phrasing in order to create humor through the disruption of a known phrasal template.[17] Additionally, phrasal irony is "conventionally used to express criticism and censure in an indirect manor."[18] Thus, by disrupting a well-known phrase, and providing replacement text that positions itself in implicit opposition to the original meaning, the reader is both chastised and entertained.

Gilmore continues the subversive variation of the phrasal template with, "A woman's place is in the Resistance," changing the ending once again. The phrasal template provides a cultural shorthand or memetic context by emphasizing the parallel of our current political situation to that of the Resistance fighting against the First Order (or the Rebellion fighting against the Empire) in *Star Wars*, that which incorporates not only a feminist critique but a political one as well. This connection is made by the visual anchor of Leia, who is a Rebellion agent and later a general in the Resistance; cementing a woman's place is not only in the resistance but also leading it.

In addition to embracing the ideology of resistance to an oppressive regime, *Star Wars* fandom has pulled two quotes from *Rogue One* (2016) and *The Last Jedi* (2017) that embody the underlying values that fuel and focus sociopolitical resistance: hope and love. In the 2017 Women's March, *Rogue One* had recently been released, though the female lead and rebellion leader Jyn Erso (Felicity Jones) did not become a visual icon for the Women's March. However, her call to battle, "Rebellions are built on hope," did become a phrasal template used in protest posters. This statement often appeared alone with only the rebellion logo for visuals or remixed with imagery of Leia and even Rey. The quote itself is used within the film as a call for action, a rallying cry for a kamikaze mission vital to the rebellion's cause. It posits that the most important resource is not military, financial, or even logistical, but emotional—of hope and the human spirit. Protesters using this quote are creating a link not only to *Star Wars* but also to previous political slogans and ideals, particularly Obama's campaign of hope in 2008.

Fig. 5.2. Rose Tico and Finn, two new characters of color in the *Star Wars* franchise, are featured in this protest poster by Anthony Breznican (2018).

Hope is essential to rebellion, for one must have hope in order to imagine something better, otherwise why bother to protest, why rebel at all? With the Anniversary March in 2018, a new installment of the *Star Wars* franchise, *The Last Jedi*, had been released and with it a new quotation fans leveraged in their protest. For the first time, it is a woman of color who provides the ideological lesson for our male protagonist and audience to learn. Rose Tico (Kelly Marie Tran) saves Finn (John Boyega) from himself and explains that the only way to win is "not fighting what we hate, but saving what we love." Many fans have celebrated and embraced the new diversity and values of the *Star Wars* franchise and leverage those ideas and beliefs into their fan activism and political protest.

The Resistance Wants You: Propaganda as Evolving Meme

Alongside traditional fan activism posters at the Women's March, there were a variety of remixed propaganda posters that rely on historical nationalism as a mimetic template for the current political protest. The intertextual use and remix of propaganda posters by protesters is a type of "political culture jamming" as described by Jamie Warner, in that the poster images work by "disseminating dissident images with messages designed to provoke the same type of dètournement or subversion of the dominant meaning . . . that culture jammers seek."[19] By using historical propaganda and political posters, the protesters-cum-culture jammers are relying on the memetic knowledge linked to these images to create new cultural links or to reframe the old ones.

Featuring Princess Leia and *Star Wars* iconography, these posters merge the real-life history of propaganda in the United States and the fictional tradition within the *Star Wars* universe. As the *Star Wars* universe is based on intergalactic war and politics, it is not surprising that there is a canonical history of propaganda within the fictional universe. There is even an in-universe book on the evolution of both Empire and Rebels/Resistance propaganda use titled *A History of Persuasive Art in the Galaxy*, written by Pablo Hidalgo as Jaynor of Bith, a character from *Star Wars* who was a propaganda artist for both sides at one time or another. Hidalgo as Jaynor states in the introduction of the book:

> An artist uses expression and symbolism as weapons, transforming
> art into propaganda. . . . Art is a reflection of civilization. So is war. Art
> in the service of war is doubly so. To dismiss propaganda as a lesser
> form of art is to deny a fundamental part of who we are.[20]

The subsequent volume outlines major propaganda campaigns from
both sides of the conflict, including the uses of symbols, icons, and language. There are four posters specifically leveraging images of Princess
Leia within the text. Through these posters, we can see the official positioning of Princess Leia by both the fictional Rebellion and the very real
Lucasfilm franchise. Early propaganda using Leia were for internal use to
bolster troop morale and featured phrases like "We Can Do It" and "May
the Force Be with You." According to Jaynor/Hidalgo, "Princess Leia was
more than just a leader. She was an inspiring symbol. . . . Leia embodied
tenacity and courage and appeared in artwork shared only within rebel
ranks."[21] Later canonical posters featured Leia in tribute to the lost Alderaan (*A New Hope*), recruitment posters based on the Battle of Endor
(*Return of the Jedi*), and Leia's failed run for Senator (*Bloodline* by Claudia
Gray).

 According to art historian Nistasha Perez, propaganda needs two
sides to work effectively.[22] Historically in war, the natural divide is
between two opposing forces and in politics, between parties. Each side
is establishing its own set of iconography and values, while demonizing
the opposition. Perez examined protest posters from the Women's March
and canon propaganda from the *Star Wars* universe and established some
of the underlying values associated with each side of the propaganda
wars. According to Perez, the Empire's underlying values are based in the
normative, mainstream, and conformity, whereas those of the Rebellion/
Resistance are based on diversity, individuality, and freedom. We can
see the mapping of these values into the Women's March propaganda
through the frequent depiction of Donald Trump as Darth Vader or
Jaba the Hutt and the use of Princess/General Leia as standard-bearer for
the protesters themselves, thus aligning the real-life opposition to their
fictional counterparts.

 Renowned comic artist Greg Horn created a protest poster reimagin-
ing the infamous J. M. Flagg's 1917 "'Uncle Sam' . . . wants you!" propaganda poster. Horne's version features Princess Leia, bun adorned, toting

a blaster in one hand and pointing out to the reader with the other at the center. At the top left corner, above Leia's head, is a planet encircled with a phrase from the film "A million voices cried out." Below Leia's pointed finger, the military propaganda text is replaced with "Don't be silent now" in bright red, with a Rebellion symbol and final tagline "Join the Rebellion" at the bottom. Though both posters are recruitment propaganda, the historical one relies solely on nationalist ideals for its appeal and lacks the humanist motivations of the *Star Wars*–based protest poster. Horn's propaganda relies on the reader knowing that the planet depicted is the destroyed Alderaan, a tribute to a fictional genocide visually connecting us to the very real Holocaust, despite the fact that the inspiration propaganda is from World War I and not World War II. The primary text message in the Leia poster is not one of recruitment as in the Flagg piece, but a reminder of the ethical need to speak for those who can't, with a secondary message of recruitment to the resistance. The text, "Don't be silent now," is another marker associating the current political climate to that of Nazi Germany, as that fascist regime began through traditional politics and made purchase by the public's apathy and the lack of vocal dissent.

The links between protest posters and historical propaganda posters continues with Leia seamlessly becoming Rosie the Riveter. Using J. Howard Miller's 1942 propaganda poster "We Can Do It!" as a base, fans have positioned Princess Leia in place of Rosie and added a Rebellion tattoo on her bicep. I've been unable to find an artist associated with this image, and it predates the Women's March by several years, with the first image circulating in 2008 for a FreakingNews.com image contest. However, it was printed and used by protesters for the March, thus replicating and disseminating the meme offline. These fan-altered propaganda-turned-into-protest-posters use the same tactic of mimicry and subversive language to create political speech. By relying on the patriotic core of the original meme, these new variants equate political protest as democratic and nationalistic imperatives at the heart of American ideals.

This connection is made explicit with protest posters using the national colors to create images of Leia against a background of the American flag with text that reads, "Resist!" and "We the people, Rebel against Hate." These posters, and particularly the image captured in Austin by Alexa Bourdage, pay homage to the iconic "Hope" poster created by

Fig. 5.3. World War I propaganda poster "Uncle Sam" (1917) by J. M. Flagg is the inspiration for comic artist Greg Horn's 2017 protest poster "Don't be silent now" (used with permission by GregHornArt.com).

Fig. 5.4. J. Howard Miller's "Rosie the Riveter" (1942) is a perennial favorite for fans to "culture jam" into the "Leia the Riveter" variant.

Shepard Fairey in support of Barack Obama's 2008 presidential campaign that used a 3-tone posterization technique. This memetic evolution pulls the *Star Wars* ideology of resistance into American nationalism. However, the use of "Hope" complicates and potentially even co-opts the yearning for equality African Americans experienced during Obama's campaign and presidential inauguration. Clearly intended to integrate the Women's March protest into the larger history of the civil rights and women's liberation movements, these posters rely on the image of Princess Leia to create a memetic bridge.

Horn's piece re-centers a traditionally male military poster as female-centric; whereas the Rosie/Leia mash-up provides a fan-driven twist to a historically iconic feminist image, and American-flag-Leia incorporates associations with racial equity and Obama's presidential campaign. These images rely on the reader's previous knowledge of US political propaganda imagery and *Star Wars* to be fully understood. Therefore, these memes link

Fig. 5.5. The "Hope" (2008) poster by Shepard Fairey has inspired so many since it was created for President Obama's campaign. It is clearly the inspiration for this poster seen in Austin, Texas, taken by Alexa Bourdage in 2017.

various ideologies from nationalist patriotism, general fandom community, *Star Wars*' "the force," and feminism.

Take This, Pass on Your Light: Intergenerational Exchange

Alongside images relying on historical propaganda, young protesters and those catering to them invoke Princess Leia in their protest memes differently. Carrie Fisher herself wrote about the intergenerational nature of *Star Wars* in *The Princess Diarist*, commenting:

> It's like you are introducing the child to a tribe; there's a ritual . . . you watch him watching *Star Wars*, trying to figure out how much you have in common with your kid, see which character he'll identify with, who he'll root for, and hope at the end of it you can still love your child the same way.[23]

For many parents, the gift of *Star Wars* is a bonding experience that not only creates a shared interest in a popular text, but it is also a sharing of values. These values are mined from the text and through the community experience of the *Star Wars* fandom. The Women's March was filled with children, as many parents found the March an important moment to teach children about civic duty and provide them with a rare opportunity to contribute to an international moment.

This intergenerational exchange is not limited to the bonds of family but is open to the bond of fandom. For instance, Ana Matronic of the band Scissor Sisters cosplayed as young Princess Leia, complete with buns and a poster reading simply "We Will Defeat the Dark Side" in the *Star Wars* title font. Matronic, in an interview with *Vanity Fair*, stated, "I knew that there was going to be lots of kids there. So, to see their idol, their princess there supporting them and who they are I thought would stick with them forever. I could inspire these kids to be activists and keep fighting."[24]

According to Cami Rowe, costuming used in political protest fulfills several functions including attention-grabbing, the branding of organizations, identities, and ideologies as well as morale-boosting. More importantly, costuming can provide a sense of the carnivalesque—an indicator of liminal performativity of political agenda.[25] Matronic's use of cosplay of such an iconic and ideologically laden character as Princess Leia is intended not only to make a political point but also to pass that political ideology on—not to the political opposition, but to the next generation of fan-activists. Matronic's cosplay presence at the Woman's March is one of many similar examples of intergenerational exchange of both fandom and activist values focused on community, persistence, and resistance.

The mother of a young Rey cosplayer and activist tweets an image of her daughter carrying a homemade sign asking, "What would Leia do?" that is adorned with the Rebellion symbol, flowers, and rainbows. The mother reports, "An older man handed A—— his lightsaber and said, 'Take this.' She is glowing. Pass on your light to the next gen."[26] *Star Wars* is unlike many modern pop texts for a variety of reasons, not the least of which is its underlying ideology to resist oppression, but perhaps, more importantly, its ability to cross generational lines. According to Janelle Vermaak, intergenerational exchange is a "second-hand fandom" that is passed from parent to child, from friend to friend. She argues that we "gift" affect or emotion through the sharing of filmic or fan experiences.[27] Similarly, parents bringing their children to protest events are doing so to instill a set of civic values, to have their children participate in history, and to bond over that shared experience.

The fannish and protestor impulse are similar in the need to exchange values, feelings, and experience between generations—strengthening traditional familial ties but also forming bonds based on choice. Unfortunately, one of the reasons that Princess Leia was so prevalent as an icon at the Women's March is due to her recent passing—reminding fans of those generational lines and encouraging the passing of the fandom and the activist torch down to younger hands.

"Carrie Fisher Sent Me": The Cultural Impact of a Feminist Hero

To fully understand the cultural space reclaimed through fan protest memes produced as posters for the Women's March on Washington, we must understand the cultural icons selected from *Star Wars*—their meaning and context. To this end, we will examine the connection between Carrie Fisher's life and the proximity of her death to the March and the character of Leia and the ideology associated with her and *Star Wars*.

Carrie Fisher was an outspoken feminist and mental health advocate through her celebrity as an actress and script doctor, and through her work as a nonfiction author. Fisher passed away on December 27, 2016, and was publicly mourned by *Star Wars* fan communities and the general public. Her death came roughly a month before the Women's March on Washington, and the news was still flooded with memorials and tributes to the star. It is no wonder that artists and protestors latched onto her as a feminist icon to leverage within a protest meme, particularly since Carrie herself was in ardent opposition to Trump's candidacy as president. Alongside posters of Princess Leia, protesters recreated anti-Trump tweets made by Carrie, like, "Trump speaking his mind isn't refreshing, it's appalling. CocaCola is refreshing."[28]

Despite Fisher's ardent real-life activism, the actress is primarily remembered for her portrayal of Princess Leia, which was originally written as a traditional "damsel in distress" stereotype, but which Fisher revised with her performance as an agented, sarcastic, and feminist heroine. Princess Leia is a major pop icon for various reasons. She has some of the funniest wisecracks in the original trilogy, with sarcastic lines like "Someone has to save our skins. Into the garbage chute, flyboy" (*A New Hope*) and "You have your moments. Not many of them, but you do have them" (*Empire Strikes Back*). Princess Leia has substantial agency as a character equally wielding her intelligence, voice, and blaster. As a feminist icon, Princess Leia is on equal footing with her male costars and is in the fray of action throughout all three of the original films. Finally, one cannot completely dismiss the stunning visuals the character provides. Leia is instantly recognizable by her double bun hairstyle, white robes, and yes the gold bikini.

One of the most iconic and problematic scenes in the *Star Wars* franchise regarding the exploitation of women appears in *Return of the Jedi*. In this scene, Leia is enslaved, wearing a gold bikini and in chains. Jabba the Hutt, an extraordinarily large and anthropomorphized wormlike alien, has taken "possession" of Leia and makes his sexual desires for her known. Clearly a metaphor for misogyny and oppression, these visuals redeem themselves, at least in part, through Leia's agency in the rest of this sequence. Leia saves herself from slavery using the chains of bondage to strangle her captor. She uses the trappings of sexist oppression to free not only herself but also to redeem her character as a feminist icon with agency and strength.

Carrie Fisher herself is very critical of this scene and has publicly spoken about the gold bikini and slave motif as being antifeminist.[29] Many feminist fans have rechristened the "slave outfit" as the "Hutt-killer" costume, as they see the only proper use of the outfit is to kill the patriarchy. Fans leverage the image of Princess Leia—Jabba Killer and Fisher's own feminist rhetoric—in their fan tributes and fan activism protest posters. One poster uses an illustrated "slave" Leia breaking her chains with "Enough" in bold letters, while many others reframe Donald Trump as Jabba the Hutt either through the incorporation of his iconic toupee or the "Make America Great Again" cap. Here we see a poster using an image of Lady Liberty dressed in the Hutt Killer costume, strangling a Jabba/Trump. Given Trump's history of misogyny and antiwomen rhetoric, it is an easy evolution from the general misogyny associated with Jabba to the specific and real danger of Trump's presidency.

As General Organa in *The Force Awakens*, the character of Leia is no less vocal or independent but has grown into a leadership position within the Resistance. Though her screen time is brief, her position and the deference afforded to her by that position speaks volumes. It is important to note that in the tactical meeting, General Organa doesn't come up with the plan to disable "Starkiller Base" but instead asks questions to highlight flaws and issues that need to be addressed to accomplish the task at hand. However, during battle General Organa is in full command of the battalion of fighters, despite her grief over the loss of Han. This depiction of leadership style is striking in its focus on feminine leadership being less abrasive but no less efficient, purposeful, and effective as the more traditional male presentations of power and leadership.

Leia's position as General complements her role as mother to her son Ben, also known as Kylo Ren, and her desire for motherhood. Her connection to the force is highlighted in the film through her connection to Han and Rey. In this way, Leia has come to model motherly performance and fulfill the mother role for the newest batch of Resistance fighters: Rey, Poe, and Finn. Her maternal affect, particularly in regard to Rey's grief over Han's death, provides complexity to her role as General and another entry for feminist interpretation.

Ultimately, the legacy of Carrie Fisher comedienne, author, mental health and feminist activist cannot be disentangled from the popular memory of the active, sharp-tongued, and agented Princess/General Leia. Fisher was an avid user of social media for political commentary, and, within the

Fig. 5.6. Twitter user @MaraJade_2017 took this photo of a protest featuring "Hutt-Slayer" Lady Liberty choking President Trump/Jabba the Hutt in Providence, Rhode Island (2017).

Star Wars canon, Princess Leia was no stranger to the use of propaganda. That both the character and the actress are so closely aligned within popular memory contributes toward the use of their image as a meme in the Women's March, as a tribute to her memory through political speech that protesters feel both Leia and Carrie would support.

The use of popular culture memes in political protest is then a reclamation of physical and cultural public space by protesters. These images rely on the underlying values of fandom culture, American democratic ideals, and the values embedded in the source media text that the meme is referencing. In doing so, fan activist posters merge two intergenerational exchange systems: fandom and protest—encouraging the communication of shared values. In this case the shared value is that of resistance and hope—foundations for freedom.

Among the specific Carrie Fisher tributes, Mark Hamill tweeted images from the protest with the comment "I know where she stood. You know where she stood. Such an honor to see her standing with you today."[30] Author Anthony Breznican tweeted an image of a protest poster that simply states "Carrie Fisher Sent Me." He commented, "Carrie Fisher isn't gone. She was alive and well at the #WomensMarch."[31] For many protesters the Princess Leia memes are as much a political protest of an oppressive regime as they are a tribute to a fallen hero, whether that hero was the fictional Leia or the very real Carrie Fisher; either way, she was a badass, feminist icon whose presence is still felt today.

Notes

1 Erica Chenoweth and Jeremy Pressman, "Estimated Women's March Attendance and Visualization" January 22, 2017, https://geographer.carto .com/viz/a229d5d2-e04a-11e6-9c98-0e98b61680bf/embed_map.

2 Barb Darrow, "More Than 1 in 100 of All Americans Were at Women's March Events," *Fortune*, January 23, 2017.

3 David A. Fahrenthold, "Trump Recorded Having Extremely Lewd Conversation about Women in 2005," *Washington Post*, October 18, 2016.

4 Henry Jenkins, "Fandom, Participatory Culture, and Web 2.0," *Confessions of an Aca-Fan*, January 9, 2010.

5 Anna Van Someren, "On Chuck and Carrot Mobs: Mapping the Connections between Participatory Culture and Public Participation," *Confessions of an Aca-Fan*, January 16, 2009.

6 Melissa M. Brough and Sangita Shresthova, "Fandom Meets Activism: Rethinking Civic and Political Participation," *Transformative Works and Cultures* 10 (March 30, 2011): 5.4.

7 Danielle Hart, "'A War for a Better Tomorrow': *Ms. Marvel* Fanworks as Protest against the 2017 Immigration Ban," Fandom and Activism Panel at the Fan Studies Network North America Conference, DePaul University, Chicago, IL, October 25, 2018.

8 Benjamin Hufbauer, "The Politics behind the Original 'Star Wars,'" *Los Angeles Review of Books*, December 21, 2015; Matt Miller, "'Star Wars' Is Not Anti-Trump, But It Is Anti-Fascism," *Esquire*, December 12, 2016.

9 Limor Shifman, *Memes in Digital Culture* (Cambridge, MA: MIT Press, 2013), 18.

10 Kevin Howley, "'I Have a Drone': Internet Memes and the Politics of Culture," *Interactions: Studies in Communication and Culture* 7, no. 2 (2016): 171.

11 Noam Gal, Limor Shifman, and Zohar Kampf, "'It Gets Better': Internet Memes and the Construction of Collective Identity," *New Media and Society* 18, no. 8 (2015): 1699.

12 Shifman, *Memes in Digital Culture*, 30.

13 Ryan Bowles Eagle, "Loitering, Lingering, Hashtagging: Women Reclaiming Public Space via #BoardTheBus, #StopStreetHarrassement, and the #EverydaySexism Project," *Feminist Media Studies* 15, no. 2 (2015): 351.

14 "Mission and Vision," Women's March on Washington, accessed March 18, 2017, https://womensmarch.com/mission-and-principles.

15 Joanna Robinson, "The Force Is with Her: How Carrie Fisher Became the Surprising Face of the Rebellion against Trump," *Vanity Fair*, January 23, 2017.

16 Gary Martin, "'Women's Place Is in the Home'—the Meaning and Origin of This Phrase," Phrasefinder, accessed March 18, 2017.

17 William Loew, "Irony in the Text or Insincerity in the Writer?," in *Text and Technology*, ed. M. Baker, G. Francis, and T. Togini-Bonelli (Amsterdam: John Benjamins, 1993), 162.

18 Alan Partington, "Phrasal Irony: Its Form, Function, and Exploitation," *Journal of Pragmatics* 43 (2011): 1799.

19 Jamie Warner, "Political Culture Jamming: The Dissident Humor of *The Daily Show with Jon Stewart*," *Popular Communication* 5, no. 1 (2007): 22.

20 Pablo Hidalgo, *A History of Persuasive Art in the Galaxy* (New York: Harper, 2016), 9.

21 Hidalgo, *History of Persuasive Art in the Galaxy*, 69.

22 Nistasha Perez, "The Resistance Is Fannish," Fandom and Activism Panel at the Fan Studies Network North America Conference, DePaul University, Chicago, IL, October 25, 2018.

23 Carrie Fisher, *The Princess Diarist* (New York: Blue Rider Press, 2016), 229.

24 Robinson, "The Force Is with Her."

25 Cami Rowe, *The Politics of Protest and U.S. Foreign Policy* (New York: Routledge, 2013), 66–67.

26 Ellie Ann. Twitter/@EllieAnnesWords: "An older man handed A . . ." January 21, 2017.

27 Janelle Vermaak, "Fan Gifting and Merchandise Collecting Practices within the Alien Film Franchise," Fan Practices and Labor Panel at the Fan Studies Network North America Conference, DePaul University, Chicago, IL, October 26, 2018.

28 Carrie Fisher, Twitter/@carrieffisher: "Trump speaking his mind isn't refreshing, it's appalling. Coca Cola is refreshing . . ." November 6, 2016.

29 Carrie Fisher, interview by Terry Gross, "Carrie Fisher Opens Up about *Star Wars*, the Gold Bikini and Her On-Set Affair," *Fresh Air*, National Public Radio, November 28, 2016.

30 Mark Hamill, Twitter/@HamillHimself: "I know where she stood . . ." (January 21, 2017).

31 Anthony Breznican, Twitter/@Breznican: "Carrie Fisher isn't gone . . ." (January 21, 2017).

II

✳ ◆ ✳ ◆ ✳

Carrie/Leia

Comedy from the Edge

CARRIE FISHER'S AUTOBIOGRAPHICAL WRITING

Linda Mizejewski

C arrie Fisher's 2008 memoir *Wishful Drinking* opens with a scrapbook-like collage of images followed by the Alcoholics Anonymous formula greeting, "Hi, I'm Carrie Fisher and I'm an alcoholic," to which she adds, "And this is a true story." AA stories are usually assumed to be true, but this odd claim is understandable given that the scrapbook images are, in chronological order, photos and headlines from the various media that have skewed Fisher's "true" story through the lenses of sentimentality, sensationalism, and melodrama. Her childhood family photo, a studio publicity shot, appears on a magazine cover that also entices readers with a story about "The Loves That Shock Hollywood." But the next scrapbook item is from a tabloid front page announcing that "the latest rumor to shock Hollywood" is about the *breakup* of that studio-perfect family by glamour queen Elizabeth Taylor. On the same tabloid page, a headline also promises a story on how "You will soon be eating insects and loving it." Another headline announces a crisis from Fisher's life as if it were happening to her most famous fictional character: "Princess Leia Overdoses at Cedars-Sinai." And even the two more straightforward news headlines signal scandal and emotional crisis—a mysterious death at Fisher's home, her disclosure of bipolar disorder.[1]

The scrapbook effect brings some irony to Fisher's assertion about a true story because the truth of Fisher's life is that it was mediated by pop-culture narratives from the time she was born. Star autobiographies typically make a claim to a "real" story of their subjects, but Fisher makes no such distinction. Her memoirs show that she understands her own experience as a mash-up of gossip, Hollywood mythologies, and the fictions of Princess Leia. She notes in *Wishful Drinking* that she was prone to say she saw her father more on TV than in real life, but then she does a snarky deconstruction of that idea: "Like real life is this other thing, and we're always trying to determine what's going on in this distant, inaccessible, incomprehensible place."[2] As this suggests, Fisher was Hollywood's in-house poststructuralist, writing and rewriting her own narrative even as she realized its provisional status among multiple popular stories and images of Carrie Fisher/Princess Leia. So when she speaks of stories or headlines being "true," it's crucial to keep in mind the quip she uses in her 2004 novel *The Best Awful* and repeats in *Wishful Drinking* and in numerous interviews: "If my life wasn't funny, then it'd just be true, and that would be totally unacceptable."[3]

Fisher's quip provides a rich entry to her writing because it situates comedy, truth-telling, and resistance as the animating tensions of her fictions and her memoirs. Her use of comedy enables Fisher to refute the "totally unacceptable" narratives that define female stars by their bodies, scandals, and pathologies. Also important throughout Fisher's writing is her postmodern inclination to see her experience as a pastiche of pop-culture materials and to serve as their savvy curator and commentator. Keenly aware of the demands of glamour and the fetishization of "bad" star behavior, she pitches her own story as the funny counterpoint to fabulous stardom— that is, as camp. Through camp, Fisher embraces the "bad objects," failures, and excesses of her life; in the memoirs, they show up as her personal archive of magazine covers, posed studio shots, and outrageous headlines: "the latest rumor to shock Hollywood"; "Princess Leia Overdoses at Cedars-Sinai." These pop-culture archives are central to Fisher's project of acknowledging, resisting, and lampooning her own Hollywood history—her childhood story nationally circulated in a venue that also warned us we'll all soon be living on insects.[4]

Fisher's memoirs openly engage the issues that trouble her own stardom, but she also wrote four transparently autobiographical novels dealing with her experiences of addiction, divorce, celebrity, and mental illness: *Postcards from the Edge* (1987), *Surrender the Pink* (1990), *Delusions of Grandma* (1993), and *The Best Awful* (2003). All four satirize celebrity culture and celebrate heroines who barely survive it. They also draw on comedy as a utopian mode of storytelling, a perspective that locates suffering as part of a larger, life-affirming picture. Kathleen Rowe discusses this "long view" of the comic mode as a key to its utopianism, its inclusion of the sad with the silly: "Comedy not only requires a certain emotional detachment from the fate of the individual—ultimately death—but makes such detachment possible by showing that fate in a broader perspective."[5] In the novels,

Fig. 6.1. Carrie Fisher, on the set of her 2008–2010 stage play *Wishful Drinking*, curates her archive of Hollywood images to pitch her own campy account of stardom (AF archive/Alamy).

the heroine's crises sometimes play out in plot lines about soap opera and B-movies, for example, so that what we take seriously—the suffering of the heroine—is also reflected in tacky versions of the same story.

In the last decade of her life, Fisher dropped the apparatuses of fiction and turned to memoirs, the first of which, *Wishful Drinking*, was the book version of her 2008–10 one-woman show of the same name, so it's structured through the punchlines and snappy anecdotes of stand-up comedy. John Limon has characterized stand-up comedy's self-deprecating style as "standing up" to abjection, reclaiming the most humiliating aspects of our experiences and our bodies, speaking back to shame.[6] "Okay, have it your way, I'm a drug addict," she deadpans. "You know how they say that religion is the opiate of the masses? Well, I took masses of opiates religiously."[7] Her next memoir, *Shockaholic* (2011), is structured more conventionally as a series of essays but, like the novels, achieves comedy's more sublime effect of perspective on pain. Fisher writes frankly about her shame in relapsing and her despair in losing custody of her daughter Billie. Within the same passages, though, she also writes about how her relapse was spurred by the overdose death of her friend Greg Stevens, a gay Republican operative who happened to be in her bed when he died. So Fisher's grim story of relapse includes the darkly funny details of advice from a psychic who helped her figure out why Greg might be haunting her house. The totally unacceptable versions of this story, to use Fisher's terms, would be scandal and melodrama; they would include the overdose, the relapse, and the loss of the daughter, but would omit the absurdist details of the ghost and the psychic, which attest to the way tragedy and goofiness stubbornly occupy the same space—or in this case, Fisher's haunted house. Her final memoir, *The Princess Diarist* (2016), describes her experience making *Star Wars* (1976), when, at the age of nineteen, she became Princess Leia for the rest of her life. Embedded in this memoir are raw pages from her diary of those days, when she was having an on-set affair with her costar Harrison Ford, her first serious and heartbreaking relationship. The diary pages are bookended by witty reflections on the Ford and *Star Wars* debacles that put them into sharp perspective, but the pain chronicled in the diary excerpts is sharp, too.

So, despite her one-liner about the truth being unacceptable, Fisher's engagement with the "true" is cagey and not entirely dismissive in her novels and memoirs. Also, the true stories with which she grapples are often about addiction and mental illness, the latter of which she positions as both the key to her identity and its perplexing undoing. She laments her loss of memories after electroshock therapy, so part of her agenda in her later writing is to ascertain a history and establish herself as a quirky but nevertheless authoritative narrator. And ironically, once she turns from fiction to memoir, fiction becomes one of her primary topics: her sci-fi alter ego Princess Leia, exploited as merchandise and pornography but also intrinsic to Fisher's identity, commingling fiction with the profoundly true.

The Funny, the True, the Totally Unacceptable

Taking control of her own story by writing it first as fiction and then as memoir, Fisher privileges wit and voice over body, challenging the very basis of Hollywood's standard treatment of women. No matter how fiercely feminists claim Princess Leia as an icon, one of her most iconic images remains her pinup moment in *Return of the Jedi* (1983), when she writhes in captivity wearing her metallic bikini. Yet Fisher reports her realization at the age of ten that she would inherit the fame but not the beauty of her movie-star mother Debbie Reynolds: "I would not be, and was in no way now, the beauty that my mother was," she writes in *Wishful Drinking*. "I decided then that I'd better develop something else—if I wasn't going to be pretty, maybe I could be funny or smart."[8] In previous work, I've pinpointed the pretty versus funny dynamic as central to cultural perceptions of women and comedy and also to feminist resistance to that dynamic—that is, women comedians often target "pretty" by lampooning femininity and glamour.[9] The edginess of this comedy is not only its defiance of female norms but also its acknowledgment of the stakes—the pain of going with not-pretty in a culture where "pretty" will go anywhere.

In *Shockaholic*, Fisher quotes a mocking internet troll: "Whatever happened to Carrie Fisher? She used to be so hot. Now she looks like Elton John." Fisher replies with the cliché that most commonly condemns a woman who doesn't pay attention to her appearance: "I let myself go," she agrees, but directs us away from the loose, jowly bodies to the more pleasurable images of where, exactly, these bodies can be found and why. "Where all fat, jowly, middle-aged women go—refrigerators and restaurants (both fine dining and drive-thru)."[10] Fisher was the very best at what is valued least in Hollywood culture, where attention goes to the body in the metallic bikini, not the one cracking jokes about it.

Fisher brought the same wit to her own stories of addiction and mental illness, using comedy to refute the popular narrative of female stardom as pathology and abjection. Steven Cohan points out how "Hollywood has perpetuated its own mystique" by exploiting the female pathology narrative; he pinpoints its culmination in the postwar era bookended by Judy Garland's suicide attempt in 1950 and the deaths of Marilyn Monroe and Garland in 1962 and 1969, respectively. Their stories were "flagship moments in a new era of scandalous sexual revelations and gossipy half-truths about stars' alcoholism, drug use, secret affairs, and infidelities," he writes. The result was attention deflected away from a star's talent, focusing instead on "her driving ambition, which is, in turn, portrayed as unhealthy and excessive, hence 'monstrous,' female desiring," a pattern which he sees continuing into the present day.[11] Fisher reveals her awareness of this "monstrous" pathology narrative beginning with *Postcards from the Edge*, in which the heroine's mother brings her a Garland biography while she's in rehab. Her heroine Suzanne names Garland and Monroe as among the stars who have had the most impact on her life, all of them dead from suicide or overdose. She notes that the stars who "don't make it" are considered "heroes," as if "killing yourself like that isn't so bad. All the interesting people do it, the extraordinary ones." Suzanne herself admires the famous alcoholics and drug addicts, she admits, and her highly publicized overdose admits her to their "club": "Wow, I'm hip now, like the dead people. Romancing the stoned."[12]

Fisher's novels and memoirs deflate romantic notions of self-destruction, but Judy Garland in particular threatens to preside over Fisher's life like the bad fairy godmother showing up to predict catastrophe and woe. In *The Princess Diarist* Fisher recounts offering her Judy Garland imitation as a way to amuse Harrison Ford during the filming of *Star Wars*. She cautions him that, "It's pretty loud and includes some dancing and a lot of makeup"—clearly more drag queen tribute than party trick.[13] Garland, like Fisher, had grown up in show business but was never at home there. By the time Fisher was writing her memoirs, there were many more parallels, not only because of her struggle with addiction, but also because she too had married a gay man, had made repeated spunky comebacks after disasters, and, as Richard Dyer has said of Garland, had a failed relationship to glamour despite her moment as the sci-fi pinup in a metallic bikini.[14]

There's no extant footage of Fisher channeling Garland, but she opened the stage performance of *Wishful Drinking* singing "Happy Days Are Here Again," the song Barbra Streisand sang with Garland in a famous duet medley during Streisand's 1963 appearance on *The Judy Garland Show* (CBS; 1963–64). In her own *Wishful Drinking* show, Fisher sang "Happy Days" as an ironic and bittersweet accompaniment to a montage of alarming headlines like "Fisher Spends Months in Psych Ward" projected on a screen onstage. The song is quoted at the beginning of the opening scrapbook montage in the book version, too. Garland's apparition also haunts the *Wishful Drinking* photos of Fisher as a young girl performing a cabaret act with her mother; the two of them uncannily double the well-known images of Garland performing with her daughter Liza Minnelli. The mother-daughter photos of Fisher and Reynolds are especially poignant given their close relationship and the proximity of their deaths. But unlike Garland or Monroe, Fisher provides her own accounts of her struggles with sobriety and mental health.

Fictional Carrie Fishers

All four of Fisher's novels feature a heroine who is transparently an avatar for Fisher herself—a brilliant, troubled actress or writer, in recovery and in therapy, unlucky in love, sometimes unstable and occasionally as crazy as the celebrity culture in which she's immersed. The through line of all four books is the heroine's piercing, witty perspective on herself and on this culture, a device that repudiates the Judy Garland/Marilyn Monroe narrative of pathology because it centralizes the female star's intelligence and agency. Her first novel, *Postcards from the Edge*, directly refutes a popular version of the fallen-star narrative, Jacqueline Susann's 1966 bestseller *Valley of the Dolls*, a backstory of stars who use "dolls"—amphetamines, and barbiturates—to relax, sleep, work, and blunt personal pain. In the following essay in this anthology, Ken Feil explores Fisher's citations of this Susann novel—including Fisher naming her own heroine Suzanne Vale—and her use of Susann's camp sensibility.

Unlike *Valley of the Dolls*, *Postcards* seizes the topic of celebrity substance abuse as satire instead of melodrama. It also centralizes the heroine's authoritative voice. The first third of the book consists of her journal entries, one for each of the thirty days Suzanne spends in rehab. The narrator acknowledges she's smart but must have used "the wrong parts of my brain," she writes, "the parts that said, 'Take LSD and painkillers. This is a good idea.' I was into pain reduction and mind expansion, but what I've ended up with is pain expansion and mind reduction."[15] Fisher is also attuned to the ways recovery doesn't solve all personal problems. One of the running jokes in the novel is about a scriptwriter who meets Suzanne in rehab, learns nothing from his experience there, and writes a terrible screenplay for a movie called *Rehab!*, which is successful enough that *Beyond Rehab!* is in the works too. This cunning, funny take on addiction and recovery is evident today in the comedy of Rob Delaney and in the insider-recovery humor on the sitcom *Mom* (CBS; 2013–), but it was new in 1987 when fiction on this topic inclined toward sensationalism.

Suzanne gets out of rehab to find the same absurd celebrity world that had pushed her over the edge into drug use. But unlike *Valley*'s depiction of over-the-top crises, infidelities, and scandals, *Postcards* is structured as a series of cringe-worthy minor moments, like Suzanne's work on a low-budget movie filmed in the desert, where Suzanne has to take a drug test and then be tied to a fake cactus. During the filming, she's asked if she'll stay in show business, and she replies, "Do you mean this show business or the glamorous, fun show business?"[16] All four of Fisher's novels lampoon the mythology of a "glamorous, fun show business" through heroines who, no matter how depressed or addicted, understand that the warped culture around them exceeds their own maladies. This stance powerfully disclaims the female-pathology narrative, which, as Cohan argues, reinforces the "mystique of Hollywood as the epitome of consuming, leisure, sexual freedom, class mobility, and modernity" by faulting the star's ambition instead of the culture's impossible ideals.[17]

Postcards ends with Suzanne still sober, modestly successful, and in a stable relationship, but the novel never wavers from its reminders of her ongoing depression. Suzanne's despair about the flimsiness of Hollywood overlaps with her own despair about her experience of herself as insubstantial and incomplete. The epilogue is a witty letter to the doctor who had pumped her stomach after her overdose, and she asks him if, all those years ago, she had thrown up something she might need: "Some small but trivial thing that belonged inside? I distinctly feel as though I'm missing something. But then, I always have."[18] This vomit joke about the double meanings of emptiness is the book's last word on celebrity overdose, handled with droll existential humor. The star heroine may be damaged and vulnerable, but the focus is her keen self-awareness and her ability to tell her own story with humor instead of pathos.

Fisher's next two novels are romans à clef that engage and resist two of pop culture's favorite stories about female stardom: the disastrous marriage and single motherhood in Hollywood. *Surrender the Pink*, based on Fisher's marriage to and divorce from Paul Simon, cites the Marilyn Monroe story by fictionalizing Simon as a New York playwright, calling to mind Monroe's unhappy marriage to Arthur Miller. But heroine Dinah Kaufman, far from being a sex symbol, is a writer who thinks of her manic-depressive mood swings as competing fictions, "the fiction of existential pain and horror" as opposed to the one that was "a lighthearted read, a book called Isn't it Darling to be Human—How Exciting to Be Alive!"[19] Dinah is the writer of a soap opera, *Heart's Desire*, a thinly disguised version of her marriage and divorce from the playwright Rudy, so there's a fictionalization within a fictionalization in this novel. The soap opera version of Dinah Kaufman/Carrie Fisher has campy-dreadful lines about love: "my goal is to love you like people love their country. . . . And I don't mean my own country. No, no. I mean like part of Scandinavia maybe . . . Or Pakistan."[20] In a final metatextual twist, Dinah ends up with the soap-opera actor who plays the fictionalized version of the estranged playwright Rudy. So, the painfulness of Dinah's story is couched in a comic mise en abyme in which "real" stories and their melodramatic fictions are endlessly embedded. The saga of Dinah and Rudy "went on without them, leaving them behind."[21]

Delusions of Grandma continues this self-conscious approach to narrative. The heroine, Cora, is a script doctor, hired to rewrite screenplays, archly aware of how the best stories and characters must, above all, be packaged to exacting commercial formulas. Her job, she says, is to make the characters "more defined, insightful, funny, compelling—in a word, make their conflict worth attending to for up to, but God forbid not beyond, two big-budget hours."[22] Hollywood's narratives are unlikely to be deep or thoughtful, Cora points out, because it was a place where "people were known instead of knowing, incendiary as opposed to insightful or incisive."[23] In light of this dynamic, *Delusions* cites and evades the paths of both melodrama and romantic comedy in telling the story of Cora's romance with the young lawyer Ray and her resulting unintended pregnancy. The context of this story is the AIDS crisis, and Cora has taken in a gay friend who is dying. So, the cliché of the gay best friend takes on some depth as well as putting the Cora/Ray story in perspective. The romance does not in fact end happily even though the narrative does, in a slapstick comedy subplot about sneaking Cora's grandfather out of a nursing home so he can end his days at home. The madcap final chapters and the ceaseless references to high and low cultural texts—from Hitchcock movies to soap opera to the metaphysical poet John Dryden—make for a dizzying ride. The jarring effect comes from *Delusions'* ambition to encompass death and sadness as part of the utopian perspective of comedy.

Fisher's final novel, *The Best Awful*, adheres to stardom's decline-and-comeback story, but the "decline" is the heroine's full-blown psychotic breakdown, and her comeback is her decision to become an advocate for "subjects ranging from mental illness to gay pride."[24] This novel is based on a turbulent time in Fisher's life in the late 1990s after her partner and father of her child left her for another man. *The Best Awful* engages every hoary cliché of female stardom gone downhill: the middle-aged star reduced to talk-show host, a tabloid-fodder divorce, relapse into drug addiction, psychosis, institutionalization. But as she does in her previous fiction, Fisher demystifies this Valley-of-the-Dolls narrative and breaks through its clichés through the critical observations of a highly intelligent and funny heroine—again Suzanne Vale, decades older: "She'd probably end up a poor man's Norma Desmond, watching reruns of herself on late-night TV," Suzanne thinks, "but with no butler, no younger man caged above her garage writing *Salome* for her."[25] To the very end, *The Best Awful* is acutely conscious of its own narration as the counterpoint of popular versions of female celebrity addiction and scandal. In its last pages, Suzanne enjoys a peaceful moment with her ex-husband and imagines them getting together again, but with the possibility "they would Hollywood get together—meaning they'd appear to get back together" through a series of coy photographs and breezy interviews[26]—that is, through media and pop culture versions of their story.

In a sly grand-finale gesture, *The Best Awful* includes in its penultimate chapter a big public comeback event for Suzanne, but far from being a glamorous reentry into show business, it's her speech at a fundraiser in which she pleads for recognition of bipolar disorder as a mental illness that needs to be treated with openness and compassion rather than secrecy and shame. Suzanne's speech makes it clear that she herself will treat it with humor too, imagining a Bipolar Pride Day: "I mean, can you imagine the parades?"[27] The comeback-event chapter is called "Boo Radley's Tree," citing Harper Lee's *To Kill a Mockingbird* and its shy recluse who leaves trinkets in a tree hollow as gifts, stepping out of the shadows only at the end of the book. By the time *The Best Awful* was published in 2004, Fisher had already stepped into the public spotlight with the story of her bipolar disorder and her horrific 1997 breakdown and institutionalization fictionalized in this final novel.[28] For the rest of her life, she would work as an advocate and fundraiser for mental illness, always with the comic and irreverent tone of Suzanne's grand speech in the last pages of this book, which includes the line Fisher would herself use for the rest of her life, about funniness as the only alternative to the "totally unacceptable."[29]

Camp and the Archive

The scrapbook opening of *Wishful Drinking* introduces the strategy and comic approach that shape all three of Fisher's memoirs. In the first two, Fisher curates her personal history through tabloid headlines, fan magazine covers, and studio publicity shots alongside her own family photos, with the ironic acknowledgment that the staged shots of her parents as America's Sweethearts really *are* her family photos, the fictions that shaped and still inform her self-identity. Her third memoir, *The Princess Diarist*, which deals with her experience of becoming Princess Leia, assembles publicity shots and excerpts from her 1975–76 journals. Fisher's funny and ironic take on these archives draws on the comedy of camp and also on a rich autobiographical practice. Producing these archives alongside her commentary on them, Fisher participates in the tradition described by Amelie Hastie as the work of female stars who "reflect upon themselves as images" and use autobiography "to produce their own theoretical and historical models about their work and the industries they have been engaged in."[30]

Following Hastie, we can see Fisher's often-used quip about comedy, truth, and the "totally unacceptable" as her theorization of her own experience, which she sees as a nexus of contending narratives in Hollywood history and popular culture. Hastie argues that stars' personal archives—their collections and scrapbooks of their own careers—function as autobiographical practices that contribute to film and star history. Curating these collections, the star "has a peculiar temporal and affective relation to the production of history. She collects objects and materials of the present so that her history may be retrieved and guarded in a future time." This concept of the star "guarding" her history is especially resonant with Fisher's awareness of the toxic narratives through which her own story could be told. Hastie argues that stars' collected materials reveal "layers of historical production colliding," but Fisher is interested in the unintended humor of these colliding histories with an eye toward the excesses and absurdities of star discourses.[31]

The colliding histories in Fisher's memoirs often pit materials from fan magazines and studio publicity against Fisher's autobiographical commentaries. In *Wishful Drinking*, staged photos show her beaming parents, movie star Debbie Reynolds and singing sensation Eddie Fisher, doting on three-year-old Carrie. But Fisher accompanies the photos with her story of what was actually happening during this time, when her father left home to comfort the newly widowed Elizabeth Taylor: "my father flew to Elizabeth's side, gradually making his way slowly to her front. He first dried her eyes with his handkerchief, then he consoled her with flowers, and he ultimately consoled her with his penis."[32] At other times, Fisher's curation shows how the same popular discourse can shape both celebration and tragedy as seamless narratives representing the "real" life of a star. In *Shockaholic*, she offers the star life of her mother through the covers of fan magazines such as *Modern Screen*, *Photoplay*, and *Screenland*, which picture Debbie Reynolds first as part of an adorable romantic couple and then as an exuberant young mother: "Debbie and Eddie!"; "Debbie's Thrilling Morning with the Stork." However, a year later, the same magazines represent "Debbie" as melodramatic heroine, bravely raising her two children alone: "What I tell My Children about Liz and Eddie"; "Debbie Answers Her Daughter's Question: Won't Daddy Be With Us *All* the Time?"; "Debbie's Own Story: The Night My Children Kept Me from Dying!"[33] Fisher emphasizes how thoroughly her parents were shaped by these Hollywood discourses to the point that they "weren't really people in the traditional sense . . . they were stars before their peopleness had a chance to form itself. The studio essentially designed my mom—they taught her to talk, had her ears surgically pinned back, shaved her eyebrows."[34] Fisher understands stardom's power to "design" individuals not just physically but ontologically—as their "peopleness," their way of experiencing the world.

And this includes her own experience of stardom, which she documents in these memoirs not as history but as wily exposure of the sentimental, gossipy, pseudosolicitous discourses that purport to reveal that history. Fisher's "scrapbook" of these curated images is instantly recognizable to fans of camp and Hollywood scandal because it mimics Kenneth Anger's 1959 camp classic book *Hollywood Babylon*, in which gossipy accounts of Hollywood scandals are accompanied by lurid tabloid clippings, sensational headlines, and publicity/news photos. Following the Anger book, Fisher presents an archive of images intended to be consumed with rolling eyes and shameless enjoyment of excess and artifice—that is, consumed as camp. She offers the romantic/melodramatic/sentimental magazine covers and studio shots to evoke camp's ironic double readings, exposing how stardom is constructed through those sensational discourses. Matthew Tinkcom, in his book on camp and gay male history in Hollywood, describes how the archive materials in *Hollywood Babylon* ask readers "to try to imagine the alternative 'straight' reading of the material, an exercise in which the ideological fissures of star imagery begin to emerge with dizzying effect." Tinkcom emphasizes the concurrent strands of disdain and pleasure in Anger's text, "the strategies of dissemblance, subterfuge and ironic play" but also "a simultaneous delight in the gossip in which Anger traffics and use

Fig. 6.2. Debbie Reynolds, Eddie Fisher, and daughter Carrie circa 1956: Fisher's memoirs offer colliding histories of her much-publicized childhood and family drama (© 2000 Globe Photos/ZUMA Press, Inc./Alamy).

of gossip-driven fan accounts." The "delight" is the pleasure of consuming a "counterhistory to an idealized Hollywood," which is especially significant for queer consumers lovingly engaged in a cinema tradition that excludes them.[35]

Like Kenneth Anger, Carrie Fisher presents a "counterhistory to an idealized Hollywood" through an archive that both articulates and excludes her in its sensationalism, consumerism, and gossip. Her stance toward these campy excesses of stardom and celebrity is sometimes overt mockery. In *Wishful Drinking*, for instance, she describes how her alter ego Princess Leia has materialized as camp objects: a plastic doll, shampoo bottle, wrist-watch face, sex toy, and Pez dispenser. *Wishful Drinking* also includes real headlines in its opening pages ("Princess Leia Overdoses at Cedars-Sinai") and fake headlines on the back cover ("Carrie Fisher Selected as Runner Up Bipolar Woman of the Year"), making the point that both are equally outrageous and funny.

But Fisher shows her exasperation with these artifacts and discourses, too, given her deep and personal presence in their "true" elements. She did in fact overdose at Cedars-Sinai, and she disclosed her bipolar disorder within a culture that generally treats mental illness in reductive ways, such as disease-of-the-month proclamations instead of resources directed at treatment. Likewise, the fake headlines are accompanied by artificially posed but nevertheless "true" photos of Fisher with her mother, Fisher with Elizabeth Taylor, and a toddler Fisher in the arms of her father. In *Shockaholic*, the magazine covers featuring Debbie Reynolds as a newly abandoned mother include two-year-old Carrie Fisher in the photos, an unwitting participant in a narrative being conveyed as maternal melodrama. Fisher writes in *Princess Diarist* that as a child, she hated being photographed this way as a prop to a story about her mother's heartbreak.[36] Her anger about the exploitation of her image is evident, too, in her descriptions of how George Lucas holds the copyright to Princess Leia, so Fisher had no control over how her image was used. As she says in *Wishful Drinking*, "he owns my *likeness*" (italics hers), and reports her shock at seeing a Leia doll with an anatomically correct peek-a-boo feature at a comic book convention.[37]

So, there's an edge to this campy archival strategy, a sadness and anger poised in the tension between the "true" and the "totally unacceptable." Fisher's story includes a "true" loss of a father but also the "totally unacceptable" version of that loss as tabloid hype. The magazine covers are a campy joke but they also document Fisher's history. This edginess is intrinsic to camp comedy's historical roots in gay male survival of homophobia and the isolation of the closet. The campiness of *Hollywood Babylon*, Tinkcom argues, emerges from Anger's "critical sense of Hollywood's near-total exclusion of images of homoerotic desire" as much as "his loving embrace of Hollywood iconography." The critical debate about camp's political valence has centered on this issue of the outsider perspective, specifically the perspective of gay male culture, being essential to its identity as both an aesthetic and a critique.[38]

Arguing against this characterization of camp as an exclusively gay male phenomenon, Pamela Robertson has made an eloquent argument for the inclusion of female authorship in camp culture, emphasizing camp's alliance with feminism as a related outsider critique and claiming camp as a queer discursive space not limited to the province of gay men.[39] Feil taps this assumption of female camp authorship in describing the ways Fisher draws on Jacqueline Susann to lampoon the tropes of the backstage story in *Postcards from the Edge*, particularly in the campy embrace of the failures of career and glamour. Citing Jack Halberstam on the queer artist's engagement with failure, Feil is attentive to "the darkness" of the camp aesthetic, which for the purpose of my own analysis shows up in Fisher's memoirs as her engagement with the "totally unacceptable."

However, the edginess of Fisher's humor aligns her with camp's power of empathy and reparation as well as with camp's historical basis in abjection. Cynthia Barounis points out that, emerging from homophobic persecution and marginalization, "camp has always, to some extent, urged us to take trauma and its aftermath seriously," albeit with laughter rather than tears. While much scholarship on camp focuses on performance and theatricality, Barounis explores the interiority and affect of camp, drawing on disability studies to argue for what she calls a "crip approach to camp that privileges less visible disabilities, including psychiatric impairments."[40]

The cover illustrations of Fisher's first two memoirs tap this affect with kitschy but disturbing drawings of Princess Leia collapsed with a martini glass still in her hand (*Wishful Drinking*) and manufactured into a plastic doll, her hands covering her face in a gesture of horror (*Shockaholic*). Given Fisher's advocacy for mental health, particularly her efforts to dispel the stigma of bipolar disorder through her candid self-disclosures, these illustrations are fitting ways to signal her alliance with camp comedy through a crip approach, as Barounis suggests. And this alliance in turn illuminates Fisher's use of archival material and camp in her final memoir, *The Princess Diarist*.

The Princess Diarist is built around the archive of Fisher's own journal during the months she was filming *Star Wars* and having her first serious affair, a relationship with her costar Harrison Ford, who was a father and married man fourteen years older than Fisher. Wholly without irony or humor, these diary pages depict Fisher struggling with her feelings for a man who was emotionally unavailable and who reduced her to awkward silences. So the sadness of these journals resides not only in the heartbreak of the affair but also in Fisher's reports of her clumsy lack of words in Ford's presence. The absence of language, a characteristic of abjection, is shockingly counter to Fisher's popular image as a witty quipster and to Princess Leia's image as the smart aleck who talks back to Darth Vader. The diary pages exhibit glimpses of Fisher's wit and insight, but they are remarkable mostly for their painful rawness; they exhibit, too, glimpses of the despair that Fisher would later in her life find overwhelming. Already she describes an "old familiar feeling of hopelessness. That vague sense of desperation; fighting not to lose something before you've decided what you've got."[41] While Fisher's first two memoirs offer an archive of camp Hollywood objects that make the "true" and "totally unacceptable" story funny, this final memoir includes an archive that flatly lays out the pain, the abjection, the totally unacceptable.

Nonetheless, the archive pages of this memoir are bookended by Fisher's story of the affair from her perspective forty years later and by her ruminations on the making of *Star Wars* and the long-term effects of becoming Princess Leia. Here we find Fisher's sly, campy takes on the infamous hairstyle—"the hairy earphone configuration,"[42] the original *Star Wars* script that introduced the captive Leia "upside down and unconscious with yellow eyes,"[43] and the humbled life of the aging icon: a little girl at a fan convention wailing "I want the other Leia, not the old one!"[44] As a behind-the-scenes story of the production of *Star Wars*, much of this book offers a feminist critique of filmmaking culture as "a man's meal, with women generously sprinkled through it like overqualified spice."[45] Within the demands of that world, she was sent to a fat farm to lose ten pounds even though she only weighed 110. These opening and closing chapters deliver sharp critiques of Hollywood sexism, in vivid contrast to the diary pages that deliver the voice of an obsessed young fan in love with an unobtainable movie star. Given the snappy power of the opening and closing chapters of this book, why include the writings of a hurt and bewildered young woman who has not yet come fully into this wiser and stronger voice?

First, Fisher's reclaiming of this archive with all its awkward self-revelation evokes what Barounis describes as the "salvaging" power of camp, its attention to what's been discarded and neglected by mainstream culture. Barounis points out the appeal of camp comedy for people with disabilities who have been likewise designated as broken and out of place. The transformative power of camp, she says, enables it to reclaim discarded objects and turn them into "belongings" that are valued and loved.[46] Claiming her naive and vulnerable younger self enables Fisher to retrieve it from abjection. It's a risky move. The unguarded writing in the journals works at odds within an otherwise sharply crafted narrative that takes campy swipes at the George Lucas franchise and male fan culture. The diary doesn't seem to belong. But that's the whole point. As Barounis suggests, camp can be about loving the unlovable. It can make us cringe.

Second, Fisher's inclusion of this archive lays bare the element of affect in her take on stardom and the film industry in this memoir. By including the sadder, cringe-worthy diaries as well as her sharp-tongued rebukes of Hollywood culture, Fisher makes a compelling case for the importance of human vulnerability and affect in her juggling of truth, comedy, and the "totally unacceptable." The campy tabloid headlines, sensational magazine covers, and Pez dispensers refer to and revolve around a real person with feelings, the person we access through the diary. Fisher refuses to render this archive as anything but "true"—that is, not funny but also not "totally unacceptable." In this final model of her own stardom, Fisher acknowledges abjection, shame, and silence as part of her story, even as she refuses to allow this version of herself as the final word.

Instead, *The Princess Diarist* concludes with three chapters ruminating with pithy humor on what stardom has entailed for her not as a classic Hollywood movie star but as the sci-fi confection Leia. Lest we postulate a "real" Carrie Fisher in the diaries against a fictional *Star Wars* character, these final chapters insist that no such delineations are possible. When someone shouts "Princess" at an airport, she feels obliged "to turn around and politely respond 'Yes?,'"[47] a move that postmodern thinkers will appreciate as her profound recognition of herself within a fictional ideology. In a scintillating tour de force, Fisher writes expansively on the question of who she would be if she were *not* Princess Leia and did *not* have a full lifetime dealing with the absurdities and indignities of a particularly outlandish alter ego. "I'd be me," she concludes. "You know, Carrie. Just me."[48] But this is a campy wink toward the outsize history of herself as Leia in the previous pages.

One of her final archive photos in this book illustrates her humorous embrace of "Princess Leia me," as she calls herself, enshrined as a wax figure at the Madame Tussauds Wax Museum. The wax figure embodies Leia in the famous bikini, the monster Jabba the Hutt hovering behind her. In the photo, the middle-aged Carrie Fisher sits next to her, holding her beloved bulldog Gary, his tongue lolling out, every bit as ugly as Jabba—a delectably campy family photo. In *Shockaholic*, Fisher draws on this infamous *Return of the Jedi* scene when she predicts that her legacy will include her own writings but will be dominated by her fictional alter ego in the bikini:

> What you'll have of me after I journey to that great Death Star in the sky is an extremely accomplished daughter, a few books, and a picture of a stern-looking girl wearing some kind of metal bikini lounging on a giant drooling squid, behind a newscaster informing you of the passing of Princess Leia after a long battle with her head.[49]

Fisher's dark postmodern humor allows her to imagine her death not as melodrama but as a newscast that comically gets it wrong, confusing the woman with icon, which is both funny and true. Fisher camps up her self-obituary with the giant squid image and the vision of her journey as epic and galactic, but the poignancy of this passage is her prediction of mental illness and addiction—"a battle with her head"—as her final struggle. Yet in its sly humor, this contemplation of her own death typifies the tone of all three memoirs, in which catastrophes and disappointments are recounted with a voice inflected by comic aplomb instead of despair.

Notes

1 Carrie Fisher, *Wishful Drinking* (New York: Simon & Schuster, 2008).
2 Fisher, *Wishful Drinking*, 6.
3 Carrie Fisher, *The Best Awful* (New York: Simon & Schuster, 2004), 262. The quip also appears in *Wishful Drinking*, 17.
4 Fisher's campy curation of outrageous objects is evident in the documentary *Bright Lights*, in which she offers a tour of her house, which includes the life-size Princess Leia sex doll in the exercise room, the piano in the bathroom, and her collection of "portraitures of ugly children," as she puts it.
5 Kathleen Rowe, "Comedy, Melodrama, and Gender: Theorizing the Genres of Laughter," in *Classical Hollywood Comedy*, ed. Kristine Brunovska Karnick and Henry Jenkins (New York: Routledge, 1995), 39–59, at 48. Rowe uses Northrup Frye's concept of comedy as utopian in making the case for comedy as a mode that can express women's experience.
6 *Stand-up Comedy in Theory, or, Abjection in America* (Durham, NC: Duke University Press, 2000), 4–7.

7 Fisher, *Wishful Drinking*, 99.

8 *Wishful Drinking*, 50.

9 Linda Mizejewski, *Pretty/Funny: Women Comedians and Body Politics* (Austin: University of Texas Press, 2014).

10 Carrie Fisher, *Shockaholic* (New York: Simon & Schuster, 2011), 26.

11 Steven Cohan, "'This Industry Lives on Gossip and Scandal': Female Star Narratives and the Marilyn Monroe Biopic," *Celebrity Studies* 8, no. 4 (2017): 528, 530.

12 Carrie Fisher, *Postcards from the Edge* (New York: Simon & Schuster, 1987), 34.

13 Carrie Fisher, *The Princess Diarist* (New York: Blue Rider Press, 2016), 100.

14 Richard Dyer, *Heavenly Bodies: Film Stars and Society* (New York: Routledge, 1986), 163.

15 Fisher, *Postcards from the Edge*, 13–14.

16 *Postcards from the Edge*, 136.

17 Cohan, "This Industry Lives," 540.

18 Fisher, *Postcards from the Edge*, 226.

19 Carrie Fisher, *Surrender the Pink* (New York: Simon & Schuster, 1990), 23.

20 Fisher, *Surrender the Pink*, 81.

21 *Surrender the Pink*, 279.

22 Carrie Fisher, *Delusions of Grandma* (New York: Simon & Schuster, 1994), 23.

23 Fisher, *Delusions of Grandma*, 22.

24 Fisher, *Best Awful*, 260.

25 *Best Awful*, 160.

26 *Best Awful*, 268.

27 *Best Awful*, 261.

28 Fisher's interview with Diane Sawyer on *60 Minutes* took place in 2000. For an example of her follow-up interviews, see Lybi Ma, "Carrie Fisher," *Psychology Today* (November/December 2001): 32–37+.

29 Fisher, *Best Awful*, 262.

30 Amelie Hastie, *Cupboards of Curiosity: Women, Recollection, and Film History* (Durham, NC: Duke University Press, 2007), 2–3.

31 Hastie, *Cupboards of Curiosity*, 23–24, 5.

32 Fisher, *Wishful Drinking*, 33–34.

33 Fisher, *Shockaholic*, 126, 135–44.

34 *Shockaholic*, 137.

35 Matthew Tinkcom, *Working Like a Homosexual: Camp, Capital, Cinema* (Durham, NC: Duke University Press, 2002), 148, 141.

36 Fisher, *Princess Diarist*, 210.

37 Fisher, *Wishful Drinking*, 87.

38 Tinkcom, *Working Like a Homosexual*, 141. For a detailed overview of the decades-long debate about camp politics, see Fabio Cleto, "Introduction: Queering the Camp," in *Camp: Queer Aesthetics and the Performing Subject* (Edinburgh: Edinburgh University Press, 1999), 1–43. Writing of the contradictory definitions of camp as an aesthetic style, a politics, and a queer perspective, Fabio Cleto in the introduction to his anthology on this topic suggests that we understand camp as a "site of debate, rather than of consensus," 4. Also see in that volume Caryl Flinn's argument for the inclusiveness of camp politics beyond those of gay men, "The Deaths of Camp," 433–57.

39 Pamela Robertson, *Guilty Pleasures: Feminist Camp from Mae West to Madonna* (Durham, NC: Duke University Press, 1996). See Robertson's introduction, 3–22, and her discussion of camp's feminist impact in her chapter on Madonna, 117–38.

40 Cynthia Barounis, "Witches, Terrorists, and the Biopolitics of Camp," *GLQ: A Journal of Lesbian and Gay Studies* 24, no. 2/3 (2018): 217, 219.

41 Fisher, *Princess Diarist*, 115.

42 *Princess Diarist*, 40.

43 *Princess Diarist*, 28.

44 *Princess Diarist*, 225.

45 *Princess Diarist*, 33–34.

46 Barounis, "Witches, Terrorists, and the Biopolitics of Camp," 221.

47 Fisher, *Princess Diarist*, 246.

48 *Princess Diarist*, 246.

49 Fisher, *Shockaholic*, 74–75.

Postcards from the Valley of the Broads

CARRIE FISHER, JACQUELINE SUSANN, AND FEMINIST CAMP AUTHORSHIP

Ken Feil

Carrie Fisher punctuated the film adaptation of her autobiographical novel *Postcards from the Edge* (directed by Mike Nichols, 1990) with a revealing movie reference. Toward the conclusion, Fisher's alter ego Suzanne Vale (Meryl Streep)—a young movie star fresh out of rehab after an overdose, now making a comeback—locks horns with her mother Doris (Shirley MacLaine), a former Hollywood movie star. Their climactic argument airs a blend of familial and professional history that echoes Fisher's own history, including her upbringing by mother Debbie Reynolds and the fallout from father Eddie Fisher's affair with Elizabeth Taylor. Gossipy revelations fly back and forth related to mother and daughter's competition as performers and their shared substance abuse problems. Suzanne states to Doris, "*You're* the performer. I can't possibly compete with you. What if somebody won?" Recalling Suzanne's thirteenth birthday and Doris's inebriated misbehavior, Doris admits that "my skirt accidentally twirled up," to which Suzanne quietly replies, "And you weren't wearing any underwear." "Well . . ." Doris ripostes. Their quarrel reaches a breaking point, after which Suzanne nearly breaches her sobriety and Doris gets into a drunken car accident. A frail-looking Doris greets Suzanne in her hospital room, deprived of her wig and cosmetics, head bare and bandaged; as the two make up, Suzanne helps Doris reapply her makeup. Anticipating the swarm of paparazzi in the waiting room (cameras cocked and ready), Doris ties a scarf over her head (aided by Suzanne), dons her fur, and, having restored her glamorous facade, meets the press. Marveling in her mother's rebound in the hospital hallway, Suzanne runs into the same doctor who just weeks before had pumped her stomach and sent her get well flowers, and who now asks the actress out on a date. Suzanne kids, "Okay. We could go see *Valley of the Dolls*."[1]

Carrie Fisher's screenplay altered her novel considerably for the film version, and by including these sequences between Suzanne and Doris as well as topping them with the ironic movie reference, Fisher crystallizes an illuminating network of connections to Jacqueline Susann and *Valley of the Dolls*, her notoriously popular roman à clef and its 1967 film adaptation. Like *Postcards from the Edge*, *Valley of the Dolls* spotlights showbiz women managing substance abuse, career, fame, and sexuality, and the film has endured as a longtime favorite in gay camp culture.[2] Susann famously modeled her characters on actual celebrities, the gist of the roman à clef, and employed a legendary "guessing game" to attract and engage readers. Judy Garland apparently engendered the pill-addicted, wisecracking, golden-voiced super-starlet Neely O'Hara; Ethel Merman reputedly stopped speaking to Susann over the character Helen Lawson, a Broadway grandam drawn to brass, booze, and obscenities; Marilyn Monroe and Jayne Mansfield reverberate in the character Jennifer North, the sophisticated bisexual show girl, art film star, and doyen of the gossip columns; and Grace Kelly supposedly inspired Susann's protagonist, the quietly transgressive New England girl Anne Welles, who soars to success as a fashion model and businesswoman. Susann also dropped numerous clues in widespread promotional appearances that her own life informed the gossipy narrative, as did those of her showbiz girlfriends.[3]

Fisher's foray into the celebrity *film à clef* plays a similar guessing game with the audience, and in the confrontation scene at home and the reconciliation at the hospital, revises one of the iconic camp sequences of the novel *Valley of the Dolls* and especially the film version, the washroom scene between Neely O'Hara (Patty Duke) and Helen Lawson (Susan Hayward). Nursing an old rivalry, the two trade insults in a nightclub powder room, in front of the makeup mirror: Neely ridiculing Helen's new show, the elder diva mocking Neely's stint in "the nuthouse" and attempt to make a comeback, and both of them deriding each other's reliance on "fags" for consorts. A skirmish ensues that spills into the washroom wherein Neely rips off Helen's wig and flushes it down the toilet. Facing her age in the bathroom mirror—the shock of gray hair formerly concealed by the wig—the elder star considers beating a covert retreat through the kitchen, but instead,

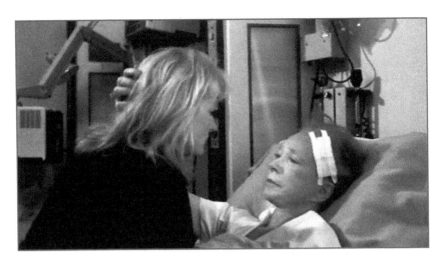

Fig. 7.1. Suzanne (Meryl Streep) commiserates with Doris (Shirley MacLaine) without her wig; and Doris is reborn for her audience with Suzanne by her side in *These Old Broads* (2001; Sony Pictures).

grandly recuperates her glamour. "I'll go out the way I came in," Helen affirms with her patented rhythmic articulation, then whips off her neck scarf and adroitly wraps it over her crown, grandly exiting the lounge to reunite with her public.

Fisher's homage to this scene in the concluding scenes of her *Postcards* screenplay underscores how Fisher positions herself in the camp legacy of *Valley of the Dolls*, crafting Suzanne and Doris as latter-day variations on Neely and Helen and citing the film title, in addition to the clever proximity of "Suzanne Vale" to "Susann" and "*Valley.*" Fisher also situates herself in Susann's legacy as maestro of the celebrity *film à clef*, its playful blurring of truth and fiction, and in particular, its comedy of gossip.[4]

Fisher's deployment of the celebrity roman à clef in addition to her citations of Susann and *Valley of the Dolls* explain her strategies for adapting the episodic, anecdotal novel *Postcards from the Edge*, tactics that she would magnify a decade later for the TV movie *These Old Broads* (Diamond, ABC; February 12, 2001). Fisher promoted *Broads*, which she cowrote with Elaine Pope, as a gift to three of the film's featured players: her mom Debbie Reynolds, Shirley MacLaine, and Elizabeth Taylor. Fisher's tribute flaunts numerous fictionalized details of these stars' lives, and at the same time, honors comedic tropes, themes, and tactics endemic to Susann's work yet often dismissed. *Broads* strikes a material link to Susann's legacy in addition to her gay camp reception, something that the casting of Joan Collins further accentuates. Collins's notoriety as Alexis in *Dynasty* made her a favorite of 1980s gay culture, and her sister Jackie Collins followed closely in Susann's footsteps with numerous bestselling showbiz romans à clef, notably *Hollywood Wives*.[5] Quotations of the film version of *Valley of the Dolls* and other Hollywood camp films fill out the many in-jokes implanted by Fisher and Pope that cite gay camp culture. *Broads* also intervenes into certain problems evident in the camp reception of Jacqueline Susann and *Valley of the Dolls*, regarding misogynistic assumptions about women's agency as camp performers solidified in the figure of the "aging diva," in addition to the limits that Susann imposes on her own aging diva's theatrical, comedic agency. Fisher turns *These Old Broads* into a feminist camp corrective that expands the camp meanings of *Valley of the Dolls* as well as the comedy of manners intrinsic to Susann's authorship.

Fisher further structures her streamlined adaptation of *Postcards* around a central feature of *Valley of the Dolls'* enduring camp appeal, then

Fig. 7.2. Neely (Patty Duke) grabs Helen's wig (Susan Hayward); and Helen dons her scarf in camp triumph in *Valley of the Dolls* (1967, Twentieth Century Fox).

redoubles this strategy for her 2001 TV movie *These Old Broads*: the inter-generational clash between female stars struggling with celebrity, addiction, sexuality, and their aging bodies. This recurrent genre trope remains germane to backstage "women's pictures" such as *All About Eve* (1950), and especially in what Steven Cohan calls the "back studio picture," movies about Hollywood filmmaking and stardom such as *Valley of the Dolls*.[6] As back studio pictures, *Postcards* and *Broads* each features central women characters—and tellingly in *Broads*, a gay man—whose face-off revises the famously feuding divas in *Valley of the Dolls*.

The made-for-television back studio comedy *These Old Broads* queers the trope of intergenerational conflict along with magnifying another feature of Susann's *Valley of the Dolls*, one that the film adaptation woefully down-played: the intimate and ambiguous relationships among a trio of showbiz women seeking careers and sex lives, theatricalized by the showbiz context and their performances for the male gaze as well as each other's.[7] The film centers on the efforts of young Wesley Westbourne (Jonathan Silverman) to mount a network TV special reuniting the three female stars of a recently rediscovered Hollywood classic, *Boy Crazy*, one of whom is the aspiring producer's estranged, adopted mother. Pitting erstwhile Hollywood star Kate Westbourne (Shirley MacLaine) against her adopted son, in addition to her costars Piper Grayson (Debbie Reynolds) and Addie Holden (Joan Collins), the film outs Wesley and reveals Kate as his biological mother in a climactic, spectacular comedic sequence that includes Piper losing her wig. *Broads* links the trope of intergenerational clash with Susann's frequent characterizations of showbiz women companioned with gay compatriots (*Valley of the Dolls, The Love Machine, Dolores*).[8] More importantly, *Broads* focuses on the relationships among Kate and her aging Hollywood cohorts in addition to their longtime agent Beryl Mason (Elizabeth Taylor), all alienated from each other over sexual and career competition from decades past.

By concentrating on aging showbiz women in *These Old Broads* and their desire for revived careers and sex lives, Fisher combines and reworks Susann's central characters in *Valley*: the isolated, elder female celebrity Helen Lawson, vulgar and sex-starved; and the sexually adventurous, younger female comrades seeking careers in show business, the trio of Neely, Anne Welles, and Jennifer North. *Broads* confers its elder divas with a back-story comparable to the young heroines of *Valley* and further evokes that film and its camp appeal through the bitchy backbiting among the actresses, including comparing each other to drag queens, and their aforementioned epic battle on the studio backlot in which sexual affairs are revealed and a wig is uprooted. The caustic battles of Susann's dueling divas and "bitchy fags" (as Jennifer puts it in *Valley*) get a softer touch, though, in Fisher's deployment of feminist camp irony. *Broads* provides a comedic happy ending, as does *Postcards*, conspicuously absent in Susann's *Valley of the Dolls*, with scenes of reconciliation that privilege female desire and celebrate the failure of normative gender roles, all while sustaining Susann's choice to squelch heterosexual romance. Fisher restores mother-child intimacy as well as sisterhood among the *Old Broads*, but reconciliation necessarily involves the comedy-of-manners trope of over-the-top, often humiliating clashes and only prospers through asserting self-ironic awareness of gender performance, star gossip, and genre conventions.

Cut from the Same *Clef*: *Valley* Girls' Gossip, the Feminist Comedy of Manners, and Camp

Both Jacqueline Susann and Carrie Fisher deploy celebrity gossip with the "purpose," paraphrasing Patricia Meyer Spacks, "to generate comedy."[9] Although Spacks narrows the association of comedy and gossip to theatrical Restoration comedies of manners, in which the activity of gossip figured into the narrative formula and moral themes of numerous plays, Susann understood the humorous fun of gossip intrinsic to the showbiz roman à clef: the genre's "infectious" appeal, as Sean Latham characterizes it, to read between the lines for clues to the characters' real-world identities, and the opportunity to discern parodic portraits of celebrities both outrageously mismatched with their popular personas and consistent with the gossip that precedes them.[10] The theatricalized gossip and scandal narratives typical of the roman à clef provided fertile sources for comedy, as did the genre's playful and duplicitous dance at the borders between fact and fiction, confession and creation, gossip and art, frivolity and seriousness.[11]

In *Valley of the Dolls*, Susann played a guessing game with readers to recognize the celebrity sources for her characters, a strategy centralized in promoting the book. As Winzola McLendon characterized it in a 1966 *Washington Post* piece: "Show business has a new guessing game. It's 'Who are the main characters in Jacqueline Susann's just-out novel, Valley of the Dolls?'"[12] Susann's "guessing game" captured the genre's delights, what Latham articulates as the "tantalizing anonymity" regarding celebrity characters and their scandalous activities, the "confusion of fact and fiction," the "confusing configuration of secrecy and disclosure."[13] As Susann routinely and playfully teased, for example, concerning Merman and *Valley of the Dolls*, "She didn't speak to me before I wrote the book. Now she's not speaking to me, only louder."[14]

Fisher unearths and magnifies the constitutive humorousness of the celebrity roman à clef in the move to *film à clef* and "back studio picture." By amplifying the comedic dimensions of Susann's dissection of Hollywood, its portrayals and treatment of women, Fisher defines her own authorial agency while shining light on Susann's, too often overshadowed by her reputation for unintentionally funny, naive camp, a misperception compounded by the camp reception of the film adaptation of *Valley of the Dolls*.[15] Susann and Fisher each play a guessing game with audiences over the true identity of their characters, and both generate a feminist comedy of manners about gender, taste, and Hollywood.

The feminist comedy of Susann's and Fisher's "exposés" plays off of what Linda Mizejewski refers to as "the dynamic of pretty versus funny, the default description of how women are usually perceived in the history of comedy."[16] Both Susann and Fisher mock Hollywood's production of "pretty" as "the ideal that is exposed as funny."[17] Mizejewski explores the comedy of a kindred spirit to Susann and Fisher, Kathy Griffin, whose modus operandi likewise revolves around demystifying celebrity and glamour. Griffin, like Susann and Fisher, derives comedic agency from a range of deviations from the feminine ideal: "gender failure," "failure at mainstream stardom," and a "failure at glamour"; this amalgamation combines with Griffin's stockpile of "vulgar language," "queer politics," and star "gossip" to commit the "primary subversion . . . heterosexuality itself."[18] If vulgar femininity remains a sign of failure and a cue for contemptuous mockery, Griffin can appropriate it to mock and defy "pretty" with the knowledge that failure is "funnier and more interesting than success."[19] Griffin even shares with Fisher a camp appreciation for *Valley of the Dolls* and its celebrations of unflattering, unpretty celebrity women. In her 2016 memoir *Kathy Griffin's Celebrity Run-Ins: My A–Z Index*, Griffin recounts a "celebrity run-in" with Barbara Walters in "the bathroom at *The View*": "When I replay this scene in my head, it's eerily similar to the bathroom scene in *Valley of the Dolls*. (I admit I do go back and forth on which of us gets to be Neely O'Hara and Helen Lawson. Please submit your answers to www.KathyGriffin.com.)"[20]

Susann and Fisher likewise underscored the interconnections of funny women and the failure of "pretty" by telling stories about women stars navigating the norms of social behavior related to gender, taste, and celebrity. On the one hand, both authors engaged what Claire Knowles detects in the work of Susann and her predecessor Grace Metalious (*Peyton Place*) as the "deployment of the logic of gossip and scandal to make visible the sufferings of women in the patriarchal culture of the post-war United States," in addition to "the callous reality of a patriarchal industry that has a vested interest in promoting one (rather damaging) version of femininity."[21] Knowles underestimates the manner in which Susann deploys the same elements for comedic ends, not to mock women's "suffering" but to demonstrate and celebrate the "unpretty" means by which the same celebrity women defy that "damaging version of femininity." Fisher locates this element germane to the pleasures of Susann's texts, the comedy of manners. A genre that also turns scandal into entertainment, the comedy of manners typically features anti-romantic narratives propelled by characters preoccupied with sex, money and status, and often gossip, narratives in which the assertion of style correlates with critiques of "conventional values," closeted or disguised by the facade of fiction or theater.[22] Through their fictionalized celebrity characters, Susann and Fisher performed a variation on the comedy of manners in which gossip provided the vehicle to showcase showbiz career women who turn "failure" into a style of gender performance, both empowering and funny.

In *Valley of the Dolls*, Susann integrates manners comedy, wit, playfulness, and vulgarity to serve a *serious* function: saving her women from full entrapment in their socially constructed roles as bodies, beauties, and machines of entertainment. Far from being the naive creator of "so-bad-its-good" popular fiction, Susann mined the incongruity of pretty/funny and its connections to success/failure as well as tasteful/vulgar. One of Susann's primary means for mocking or challenging prevailing notions of "pretty" remains the assertion of vulgarity, a strategy that personifies what Jack Halberstam calls, with regard to the camp comedy of Quentin Crisp, "the crucial link between failure and style."[23] In the comedy of manners, style remains central to the narrative and functions as a vehicle to smuggle in subversive perspectives. As David Hirst explains, "style is meant not merely [as] a superficial manner of expression but a definition of behavior," in a contest among the characters in which the "winners are always those with the most style," and transgressive behaviors can reign depending on how "they are performed, or more often the style with which they are concealed."[24] As the criterion of style remains paramount in the estimation of victory and expressive of a subversive moral sensibility, Halberstam's "failures" easily align with Hirst's "winners," even when a narrative such as *Valley of the Dolls* fails to render characters conventionally heroic or triumphant. The flamboyantly vulgar style of Helen Lawson, Neely O'Hara, and Jennifer North in *Valley of the Dolls* challenges the protocols of gender and taste; resisting the propriety of passive "femininity" serves as a necessary component of advancing in a male-dominated industry as well as provides a source of pleasure and bonding among women.

Helen Lawson, for instance, brazenly challenges the male gaze through usurping diverse signs of male privilege: artistic control, sexual desire, and the continued use of obscenities. When the director of her latest show disputes Helen's idea to recast the beautiful ingenue with an unglamorous actress (Neely O'Hara), the next line of dialogue that Susann gives to the diva proves hilariously iconoclastic, considering that this is the great Ethel Merman talking, and critical of the male gaze: "Helen's eyes narrowed. 'And what should an ingenue look like? A fucked-out redhead with big tits?' "[25] Helen transgresses the "polite" rules of female discourse in the very act of criticizing the pressures of women to meet a patriarchal beauty fantasy, and she incorporates her public appropriation of male privilege into her personal life. In hot romantic pursuit of a middle-aged bon vivant, Helen wonders to Anne about his lack of reciprocation; Anne speculates that "he has respect for you," but Helen retorts, "Who wants respect? I want to get laid!" Anne's subsequent reaction serves as the punchline in this round of Helen's "comedy of bad manners": "Anne's gasp was audible."[26] Although Helen's "off-color jokes" repeatedly embarrass Anne, they also endear Helen to her, a form of community that Anne identifies when she joins Helen during a night on the town: "Anne quickly caught the mood of hilarity and even found herself laughing at some of Helen's off-color jokes. It was impossible not to like Helen."[27]

Susann's "sleazy realism" validates female impropriety and furthermore critiques the genuinely disgusting, grimly ironic vulgarity exhibited in a range of men's machinations toward women, from romantic suitors to celebrities and the administrators of the culture industry. The name that

Susann gives to a controlling, malignant Hollywood studio chief alone speaks volumes: "The Head." With a personality redolent of Louis B. Mayer at MGM and Daryl F. Zanuck at Twentieth Century-Fox in addition to a nickname that evokes both a dick and a urinal, The Head's persona as a concerned fatherly figure conceals his venality and manipulations. The Head not only cultivates Neely's pill addiction to manage her weight but also mercilessly sacks the star as the wreckage of her addiction—including a suicide attempt—becomes a financial liability. The Head's firing of Neely occurs just as he plans to recruit Jennifer North, now an international star in sexy, high-grossing French art films, to help the studio compete with the new medium of television. As The Head describes his scheme to Neely, he digresses into a misogynistic rant: "Imagine the deals I have to make and the footsies I have to play to get that naked whore to come make a movie for me. Ten years ago the Industry would have thrown her out. Now every studio is fighting for her. Something's happening to this country. We're going to go immoral. And television is doing it. I've always stood for clean American pictures, but now we have to fight television with everything we can get—tits, asses, French whores."[28] The misogynistic meanings of The Head's tirade are far from funny, but his hypocrisy and taken-for-granted vulgarity are: ridiculously offensive, self-righteous, and unselfconscious. Blaming television enables The Head to excuse himself from responsibility for incorporating sex into hitherto "clean American pictures," in addition to faulting Jennifer right in the act of exploiting her.

The film version of *Valley of the Dolls* stifles Susann's comedic as well as critical agency to effectively resuscitate the norms that the novel upsets. As Susann infiltrates classical Hollywood tropes and deromanticizes them, the film reconstructs the sprawling novel as a classical Hollywood "woman's picture" and "back studio picture," teeming with sexually titillating set pieces.[29] The film sanitizes the shocks of female indecorum and frames them through the bourgeois, male gaze of social melodrama replete with the usual tropes of the "fallen woman": victimization, redemption, and retribution.[30] By erasing Susann's deliberate humor, the film adaptation surely threatened to displace the power of "funny" with the passivity of "pretty": absenting the ironic critique of the male-dominated entertainment industry in addition to diluting the female characters' most outrageous, gender-busting wisecracking, combined with adhering to genre norms and objectifying women in Production Code–rupturing antics.[31]

Although "pretty" might trump "funny" in the "straight" interpretation of *Valley of the Dolls*, the film's camp reception locates comedy in the ironic failure of pretty and all of its institutionalized props. Susan Sontag's classic gloss on "homosexual taste" in "Notes on 'Camp'" includes the axioms that "the lover of Camp, [sic] appreciates vulgarity" and "Camp sees everything in quotation marks," dispositions drawn to the qualities of "too much," "failed seriousness," "passionate failure," and the "theme of androgyny."[32] Richard Henke opines about the failed seriousness of the film *Valley* and its queer, feminist revelations: "In its stilted and often inept use of techniques of Hollywood technologies, which consequently now appear obvious as techniques, *Valley of the Dolls* exposes its own media's manipulations in the construction of gender and sexuality."[33] The theatricalized excess of "pretty" in *Valley*, or what Henke refers to as "a seemingly endless series of clichés about femininity and stardom," is in Sontag's terms "too much," incapable of being taken seriously and gives way to "funny," campy performativity in spectacularly stylized sequences.[34] Alonso Duralde, a longtime gay film programmer and critic, provides a delighted encapsulation of Henke's assertion when commenting on Helen Lawson's musical number "I'll Plant My Own Tree," as performed by Susan Hayward. Besides the nonsensical lyrics and garish stage design—a stained-glass mobile evoking a giant tree with multicolored plates that arbitrarily and sluggishly swivel—Duralde extols Hayward's equally stylized performance of femininity, "that crazy pose where her lower torso was in one zip code and her upper is in another one" ("Gotta Get Off This Merry-Go-Round"). The film's gay reception as naive camp cultivates ironic identification with the flamboyant failure of pretty, which climaxes in the washroom clash between Neely and Helen.

Perceptions of *Valley of the Dolls* as "passionate failure" nevertheless pose some potential challenges. To begin with, the reading of the film as naive camp threatens to fold back onto estimations of the novel and its author, at the expense of Susann's deliberate camp comedy and authorial agency. The conditions of naive camp also furnish the opportunity to ridicule gender failure, and in her climactic confrontation with Neely, Helen remains vulnerable to the vicissitudes of pretty/funny and failure/success. When the younger star tears off Helen's wig, she exposes the elder diva's theatrical efforts to conceal the signs of age; theatricality and seniority now correlate with the vulgar spectacle of female failure, or as Henke remarks, "The glamorous actress becomes a feeble old woman. In fact, with her masculine crew cut, the

exposed Lawson appears as not even a woman but rather an ominously per-
verse androgyne."[35] Henke seems to be describing the scene from the novel,
when Neely blurts out after removing Helen's wig, "It looked awful on you,
Helen. I think you're much more interesting this way—crew-cut."[36] The
film, by contrast, shows Helen with a full head of gray hair. Both renderings
of Helen, though, remain problematic for the type of ridicule they appeal to,
in which laughter at female failure in the form of the "aging diva" reaffirms
normative constructs of age, gender, and desirability. Caryl Flinn explains
the process of "the 'aging diva' phenomenon," how the norms of cultural
failure and gender failure determine the "obsolescence and morbidity" of
elder women celebrities and the female body, thus rationalizing ridicule
of their "failed seriousness."[37] Pamela Robertson locates this "camp effect" in
the 1970s reception of Mae West: "obsolete and outmoded," "a burlesque of
woman, a grotesquerie, beloved for her ridiculous and narcissistic belief in
her own sexual appeal."[38] Perceiving *Valley* from this camp perspective, the
film's failed seriousness translates to the status of Helen's character and ren-
ders her laughable, laughter that reinstates the hegemonic norms governing
gender, age, relevance, and desirability.

The "queer" correlation of failure and style Halberstam explored presents an alternative camp practice, however, wherein "failure presents an
opportunity rather than a dead end; in true camp fashion, the queer artist
works with rather than against failure and inhabits the darkness. Indeed, the
darkness becomes a crucial part of a queer aesthetic."[39] In *These Old Broads*,
Fisher especially "inhabits the darkness" in her concentration on the elderly
female stars, their replays of feuds and star scandals, their identities founded
on audience adoration, and their endless displays of excessive theatricality.
Following in the footsteps of Susann and catalyzed by feminist, queer camp
identification with failure, Fisher provides what Halberstam celebrates as
"generative models of failure": cueing identification with the failure of pretty
in the face of ugly adversity and reveling in failure with a future.[40] Fisher's
screenplays for *Postcards from the Edge* and *These Old Broads* finally restore
Susann's camp comedy to the women's picture and back studio genres, dis-
combobulating them with a vulgar, feminist comedy of manners propelled
by celebrity gossip and star scandal. Although *Postcards* briefly redeems the
aging diva figure as a self-consciously camp agent, Fisher virtually structures the narrative of *These Old Broads* around the rising camp consciousness of the film's aging divas, in addition to thematizing the rapprochement

between feminist camp and gay camp. And in a final reversal of Susann, Fisher's "failures" win.

Clef Hangers: *Postcards* from Camp and *Broads* Comedy

The films *Postcards from the Edge* and *These Old Broads* parallel *Valley of the Dolls* by wringing comedy and drama from the gossipy showbiz roman à clef in which characters are modeled on actual celebrities. Commentators have traced Susann's legacy to novelist Jackie Collins, who drew from scandalous show business figures and escapades for such tomes as *Hollywood Wives*.[41] Collins extended that lineage to Carrie Fisher in 1988, simultaneous to identifying the comedic dimensions of the celebrity roman à clef; emblazoned on ads and the paperback, Collins recommended *Postcards from the Edge* as "a sharply irreverent, deliciously witty trip through Hollywood-land."[42] The *New York Times* evoked Fisher's positioning in the disparaged genre of show-biz roman à clef as well as her innovations when calling *Postcards* "a kind of literate trash novel," and an "at least-autobiographical book [that] charted the chemical, sexual and emotional obsessions of a frantic, wisecracking 30-year old Hollywood actress."[43] Fisher essentially crafted a "Suzanne Vale *of the Dolls*": openly drawing from her experience of Hollywood stardom, drug addiction, and institutionalization in addition to industry machismo, pretentiousness, and paternalism, and enacting a "guessing game" about the events of her own life. Apart from Suzanne, however, the Tinseltown denizens paraded in *Postcards* fail to evoke anyone widely recognizable, and Fisher only briefly reveals Suzanne's celebrity mother Doris (presumably drawn from Fisher's mom Debbie Reynolds).[44]

For the film adaptation, however, Fisher's embrace of genre conventions—back studio picture, women's picture and *film à clef*—sharpened the clarity of her real-life models and overtly teased audiences to speculate about the real-life character models. Magnifying the role of Suzanne's aging celebrity mother and crafting tight causality among plotlines about Suzanne's recovery, professional comeback, and rocky relationship with Doris, Fisher consequently refashioned *Postcards from the Edge* into a *film à clef* about Hollywood women, despite the concerns she voiced to the *New York Times* about audiences drawing conclusions that her family might find embarrassing.[45] As Roger Ebert confirmed in 1990, Fisher fashioned a *film à clef* that "turns into a comedy of manners . . . a domestic show-biz comedy that plays up the mother-daughter rivalry," and a movie "preoccupied with gossip; we're encouraged to wonder how many parallels there are between the Streep and MacLaine characters and their originals, Fisher and Debbie Reynolds."[46] Ebert indicates the constellation of *film à clef*, women's picture, comedy of manners, and gossip, but appears immune to the fun it produces, of performance and concealment, the reversal of failure and the triumph of style. The hospital scene of the *Postcards* film exemplifies this concatenation when Suzanne cites *Valley of the Dolls* as well as admires Doris's ability to face the reporters with panache: "We're designed more for public than for private," Suzanne concludes, an acknowledgment of Doris's ultimate victory through artifice, theatricality, and style in the terms of manners comedy.

Fisher translates two functions of gay camp to Suzanne and Doris: first, what Henke refers to as "the camp spectator's project . . . to question any version of woman claiming to be genuine, and to point out the strategies and implications of affirming 'the real,' 'the natural' and 'the feminine.'"[47] And related to the first point, Fisher represents her women as self-conscious camp performers whose sense of "irony" signifies an awareness that "extends outside the diegesis," as Mark Finch encapsulates Joan Collins's camp agency playing Alexis on *Dynasty*.[48] Doris's masquerade, Suzanne's appreciation, and all the literal and figurative citations of *Valley of the Dolls* radiate such ironic self-awareness, and, coupled with the reverberation of gossip and autobiography, convey an awareness that overwhelms the immediate narrative world of *Postcards from the Edge*.

Fisher redoubles all of these elements with *These Old Broads* and, trumpeting the elements of gossip and scandal ripped from real life, mines manners comedy and camp comedy in a *film à clef* variation of the women-driven "back studio picture." The *New York Times* emphasizes the film's playful and overt blurring of reality and fabrication in the context of gossip and scandal, first by launching its review by describing the scene in which Reynolds's and Taylor's characters discuss what sounds like Taylor's home-breaking affair with Eddie Fisher, Reynolds's ex-husband and Carrie Fisher's father: "It's fact. It's fiction. It's 'These Old Broads,'" a film that "makes every effort to blur fact and fiction."[49] The *Los Angeles Times* hints at the potentially tasteless revelations created by the manners comedy of the *film à clef*: "Tonight's reunion of these living legends is made even more remarkable by the jokes Taylor's and Reynolds' characters swap about a man named 'Freddie Hunter.' . . . Where it gets just a little strange is that the jokes—some referring to Freddie's sexual prowess (or lack thereof) were penned by screenwriter Carrie Fisher. . . . Though Carrie Fisher, now 44, admits the amount of sex she included in her movie leaves her 'sort of mortified,' she couldn't resist the opportunity to exploit her family's rich history for laughs."[50] Fisher's scandalous gossip surely serves comedic purposes, recalling Spacks,[51] and as someone "designed more for public than for private," her deeply personal, utterly public divulgences hilariously and grotesquely revalue a range of private failures as perversely victorious.

Contributing to the intersection of *film à clef* with sexual comedy of manners, gay culture plays a prominent place in *These Old Broads* and coincides with Fisher's amplification of a camp address. Fisher plays with Sontag's definition of deliberate, "wholly conscious" camp: the idea that "Persons begin 'camping'" when they "respond to their audiences," for instance, Bette Davis in *All About Eve* and Mae West in general; and that "Successful Camp . . . even when it reveals self-parody, reeks of self-love."[52] Reflecting on playing Addie opposite Shirley MacLaine's Kate and Debbie Reynolds's Piper, Joan Collins attests to these sentiments about camp self-parody as an expression of self-love for an audience: "We all send each other up. This is a camp pastiche. Very naughty, very close to the mark."[53] Collins makes clear they were at least in part camping for each other, their own audience. Fisher's feminist camp takes these elements in unique directions by striking a direct identification with gay camp yet revising one of its misogynistic tropes, the "aging diva": an object of ridicule for her unintentional failure to be desirable, or as Pamela Robertson asserts, "a grotesque figure, which disqualifies her as an object of erotic desire and distances her from a female audience."[54] To these ends, Fisher's narrative develops by transforming the aging diva into a source of camp identification, from the ridiculous object of naive camp into the self-loving, self-parodying camp agent whose awareness exceeds the narrative.

Central to this progression to camp agency is the character Wesley, Karen's gay son, the director of their TV special, and this story's variation on Suzanne in *Postcards*, an estranged adult-child-of-a-celebrity. Addie, Piper, and Kate need to reconcile not just with one another but with Wesley as well. Reviewers and columnists neglected to comment that Fisher's alter ego in the film is a gay man, most likely because the narrative outs Wesley at a pivotal moment in the plot. After a disastrous dress rehearsal of the *Boy Crazy* special for network executive Gavin, a sleazy sexist who continually derides the three women as aged grotesques, Addie raises Kate's envy by affectionately, and a bit seductively, congratulating Wesley for his efforts. Noting Kate's disapproval, Addie needles her costar for being so selfish and unaware of her son, which Addie proves by informing Kate, "Wesley bats for the other team . . . your son Wesley is gay." Kate impulsively takes Wesley out of a heated meeting with Gavin to tell him she knows he is gay, and then reveals to Wesley that she had born him out of wedlock, a result of her affair with the director of *Boy Crazy* Dick Preston, and pretended to adopt Wesley to stave off scandal and maintain her Hollywood career. "And we all had little secrets," concludes Kate, to Wesley's distress. Addie overhears Kate's disclosure, which revives their longtime feud over the affections of Dick Preston, a tinderbox that Piper ignites by divulging her hitherto secret affair with the same director, verified by identifying his "freckled penis." Addie exclaims to Piper, "Pretending to be that little goodie-two-shoes virgin when you were as big a whore as we were," and after further verbal jousting, calls Piper a "silly, dried up bimbo," then grabs at Piper's hair. The surprise of Piper's wig coming off is played for laughs, as the shot continually cuts back to Piper's startled stare and gray wisps of hair, followed by Kate grabbing the wig and slapping her castmates with it until they all three fall onto the ground. Gavin breaks up the brawl and cancels the special, after which Wesley berates the divas for betraying the message of female friendship that their film *Boy Crazy* represented. All of this inspires the three stars to bury the hatchet, support one another, rectify their mistakes with Wesley, and get their special back on the TV schedule. Altruistic intentions are outweighed, however, by bonding over their shared camp code, which Piper articulates as an epiphany: "We can't be ourselves unless we're in front of an audience." A sentiment heartily affirmed by her costars, this disposition echoes what Susann refers to as "mass love" in *Valley of the Dolls*: "Protected by the footlights, Helen received love on a mass scale. . . . They were no longer an audience, they were a cult, united in the worship of Helen Lawson."[55]

While Susann denies Helen insight into her own performative reliance on an audience for sense of identity, Fisher turns Piper's camp revelation of theatricality into plot motivation, rallying Piper, Addie, and Kate to track down Wesley at a gay dance club where Piper and Addie perform "Get Happy" in front of an ecstatic audience. The club scene fulfills multiple camp functions, beginning with the play between fact and fiction in the roman à

Fig. 7.3. Addie (Joan Collins) removes Piper's (Debbie Reynolds) wig, while Kate (Shirley MacLaine) looks on; and Piper's camp awareness is expressed through direct address in *These Old Broads* (2001; Sony Pictures).

clef as well as the guessing game; here, Kate and Wesley's reunion possibly alludes to Fisher's legendary reconciliation with "ex-stepmother" Elizabeth Taylor at a lesbian-gay awards show.[56] Piper and Addie's performance of "Get Happy," moreover, overtly references the signature showstopper of gay camp icon Judy Garland, a song that she originated in her comeback film *Summer Stock* (1950).[57] (This adds to an earlier allusion to Garland's film *Girl*

Crazy, the title of Piper, Kate, and Addie's old Hollywood hit, *Boy Crazy*.) Complementing the three stars' affirmation of their performative identity— "We can't be ourselves unless we're in front of an audience"—one adoring gay male fan shouts to Kate, "I dressed like you for Halloween," all evidence of Addie, Piper, and Kate as camp characters who understand themselves "in quotation marks."

Fig. 7.4. Addie and Piper sing "Get Happy" to an adoring gay audience; and Kate joins Addie and Piper for gay applause after making up with her son Wesley in *These Old Broads* (2001; Sony Pictures).

Concluding with their triumphant television performance, the finale "What a Life," the "old broads" bond in song over career and romantic adversities in their "crazy, wacky, loony, tacky . . . fabulous life" as well as the challenge of aging: "nice things sag and you need a tuck again, what a life!" As they belt their quips, the primary gaze of joy and source of appreciative cackling that greets them from the studio audience belong to their agent Beryl, the fourth "old broad" played by Elizabeth Taylor. "Failure loves company," ponders Halberstam in the spirit of Sontag's idea that camp self-parody generates from performing for a camp audience, company in which "all our failures combined might just be enough, if we practice them well, to bring down the winner."[58] Through her comedic, camp lens, Fisher practices failure and foments a community of failure in *These Old Broads* that invokes identification with the "loser" as a means of redefining "winning." The "failures" of age, taste, gender, sexuality, and scandal transform, through the reflexive theatrics of gossip, irony, and self-parody, into a form of success that contradicts patriarchal Hollywood hegemony. If in *Postcards* Fisher's camp-inflected autobiographical celebrity gossip liberates her by "talking about herself behind her own back,"[59] the empowerment in *Broads* applies to the elder stars MacLaine, Collins, Reynolds, and Taylor, whose engagement in self-parody stems from their failure and enables their triumphant comeback (in this film and through this film). Piper, Kate, and Addie emerge as camp agents of their own self-parody.[60] And so does Fisher; recycling her own life story, family dramas, and Hollywood scandals to the point of feeling "sort of mortified," her *film à clef* combines with "camp pastiche" (as Collins put it) as well as "naughty" manners comedy to satirize a cluster of sexual norms, gender roles, and conventions of aging and motherhood alongside the particulars of celebrity, Hollywood, and its treatment of women.

Although E. Ann Kaplan detects in *Postcards from the Edge* "constructs of sad, aging stars, forced to take a back seat,"[61] something akin to Flinn's "'aging diva' phenomenon," Fisher's version of this trope nevertheless underscores the empowering self-irony underpinning funny female failure. Debbie Reynolds understood this when she gave Shirley MacLaine her blessing to portray her in *Postcards*: "The main thing about playing me is just to be funny."[62] MacLaine echoed the sentiment a decade later when she gave Fisher license to parody her in *Broads*: "Look, if you want to make fun of all my New Age beliefs, then go right ahead—as long as they're funny jokes."[63] Fisher's embrace of the camp dimensions of *Valley of the Dolls* and the back-studio woman's picture articulates a rapprochement with "funny," "failed," "femininity" that coincides with the pleasures of female community, star gossip, and genre reflexivity.[64]

Fisher's *films à clef* echo the movie version of *Valley of the Dolls* in their replays of feuding, malfunctioning female celebrities, in addition to other tropes of "failure" such as elder divas reliant on gay male admirers, and of course, the excessive style of glamorous femininity. More similarly to Susann's novel, though, Fisher's screenplays cue identification with the failure of "pretty" and routinely invest it with value: women appropriating vulgarity as a means of acquiring power and fomenting community. Embracing the gossipy, critical, comedic agency of author Jacqueline Susann and the camp dimensions of the film adaptation of her *Valley of the Dolls*, in particular the clichés of the back studio and woman's picture, Carrie Fisher devises comedies of manners celebrating the empowering irony of female failure, that funny far surpasses pretty in lifespan, style, and value.

Notes

1 This essay was first presented at the 2018 Society for Cinema and Media Studies conference. Thanks go to Linda Mizejewski and Tanya D. Zuk, whose Carrie Fisher panel generated this work, and for their smart as well as supportive feedback. Thanks also to Michael S. Keane, my Irving Mansfield, always making it possible for me to "Sparkle, Neely, sparkle."

2 Joanne Hollows, "The Masculinity of Cult," in *Defining Cult Movies*, ed. Mark Jancovich et al. (Manchester: Manchester University Press, 2003), 39; Ken Feil, "'Fearless Vulgarity': Camp Love as Queer Love for Jackie Susann and *Valley of the Dolls*," in *Queer Love in Film and Television*, ed. Pamela Demory and Christopher Pullen (London: Palgrave Macmillan, 2013), 141–51.

3 See Barbara Seaman's *Lovely Me: The Life of Jacqueline Susann* (New York: Seven Stories Press, 1996) for a thorough and researched breakdown of probable models for Susann's fictional characters.

4 In the commentary track for the 2001 DVD edition of *Postcards*, Fisher discusses how organizing the adaptation around the relationship between Suzanne and Doris gave shape and direction to her unwieldy novel.

5 Mark Finch, "Sex and Address in Dynasty," *Screen* 27, no. 6 (November–December 1986): 38–41; Ken Gelder, *Popular Fiction: The Logics and Practices of a Literary Field* (New York: Routledge, 2004), 133–41.

6 Steven Cohan, "'This Industry Lives on Gossip and Scandal': Female Star Narratives and the Marilyn Monroe Biopic," *Celebrity Studies* 8, no. 4 (2017): 527–43, at 530, 543.

7 Judith Mayne, "Lesbian Looks: Dorothy Arzner and Female Authorship," in *How Do I Look?: Queer Film and Video*, ed. Bad Object-Choices (Seattle: Bay Press, 1991), 103–35, at 116–17.

8 The straight diva's camaraderie with gay men is portrayed briefly in *Postcards*, when Doris meets Bart the drag queen and his lover Allen while visiting Suzanne at rehab. After learning that Bart performs as Doris, she explains to her daughter, "you know how much the queens love me."

9 Patricia Meyer Spacks, *Gossip* (New York: Albert A. Knopf, 1985), 136.

10 Spacks, *Gossip*, 121–22; Sean Latham, *The Art of Scandal: Modernism, Libel Law, and the Roman à Clef* (New York: Oxford University Press, 2009), 3.

11 Lauren McCoy, "Literary Gossip: Caroline Lamb's *Glenarvon* and the Roman à Clef," *Eighteenth-Century Fiction* 27, no. 1 (Fall 2014): 127–50, at 128–33; Latham, *Art of Scandal*, 3–5, 56–58.

12 Winzola McLendon, "Behind the Glamor of Show Business," *Washington Post*, February 22, 1966, B5.

13 Latham, *Art of Scandal*, 48–53.

14 Marjory Adams, "Author Susann Has 'Em Guessing on 'Dolls' Stars," *Boston Globe*, May 10, 1966, 21; Carol Bjorkman, "Features: Carol," *Women's Wear Daily*, March 28, 1966, 8.

15 This chapter compiles material from my book *"Fearless Vulgarity": Jacqueline Susann, Comedy, and Queer Culture*, forthcoming from Wayne State University Press.

16 Linda Mizejewski, *Pretty/Funny: Women Comedians and Body Politics* (Austin: University of Texas Press, 2014), 3.

17 Mizejewski, *Pretty/Funny*, 5.

18 *Pretty/Funny*, 31, 35, 52, 55–56.

19 *Pretty/Funny*, 31.

20 Kathy Griffin, *Kathy Griffin's Celebrity Run-Ins: My A–Z Index* (New York: Flatiron Books, 2016), 261–62.

21 Claire Knowles, "Working Girls: Femininity and Entrapment in Peyton Place and Valley of the Dolls," *Women: A Cultural Review* 27, no. 1 (2016): 62–78, at 63–64, 75.

22 David L. Hirst, *Comedy of Manners* (London: Methuen, 1979), 1, 4, 116; Spacks, *Gossip*, 136; Latham, *Art of Scandal*, 48.

23 Judith Halberstam (a.k.a. Jack Halberstam), *The Queer Art of Failure* (Durham, NC: Duke University Press, 2011), 96.

24 Hirst, *Comedy of Manners*, 9, 2.

25 Jacqueline Susann, *Valley of the Dolls* (New York: Grove Press, 1997).

26 Susann, *Valley of the Dolls*, 96; Hirst, *Comedy of Manners*, 60.

27 Susann, *Valley of the Dolls*, 83.

28 *Valley of the Dolls*, 278.

29 Imelda Whelehan, *The Feminist Bestseller: From* Sex and the Single Girl *to* Sex and the City (New York: Palgrave Macmillan, 2005), 38–40; Gelder, *Popular Fiction*, 132; Christine Gledhill, "The Signs of Melodrama," in *Home Is Where the Heart Is*, ed. Christine Gledhill (London: British Film Institute, 1987), 207–29, at 209; Cohan, "This Industry Lives," 530.

30 Janet Staiger, "*Les Belles Dames sans Merci*, Femmes Fatales, Vampires, Vamps, and Gold Diggers: The Transformation and Narrative Value of Aggressive Fallen Women," in *Reclaiming the Archive: Feminism and Film History*, ed. Vicki Callahan (Detroit: Wayne State University Press, 2010), 43–46; John Cawelti, "The Evolution of Social Melodrama," in *Imitations of Life*, ed. Marcia Landy (Detroit: Wayne State University Press, 1991), 44–46.

31 This absenting of comedy remains consistent with some of the back studio pictures of the same period explored by Cohan, films about Hollywood in which the aging female star, her "monstrous" behavior, and decaying or damaged body reflect tensions about both female agency and the decline of the studio system (Cohan, "This Industry Lives," 530, 532). Cohan notes that two back studio biopics from 1965 about Jean Harlow and a *film à clef* inspired by her (*The Carpetbaggers*) stifle the star's agency by denying her "genuine comedic talent" and reducing Harlow's appeal to the "currency" of her body (Cohan, "This Industry Lives," 534).

32 Susan Sontag, "Notes on 'Camp,'" in *Against Interpretation and Other Essays* (New York: Farrar, Straus and Giroux, 1966), 279–80, 284, 286–87, 289, 290, 291.

33 Richard Henke, "*Imitation of Life*: Imitation World of Vaudeville," *Jump Cut*, no. 39 (June 1994): 31–39. This also pertains to another quality of failure, its "stalling the business of the dominant," as Halberstam puts it (Halberstam, *Queer Art of Failure*, 88).

34 See also Anne's "Gillian Girl" cosmetics commercial and Jennifer's denuded appearances in sexy French art films, in addition to the montage of Neely's career that Henke analyzes in detail.

35 Henke, "*Imitation of Life*: Imitation World of Vaudeville"; Cohan, "This Industry Lives," 534.

36 Susann, *Valley of the Dolls*, 300.

37 Caryl Flinn, "The Deaths of Camp," in *Camp: Queer Aesthetics and the Performing Subject* (Edinburgh: Edinburgh University Press, 1999), 443–44.

38 Pamela Robertson, *Guilty Pleasures: Feminist Camp from Mae West to Madonna* (Durham, NC: Duke University Press, 1996), 26–27.

39 Halberstam, *Queer Art of Failure*, 96.

40 *Queer Art of Failure*, 120.

41 Whelehan, *Feminist Bestseller*, 41; Gelder, *Popular Fiction*, 130–33.

42 Advertisement: *Postcards from the Edge. New York Times Book Review*, June 12, 1988, 39.

43 Susan Linfield, "First It Was Drugs, and Now It's Mother," *New York Times*, September 2, 1990, H15.

44 Carrie Fisher, *Postcards from the Edge* (Beverly Hills: Phoenix Books, 1988), 176.

45 Linfield, "First It Was Drugs, and Now It's Mother."

46 Roger Ebert, "Postcards from the Edge Movie Review," September 12, 1990, www.rogerebert.com/reviews/postcards-from-the-edge-1990.

47 Henke, "*Imitation of Life*."

48 Finch, "Sex and Address in Dynasty," 40–41.

49 Bernard Weinraub, "For 4 Superstars, Art Is Now Imitating Life," *New York Times*, October 12, 2000, E1, E5.

50 William Keck, "Scandal's History for 'These Old Broads,'" *Los Angeles Times*, February 12, 2001, F1.

51 Spacks, *Gossip*, 49–50.

52 Sontag, Notes on "Camp," 282–83.

53 Weinraub, "For 4 Superstars, Art Is Now Imitating Life," E1.

54 Flinn, "The Deaths of Camp," 443; Robertson, *Guilty Pleasures*, 53.

55 Susann, *Valley of the Dolls*, 114. Although Susann treats the female celebrity's need for "mass love" as neurotic in *Valley of the Dolls*, Susann's own relish of her role as celebrity author and personality surely suggests her ambivalence and perception of ambiguity. Fisher rescues self-conscious performativity, however, as a valid (and inherently camp) means of self-knowledge and expression.

56 Keck, "Scandal's History for 'These Old Broads,'" F1.

57 For four classic accounts of Judy Garland and gay camp, see Richard Dyer, *Heavenly Bodies: Film Stars and Society* (London: British Film Institute/

Macmillan Education, 1986); Janet Staiger, *Interpreting Films* (Princeton, NJ: Princeton University Press, 1992); Matthew Tinkcom, *Working Like a Homosexual: Camp, Capital, Cinema* (Durham, NC: Duke University Press, 2002); Steven Cohan, *Incongruous Entertainment: Camp, Cultural Value, and the MGM Musical* (Durham, NC: Duke University Press, 2005).

58 Halberstam, *Queer Art of Failure*, 120.

59 Nick Salvato, "The Age of Gossipdom," *Modern Drama* 53, no. 3 (Fall 2010): 289–96, at 295.

60 Robertson, *Guilty Pleasures*, 10–13.

61 E. Ann Kaplan, "Wicked Old Ladies from Europe: Jeanne Moreau and Marlene Dietrich on the Screen and Live," in *Bad: Infamy, Darkness, Evil, and Slime on Screen*, ed. Murray Pomerance (Albany: State University of New York Press), 240.

62 Linfield, "First It Was Drugs, and Now It's Mother."

63 Keck, "Scandal's History for 'These Old Broads,'" F1.

64 Problems with *Postcards from the Edge*, the novel (and by extension, the film) arise over the discrepancy between gender performativity and other theatricalized expressions of difference, particularly race, as well as the erasure of lesbian desire from gender performativity. The novel racializes particular characters in ways that reflect unacknowledged power relationships, such as Carl in rehab as well as Mary, Doris's beloved housekeeper, and in the film, Julie Marsden (CCH Pounder) the rehab administrator, Suzanne's rehab roommate Aretha (Robin Bartlett), and Doris's housekeeper (Gloria Crayton, the real-life sister of Debbie Reynolds's assistant). Most troubling, Fisher describes Suzanne's aversion to "being recorded," "as if she became an African native the moment the cameras started rolling" (Fisher, *Postcards from the Edge* [Beverly Hills: Phoenix Books, 1988], 112). The complete effacement of lesbian desire also persists, such as when Fisher makes sure to supply the detail that Suzanne and her friend Lucy "slept in different rooms" (Fisher, *Postcards from the Edge*, 185), by contrast to Jacqueline Susann's braver exploration of this dimension of female relationships in *Valley of the Dolls*. One wonders if the absence of lesbian representation in *Postcards* inspired Carrie Fisher's cameo in *These Old Broads*, where she plays a sex worker in a holding cell, dressed suggestively and lying with her head in the lap of another sex worker.

"My body hasn't aged as well as I have. Blow us"

CARRIE FISHER AND THE UNRULY AGING ACTRESS

Kristen Anderson Wagner

T he last two years of Carrie Fisher's life were filled with countless press junkets, conventions, and other public appearances. The 2015 reboot of the *Star Wars* franchise brought Fisher back into the spotlight as she reprised her role of Princess—now General—Leia Organa in *The Force Awakens*, and in 2016 she was filming *The Last Jedi* (2017) while also promoting her book *The Princess Diarist* and the documentary *Bright Lights: Starring Carrie Fisher and Debbie Reynolds* (2016), which chronicles her relationship with her mother. In one interview after another, Fisher—with her dog, Gary, by her side—answered predictable questions about how it felt to play Leia again, what she thought of the new movies, and what she did to get back into character after so many years. She was also invariably asked about the fact that she lost weight—euphemistically referred to by some interviewers as "physically transforming"—for the new films. Fisher took these questions in stride, responding with a mixture of humor and vexation, as when Stephen Colbert asked, "Were you asked to physically transform at all as Princess Leia? I heard they asked you to lose weight." Fisher responded, "They did. They always do. They wanna hire part of me, not all of me. So, they wanna hire about three-fourths, and so I have to get rid of the fourth somehow. The fourth can't be with me."[1]

Indeed, Carrie Fisher's various "physical transformations"—from youth to maturity, from thin to overweight—were a focal point of public discourses about her over the last several years of her life, as fans and the media endlessly questioned whether she had "aged well," and debated her ability to continue playing Princess Leia. These discourses reveal both the extent to which the public expects actresses to conform to mainstream beauty standards

Fig. 8.1. "The fourth can't be with me." Carrie Fisher and Gary on *The Late Show with Stephen Colbert*, November 22, 2016 (CBS).

indefinitely and the way they punish those who either can't or won't make the considerable effort to appear perpetually young. The fact that Fisher wasn't, in fact, particularly old—she was just sixty when she died in 2016—was immaterial to critics. The idea of "aging well" has less to do with chronological age than with physical appearance, as a person is considered to have aged well if they adhere to youthful beauty ideals, including avoiding (or hiding) wrinkles, gray hair, and, perhaps most importantly, excess pounds. Because Fisher at sixty no longer looked young, she was, by default, considered old, proving Lois Banner's point that "we define someone as old because he or she looks old. . . . It is in this context that aging women especially become doubly 'the other.' Trivialized because they are not young, they are also derided because they stand outside of standard conventions of beauty."[2]

Fisher pushed back against the public's insistence that she either "age gracefully" or drop out of sight with biting humor, such as in this 2015 tweet: "Please stop debating about whether or not I aged well. Unfortunately, it hurts all three of my feelings. My body hasn't aged as well as I have. Blow us."[3] Not only did she use this tactic to discuss her current treatment in Hollywood and in the press but also to reevaluate her earlier experiences of sexism and exploitation in the film industry, including George Lucas's insistence that she not wear a bra under her costume in the original *Star Wars* (1977), and her discomfort with her gold bikini costume from *Return of the Jedi* (1983). Through the lens of humor, Fisher is able to reframe past experiences in her own terms as well as defy later efforts to ignore or contain her. She is able to use her insider position as a celebrity to draw attention to issues that are important to her and her outsider position as an older woman to speak uncomfortable truths.

Fisher's approach to aging can be contrasted with that of her mother, Debbie Reynolds, whose public behavior and appearance was more in line with what Hollywood and society have traditionally demanded of actresses as they grow older. While Reynolds would often use self-deprecating humor as she aged, she never repudiated the public expectation that she remain eternally young and beautiful in the same way that her daughter did. But Fisher, unlike Reynolds, pushed back against the institutional sexism that defined and constrained both actresses' careers, and in doing so called attention to inequities in Hollywood and in society at large. The use of humor to address these issues is notable because humor can be empowering, as an effective way to highlight injustices and disrupt power structures. Fisher often turned her biting humor toward areas in which she felt marginalized or exploited, because of her age, her gender, her appearance, or her history with mental illness and addiction. For Fisher, addressing these issues with a combination of humor and anger helped her to bring attention to and process her experiences, including disturbing or traumatic events: as she often quipped, "If my life wasn't funny it would just be true, and that is unacceptable."[4]

"You don't have to ask if you want to work at that age"

Fisher often said, "I think in my mouth, so I don't lie."[5] She had always been candid in discussing her struggles with everything from drug abuse and bipolar disorder to her own insecurities and misogynistic treatment in Hollywood. And so, when asked whether she needed to be convinced to reprise her role as Princess Leia for *The Force Awakens*, Fisher was quick to point out the limited opportunities available to older actresses, as in this *Good Morning America* interview from 2015:

> AMY ROBACH: I understand that George Lucas personally asked you to come back. Did it take some convincing?
> CARRIE FISHER: No. I'm a female in Hollywood over the age of, let's say 40 and then, we could also say 50. . . . You don't have to ask if you want to work at that age.[6]

In *The Princess Diarist*, she reflected on fans' reaction as she aged:

> Now the reaction I sometimes get is disappointment, occasionally bordering on resentment, for my having desecrated my body by letting my age increase so. . . . I wish I'd understood the kind of contract I signed by wearing something like that, insinuating I would and will always remain somewhere in the erotic ballpark appearance-wise, enabling fans to remain connected to their younger, yearning selves—longing to be with me without having to realize that we're both long past all of this in any urgent sense, and accepting it as a memory rather than an ongoing reality.[7]

Or, as she asks elsewhere in the book, "Why did all these men find it so easy to be in love with me then and so complex to be in love with me now?"[8]

She was similarly candid when discussing beauty standards for women in Hollywood. She openly discussed the fact that she was asked to lose weight for each of the *Star Wars* films. Despite the fact that she weighed just 110 pounds when cast in the first film, she writes, "I was awarded the part in *Star Wars* with the dispiriting caveat that I lose ten pounds, so for me the experience was less like, 'All right! I got a job!' and more like, 'I got a job and I hurt my ankle.' The minus 10 percent was an agent's fee, in flesh."[9] When asked about her weight loss for *The Force Awakens* in a *Good Housekeeping UK* interview, Fisher stated, "I'm in a business where the only thing that matters is weight and appearance. That is so messed up. They might as well say get younger, because that's how easy it is."[10] Her weight loss for the *Star Wars* sequels was discussed endlessly in the press, framed simultaneously as a triumph for Fisher over aging and as an example of Hollywood sexism. She generally responded gamely to questions about her weight loss, repeating her line about the producers only wanting to hire three-fourths of her, although in her *Good Morning America* appearance Fisher, clearly tired of talking about it, turned the question back on the interviewer:

> AMY ROBACH: You actually physically transformed for this role.
> CARRIE FISHER: Yes, I did. I did lose weight. And I think it's a stupid conversation. [Robach laughs] Not with you!
> AMY ROBACH: We'll move on!

CARRIE FISHER: Not with you! I mean it's good with you but normally I wouldn't talk about it with someone else. But you're so thin let's talk about it. How do you keep that going on? Do you exercise every day?

AMY ROBACH: I do. I work out every day.

CARRIE FISHER: And isn't it boring?

AMY ROBACH: [laughing] Yes.

CARRIE FISHER: But you love it.

AMY ROBACH: I try to put some music on to, you know, to motivate me.

CARRIE FISHER: What music makes this worthwhile? No, I wanna hear what the song is. Maybe I can go for it too.[11]

Fisher's openness about her experiences as an aging, overweight actress in Hollywood provided fodder for people who apparently found it unforgivable that she was no longer a slender young sex symbol in a metal bikini. Indeed, the public had long been fixated on Fisher's weight—as far back as 1986, in a *Tonight Show* interview, guest host Joan Rivers asked if Fisher ever exercised or dieted; Fisher said she didn't, quipping, "I'm a failed anorexic. I have all the thinking but I can't muster the behavior."[12] In 2008, when she opened her one-woman stage show based on her book, *Wishful Drinking*, the fifty-one-year-old Fisher faced a great deal of scrutiny because of her weight, as in a Gawker article that compared her to Jabba the Hutt ("Seriously—how did this seismic, evolutionary species reassignment come to pass, and do the universe's laws of equilibrium require that the slug-like crime lord now be cavorting by some Tatooinian resort pool in a bikini?").[13] The criticism reached a fever pitch with the release of *The Force Awakens*, as the fifty-nine-year-old Fisher stepped back into the iconic role she first played at nineteen. Professional writers and amateur trolls alike debated whether she had aged well and wondered if she could still convincingly play Leia, in articles with titles such as "The Force Awakens, but What Happened to Carrie Fisher's Face?" and "If Carrie Fisher Doesn't Like Being Judged on Looks, She Should Quit Acting."[14] Even her post-weight-loss physique was criticized, as the *National Enquirer* announced that "Carrie Fisher has withered away to nearly nothing after fans blasted her bloated figure in the last *Star Wars* movie . . . ! 'She's gone beyond anorexia!' said top New York internist Dr. Stuart Fischer after examining a recent photo of the 59-year-old actress."[15] These comments were further fueled by Fisher's openness about the fact that she had been asked to lose weight to play Leia—both in the original movies and in the reboot—and by her drawing attention to the fact that film roles are scarce for women over fifty. As Jennifer Fogel writes in her essay in this anthology, *New York Post* writer Kyle Smith had little sympathy for Fisher in the face of these criticisms, arguing that, as a public figure who's "made millions off being pretty" she had no room to complain about her treatment in the press. In response, Fisher tweeted, "Ok, I quit acting. NOW, can I not like being judged for my looks? Tell me what to do and who to be, oh wise New York Post columnist. You GENIUS."[16]

Youthful Aging

Carrie Fisher's experiences with this sort of sexist treatment—from the studio, from the press, and from the public—are neither surprising nor unique to her. Ageist attitudes toward women are endemic in American society, and Hollywood is notoriously unwelcoming of women past the age of forty. As is the case for many older celebrities, much of the discourse surrounding Carrie Fisher concerned whether or not she had "aged well," a nebulous standard that generally expects people to maintain a youthful appearance regardless of their chronological age. As Hilde Van den Bulck argues, the discourse of "youthful aging"

> expects both male and female celebrities to maintain their body—and thus their beauty—nonstop as part of their job and responsibility as a celebrity. Celebrities are under permanent scrutiny by media and audiences in this regard. . . . When a famous body presents the audience not with the usual constructed perfection but more true to nature, media and audiences rebel. Conversely, a famous body that appears to stand the test of time is praised.[17]

Celebrities such as Angela Bassett, Julianne Moore, Halle Berry, and Salma Hayek who manage to maintain their youthful looks are celebrated for "aging gracefully," while those whose true age is evident through physical markers such as wrinkles, cellulite, and weight gain face public derision and rejection. As Iolanda Tortajada, Frederik Dhaenens, and Cilia Willem argue, "Mature female bodies are only interesting to media and popular culture insofar as they can be used as a visible proof of a deferred ageing process; otherwise, they remain hidden from the public eye, as they are considered to be *abject* bodies that do not fit the aforementioned model of successful ageing."[18] Of the many visible markers of aging, weight gain is perhaps the least forgivable in the public eye. While Fisher was criticized for numerous ways in which her appearance had changed in the decades following *Star Wars*, she was most relentlessly disparaged for gaining weight. By contrast, Helen Mirren was widely praised when photos surfaced of the then-sixty-three-year-old actress wearing a bikini, revealing, as one article put it, "an extremely toned Helen," and "cementing her image in front of the world as the ultimate sex symbol."[19] Despite their visible wrinkles and graying hair, actresses such as Mirren, Jane Fonda, and Jessica Lange are held up as examples of youthful aging largely because of their slim figures, proving that staying thin is inextricably linked to societal conceptions of youth and beauty.

In her work on celebrity, aging, and gossip culture, Kirsty Fairclough argues that the gossip industry, which in turn influences advertising and other mass media, closely scrutinizes female celebrities, identifying a narrow space in which women can be said to have "aged well." According to Fairclough, "the primary function of the celebrity gossip industry is the hyperscrutiny of the female celebrity, where they are examined in terms of how effectively they lock into prescribed notions of post-feminist beauty norms of which the invisibility of ageing is a fundamental component."[20] Not only are women expected to keep all signs of aging invisible, they're also expected to hide the labor required to maintain mainstream beauty standards. A woman who has aged well must be properly feminine and must maintain a youthful appearance (seemingly) without effort. As Fairclough explains, "In gossip culture these discourses can be deeply contradictory where not to engage in practices of transformation means certain descent into career oblivion and engaging in too 'obvious' a way suggests desperation. Famous women are not considered 'true stars' if they make the signs of labor too obvious in the gossip industry."[21]

Fisher's disclosure of the studio's demands that she lose weight, along with changes in her appearance attributed to often rumored but never confirmed cosmetic procedures, were clearly interpreted by many as signs of desperation, of not aging in a culturally sanctioned way, and contributed to public criticism about her aging. A rather typical example of this occurs in an online article that purports to defend Fisher and other aging actresses by asking, "Would it really have been too much for audiences to cope with an older (and fatter) Princess Leia? Shouldn't midlife take its natural course?" However, the writer ultimately derides Fisher in the same language used by her harshest critics, as she claims that she was "startled and somewhat perplexed by the appearance of Carrie Fisher [in *The Force Awakens*]. Had Andy Serkis donned a motion capture suit to play her face? While Botox and plastic surgery are de rigueur for any actress over thirty-five these days, Fisher's skin was so shiny and flawless it could be mistaken for a new life form. Or one of those freaky aliens from the numerous bar scenes in the franchise."[22] Here, the criticism isn't that Fisher took steps to change her appearance (there is, after all, no mention of her weight loss in the article), but rather that some of the steps she took weren't "natural." It's acceptable for actresses to age, then, but they must continue to look "authentically" young, and they can't take any obvious interventions to maintain their youthful appearance.

This emphasis on actresses "aging well" is reflective of a double standard in Western culture in which men are allowed to grow older while women are expected to remain eternally youthful. This is evident in the treatment that Fisher's *Star Wars* costars, Mark Hamill and Harrison Ford, received in the press on the release of *The Force Awakens* and *The Last Jedi*. While social media and the press were rife with criticisms about Fisher's looks, Ford "looks like he's been 'round the galaxy a few hundred times, but damned if he doesn't wear it well," and Hamill is described as having "a handsome grizzle to him, with a rather endearing paunch. He is a little shambly and a lot rambly, and where he once looked callow, he now looks kind."[23] Of course, all three actors had aged in the nearly forty years between *Star Wars* and its sequels. But while Fisher (who was five years younger than Hamill and fifteen years younger than Ford) was widely criticized for simply looking her age, Ford is seen as weathered rather than wrinkled, and Hamill is endearingly paunchy rather than fat. Indeed, actresses are expected to conform to youthful beauty standards well into middle age, while male actors enjoy a much greater latitude in what's considered acceptable aging. As Deborah Jermyn argues,

> Hollywood has long stood as a kind of exemplary instance of popular culture's erasure of older women and it has become a truism to note that women "of a certain age" in mainstream film see their roles run out long before their male counterparts do. While these women fade

away from the public eye, male actors can expect to keep playing the romantic Hollywood hero—to a much younger woman protagonist, naturally—well into their fifties and beyond.[24]

This dynamic explains why Ford has played action and romantic leads well into his seventies, while Fisher found few leading roles after her thirties, instead appearing in films and on television in a series of supporting roles and cameos as kooky moms and foul-mouthed agents and developing a behind-the-scenes career as a writer and script doctor.

"Get CGI, perspective, and deal with it"

Fisher didn't take these criticisms lying down. Instead, she pushed back against critics, using humor as a strategy to defuse trolls and reframe her narrative on her own terms. In her writings, her interviews, and on social media Fisher uses humor to critique cultural norms and deflate power structures. She railed against ageism and narrow beauty standards on Twitter, saying, for example, "Youth and beauty are not accomplishments. They're the happy biproducts of time and/or DNA. Don't hold your breath for either. If you must hold air, take Gary's"—referring to her beloved French bulldog.[25] On the revelation that Fisher wasn't asked to do motion capture for young Princess Leia in *Rogue One: A Star Wars Story* (2016) (a younger actress was cast, with CGI used to make her more closely resemble Fisher), she shared an article with the headline, "Rogue One's CGI Princess Leia: The sands of time are so cruel you can't even do motion capture for your younger self," and tweeted, "Is your body decaying and death marching ever closer? Are the sands of time so cruel they should be arrested and sent to a cardiac beach? Get CGI, perspective and deal with it."[26] Elsewhere, Fisher pointed out that "we treat beauty like an accomplishment and that is insane."[27] And yet, she observes, "given a choice between youth and beauty or age and wisdom, I'll let you guess which one most of us would opt for."[28]

An undercurrent of anger courses through much of Fisher's humor on this topic, as she exposes injustices that she's experienced, both past and present. In her later years she spoke out about a variety of issues, from minor indignities to perceived exploitation, that she suffered while filming the original *Star Wars* trilogy, including Leia's unflattering hairstyle and

George Lucas's insistence that she not wear a bra while filming the original *Star Wars*, and being made to wear a skimpy gold bikini in *Return of the Jedi*. For example, in her speech at George Lucas's AFI Life Achievement Award Ceremony, she riffed on the Padmé Amidala character played by Natalie Portman in the prequels: "you had the unmitigated gall to let that chick, the new girl who plays my mother, Queen Armadillo, or whatever her name is? She wears a new hairstyle and outfit practically every time she walks through a door! I mean, I bet she even got to wear a bra, even though you told me I couldn't, because there was no underwear in space!"[29] She frequently railed about having to wear "that fucking bikini" in *Return of the Jedi* ("what super-models will eventually wear in the seventh ring of hell"[30]), and expressed her displeasure at the fact that in the *Star Wars* installation at Madame Tussauds Wax Museum in London, "The main thing you notice . . . about wax Leia is that I'm almost naked."

> Everyone else got to wear their regular outfits from the first movie. I had to wear my outfit that Jabba picked out for me. Jabba the Hutt—the fashionista. Jabba the Hutt—the Coco Chanel of intergalactic style. Trendsetter, fashion maven, leader of women's looks in his world, on his planet and the next. In wax, I would forever be outfitted by outlaw Jabba.[31]

When asked by an interviewer what she would recommend parents tell their children about the gold bikini, she said, "Tell them that a giant slug captured me and forced me to wear that stupid outfit, and then I killed him because I didn't like it. And then I took it off. Backstage."[32]

Fisher also frequently commented on the fact that Lucas owned all merchandising rights to the *Star Wars* franchise, as discussed by Jennifer Fogel and Andrew Kemp-Wilcox in this anthology. Fisher thus wasn't able to profit from the relentless commodification of her image over the last forty years of her life, demonstrating how she and costars Mark Hamill and Harrison Ford didn't have the clout at the time to negotiate more favorable deals for themselves when the first *Star Wars* film was made. And so, in *The Princess Diarist* she writes, "Had I known [*Star Wars*] was going to make that loud of a noise, I would've dressed better for those talk shows and definitely would have argued against that insane hair (although the hair was, in its own modest way, a big part of that noise). And I certainly wouldn't have ever just blithely signed away any and all merchandising rights relating to my image and otherwise."[33] Fisher clearly felt that the studio took advantage of her youth and inexperience when drafting her contract: "Holding out for points or a piece of the merchandising was not an option for—or even something that would ever have occurred to—a nineteen-year-old signing on for her first lead role in a little space movie."[34] And when Kathie Lee Gifford asks in a 2015 *Today Show* interview whether she will "have a little piece of the action" from *The Force Awakens*, Fisher responds, "No one gets pieces of anything. . . . Because they could just say, 'Oh, you want a piece of it? We'll get that girl over there. She's not as old as you are.'"[35]

Fisher approached fame itself with this same blend of humor and cynicism. She quipped that *Star Wars*, the franchise that made her a star and that is beloved by countless fans, "followed me around like a vague exotic smell."[36] She was clear-eyed about the fleeting nature of fame, "the almost invisible diminishment over time of one's popularity,"[37] a fact that she attributed to watching her parents' stars fade as they grew older:

> I had missed the early giddy portion of my parents' rise to success. I arrived on the scene when my mother, Debbie Reynolds, was still making good, big-budget films at MGM. But as I grew up and my consciousness all too slowly snapped into focus, I noticed that the films were not what they had originally been. Her contract expired when she was in her late thirties.[38]

Fisher's firsthand exposure to her parents' difficulty maintaining their stardom as they aged, along with her own experiences fending off criticism as she grew older in the public eye, certainly colored her views of celebrity. In a 2016 NPR interview, Fisher further elaborated on her reluctance to follow in her mother's footsteps as an actor:

> CARRIE FISHER: And I knew that it was a heartbreaking—you know, that show business is a heartbreaking career.
> KELLY MCEVERS: What do you mean?
> CARRIE FISHER: The rejection—you know, the criticism, especially now with the internet. You know, it used to be that you're your own worst enemy—no longer. The internet is. And they say really, really vicious things about you based in some sort of truth.

So it's painful. And eventually it's going to dump you. Eventually it's going to say, you look old. You look fat. It's over. And there's no escaping it.[39]

Fisher was uniquely positioned to understand the likelihood of her future downward career trajectory, and she used this knowledge to ensure that she never took her own fame too seriously. The irony, of course, is that while Fisher's acting career may have stalled post–*Star Wars*, her celebrity didn't. Princess Leia's enduring popularity left Fisher with a large and devoted fan base, although she noted the dissonance that could be created for fans when their cherished image of a young Leia was contrasted with the reality of the then middle-aged actress who portrayed her. Fisher writes about her experience signing autographs at conventions, being constantly asked to sign pictures of her younger self:

We have gone on—aged, and in some cases (like my own) waists have thickened a bit—but the images have not changed. In the photos we are stopped in our tracks. . . . That souvenir, now yours forever, captures two instants: the long-ago one when the photo was taken, and the more recent one when that signature was written just for you. . . . Two moments, decades apart, now joined forever.[40]

Victoria Bazin and Rosie White have written that "age seems to be the last difference, the unspoken but inevitable site of a difference not only *between* subjects but also a difference *within* subjects as they are exiled from their younger selves."[41] This is evident in Fisher's description of the "two moments . . . joined together." Fisher's advancing age separated her from the younger iteration of herself represented by young Princess Leia, and yet the process of signing autographs allowed the older Fisher and the younger Leia to coexist and give meaning to each other.

Fisher spoke about aging—and specifically about public comments about her age and appearance—with the same type of anger-infused humor with which she spoke about her past experiences. She writes at length about her age and appearance in *Shockaholic*:

What I didn't realize, back when I was this twenty-five-year-old pinup for geeks in that me myself and iconic metal bikini, was that I had

Fig. 8.2. "Two moments, decades apart, now joined forever." Still from *Bright Lights* (2017, Bloomfish Pictures).

signed an invisible contract to stay looking the exact same way for the next thirty to forty years. Well, clearly I've broken that contract. . . .

But come the fuck on, how many women do you know who are over forty-five, or over fifty—and don't get me started on over fifty-five—how many women of this ever-advancing age do you know who are effortlessly lean and impishly lithe? . . . There are two choices post forty-five: letting ourselves go or making ourselves sit like good, well-groomed, obliging pets, coats smooth and wrinkle-free, stomachs flat, muscles taut, teeth clean, hair dyed, nails manicured—everything just so . . . not only is this completely unnatural . . . but it demands a level of discomfort you have to be willing to live with 'til death by lap band or liposuction.[42]

Here Fisher expresses myriad frustrations, with internet trolls, toxic fandom, mainstream beauty standards, and aging itself. In her writings, in interviews, and on social media she felt free to confront and critique these and other issues, often using biting humor to make her point. And so on Twitter she writes, "The best ways to make sure people think you've aged well is A) good lighting B) no facial expressions when being photographed C) a cool photographer D) an editor who loves you."[43] In another instance she writes, "I identify more with who I feel myself to be than what I look like. Either way, am I obliged to entertain you with my appearance?"[44] She also joked about the controversy over the CGI version of Leia in *Rogue One*: accompanying pictures of herself and Gary in Belgium, she tweeted, "In Bruges looking for a theater that's playing Rogue One. Gary heard I do some of my best work in it," and later, "Seeing Rogue One this weekend. Saw CGI me though. Like uber botox only more persistent."[45] Whether reevaluating her early experiences as a young actress or speaking bluntly about her later experiences as an aging woman in Hollywood, Fisher uses biting humor to expose truths about the ways that the film industry, the press, and the public treat women, and especially older women.

Debbie and Carrie

Carrie Fisher's approach to aging is especially interesting when compared with her mother, Debbie Reynolds. Reynolds exuded old Hollywood glamour—as her son, Todd Fisher, put it, "She went to school at MGM where they trained you how to behave. And so it's in her consciousness to be at her best at all times."[46] In public appearances, including the cabaret acts that she performed into her eighties, Reynolds made every attempt to evoke her younger self, from her glittering gowns and perfectly coiffed blonde hair, to her performances of her former hit songs. Each actress approached aging in widely divergent ways, with Reynolds following a more traditional trajectory for an aging actress in Hollywood and Fisher using the freedom that comes with aging to lash out at Hollywood double standards.

Debbie Reynolds was a product of the Hollywood studio system. She made her film debut at the age of sixteen, and for most of the next two decades every aspect of her life was shaped by the studio. Reynolds points out that "MGM was my university. . . . The studio educated me, chose my escorts for premieres, managed my press, and advanced my career by having me make special appearances."[47] As Linda Mizejewski notes in her essay in this anthology, Fisher understood the degree to which this early training formed her mother's physical appearance and public persona, and even, to some extent, her private personality. Because her parents "were stars before their peopleness had a chance to form itself," Fisher argues that the studio was able to mold them into the ideal image of classical Hollywood movie stars.[48]

Reynolds took this early training to heart, continuing to present herself in a studio-sanctioned way for the rest of her career. Whether in movies, television, or cabaret acts Reynolds continually referenced her younger self in her appearance, manner, and material. The 2016 documentary *Bright Lights* offers a glimpse of this, as the then eighty-two-year-old actress plans a number of stage performances despite her increasingly frail health. In one compelling sequence, we see Reynolds preparing to go onstage to perform her cabaret act. Clips of a much younger Reynolds onstage are shown, and it's striking to note how little her appearance has changed, from her blonde hair and thick false eyelashes to her dazzling beaded gown. (Fisher claims that the gown "weighs more than she does"; Reynolds concedes that "it does weigh about 50 pounds, but it's so beautiful!") But while her appearance evokes her younger self, she is clearly feeling her age, a fact that's emphasized by the juxtaposition of clips of a younger Reynolds dancing and energetically working the audience, and a present-day Reynolds sitting in her chair while an assistant adjusts her stockings and puts her shoes on. "I used to go out in the audience, I used to do that. I used to wear a girdle, too, and I don't do that anymore," Reynolds says. "It's like the old days in a way, but I'm like the old days, so . . ."[49] However, any frailty evident offstage disappears once she steps in front of her audience, as she's instantly lively and engaging the moment the spotlight hits her. Her act is, indeed, like the old days, including jokes about Eddie Fisher, clips from her movies, and performances of songs from her film career, including a lovely rendition of her 1957 hit song "Tammy" to close the show. The audience—which appears to be composed primarily of senior citizens who likely remember her early stardom—clearly adores her, and she basks in their applause. And then, once she's offstage, she removes her shoes and slowly and carefully descends a set of stairs with the help of two assistants. It's as if she ages twenty years as soon as she leaves the stage.

This sequence illustrates the lengths to which Reynolds went to give the appearance of youth, even as her body was feeling the effects of aging. Throughout *Bright Lights* her children comment on how difficult it is for Reynolds to accept any limitations related to her age, which Reynolds acknowledges: "For me, the hardest part of getting older is that I think I'm thirty. Then I look in the mirror and see somebody else looking back. It still startles me."[50] As Todd Fisher recalls, "Mom's edict to all of us when we were out in public: 'Go ahead and put your arm around me, but never let it look as if you're holding me up.'"[51] Unlike Carrie Fisher, who spoke out against societal expectations for women to "age gracefully," Reynolds followed a more traditional path for aging actresses in Hollywood. She made

Fig. 8.3. Debbie Reynolds and Carrie Fisher performing in Las Vegas in 2014. Still from *Bright Lights* (2017, Bloomfish Pictures).

a considerable effort to maintain her youthful appearance and hide visible traces of aging well into her senior years, and when she did speak about her age it was with gentle, self-deprecating humor; for example, "I love England; everything there is at least five hundred years older than I am," and "I plan on entertaining you as long as I can—which, looking at my watch, could be another twenty minutes."[52]

Reynolds's and Fisher's disparate approaches to aging can be attributed, to some extent, to the cultural and industrial differences between old and new Hollywood. MGM fostered and protected Reynolds's persona as the wholesome girl next door, casting her in family-friendly musicals and clean-cut comedies, and the press perpetuated this image. Even when she was caught up in scandal after her husband left her for Elizabeth Taylor, Reynolds was depicted by the studio and in the press as the virtuous and long-suffering wife and mother, leaving her wholesome reputation intact. Although she was certainly subject to unflattering press from time to time, she didn't experience the intense and often misogynistic public scrutiny that Fisher did for much of her career.

By the time Fisher began her acting career, the studios and the press no longer enjoyed the cozy reciprocal relationship that they did during the classical era. Movie stars in the 1970s faced a paparazzi- and tabloid-driven press that was increasingly intent on uncovering salacious details about celebrities, and actors could no longer rely on the protective cover of studio publicity machines to help smooth over scandals or negative publicity. The monumental success of *Star Wars* meant that Fisher was the focus of intense and invasive media and fan attention throughout her career, and, thanks to *Return of the Jedi*'s infamous gold bikini costume, much of that attention was objectifying and demeaning. Given these disparities in the ways each actress was treated by the studios, by the press, and by fans, it's understandable that Fisher would want to push back against the gendered expectations and sexist scrutiny she experienced, while Reynolds would be comfortable with maintaining her studio-crafted image long after her MGM contract expired.

Reynolds made "aging well" look effortless; Fisher, by contrast, drew attention to the considerable work necessary to look eternally young and therefore challenged the idea that a youthful appearance was a necessary component of "aging well." Reynolds maintained a facade of perpetual youth and beauty throughout her career, a performance of femininity as glamorous but also illusory and unachievable for most women. Rather than emulating her mother's old Hollywood version of glamour, Fisher chose to expose its artifice. In her writings and interviews she reveals the truth behind the illusion, from describing her childhood experience of watching her mother make use of a "Shrine of Wigs" and "hundreds and hundreds of lipsticks and eyebrow pencils and false eyelashes" to transform herself from mom to movie star ("When our mother dressed, the man behind the curtain became the great and powerful Oz"[53]) to openly sharing her bluntly honest thoughts on her own appearance and her experiences in the film industry.

Fisher saw firsthand that adherence to mainstream beauty standards and maintaining a youthful appearance were not enough to keep her mother's star from fading over time, and she took those lessons to heart. In *Wishful Drinking* she writes of recognizing at an early age that she was not as beautiful as her mother and deciding that instead she would be "funny or smart—someone past caring. So far past caring that you couldn't even see it with a telescope."[54] But later in the same book she admits that "I've always wished that I was someone who really didn't care what I looked like, but I do. And yet, even though I end up caring about it almost more than absolutely anything, it takes way more than a lot to get me to do anything about it."[55] It's in these contradictions that Fisher's tremendous appeal lies, in her willingness to expose her complicated insecurities and messy incongruities, and in the admission that she cared about mainstream beauty standards but refused to allow them to dominate her life. Fisher wrote, "if there's any kind of a vibe that I emanate, it's the one of not being enthused about being a celebrity. Actually, that's not quite accurate. It's not that I don't care about it, it's that I don't trust it."[56] This dynamic of simultaneously caring but not trusting is evident in the way she used anger-infused humor to hold celebrity, glamour, and public opinion at arm's length, and in her ultimate refusal to define herself and her worth according to narrow beauty ideals.

Conclusion

Hilde Van den Bulck argues that "aging—and particularly influencing and resisting it—is today presented in popular and celebrity culture as a life choice rather than a biological certainty."[57] Kirsty Fairclough similarly sees growing old as something that popular culture presents as optional:

> Ageing is configured in contemporary society as a kind of narcissistic problem and exists as an embarrassing reminder to a celebrity-obsessed transformation focused society that ultimately there is no successful way to fight it. Audiences are constantly bombarded with ways to overcome the ageing "problem" through advertising, marketing, the visibility of youthful older people in celebrity culture and through the promotion of a lifestyle trajectory that suggests there is no need to succumb to old age any longer, as the technologies exist to stave it off or at least keep it at bay.[58]

This idea of aging as a "life choice" and a "narcissistic problem" could certainly explain a lot of the vitriol directed at Carrie Fisher as she grew older. Fans who yearned for *Star Wars*–era Princess Leia blamed Fisher for "letting herself go," for not making every possible effort to keep herself looking eternally nineteen. While many celebrities, including Debbie Reynolds, do go to considerable lengths to attempt to maintain some semblance of their youthful appearance, looking eternally young is not possible or even desirable for everyone.

Fisher pushed back against public criticism that she didn't "age well," that she allowed herself to age at all. She opened up about her struggles with her weight and aging, thoroughly rejecting the unspoken requirement that actresses must appear perpetually youthful, and she spoke out against sexist treatment that she experienced in Hollywood. The fact that she used humor so effectively helped make her truths more palatable to many listeners, and the fact that her humor was frequently suffused with anger made her comments that much more cutting and incisive. Fisher was therefore effectively able to use this combination of humor and anger to challenge expectations for aging actresses and to reframe past events on her own terms. In *Wishful Drinking* Fisher writes, "There are a couple of reasons why I take comfort in being able to put all this in my own vernacular and present it to you. For one thing, because then I'm not completely alone with it. And for another, it gives me a sense of being in control of the craziness."[59] Putting her experiences into "her own vernacular"—biting humor—gives her the power to reframe her narrative on her own terms as well as push back against efforts to ignore, contain, or shame her. Or, in Carrie Fisher's words, "if my alleged resemblance to Elton John turns out to be a problem for anyone out there, all I can really say (politely and in a sing-song voice) is 'blow my big bovine, tiny dancer cock!' Or you could just skip the whole thing—your choice."[60]

Notes

1 *The Late Show with Stephen Colbert*, CBS, November 21, 2016.
2 Lois Banner, *In Full Flower: Aging Women, Power, and Sexuality* (New York: Alfred A. Knopf, 1992), 15.
3 Carrie Fisher (@carrieffisher), "Please stop debating about whetherOR not [I]aged well.unfortunately it hurts all3 of my feelings.My BODY hasnt aged as well as I have.Blow us." December 28, 2015, Tweet.
4 Carrie Fisher, *Wishful Drinking* (New York: Simon & Schuster, 2008), 17–18. Linda Mizejewski, in her essay in this anthology, likewise finds this quip central to Fisher's comedy and persona.
5 *Good Morning America*, ABC, December 4, 2015.
6 *Good Morning America*, ABC, December 4, 2015.
7 Carrie Fisher, *The Princess Diarist* (New York: Blue Rider Press, 2016), 227–28.
8 Fisher, *Princess Diarist*, 38.
9 *Princess Diarist*, 34. She reports that she never actually lost the ten pounds: "When we started filming, I tried to keep myself well under the radar so that the powers that be wouldn't notice that I hadn't lost the weight they'd asked me to." *Princess Diarist*, 35.

10 Michelle Hather, "If My Life Wasn't Funny It Would Only Be True," *Good Housekeeping UK*, January 2016, 18–22.

11 *Good Morning America*, ABC, December 4, 2015.

12 *The Tonight Show with Johnny Carson*, NBC, March 3, 1986.

13 Seth Abramovitch, "Carrie Fisher Comes Full Circle," *Gawker*, December 10, 2008, https://gawker.com/5106681/carrie-fisher-comes-full-circle.

14 Sue Bell, "The Force Awakens, but What Happened to Carrie Fisher's Face?" *midlifexpress*, http://midlifexpress.com/the-force-awakens-but -what-happened-to-carrie-fishers-face/; Kyle Smith, "If Carrie Fisher Doesn't Like Being Judged on Looks, She Should Quit Acting," *New York Post*, December 30, 2015, https://nypost.com/2015/12/30/if-carrie-fisher -doesnt-like-being-judged-on-looks-she-should-quit-acting/.

15 "Carrie Fisher—Anorexia Fears over *Star Wars* Pressure," *National Enquirer*, May 17, 2016, www.nationalenquirer.com/photos/carrie-fisher -star-wars-weight-loss-studio-pressure/.

16 Smith, "If Carrie Fisher Doesn't Like"; Carrie Fisher (@carrieffisher), "Ok, I quit acting. NOW,can I not like being judged for my looks?Tell me what to do & who to be, oh wise New York post columnist.u GENIUS." December 30, 2015, Tweet.

17 Hilde Van den Bulck, "Growing Old in Celebrity Culture," in *Aging, Media, and Culture*, ed. C. Lee Harrington, Denise D. Bielby, and Anthony R. Bardo (Lanham, MD: Lexington Books, 2014), 71.

18 Iolanda Tortajada, Frederik Dhaenens, and Cilia Willem, "Gendered Age- ing Bodies in Popular Media Culture," *Feminist Media Studies* 8, no. 1 (2018): 2, emphasis in original.

19 Pritha Paul, "Helen Mirren Opens Up about Sexy Bikini Photo, Says She Tried to Look Good for the Paparazzi by 'Sucking In' Her Tummy," *Meaww*, September 13, 2019, https://meaww.com/helen-mirren-opens-up-about -viral-bikini-picture-from-2008-made-her-a-sex-icon-overnight.

20 Kirsty Fairclough, "Nothing Less Than Perfect: Female Celebrity, Age- ing and Hyper-scrutiny in the Gossip Industry," *Celebrity Studies* 3, no. 1 (2012): 90.

21 Fairclough, "Nothing Less Than Perfect," 96.

22 Bell, "The Force Awakens."

23 Stephanie Zacharek, "*The Force Awakens* Is Everything You Could Hope for in a *Star Wars* Movie—and Less," *Time*, December 16, 2015, https:// time.com/4150168/review-star-wars-the-force-awakens; Hadley Freeman,

"*Star Wars*' Mark Hamill: 'I said to Carrie Fisher: I'm a good kisser—next, we're making out like teenagers!" *The Guardian*, December 15, 2017, www .theguardian.com/film/2017/dec/14/star-wars-the-last-jedi-mark-hamill -carrie-fisher-good-kisser.

24 Deborah Jermyn, "'Get a life, ladies. Your old one is not coming back': Ageing, Ageism and the Lifespan of Female Celebrity," *Celebrity Studies* 3, no. 1 (2012): 3.

25 Carrie Fisher (@carrieffisher), "Youth&BeautyR/NOT ACCOMPLISH-MENTS,theyre theTEMPORARY happy/BiProducts/of Time&/or DNA/ Don't Hold yourBreath4either/ifUmust holdAir/takeGarys," December 29, 2015, Tweet.

26 Carrie Fisher (@carrieffisher), "IsYRbody DKaying + deth marching ever closer? Rthe sands of time so cruel they shud B arrested + sent 2 a cardiac-beach?Getcgi, perspective + deal w/it," December 21, 2016, Tweet.

27 Hather, "If My Life Wasn't Funny," 22.

28 Carrie Fisher, *Shockaholic* (New York: Simon & Schuster, 2011), 31.

29 "Carrie Fisher Roasts George Lucas at AFI Life Achievement Award," http://video.afi.com/videos/play/lZ97s396kb0/carrie-fisher-roasts-george -lucas-at-afi-life-achievement-award/.

30 Carrie Fisher, "Carrie Fisher in 1999: '*Star Wars* Taught Me Everything," *Newsweek*, December 27, 2016, www.newsweek.com/carrie-fisher-star -wars-essay-167072.

31 Fisher, *Princess Diarist*, 242–43.

32 Quoted in Melissa Locker, "The Tao of Carrie Fisher: 37 Great Quotes from the Actress and Author," *Rolling Stone*, December 27, 2016, www .rollingstone.com/culture/culture-news/the-tao-of-carrie-fisher-37-great -quotes-from-the-actress-and-author-129633/.

33 Fisher, *Princess Diarist*, 194–95.

34 *Princess Diarist*, 218–19.

35 *The Today Show*, NBC, December 14, 2015.

36 Brian Hiatt, "Carrie Fisher on *The Force Awakens*: 'I've Always Been in *Star Wars*,'" December 9, 2015, www.rollingstone.com/movies/movie-features/ carrie-fisher-on-the-force-awakens-ive-always-been-in-star-wars-55662/.

37 Fisher, *Princess Diarist*, 9.

38 *Princess Diarist*, 10.

39 "Carrie Fisher Draws from Her Personal Journals in *The Princess Diarist*," *All Things Considered*, NPR, November 22, 2016, www.npr.org/2016/11/

22/503052653/carrie-fisher-draws-from-her-personal-journals-in-the
-princess-diarist.

40 Fisher, *Princess Diarist*, 220–21.

41 Victoria Bazin and Rosie White, "Generations: Women, Age, and Difference," *Studies in the Literary Imagination* 39, no. 2 (Fall 2006): ii.

42 Fisher, *Shockaholic*, 26–27, 30.

43 Carrie Fisher (@carrieffisher), "theBESTways2makeSURE ppl thinkU've
agedWELL is A)Good lightingB)NOfacialXpressions whenB-ing photo-
graphedC)a cool fotographerD)AN editor who lovesU," January 13, 2016,
Tweet.

44 Carrie Fisher (@carrieffisher), "I identify more w/who I feel myself 2be
than what I look like.Either way,Am I obliged 2entertain U w/ my appearance?" December 30, 2015, Tweet.

45 Carrie Fisher (@carrieffisher), "In Bruges looking for a theater that's playing Rogue One. Gary heard I do some of my best work in it," December 20,
2016, Tweet; "C-ing Rogue One this weekend. Saw CGI me though. Like
uber botox only more persistent," December 20, 2016, Tweet.

46 Todd Fisher, *Bright Lights: Starring Carrie Fisher and Debbie Reynolds*,
directed by Alexis Bloom and Fisher Stevens, Bloomfish Pictures, HBO
Documentary Films, Insurgent Docs, and RatPac Documentary Films,
2016.

47 Debbie Reynolds and Dorian Hannaway, *Unsinkable: A Memoir* (New
York: HarperCollins, 2013), 199.

48 Fisher, *Shockaholic*, 137.

49 Debbie Reynolds, in *Bright Lights*.

50 Reynolds and Hannaway, *Unsinkable*, 177.

51 Todd Fisher with Lindsay Harrison, *My Girls: A Lifetime with Carrie and
Debbie* (New York: HarperCollins, 2018), 341.

52 Reynolds and Hannaway, *Unsinkable*, 158, 181.

53 Fisher, *Wishful Drinking*, 48, 50.

54 *Wishful Drinking*, 50–51.

55 *Wishful Drinking*, 314.

56 Fisher, *Shockaholic*, 59–60.

57 Van den Bulck, "Growing Old in Celebrity Culture," 68.

58 Fairclough, "Nothing Less Than Perfect," 92.

59 Fisher, *Wishful Drinking*, 121.

60 Fisher, *Shockaholic*, 29.

"Stay afraid, but do it anyway"

Carrie Fisher's Mental Health Advocacy

Cynthia A. Hoffner and Sejung Park

arrie Fisher may be best known for her legendary role as a Princess/ General Leia Organa, but she was also a mental health champion who dedicated her life to combating stigma.[1] Her advocacy efforts began with her first novel, *Postcards from the Edge*,[2] which fictionalized her own struggles with addiction. But it was her disclosure of bipolar disorder on *Primetime* with Diane Sawyer in 2000 that really launched her groundbreaking efforts to dismantle stigma related to mental illness. In interviews and candid memoirs (e.g., *Wishful Drinking, Shockaholic*), Fisher openly discussed her personal mental health experiences. Her status as a cultural icon meant that many people felt some degree of emotional attachment or parasocial bond with her. She used her connection with fans and the public to demystify mental illness, cultivate hope and resilience, encourage treatment, and challenge stigma. Her personal disclosures may have been especially meaningful to women, who face unique issues when dealing with mental illness. When she died in December 2016, much of the media coverage and social media discussion (such as the Twitter hashtag #InHonorOfCarrie) addressed her work as a mental health advocate.[3]

Fisher's mental health advocacy may be her greater personal legacy. According to the World Health Organization, mental health advocacy includes efforts "to place mental health on the public agenda, to promote a greater acceptance of persons with mental disorders, to protect their human rights and to reduce the pervasive effects of stigma."[4] Advocacy for social change often focuses on public policy and funding, but equally important are efforts to challenge public stigma and empower people dealing with mental health issues. These are the areas that Fisher focused on, although she also spoke at rallies and other venues in support of increased public funding and access to mental health care.[5] Fisher's advocacy was media-based, primarily through her writing and interviews and related media coverage. As a key element of her advocacy, she worked to promote awareness of mental health issues and to change the "default frames" for mental illness from those associated with weakness, blame, and incompetence to those emphasizing empowerment, pride, and competence.[6]

This chapter reviews Carrie Fisher's role as a mental health advocate during her life as well as media coverage and audience response on social media following her death. Her mental health advocacy is discussed in the context of scholarly work on related topics, including mental illness stigma, media coverage of mental health issues, and the role of celebrities in public communication about health. Our analysis then draws on Fisher's own work (e.g., her writing, interviews), news coverage, social media response, and a survey conducted by the first author two weeks after Fisher's death to understand her legacy as a mental health advocate. The survey was posted on Amazon's MTurk site and was completed by a total of 305 participants (ages twenty to seventy-three). They reported on their perceptions of and feelings toward Fisher prior to her death as well as their emotional and behavioral responses following her death. Results of the survey are reported in two papers that will be referenced in this chapter.[7]

Mental Illness Stigma and Media Coverage

Stigma related to bipolar disorder, depression, addiction, and other mental health conditions is a major public health concern.[8] Grounded in Erving Goffman's foundational work,[9] stigma has been defined as a mark or label that associates negative, socially discrediting attributes with a person or social group, leading to disapproval and social rejection. Models of mental illness stigma include stereotyping, social separation, emotional responses, status loss, and discrimination.[10] Stigma may also be internalized by people with mental illness. Self-stigma is associated with negative emotional responses such as shame, low self-esteem, and low self-efficacy. For people with mental illness, stigma—both self-stigma and perceived public stigma—presents a barrier to social connection, to seeking or continuing mental health care, and to pursuing life goals.[11]

Some stigmatized attributes may be visible or readily apparent (e.g., certain physical attributes), but concealable stigmas are "invisible" and can be kept hidden. Many health issues, including mental illness, may be concealable. Goffman referred to people with a concealable stigma as "discreditable," meaning that revelation of their stigmatized identity would lead to social devaluation and rejection.[12] Mental health issues are often not revealed due to fear of blame, rejection, or other adverse consequences. Yet cues suggesting that a health condition should be secret or not openly discussed reinforce stigma.[13] Those who conceal a stigmatized health issue experience greater isolation, receive less social support, and cope less effectively with stress.[14]

Stigmatizing messages associated with mental health issues are pervasive in the media, which may motivate people to keep mental health diagnoses concealed from others. Fictional and news portrayals often suggest that people with mental illness are strange, unpredictable, incompetent, and/or dangerous.[15] In a recent analysis, McGinty and colleagues found that the majority of news stories that mentioned mental illness also referenced violence, and that successful treatment and recovery were rarely covered. Such depictions perpetuate stereotypes and contribute to stigmatization. However, positive media portrayals that challenge stereotypes and evoke empathy and understanding have the potential to reduce stigma.[16] The way media portray mental health treatment, including therapy and medication, also can affect whether individuals are willing to seek or continue treatment.[17] Negative portrayals may lead people to devalue treatment or perceive it as ineffective and can increase self-stigma associated with help-seeking. Both self-stigma and perceived public stigma may lower people's willingness to seek mental health treatment.[18]

Role of Celebrities in Public Communication about Mental Health

Health topics that are connected with celebrities are more likely to draw the attention of the public and policy makers. Celebrity involvement in health issues can have a powerful influence on attitudes, interpersonal communication, personal health behaviors, and policy support.[19] When a public figure shares a stigmatized health condition—such as HIV, lung cancer, or a mental illness—the disclosure also has the potential to lower stigma.[20]

Carrie Fisher was among the first celebrities to openly discuss her experiences with serious mental illness, and she was deeply committed to changing the conversation about mental health.[21] In a December 2000 interview on *Primetime* with Diane Sawyer, Fisher talked frankly about her struggle with bipolar disorder. She told Sawyer: "I am mentally ill. I can say that. I am not ashamed of that. I survived that, I'm still surviving it, but bring it on."[22] Fisher was initially diagnosed with manic depression in her mid-twenties, but it took her years to fully accept the diagnosis and begin appropriate treatment.[23] In her *Primetime* interview, she told Sawyer: "I thought they told me I was manic depressive to make me feel better about being a drug addict."[24] Bipolar disorder is a serious mental illness characterized by marked changes in mood, energy, and activity level. Although there are several types, people with bipolar disorder usually experience episodes of depression that may be debilitating and episodes of mania that involve extreme high energy, poor judgment, and risky behavior.[25] Fisher described her illness metaphorically, in a way that was easy to understand: "I have two moods. One is Roy, rollicking Roy, the wild ride of a mood. And Pam, sediment Pam, who stands on the shore and sobs. . . . Sometimes the tide is in, sometimes it's out."[26] In the years following her public disclosure of bipolar disorder, Fisher was remarkably open about her mental health experiences, and she became a passionate and outspoken mental health advocate.

Fisher followed the lead of Patty Duke, who discussed her bipolar disorder in her 1987 autobiography.[27] In recent years, many celebrities have shared their mental health issues,[28] including several dealing with bipolar disorder, such as Demi Lovato, Mariah Carey, and Representative Patrick Kennedy.[29] When public figures disclose their mental health experiences, their disclosures can help to normalize mental illness and treatment and can increase public awareness that people with mental illness can live meaningful, productive lives. Such disclosures have the potential to lower both public stigma and self-stigma of people living with mental illness.[30]

Revelation of a stigmatized identity may have greater potential to reduce stigma if it comes from someone with whom a close bond already exists. A parasocial relationship (PSR) refers to the sense of a real, deeply felt emotional bond with a media figure, such as an actor, athlete, or fictional character.[31] People develop close attachments to media figures through mediated contact as well as interaction with and/or about them online. PSR with a fictional character—such as Princess Leia—can enhance the development of a parasocial bond with the actor who plays the role.[32]

Parasocial relationships have emotional significance and value and can potentially impact people's attitudes, beliefs, and behaviors.[33] According to the parasocial contact hypothesis, sustained media exposure to positive portrayals of social group members, especially those with whom viewers form PSRs, can lead to more favorable attitudes and behaviors toward that group.[34] Research indicates that PSR with celebrities who disclose mental health issues is associated with lower mental illness stigma and with a greater intention to seek treatment if needed, possibly due to increased self-efficacy.[35] There can be no doubt that many people felt parasocially attached to Carrie Fisher to varying degrees, through her iconic *Star Wars* character and/or her public persona. Fisher's self-confidence, resilience, and positive self-presentation made her an ideal person to challenge the stigma associated with mental illness and promote a positive view of mental health treatment.

Carrie Fisher's Mental Health Advocacy

Fisher's openness about her mental health struggles and her positive perspective were among her most significant contributions in her fight against stigma. With candor and a unique brand of humor, she used her artistic creations—including fiction, memoirs, and the Broadway version of her popular book, *Wishful Drinking*—to stimulate conversations about mental health, challenge stereotypes, and empower people dealing with mental illness.

Fisher also advocated for public mental health funding and access to mental health care. She appeared at public events and rallies benefiting mental health and spoke on the floor of the US Senate to urge increased funding for mental health services.[36] (At the time of her death, she was writing an advice column for *The Guardian*, called "Advice from the Dark Side," which addressed mental health issues, among other topics.)[37]

Why was Fisher's advocacy so powerful? In part, she was able to reach and connect with people due to her celebrity and the parasocial bond many people felt to her through her role as Princess Leia. But also critical was the fact that she spoke openly about mental health issues that many keep secret. She maintained a positive, hopeful perspective, lived life fully despite challenges, and made brilliant use of humor. Finally, she always emphasized the

Fig. 9.1. A still from the HBO recording of the one-woman show *Wishful Drinking*, featuring an older Carrie and the *Abnormal Psychology* textbook page that features Princess Leia's image (2010, AF Archive/Alamy Stock Photo).

importance of seeking help and receiving treatment for mental health problems. Her openness, positive perspective, and commitment to treatment are addressed in more detail further on.

Openness and Candor about Mental Health Issues

A central feature of Fisher's mental health advocacy was simply her striking openness and candor in discussing her experiences with addiction and bipolar disorder, including her struggles and setbacks. Stigma is reinforced by the suggestion that a health condition should not be revealed.[38] Despite risks associated with disclosure, concealing a mental illness can increase isolation, reduce the likelihood of support and encouragement, and promote self-stigma.[39] In an interview with *Vanity Fair*, Fisher captured this point in typically colorful language: "If you claim something, you can own it. But if you have it as a shameful secret, you're fucked."[40]

Fisher also noted the benefits of finding a community of people dealing with similar issues. "I find that I frequently feel better about myself when I discover that we're not alone, but that there are, in fact, a number of other people who ail as we do—that there are actually a number of 'accomplished' individuals who find it necessary to seek treatment for some otherwise insurmountable inner unpleasantness."[41] Her own personal disclosures meant that she served this role for others, who found solace, comfort, and a sense of connection from learning that she had struggles similar to theirs. Wrote one woman after Fisher's death: "Thank you for using your position and your voice to not only make a difference, but to remind others struggling with a mental illness or addiction that they are not 'bad' or 'crazy,' they are not hopeless, and they are not alone."[42] This comment suggests not only the value of openness but also the importance of how Fisher talked about mental health issues.

Positive Perspective, Pride, and Humor

Fisher was candid about her life challenges but generally offered a positive, optimistic perspective on dealing with mental health issues. She also infused nearly all of her public communication with humor and openly rejected the stigmatizing frames often applied to people with mental illness. Rachel Smith discussed how several media features, such as labels, attribution of responsibility, and threat cues, contribute to the development and sharing of stigma.[43] In her analysis of health messages, Smith found that formats tended to emphasize either stigma (e.g., blame, isolation, danger) or challenge (e.g., optimism, normal activities, treatment).[44] Carrie Fisher's framing of her own experiences, in her writing and interviews, clearly defied stigma and embraced challenges. Much of the media coverage she received reflected her own framing, often via quotes, by focusing on her openness and her personal strength and pride.[45]

Fisher was committed to empowering people with mental illness. Underlying the humor, her intent was serious when she wrote: "I thought I would inaugurate a Bipolar Pride Day. You know, with floats and parades and stuff!"[46] In a note at the end of *Wishful Drinking*, she explained further, writing: "At times, being bipolar can be an all-consuming challenge, requiring a lot of stamina and even more courage, so if you're living with this illness and functioning at all, it's something to be proud of, not ashamed of. They should issue medals along with the steady stream of medication."[47] This is a message she continued to share in her writing, interviews, and public appearances. In a 2013 interview, she offered advice to people who are "afraid to pursue their dreams" due to mental health issues: "Stay afraid, but do it anyway. What's important is the action. You don't have to wait to be confident. Just do it and eventually the confidence will follow."[48] In 2016, she told an audience on the Harvard University campus, "I've never been ashamed of my mental illness; it never occurred to me. . . . Many people thank me for talking about it."[49]

Humor shaped the way Fisher approached life and how she talked about mental health issues. "If my life wasn't funny it would just be true, and that is unacceptable," she wrote.[50] The use of humor can be a double-edged sword, with both benefits and drawbacks. Approaching difficult or stressful topics with humor can make them less threatening and easier to handle.[51] Freud argued that the use of humor can signal and promote confidence by suggesting that a person feels comfortable and at ease in dealing with challenges.[52] Asked what it was like to be a "poster child" for bipolar disorder, Fisher quipped: "Well, I am hoping to get the centerfold in *Psychology Today*."[53] Referring to a time she was hospitalized, Fisher wrote: "about a year after that, I was invited to go to a mental hospital. And, you know, you don't want to be rude, so you go. Okay, I know what you must be thinking—but this is a very exclusive invitation."[54] For people dealing with mental illness, seeing someone who can find humor in their difficult experiences may help them feel better and more self-confident.[55] However, humor also has the potential to trivialize serious topics, especially if the audience does not recognize irony or satire.[56] In *Wishful Drinking*, Fisher wrote: "You know how most illnesses have symptoms you can recognize? Like fever, upset stomach, chills, whatever. Well, with manic depression, it's sexual promiscuity, excessive spending, and substance abuse—and that just sounds like a fantastic weekend in Vegas to me!"[57]

Hoffner reported survey results that addressed respondents' perceptions of Fisher's disclosures in her writing and interviews.[58] The study found that a substantial minority (42 percent) felt her humor sometimes minimized the seriousness of mental illness. But most respondents also reported that her humor made mental illness seem less threatening (82 percent) and helped people feel more comfortable talking about mental illness (86 percent). Intriguingly, those who found Fisher more amusing were also more willing to seek mental health treatment, if needed. Overall, these findings suggest that Fisher's humor may have demystified mental illness, lowering fear and discomfort related to mental health issues.

Emphasis on the Need for Mental Health Treatment

Fisher's emphasis on the importance of treatment was another significant contribution of her advocacy. She spoke positively about her own mental health treatment, including talk therapy, medication, and twelve-step programs, and she advocated for the need to seek appropriate treatment. Speaking about her own experience, she stated: "There is treatment and a variety of medications that can alleviate your symptoms if you are manic depressive or depressive. You can lead a normal life, whatever that is."[59] After a setback in 2013, she talked about her recovery and reiterated the value of treatment. "The only lesson for me, or anybody, is that you have to get help," she said.[60]

In *Shockaholic*, Fisher discussed her decision to undergo electroconvulsive therapy (ECT) to treat her severe depression.[61] This controversial procedure is now regarded as safe and effective by many medical professionals but is best known to the public from the horrifying portrayal in *One Flew Over the Cuckoo's Nest*.[62] Fisher has been praised for her honesty about her experience with ECT, which included the adverse effect on memory that many patients experience. For example, she wrote: "I've found that the truly negative side effect of ECT is that it's incredibly hungry and the only thing it has a taste for is memory."[63] For her, however, the ability of ECT to disrupt her depression and keep it at bay was worth adverse effects on her memory. "I couldn't fix [my depression]. Medication couldn't fix it. Therapy couldn't fix it. That did," she said.[64]

Public Responses to Fisher's Advocacy

Fisher reached a wide swath of the public with her interviews and writing, due in part to her career-defining role as Princess Leia. The survey conducted by the first author revealed the powerful impact of her advocacy on public stigma related to mental illness as well as on self-stigma of people dealing with a mental health condition.[65] Her role as Princess Leia was the primary factor in most respondents' attachment to her, with two-thirds (66 percent) of the sample stating that this was how they felt most connected to her.[66] Overall, Hoffner reported that respondents felt Fisher had openly disclosed her mental health issues and that her disclosures had helped lower public stigma.[67] Their bond with Fisher may have been a key conduit through which her mental health advocacy contributed to positive change.

Those who had a stronger PSR with her and those who had a mental health condition were more likely to believe she had made it OK to talk about mental illness, and that she had helped reduce stigma. Further, the survey showed that people who reported having a mental health condition tended to regard Fisher as a role model and believed that she was more open and candid in her personal disclosures. They also perceived a greater reduction in public stigma due to her disclosures. These findings are consistent with anecdotal evidence that her openness and activism related to mental health resonated with people who identified with her mental health challenges.[68] Yet Fisher's message also resonated with survey respondents who had not personally experienced mental illness. For these people, perceiving Fisher as more open and honest in her discussion of her own mental health was associated with lower mental illness stigma, perhaps as a result of vicariously sharing her experiences.[69]

Even after her death, Fisher's message continued to have an impact. In 2017, after seeing Fisher in the documentary *Stephen Fry: The Secret Life of the Manic Depressive*,[70] a contributor to the website *The Mighty* wrote: "The way she spoke about her illness with such confidence really inspired me. . . . She made me feel 'normal' for having bipolar disorder and allowed me to realize manic episodes were nothing to be ashamed of. Carrie showed me even though I am mentally ill, I deserve to be treated with respect and equality."[71]

Fisher Received Numerous Honors for Her Mental Health Advocacy

In *Wishful Drinking*, Fisher wrote: "So having waited my entire life to get an award for something, anything (okay fine, not acting, but what about a tiny little award for writing? Nope), I now get awards all the time for being mentally ill. I'm apparently very good at it and am honored for it regularly."[72] In fact, she was extremely good at being a public advocate for mental health, and she did receive numerous awards during her lifetime for her advocacy work. The National Alliance on Mental Illness (NAMI) gave Fisher the Rona and Ken Purdy Award in 2001 for "making a significant, national contribution to end discrimination" related to mental illness.[73] She received the Erasing the Stigma Leadership Award from Didi

Hirsch Mental Health Services in 2002.[74] In 2004, Fisher was on the cover of the premiere issue of *bp Magazine*, a publication devoted to bringing information, hope, and empowerment to people with bipolar disorder.[75] According to the magazine's publisher, "It says a lot that [Fisher] agreed 'sight unseen' to be featured in a publication dedicated to serving the bipolar community."[76] She continued her work fighting stigma and communicating a message of hope and pride for the rest of her life. Fittingly, in April 2016, she received the Outstanding Lifetime Achievement Award in Cultural Humanism from Harvard College for her openness about addiction and bipolar disorder and "her efforts to destigmatize mental illness."[77] In 2017, she was posthumously awarded a Voice Award from the Substance Abuse and Mental Health Services Administration "for raising awareness and understanding of behavioral health issues and encouraging others to seek help."[78]

Media Response to Fisher's Death Amplified Her Advocacy Message

Carrie Fisher's death on December 27, 2016, prompted extensive media attention, including online, print, and television news coverage and discussion on social media. News stories reviewed her life and career, including her role as Princess Leia and her acclaim as writer and memoirist. Her struggle with addiction and bipolar disorder was also extensively covered, often with a focus on her mental health advocacy. In fact, nearly every major news outlet in the United States—including the *New York Times*, the *Washington Post*, *Time* magazine, *Newsweek*, *U.S. News and World Report*, *Rolling Stone*, *People* magazine, *CNN*, *ABC News*, and *CBS News* as well as numerous online news sites—ran stories focused on Fisher's mental health advocacy and her fight against stigma.[79]

News stories that addressed Fisher's mental health experiences generally presented them in a positive light, emphasizing her openness and candor about her mental health issues, her strength and pride, and her longtime efforts to reduce stigma and encourage treatment. Wrote the *New York Times*: "In her long, openhearted life, the actress and author Carrie Fisher brought the subject of bipolar disorder into the popular culture with such humor and hard-boiled detail that her death on Tuesday triggered a wave of affection on social media and elsewhere, from both fans and fellow bipolar travelers, whose emotional language she knew and enriched."[80] The title of a story in *People* magazine characterized Fisher's impact this way: "Inside Carrie Fisher's revolutionary openness about her mental illness: 'She changed the world.'"[81]

Sharing on Social Media in Response to Fisher's Death

When Fisher died, Twitter and other social media platforms were flooded with posts that remembered her life, celebrated her role as Princess Leia, and honored her mental health advocacy.[82] Fellow *Star Wars* actors and many other celebrities reacted emotionally to her death and expressed their grief on their social media accounts. Most focused on her legendary role in Hollywood, mourning the loss of her talent, personality, and distinctive sense of humor. Some celebrities also noted her dedication to mental health awareness and empowerment of women.[83] For example, comedian Margaret Cho tweeted: "We just lost a great ally for mental health and addiction. Be strong, be as strong as she'd want you to be. Rest in paradise @carrieffisher." Singer/songwriter Halsey tweeted: "Carrie Fisher dedicated her platform to mental health awareness & female empowerment. She is a reason + reminder to keep up your fight. RIP." Many celebrity posts went viral, liked and retweeted by thousands of users, which stimulated online conversations about Fisher's death and her contribution to society.[84]

Similarly, fans and others memorialized her on social media as Princess Leia but often went further, commenting on her role as a writer and a mental health ally. Many stated that Fisher inspired them to disclose their mental health experiences and expressed gratitude that she had helped combat mental illness stigma. Examples of tweets that illustrate the impact of Fisher's mental health advocacy include: "Carrie Fisher inspired me to write openly about my battles w/ mental illness. I wish I could have told her in person what she meant to me"; "Carrie Fisher spoke openly about her struggles w mental health. To me she was a hero—not only in the stars—but here on Earth as well"; and "If we want to honor Carrie Fisher's legacy, let's work to destigmatize mental illness in ways both big and small. It's up to us."[85] People also reacted emotionally to her death by creating memes and tributes that were shared across various social media platforms, including Twitter, Facebook, YouTube, and Instagram.[86] Many of these posts referenced her sage advice, her optimism and confidence about dealing with mental illness, and her vocal advocacy for mental health.

People also were motivated to share information about mental health on social media following Fisher's death. Hoffner found that survey respondents who felt a stronger parasocial bond with Fisher and those who felt more grief in response to her death were more inclined to post about mental health topics on social media.[87] Her fans may have attempted to cope with their loss by connecting with others on social media, and by discussing and supporting the cause she advocated. Since Fisher was a heavy user of social media and often posted messages about mental health issues, social media might have been seen as an ideal channel for fans to share their emotions with others. These findings and news coverage of the public response suggest that Fisher's mental health advocacy was amplified by sharing on social media.

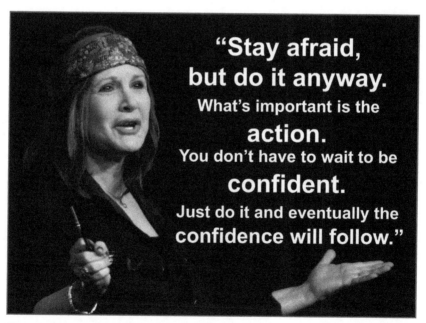

Fig. 9.2. Recreated meme using an image from the 2012 San Diego Comic Con by Gage Skidmore and an inspirational quote from Carrie.

Social Media Hashtags Following Fisher's Death

Fisher's death also inspired social media activism focused on reducing stigma and promoting mental health awareness. Fans honored Fisher by tweeting their own mental health challenges using the hashtag #InHonorOfCarrie.[88] This hashtag appeared within a few hours of Fisher's death, after political columnist Ana Marie Cox tweeted about her own bipolar disorder to honor Fisher, writing: "I'm pretty open about being in recovery; I've been more circumspect about mental illness. In honor of Carrie Fisher: I'm bipolar, too." The hashtag #InHonorOfCarrie was created less than an hour later by a Chicago radio personality, Julie DiCaro.[89] Within two weeks of Fisher's death, there were a total of 2,160 tweets that included the hashtag, including 1,157 original tweets. An analysis of tweets using this hashtag by Park and Hoffner revealed the powerful role of Fisher's personal example and mental health advocacy.[90] Major themes in the full sample of tweets included honoring Fisher's role in mental health advocacy, sharing personal mental health disorders, and framing mental illness in a positive way. The hashtag quickly became a symbol of mental health activism on Twitter.[91]

In the original tweets, the hashtag #InHonorOfCarrie was used mainly as a vehicle for "coming out" publicly about mental illness and to voice antistigma sentiments. Indeed, nearly half of these tweets (41 percent) included reports of the user's own mental health conditions.[92] This means that many people used the hashtag to follow Fisher's lead by sharing their personal stories and self-disclosing their own mental health issues. Users reported a wide range of mental health conditions, including depression, anxiety, bipolar disorder, posttraumatic stress disorder, obsessive compulsive

Fig. 9.3. Tweet by *Deadspin* editor, Julie DiCaro, creating a hashtag for Carrie and mental health awareness (Dec. 27, 2016; used with permission).

disorder, and panic disorder. They also paid tribute to Fisher's candor and openness in motivating their own self-disclosure.[93]

Most of the original tweets addressed Fisher's openness and honesty, her antistigma efforts, and her inspiration to others as well as the value of the hashtag. It is noteworthy that while users often reported personal difficulties or challenges dealing with mental health issues, negative internal self-references were rarely used. Instead, modeling Fisher's approach, positive internal self-references and personal successes and achievements in life or therapy were more commonly addressed. In fact, users often denied negative emotions and negative associations with mental illness (e.g., "I am not and never will be ashamed"; "Bipolar disorder will not beat me"). Rather, they associated mental illness with positive emotions, such as feeling "proud" and "strong" and having self-esteem and confidence in their ability to deal with their mental health issues (e.g., "I'm proud of how far I've come"; "I finally feel like I'm able to win"). Negative self-references were rare.[94] The messages shared on the hashtag #InHonorOfCarrie amplified Fisher's advocacy by echoing her challenge metaphor regarding mental illness and by modeling her example of honesty and personal pride.[95] The social activism displayed on the hashtag, ignited by Fisher's own openness and mental health advocacy, shifted the framing of mental illness from a negative, stigmatizing lens to a positive, empowering lens.

In addition to #InHonorOfCarrie activism, there were some other campaigns in response to Fisher's advocacy. For example, a social media campaign using the hashtag #EndTheStigma was started by a mental health advocate from North Carolina three days after Fisher's death.[96] This campaign encouraged people with mental illness to post online badges, signifying that they have a mental illness (e.g., "I have bipolar disorder"; "I have depression"; and "I have schizophrenia") and to share their experiences of living with mental disorders. The campaign was intended to reduce shame and correct misunderstanding about people with mental illness.[97]

Conclusion

Carrie Fisher's personal example and mental health advocacy changed the public conversation about mental illness. She directly challenged stigma with her groundbreaking openness, expressions of personal confidence and pride, and commitment to treatment, despite difficulties and setbacks.

Through her work, she empowered people with mental health conditions and motivated others to continue her legacy. In her final advice column in the British newspaper *The Guardian*, published November 30, 2016, Fisher shared a message of support and encouragement with a young person who was struggling with bipolar disorder: "We have been given a challenging illness, and there is no other option than to meet those challenges. Think of it as an opportunity to be heroic—not 'I survived living in Mosul during an attack' heroic, but an emotional survival." After noting that life challenges might lead to feeling "defeated and hopeless," she concluded: "Move through those feelings and meet me on the other side. As your bipolar sister, I'll be watching. Now get out there and show me and you what you can do."[98]

When Fisher died of a cardiac event in December 2016, there was speculation about whether her mental health issues had contributed to her death. After a toxicology report revealed that there were several drugs in Fisher's system when she died, her daughter Billie Lourd released a statement that reinforced her mother's legacy as a mental health advocate: "My mom battled drug addiction and mental illness her entire life. She ultimately died of it. She was purposefully open in all of her work about the social stigmas surrounding these diseases. . . . I know my Mom, she'd want her death to encourage people to be open about their struggles. Seek help, fight for government funding for mental health programs. Shame and those social stigmas are the enemies of progress to solutions and ultimately a cure."[99] As a passionate mental health advocate, Fisher fought stigma throughout her life and left a legacy that is motivating others to continue her work.

Notes

1 Maria Yagoda, "Inside Carrie Fisher's Revolutionary Openness about Her Mental Illness: 'She Changed the World,'" *People*, December 28, 2016, http://people.com/celebrity/impact-carrie-fisher-mental-illness/, para. 1–5; Emily Yahr, "Carrie Fisher, the Inspiring Mental Health Advocate: 'I Am Mentally Ill . . . I Am Not Ashamed of That,'" *Washington Post*, December 27, 2016, www.washingtonpost.com/news/arts-and-entertainment/wp/2016/12/27/carrie-fisher-the-inspiring-mental-health-advocate-i-am-mentally-ill-i-am-not-ashamed-of-that/, para. 4–5.

2 Carrie Fisher, *Postcards from the Edge* (New York: Simon & Schuster, 1987).

3 See Ryan Burleson and Tara Parker-Pope, "Fans Tweet about Mental Illness to Honor Carrie Fisher," *New York Times*, December 27, 2016, www.nytimes.com/2016/12/27/arts/carrie-fisher-bipolar-disorder.html?_r=0; Yagoda, "Inside Carrie Fisher's Revolutionary Openness."

4 World Health Organization, "Mental Health Policy and Service Guidance Package: Advocacy for Mental Health," World Health Organization, 2003, www.who.int/mental_health/policy/services/1_advocacy_WEB_07.pdf?ua=1, p. 15.

5 Lybi Ma, "Interview: The Fisher Queen," *Psychology Today* (November/December 2001): 32+, at para 18; Emily Shapiro, "Carrie Fisher Was a Mental Health Advocate Inspired by Her Own Struggles," *ABC News*, December 27, 2016, https://abcnews.go.com/Entertainment/carrie-fisher-mental-health-advocate-inspired-struggles/story?id=44418344, at para. 11.

6 Lori Dorfman, and Ingrid Daffner Krasnow, "Public Health and Media Advocacy," *Annual Review of Public Health* 35 (2014): 293–306, at 296.

7 Cynthia A. Hoffner, "Responses to Carrie Fisher's Personal Disclosures about Mental Health: Identification, Humor, and Perceived Influence on Public Stigma," presented at the International Communication Association conference, Prague, Czech Republic, May 24–29, 2018; Cynthia A. Hoffner, "Sharing on Social Network Sites Following Carrie Fisher's Death: Responses to Her Mental Health Advocacy," *Health Communication* 35, no. 12 (2020): 1475–86.

8 Patrick W. Corrigan and Kristin A. Kosyluk, "Mental Illness Stigma: Types, Constructs, and Vehicles for Change," in *The Stigma of Disease and Disability: Understanding Causes and Overcoming Injustices*, ed. Patrick W. Corrigan (Washington, DC: American Psychological Association, 2014), 35–56, at 35.

9 Erving Goffman, *Stigma: Notes on the Management of Spoiled Identity* (New York: Simon & Schuster, 1963), 3.

10 Corrigan and Kosyluk, "Mental Illness Stigma," 36–37; Bruce G. Link and Jo C. Phelan, "Labeling and Stigma," in *Handbook of the Sociology of Mental Health*, ed. Carol S. Aneshensel, Jo C. Phelan, and Alex Bierman (New York: Springer, 2013), 524–41, at 529–31.

11 Patrick W. Corrigan and Deepa Rao, "On the Self-Stigma of Mental Illness: Stages, Disclosure, and Strategies for Change," *Canadian Journal of Psychiatry* 57, no. 8 (2012): 464–69, at 464–66; Claire Henderson, Sara

Evans-Lacko, and Graham Thornicroft, "Mental Illness Stigma, Help Seeking, and Public Health Programs," *American Journal of Public Health* 103, no. 5 (2013): 777–80, at 777.

12 Goffman, *Stigma*, 4.

13 Vanessa Boudewyns, Itai Himelboim, Derek L. Hansen, and Brian G. Southwell, "Stigma's Effect on Social Interaction and Social Media Activity," *Journal of Health Communication* 20, no. 11 (2015): 1337–45, at 1338–39; Jessica Gall Myrick, "Public Perceptions of Celebrity Cancer Deaths: How Identification and Emotions Shape Cancer Stigma and Behavioral Intentions," *Health Communication* 32, no. 11 (2017): 1385–95, at 1386.

14 Stephenie R. Chaudoir, Valerie A. Earnshaw, and Stephanie Andel, "'Discredited' versus 'Discreditable': Understanding How Shared and Unique Stigma Mechanisms Affect Psychological and Physical Health Disparities," *Basic and Applied Social Psychology* 35, no. 1 (2013): 75–87, at 80–81; Patrick W. Corrigan, Kristin A. Kosyluk, and Nicolas Rüsch, "Reducing Self-Stigma by Coming Out Proud," *American Journal of Public Health* 103, no. 5 (2013): 794–800, at 794–95; Corrigan and Rao, "On the Self-Stigma of Mental Illness," 464–66.

15 Emma E. McGinty, Alene Kennedy-Hendricks, Seema Choksy, and Colleen L. Barry, "Trends in News Media Coverage of Mental Illness in the United States: 1995–2014," *Health Affairs* 35, no. 6 (2016): 1121–29; Jane R. Pirkis, Warwick Blood, Catherine Francis, and Kerry McCallum, "On-screen Portrayals of Mental Illness: Extent, Nature, and Impacts," *Journal of Health Communication* 11, no. 5 (2006): 523–41, at 528–29.

16 Lisa D. Hawke, Erin E. Michalak, Victoria Maxwell, and Sagar V. Parikh, "Reducing Stigma toward People with Bipolar Disorder: Impact of a Filmed Theatrical Intervention Based on a Personal Narrative," *International Journal of Social Psychiatry* 60, no. 8 (2014): 741–50, at 747–48; Cynthia A. Hoffner and Elizabeth L. Cohen, "Responses to Obsessive Compulsive Disorder on *Monk* among Series Fans: Parasocial Relations, Presumed Media Influence, and Behavioral Outcomes," *Journal of Broadcasting and Electronic Media* 56, no. 4 (2012): 650–68, at 663; Cynthia A. Hoffner and Elizabeth L. Cohen, "Portrayal of Mental Illness on the TV Series *Monk*: Presumed Influence and Consequences of Exposure," *Health Communication* 30, no. 10 (2015): 1046–54, at 1052; Robert McKeever, "Vicarious Experience: Experimentally Testing the Effects of Empathy for Media

Characters with Severe Depression and the Intervening Role of Perceived Similarity," *Health Communication* 30, no. 11 (2015): 1122–34, at 1129–30.

17 Julia A. Maier, Douglas A. Gentile, David L. Vogel, and Scott A. Kaplan, "Media Influences on Self-Stigma of Seeking Psychological Services: The Importance of Media Portrayals and Person Perception," *Psychology of Popular Media Culture* 3, no. 4 (2014): 239–56, at 252–53; David L. Vogel, Douglas A. Gentile, and Scott A. Kaplan, "The Influence of Television on Willingness to Seek Therapy," *Journal of Clinical Psychology* 64, no. 3 (2008): 276–95, at 287–89.

18 Nicolas Rüsch, Matthias C. Angermeyer, and Patrick W. Corrigan, "Mental Illness Stigma: Concepts, Consequences, and Initiatives to Reduce Stigma," *European Psychiatry* 20, no. 8 (2005): 529–39, at 533–34.

19 See Peter Cram, A. Mark Fendrick, John Inadomi, Mark E. Cowen, Daniel Carpenter, and Sandeep Vijan, "The Impact of a Celebrity Promotional Campaign on the Use of Colon Cancer Screening: The Katie Couric Effect," *Archives of Internal Medicine* 163, no. 13 (2003): 1601–5; Hoffner and Cohen, "Responses to Obsessive Compulsive Disorder on *Monk*"; Myrick, "Public Perceptions of Celebrity Cancer Deaths"; and Seth M. Noar, Jessica Fitts Willoughby, Jessica Gall Myrick, and Jennifer Brown, "Public Figure Announcements about Cancer and Opportunities for Cancer Communication: A Review and Research Agenda," *Health Communication* 29, no. 5 (2014): 445–61.

20 Diane B. Francis, Elise M. Stevens, Seth M. Noar, and Laura Widman, "Public Reactions to and Impact of Celebrity Health Announcements: Understanding the Charlie Sheen Effect," *Howard Journal of Communications* 30, no. 5 (2019): 479–94, at 490–91; Myrick, "Public Perceptions of Celebrity Cancer Deaths," 1386–87; Norman C. H. Wong, Kathryn L. Lookadoo, and Gwendelyn S. Nisbett, "'I'm Demi and I Have Bipolar Disorder': Effect of Parasocial Contact on Reducing Stigma toward People with Bipolar Disorder," *Communication Studies* 68, no. 3 (2017): 314–33, at 328–30.

21 Karen Karbo, *In Praise of Difficult Women: Life Lessons from 29 Heroines Who Dared to Break the Rules* (Washington, DC: National Geographic, 2018), 317, 325.

22 ABC News, "PrimeTime: Carrie Fisher Interview," *ABC News*, December 21, 2000, https://abcnews.go.com/Primetime/story?id=132315&page=1, para. 14.

23 Shapiro, "Carrie Fisher Was a Mental Health Advocate," para. 3.

24 ABC News, "PrimeTime: Carrie Fisher Interview," para. 10.

25 National Alliance on Mental Illness, "Bipolar Disorder," *National Alliance on Mental Illness*, 2017, www.nami.org/learn-more/mental-health-conditions/bipolar-disorder.

26 ABC News, "PrimeTime: Carrie Fisher Interview," para. 4.

27 Patty Duke and Kenneth Turan, *Call Me Anna: The Autobiography of Patty Duke* (New York: Bantam Books, 1988).

28 Sara Evans-Lacko, Elizabeth Corker, Paul Williams, Claire Henderson, and Graham Thornicroft, "Effect of the Time to Change Anti-stigma Campaign on Trends in Mental-Illness-Related Public Stigma among the English Population in 2003–13: An Analysis of Survey Data," *Lancet Psychiatry* 1, no. 2 (2014): 121–28; Anna Gekoski and Steve Broome, *What's Normal Anyway? Celebrities' Own Stories of Mental Illness* (London: Constable, 2014).

29 See John Carucci, "Celebrities Highlight Mental Health Issues," *U.S. News and World Report*, May 17, 2018, www.usnews.com/news/healthiest-communities/articles/2018-05-17/celebrities-bring-awareness-to-mental-health-issues; Wong, Lookadoo, and Nisbett, "I'm Demi and I Have Bipolar Disorder."

30 Corrigan and Kosyluk, "Mental Illness Stigma," 42–43; Wong, Lookadoo, and Nisbett, "I'm Demi and I Have Bipolar Disorder."

31 Donald Horton and R. Richard Wohl, "Mass Communication and Parasocial Interaction: Observations on Intimacy at a Distance," *Psychiatry* 19, no. 3 (1956): 215–29, at 215.

32 Nurit Tal-Or and Yael Papirman, "The Fundamental Attribution Error in Attributing Fictional Figures' Characteristics to the Actors," *Media Psychology* 9, no. 2 (2007): 331–45, at 343.

33 Jonathan Cohen, "Mediated Relationships and Media Effects: Parasocial Interaction and Identification," in *The Sage Handbook of Media Processes and Effects*, ed. Robin L. Nabi and Mary B. Oliver (Thousand Oaks, CA: Sage, 2009), 223–36, at 226–27; Gayle Stever, "Parasocial Theory: Concepts and Measures," in *International Encyclopedia of Media Effects*, ed. Patrick Rössler, Cynthia A. Hoffner, and Liesbet van Zoonen (Boston: Wiley-Blackwell, 2017), 1457–68, at 1460.

34 Edward Schiappa, Peter B. Gregg, and Dean E. Hewes, "The Parasocial Contact Hypothesis," *Communication Monographs* 72, no. 1 (2005): 92–115, at 97–98.

35 Hoffner and Cohen, "Responses to Obsessive Compulsive Disorder on *Monk*," 1578–79; Parul Jain, Uma Shankar Pandey, and Enakshi Roy, "Perceived Efficacy and Intentions Regarding Seeking Mental Healthcare: Impact of Deepika Padukone, A Bollywood Celebrity's Public Announcement of Struggle with Depression," *Journal of Health Communication* 22, no. 8 (2017): 713–20, at 717; Wong, Lookadoo, and Nisbett, "I'm Demi and I Have Bipolar Disorder," 326–29.

36 Elizabeth Johnson, "Carrie Fisher Talks about Mental Illness and Career," *Herald-Tribune*, April 20, 2013, http://health.heraldtribune.com/2013/04/20/14065/, para. 1; Lybi Ma, "Interview: The Fisher Queen," *Psychology Today* (November/December 2001): 32+ at para. 18; Massachusetts Psychiatric Society, "APA Annual Meeting 2010 Convocation Speaker Carrie Fisher," *Massachusetts Psychiatric Society Bulletin*, April 2010, 7; Shapiro, "Carrie Fisher Was a Mental Health Advocate," para 11.

37 Carrie Fisher, "Ask Carrie Fisher: I'm Bipolar—How Do You Feel at Peace with Mental Illness?," *The Guardian*, November 30, 2016, www.theguardian.com/lifeandstyle/2016/nov/30/carrie-fisher-advice-column-mental-illness-bipolar-disorder.

38 Boudewyns et al., "Stigma's Effect on Social Interaction and Social Media Activity," 1338; Myrick, "Public Perceptions of Celebrity Cancer Deaths," 1385.

39 Chaudoir, Earnshaw, and Andel, " 'Discredited' versus 'Discreditable,' " 80–81.

40 Leslie Bennetts, "Carrie on Baggage," *Vanity Fair*, November 2009, www.vanityfair.com/news/2009/11/carrie-fisher-200911, para. 4.

41 Carrie Fisher, *Wishful Drinking* (New York: Simon & Schuster, 2008), 11.

42 Kimberly Zapata, "Remembering Carrie Fisher & Her Contributions to Mental Health," Greater Than Illness, December 27, 2019, https://greaterthanillness.com/2019/12/27/remembering-carrie-fisher-her-contributions-to-mental-health/.

43 Rachel A. Smith, "Language of the Lost: An Explication of Stigma Communication," *Communication Theory* 17, no. 4 (2007): 462–85, at 467–72.

44 Rachel Smith, "Media Depictions of Health Topics: Challenge and Stigma Formats," *Journal of Health Communication* 12, no. 3 (2007): 233–49, at 245.

45 Jeffrey Blackwell, "Carrie Fisher of 'Star Wars' Fame Continues the Battle," *Harvard Gazette*, April 2016, https://news.harvard.edu/gazette/story/

2016/04/carrie-fisher-of-star-wars-fame-continues-the-battle; Yahr, "Carrie Fisher, the Inspiring Mental Health Advocate," para. 14, 17, 18.

46 Fisher, *Wishful Drinking*, 127.

47 *Wishful Drinking*, 159.

48 Johnson, "Carrie Fisher Talks about Mental Illness and Career," para. 21.

49 Blackwell, "Carrie Fisher of 'Star Wars' Fame Continues the Battle," para. 2.

50 Fisher, *Wishful Drinking*, 17.

51 Marie Ilic, Jost Reinecke, Gerd Bohner, Hans-Onno Röttgers, Thomas Beblo, Martin Driessen, Ulrich Frommberger and Patrick William Corrigan, "Protecting Self-Esteem from Stigma: A Test of Different Strategies for Coping with the Stigma of Mental Illness," *International Journal of Social Psychiatry* 58, no. 3 (2012): 246–57, at 255; Rebecca Meisenbach, "Stigma Management Communication: A Theory and Agenda for Applied Research on How Individuals Manage Moments of Stigmatized Identity," *Journal of Applied Communication Research* 38, no. 3 (2010): 268–92, at 279.

52 Sigmund Freud, "Humor," *International Journal of Psychoanalysis* 9 (1928): 1–6, at 2–3.

53 Lauren P. Kennedy, "20 Questions for Carrie Fisher," *WebMD*, 2010, www.webmd.com/mental-health/addiction/features/questions-for-carrie-fisher #1, para. 6.

54 Fisher, *Wishful Drinking*, 113.

55 See Robin L. Nabi, Jiyeon So, and Abby Prestin, "Media-Based Emotional Coping: Examining the Emotional Benefits and Pitfalls of Media Consumption," in *The Routledge Handbook of Emotions and Mass Media*, ed. Katrin Doveling, Christian V. Scheve, and Elly A. Konijn (New York: Routledge, 2010), 116–33, at 128.

56 Howard Giles, Richard Y. Bourhis, Nicholas J. Gadfield, Graham J. Davies, and Ann P. Davies, "Cognitive Aspects of Humour in Social Interaction: A Model and Some Linguistic Data," in *Humour and Laughter: Theory, Research, and Applications*, ed. Anthony J. Chapman and Hugh C. Foot (London: Wiley, 1976), 139–54, at 143–45; Emily Moyer-Gusé, Chad Mahood, and Sarah Brookes, "Entertainment-Education in the Context of Humor: Effects on Safer Sex Intentions and Risk Perceptions," *Health Communication* 26, no. 8 (2011): 765–74, at 767–68.

57 Fisher, *Wishful Drinking*, 114.

58 Hoffner, "Responses to Carrie Fisher's Personal Disclosures."

59 Adele Slaughter, "Carrie Fisher 'Strikes Back' at Mental Illness," *USA Today*, May 29, 2002, http://usatoday30.usatoday.com/news/health/spotlight/2002/05/29-fisher.htm, para. 27.

60 Elizabeth Leonard, "Carrie Fisher's Bipolar Crisis: 'I Was Trying to Survive,'" *People*, March 25, 2013, https://people.com/archive/carrie-fishers-bipolar-crisis-i-was-trying-to-survive-vol-79-no-12/, para. 11.

61 Carrie Fisher, *Shockaholic* (New York: Simon & Schuster), 4–5.

62 Jonathan Sadowsky, "Electroconvulsive Therapy: A History of Controversy, but Also of Help," *The Conversation*, January 12, 2017, www.scientificamerican.com/article/electroconvulsive-therapy-a-history-of-controversy-but-also-of-help/, para. 4, 8.

63 Fisher, *Shockaholic*, 19.

64 Andy Greene, "The Last Word: Carrie Fisher on LSD, Death, and Sex with Han Solo," *Rolling Stone*, November 28, 2016, www.rollingstone.com/movies/movie-features/the-last-word-carrie-fisher-on-lsd-death-and-sex-with-han-solo-117225, para 33.

65 Hoffner, "Responses to Carrie Fisher's Personal Disclosures"; Hoffner, "Sharing on Social Network Sites Following Carrie Fisher's Death."

66 Hoffner, "Sharing on Social Network Sites Following Carrie Fisher's Death," 1479.

67 Hoffner, "Responses to Carrie Fisher's Personal Disclosures."

68 Burleson and Parker-Pope, "Fans Tweet about Mental Illness to Honor Carrie Fisher."

69 Hoffner, "Responses to Carrie Fisher's Personal Disclosures."

70 *Stephen Fry: The Secret Life of the Manic Depressive*, directed by Ross Wilson (London: IWC Media, 2006).

71 Victoria Citter, "Thank You to Carrie Fisher, Who Gave Me Courage to Fight Bipolar Disorder," *The Mighty*, February 7, 2017, https://themighty.com/2017/02/carrie-fisher-bipolar-disorder-thank-you/, para. 2.

72 Fisher, *Wishful Drinking*, 130–31.

73 National Alliance on Mental Illness, "NAMI Honors Hollywood Actors for Confronting Mental Illness in Drama and Real Life," *National Alliance on Mental Illness*, June 14, 2001, www.nami.org/Press-Media/Press-Releases/2001/NAMI-Honors-Hollywood-Actors-for-Confronting-Menta, para. 3.

74 Slaughter, "Carrie Fisher 'Strikes Back' at Mental Illness," para. 6.

75 David Staba, "Hollywood Kid Carrie Fisher and Her Best Awful," *bp Magazine*, November 7, 2004, www.bphope.com/hollywood-kid-carrie-fisher-and-her-best-awful/.

76 *bp Magazine*, "bp Magazine's Tribute to Carrie Fisher," *bp Magazine*, December 29, 2016, www.bphope.com/hope-harmony-headlines-bp-magazines-tribute-to-carrie-fisher/, para. 5.

77 Blackwell, "Carrie Fisher of 'Star Wars' Fame Continues the Battle," para. 8.

78 Substance Abuse and Mental Health Services Administration (SAMHSA), "SAMHSA to Recognize Behavioral Health Champions at 2017 Voice Awards," SAMHSA, August 16, 2017. www.samhsa.gov/voice-awards/award-winners/2017, para 1.

79 See Laura Barcella, "How Carrie Fisher Championed Mental Health," *Rolling Stone*, December 28, 2016, www.rollingstone.com/culture/culture-news/how-carrie-fisher-championed-mental-health-115009/; Benedict Carey, "Carrie Fisher Put Pen and Voice in Service of 'Bipolar Pride,'" *New York Times*, December 28, 2016, www.nytimes.com/2016/12/28/health/carrie-fisher-bipolar-disorder.html; Rachel Dicker, "Carrie Fisher's Struggle with Bipolar Disorder Inspired Many," *U.S. News and World Report*, December 28, 2016, www.usnews.com/news/articles/2016-12-28/carrie-fishers-struggle-with-bipolar-disorder-inspired-many; Adam Howard, "Carrie Fisher Was a Feminist Force to Be Reckoned With," *NBC News*, last modified December 27, 2016, www.nbcnews.com/news/us-news/carrie-fisher-was-feminist-force-be-reckoned-n700531; Mary B. Marcus, "Carrie Fisher's Honesty about Bipolar Disorder, Addiction Helped Fight Stigma," *CBS News*, December 28, 2016, www.cbsnews.com/news/carrie-fisher-bipolar-disorder-addiction-mental-health-stigma/; Vikram Murthi, "Carrie Fisher's Honesty with Mental Illness Inspired '#InHonorOfCarrie' Social Media Movement," *IndieWire*, December 28, 2016, www.indiewire.com/2016/12/carrie-fisher-dead-mental-illness-honesty-social-media-movement-1201763248/; Shapiro, "Carrie Fisher Was a Mental Health Advocate"; Justin Worland, "Carrie Fisher Didn't Just Break Boundaries Onscreen. She also Fought the Stigma of Mental Illness," *Time*, December 27, 2016, www.time.com/4618486/carrie-fisher-dead-mental-health-legacy/; Yagoda, "Inside Carrie Fisher's Revolutionary Openness"; Yahr, "Carrie Fisher, the Inspiring Mental Health Advocate."

80 Carey, "Carrie Fisher Put Pen and Voice in Service of 'Bipolar Pride,'" para. 3.

81 Yagoda, "Inside Carrie Fisher's Revolutionary Openness."

82 Burleson and Parker-Pope, "Fans Tweet about Mental Illness to Honor Carrie Fisher"; Murthi, "Carrie Fisher's Honesty with Mental Illness Inspired '#InHonorOfCarrie' Social Media Movement."

83 Devon Ivie, "Harrison Ford, Mark Hamill, and Other Celebrities Mourn the Death of Carrie Fisher," *Vulture*, December 27, 2016, www.vulture .com/2016/12/celebrities-react-to-carrie-fishers-death.html.

84 Ivie, "Harrison Ford, Mark Hamill, and Other Celebrities Mourn the Death of Carrie Fisher."

85 Dicker, "Carrie Fisher's Struggle with Bipolar Disorder Inspired Many."

86 Natalia Lusinski, "15 Carrie Fisher Memes and Tributes to Share When You Just Miss Her Too Much," *Bustle*, December 27, 2016, www.bustle.com/ p/15-carrie-fisher-memes-tributes-to-share-when-you-just-miss-her-too -much-26461.

87 Hoffner, "Sharing on Social Network Sites Following Carrie Fisher's Death," 1481–82.

88 Burleson and Parker-Pope, "Fans Tweet about Mental Illness to Honor Carrie Fisher"; Murthi, "Carrie Fisher's Honesty with Mental Illness Inspired '#InHonorOfCarrie' Social Media Movement."

89 Burleson and Parker-Pope, "Fans Tweet about Mental Illness to Honor Carrie Fisher," para. 3–8.

90 Sejung Park and Cynthia A. Hoffner, "Tweeting about Mental Health to Honor Carrie Fisher: How #InHonorOfCarrie Reinforced the Social Influence of Celebrity Advocacy," *Computers in Human Behavior* 110, article 106353 (2020): 1–11.

91 Park and Hoffner, "Tweeting about Mental Health to Honor Carrie Fisher," 1.

92 "Tweeting about Mental Health to Honor Carrie Fisher," 7.

93 "Tweeting about Mental Health to Honor Carrie Fisher," 7–8.

94 "Tweeting about Mental Health to Honor Carrie Fisher," 8.

95 Smith, "Media Depictions of Health Topics: Challenge and Stigma Formats," 239.

96 Katie Dupere, "These Simple Badges Are Helping Social Media Users Talk about Mental Illness," *Mashable*, January 6, 2017, https://mashable.com/ 2017/01/06/mental-illness-badges-endthestigma/.

97 Dupere, "These Simple Badges Are Helping," para. 2–3.

98 Fisher, "Ask Carrie Fisher," *The Guardian*, November 30, 2016, para. 6–8.

99 Jess Cagle and Julie Jordan, "Carrie Fisher Died of Sleep Apnea and Used Drugs, Report Reveals—as Daughter Billie Releases Emotional Statement," *People*, June 16, 2017, https://people.com/movies/carrie-fisher-cause-of -death/, para. 5–6.

Threshold Guardian to Space Mom

HERE, BUT FOR THE SAKE OF CARRIE, GO I

Slade Kinnecott

O n the morning of December 27, 2016, I was looking forward to the appointment I had scheduled for a massage. One of my best friends was in town visiting for a couple days. It was another day of my Christmas break, a long-awaited reward at the end of a particularly taxing year at work. Right before the massage therapist was due to return to the room, I heard my phone notify me of an incoming text. My friend Joe's message read, "Carrie Fisher RIP :-(."

The instant I comprehended the news, I felt my heart plunge and my body harden into a cold shock. I staggered to the massage table where I would lie feeling trapped for the next hour. My body was rigid with tension and the concerted effort it required to stifle my emotions. I waited minute after minute for it to be over so I could be alone to process the news. The moment after I paid, I walked out the door in finally free-flowing tears.

The next morning, December 28, 2016, my friend was due at the airport. I dropped him off and with a great sigh of relief returned to my empty house. Social media was blowing up with commentaries, tributes, and collective grief. Then, as evening drew closer, I glanced at the news online and found a beautiful, smiling photo of Debbie. She was wearing a stunning, vivid emerald green outfit I recognized from an interview.[1] I thought, poor Debbie, what must she be going through, yet I also felt a wave of reprieve. She would be able to help us all understand this. I thought and felt all these things in a split second. In the next split second, my eyes lowered to the copy accompanying the image. "Debbie Reynolds dead at 84." OMG. NO. I felt another blow, except this time there was no point in trying to process any of it anymore. I sat stunned as night fell while my fiancée and Joe attended our weekly pub trivia without me. The team name they played under that night was "Everybody's Dead."

I don't remember much from those first raw hours but spending what energy I had left pretending to be fine. But I wasn't fine. Both of these women had been professional and personal role models integral to my core self. We lost two iconic individuals as well as a formidable mother and daughter duo. And what could be more visceral than it happening on subsequent days? All at once the "survivor" didn't survive and the "unsinkable" submerged.[2]

I had always prided myself on my ability to analyze fame and fandom from an impartial distance. But Carrie's death in particular affected me to a troubling degree. Over the next year and a half I found myself unable to get past a constant dull heartache over the sudden loss. I found my emotions embarrassing and frustrating, but they did not subside. I felt alone at first, but then knew I wasn't. All along I watched popular culture grieve also, with no less intensity. And in her egregious absence her legacy began to crystallize.

The world misses Carrie Fisher for so many different reasons. These are mine.

Before I loved Carrie, I loved Debbie. Not because I was of Debbie's generation, or Carrie's for that matter. In fact, I am part of what some generational analysts refer to as a "micro generation" called xennials.[3] A defining characteristic is to be born between 1977 and 1983, that is, within the release years of the original *Star Wars* trilogy. No, I loved Debbie because years before I hit puberty I had become obsessed with film history. I didn't know how it would happen or what it would look like yet, but I wanted a career devoted to classic movies. In the thirty years since I have worked in film and television production, film preservation, and media archiving. I am a scholar of the American studio system era of the 1920s to 1950s. My favorite folklore is that of Metro-Goldwyn-Mayer.

To me, the study of being a celebrity was as fascinating as the craft of filmmaking itself. The irresistible allure of film was in its dichotomous nature. Behind the scenes it was a technical, gritty, and dispiriting business. But what it was capable of creating was a pure, emotionally charged shared experience. The ritual of filmgoing revolutionized the world through mass communication and media culture.

In *Postcards from the Edge*, Carrie described the entertainment business as "mining for celluloid gold."[4] To me, that's how it felt to learn about the history of film. It's important to point out that I did not accumulate my knowledge in an era of Turner Classic Movies (TCM), eBay or IMDb. I spent my teens feeding my appetite by tracking down old books and fan magazines at flea markets. I would scour network television listings for anything airing that I hadn't seen. I would check out every movie star biography and the earliest films on VHS at the public library. Film history became a mental open-world role-playing game. As I learned the stories behind the films, I unlocked new knowledge of more and more players. Everyone's career, everyone's life connected in the giant, intertwining universe of Hollywood.

I don't remember exactly how I came to know who Debbie Reynolds was. It wasn't *Singin' in the Rain* (1952). It was likely an appearance on *Entertainment Tonight* or a talk show interview. What I do remember is that I knew very early on that she was a proud alumna of MGM. She exuded both pride and gratitude at having been a part of the era I felt a special kinship toward. She was a connection to the past, but she was living in the present like me.

She was still very active in the modern entertainment world. Her perfect casting in *Mother* (1996) led to a Golden Globe nomination. I saw *In & Out* (1997) in the theaters because of her. I was past the target age of Disney's cult classic *Halloweentown* (1998) but delighted in her off-screen "cameo" in *Fear and Loathing in Las Vegas* (1998). Then came *These Old Broads* (2001), a riotous project uniting Debbie with Elizabeth Taylor, Shirley MacLaine, and Joan Collins. It was written by someone of whom I had a vague awareness, her daughter. After that she did a lot of voice-over and television work, most of which I did not see. But I was entranced by her performance as a woman she had known, Liberace's mother, in *Behind the Candelabra* (2013). And so proud when she would finally receive a Life Achievement Award from the Screen Actors Guild in 2015, and the Jean Hersholt Humanitarian Award from the Academy of Motion Picture Arts and Sciences in 2016.

I had always known of Debbie's dream to have a Hollywood Motion Picture Museum. Her commitment to keep iconic costumes, props, and set pieces from being scattered around the world and into the hands of only the highest private bidders began in 1970 with the liquidating of MGM's back lots and warehouse assets. She spent day after day, week after week attending the auctions and buying as much as she could afford to amass. She did the same thing later at Twentieth Century Fox. Her vision, for movie fans of generations to come, to behold artifacts from some of the greatest films of the classic era, was inspired in part by her friendship with Walt Disney. A hybrid of movie star, entertainment historian, and fan, Debbie had talked about this concept at length in interviews when I was growing up. I was thrilled as a teenager, waiting to see this institution come to fruition. I envisioned this magical tribute to old Hollywood thriving in the modern world and could think of no place I'd rather visit.

And yet after an unconscionable number of setbacks over decades, including sabotage from her third husband, it never fully came together. I remembered in real time the Profiles in History auctions, not quite yet grasping that it was with great torment she dismantled her acquisitions. Now as an adult, an MGM historian and archivist, I admire Debbie's dedication and love of film history on an even deeper level. She was always right. The community of TCM fans blossoming twenty-five years since the station's debut in the mid-1990s proves the audience she thought would be there for this museum still is. Only Todd Fisher knows precisely what is left of her lot now. My inner child still holds out a glimmer of hope that somehow, someday, I might still have the opportunity (and great honor) to help preserve what remains of Debbie's collection.

Carrie and Todd Fisher were born of "focus pullers"[5] and into a singular experience molded by Hollywood, scandal, and celebrity. Before they could have a sense of the world, it had passed judgment on their absentee father and showered their mother with sympathy and protectiveness. It was a series of events so imbued with notoriety it fundamentally shaped their lives, and society never quite forgot. In *Wishful Drinking*, Carrie says, "So in a way, movies became home movies. Home became another place on the movie star map."[6]

But whereas Todd was able to step back from the spotlight, Carrie's involvement in the most popular movie franchise of all time fated her to an entirely public life. As a child she resented the sense of ownership strangers demonstrated toward her mother, but within a generation it became a phenomenon she too experienced. As famous figures, both Debbie and Carrie walked the line between celebrity otherness and friendly accessibility to indulge the wishes of their fans.

Carrie's first novel was *Postcards from the Edge*, inspired by her real-life drug overdose. From the beginning of her writing career she tapped her own truth and vulnerability. The screenplay, a different type of writing challenge, is an extrapolation of the book, further exploring years of a tense relationship with her mother. The two types of works are admirable as similar but independent works that foreshadowed her successful career as a script doctor.

Surrender the Pink, Delusions of Grandma, and *The Best Awful* followed. Even *These Old Broads* provided real-life resolution to the rift between her mother and former stepmother. The better you know her later autobiographical works (*Wishful Drinking, Shockaholic*, and *The Princess Diarist*), the more you recognize storylines, characters and even direct quotes from her well-documented life in their earliest expressions.

Although Debbie's career began as the studio system was faltering, she was under contract to MGM throughout the 1950s. Thus, in her recollections of her mother's career Carrie is also sharing stories of Hollywood history. From famous costars to behind-the-scenes veterans, from movie sets to back lots, from Ava Gardner to Cary Grant. This unusual education gave her insight into the fickle nature of show business. In *Wishful Drinking* the HBO special, she recalled "My brother and I grew up watching our parents' once white-hot, bright star of celebrity slowly, dim, cool and fade." Also quipping, "I like to think of celebrity as just obscurity *biding* its time" (punctuated with a knowing nod to a laughing audience).

Over the decades and due to her intimate proximity to fame and its behavior-altering powers she considered herself a "war reporter on the front lines of celebrity,"[7] and she coined terms like "shine"[8] for the experience of being in the presence of celebrity. In *The Princess Diarist* she explains how her keen awareness of fame's "unpredictable half-life" tempered her enthusiasm when *Star Wars: Episode IV—A New Hope* "exploded across the firmament of pop culture,"[9] but she also shares musings about the expectations and projections of Comicon and sci-fi convention devotees, as intense as ever, forty years later.

Over time, Carrie became so embedded in popular culture and her personal backstory so well known, she was able to play herself, literally and figuratively, in film and television roles from *Sex and the City* (2000) to *The Big Bang Theory* (2014) to *Map to the Stars* (2014). One of my favorite performances, Emmy nominated for Outstanding Guest Actress in a Comedy

Series, is Rosemary Howard in *30 Rock* (2006). In mere minutes of screen time her character descends from accomplished and reserved to wild and embittered as her emotional instability is slowly revealed. She is playing a character, but the subtext is that this character is a parody of Carrie Fisher. Her final line ends with an allusion to, what else, *Star Wars*—"Help me Liz Lemon, you're my only hope!"

The circumstances of Carrie's life were entirely unique, and yet she emerged as someone informal, likeable and incredibly easy to identify with. She was often self-deprecating and apologetic about having problems at all having been born into wealth and privilege—"Oh, poor, sad Carrie!"[10]—which in turn heightened her relatability. And while her honesty may have been a result of never having the option of a private life, as a humorist and wordsmith she distilled life into ubiquitous emotions and relatable truths that made her universally loved.

Bright Lights: Starring Carrie Fisher and Debbie Reynolds premiered at Cannes in May 2016 and four other festivals over the next six months. It is a documentary in the era of reality television about the semiprivate and complex relationship between these seemingly familiar women. Originally set to air on HBO in March 2017, it moved to January 7, less than two weeks after their deaths. Astonishing in its candor, prepossessing, and bittersweet, it is a fitting final chapter to two lives lived almost exclusively in spotlights, for us all to see. Or as Carrie put it in *Surrender the Pink*, "I had a life like mine and look at me."[11]

As a child, I instinctively knew there was something going on within me that was not troubling my peers. I could sense that when I felt happy, I was in a state of jubilation, possessed by a surge of energy that was stronger than normal. I also saw no evidence others experienced sudden waves of paralyzing dread and panic. I remember moments of complete hopelessness washing over me like a darkening of my heart. These feelings came and went often unrelated to life events but frequently exacerbated by them. Considered smart, creative, shy, and sensitive, I lived an isolated life. I didn't exactly fit in at school but I was too much of an outlier to be ridiculed. However, I was rarely lonely because I had an absorbing imagination.

My parents grew up in a generation dismayed by mental abnormality. In my youth, when I tried on various occasions to talk to them about my

Fig. 10.1. Debbie Reynolds and Carrie Fisher at the Primetime Creative Arts Emmy Awards in Los Angeles, California (2011, photo by WEN).

powerful moods, they dismissed my concerns. I crawled aloofly through my teens, conflicted about what my parents were hoping I wasn't versus what I felt I must be. My response was born of my only alternative—it became something I would have to deal with on my own.

In the spring of 2001 I was reading the annual Hollywood edition of *Vanity Fair*. In it were Carrie's answers to the Proust Questionnaire. And in her interview, I found words that would change my life. The question, "When and where were you happiest?" Her response, "In my manic highs, which are too numerous to mention."

In retrospect, it's not a remarkable answer. But at the time I finally knew unequivocally that it was the way I too had always experienced the world. I had been in conflict about myself for my entire life, but I knew this answer came from a place beyond "normal." I had been to that place countless times. A transient, impalpable place that it seemed no one in my life had been to or knew what the landscape looked like. For the first time in my life, I was sure I had been right. And with that identification I bonded to a celebrity stranger, the only person I had ever witnessed unafraid of discussing being bipolar. Like Carrie's line in *Delusions of Grandma*, "Be that as it may and it looks as though it might . . ."[12] within a few months I mustered the courage to make my first appointment with a psychiatrist.

Decades later I try to empathize and understand why my parents weren't equipped to help me arrive at or acknowledge my diagnosis, but their denial set off a trajectory of compartmentalized exile that I continue to live in to this day. After all these years they view my patterns of behavior as normal and mental illness as something *other* people deal with. It is an unresolved source of inner conflict for me. They are overwhelmingly loving in every other way, but sometimes I worry what would happen if they saw my darkness, part of who I truly am.

Bipolar disorder has several subtypes and mine is cyclothymia.[13] In the 1950s Dr. John Campbell emphasized this fundamentally dynamic nature . . . by comparing the illness with a movie:

> The fluidity, change, and movement of the emotions, as they occur in the ever-changing cyclothymic process, may be compared to the pictures of the cinema, as contrasted with a "still" photograph. Indeed, the psychiatrist, observing a manic-depressive patient for the first time, or as he undergoes one of the many undulations in mood,

from melancholia to euphoria or from hypomania to a depression, is reminded of the experience of entering a movie during the middle of the story. No matter where one takes up the plot, the story tends to swing around again to the point where it started.[14]

So, looking back it's hard to know. Did film influence the development of my mind or am I drawn to film because I find psychological solace in its nature? The bond has long since been inextricable.

Pam and Roy. The meal and the check. Liquid confidence. The mood weather system. Emotional fiction. The grid. A brain set in cement. Sadness squared. Pain squared. Pain cubed. Chocolate salad. A problem versus an inconvenience. Monster in the box.[15] Carrie says in *Wishful Drinking* that verbalizing her experiences provided "a sense of being in control of the craziness."[16] She also plays it off as a pet delusion. But in fact, visualization is a powerful tool in living with bipolar. Not only in orienting yourself to your current state, but also in providing context for those around you.

Carrie began alluding to her two moods, Pam and Roy, as early as *Postcards from the Edge*, but I wasn't aware of this personification until many years later. I had been imagining my moods as objects and places. Newton's Third Law of Motion is my mantra, bracing me for what is always coming next. I imagine my typical range of mood on the path of "the pendulum." The momentum of shifting from dysthymia to hypomania is "the pinball" finally releasing from its launch. The "bottom of the well" is my old familiar stomping ground, that is, the numbing depths beyond sadness, especially acute in the winter months. And "the spinning top" is the onset of mania, when my mind moves with effortless speed and accuracy, until it inevitably begins to topple.

No one in my life, including therapists, elucidated my experiences the way Carrie did. It didn't matter that our metaphors were different. There is comfort in the precise descriptions of intangible ordeals. And perhaps even more importantly for me and millions of others who revered her outspokenness, there is validation.

My official diagnosis came well over a decade of living with my symptoms. Like I had done my entire life thus far I entered the workforce compelled to keep my illness a personal and professional secret. I still feel obliged to go to great lengths to protect my confidentiality to this day. In reality I live a life of perpetual imbalance, but I spend as much energy as necessary projecting an image of consistency. I give my all to my career Monday through Friday and spend many weekends exhausted. I self-medicate with my favorite drugs (sugar, marijuana, sleep). I deflect endless well-meaning inquiries from coworkers about whether I had a nice weekend and what I did. I even avoid the term "mental health day" when I take a day off to reset, concerned it might draw attention to my behavior.

I knew very early on in life I would not be able to handle being a mother, and it has never bothered me. I save my maternal instinct for beloved pets and animal welfare, and it is an excellent outlet for what nurturing I have to give. Over the decades people casually ask about my interest in having children, and I always feel a twinge of self-preservation as I politely divert them away from my deep and private why. After all these years, despite how far I've come in accepting myself and this life, I still have remnants of the poison of shame in me when I come up against the societal constructs I cannot satisfy. I continue to fear any misstep in my professional life could trigger a cascade of dominoes. I worry if my reputation as an employee of sound mind and reliable competence is ever unpacked from its Samsonite it could undermine everything I have ever accomplished.

As millennials have entered the workforce, I have admired their forthright approach to mental health. Anxiety, seasonal affective disorder, and obsessive-compulsive disorder among others, are all open topics. They have an inherent respect for therapy, self-care, boundaries, and emotional intelligence as pillars of well-being. To them, any view that even hints at shame is ignorant, oppressive, and antiquated. I have watched with fascination as my colleagues openly discuss their issues. I hope we continue in this direction, but I don't know if I will ever let go of my survival instinct. My entire life I've been a spy, observing how people react to things they don't understand. We've come a long way with some of the more universal challenges (grief, anxiety, unipolar depression), but being *unpredictable* is still one of the cardinal sins of civilization.

Carrie would say, "we're only as sick as our secrets."[17] Maybe I can live up to that someday, but I continue to lean on the privilege of my privacy. If society really can embrace mental illness in all its forms one day, Carrie will be one of the first people to thank. She was a teacher and a cheerleader.

She offered knowledge, perspective, and encouragement. She spoke to sufferers as well as the average person. She scolded derisive attitudes toward mental illness, took the sting out of its life sentence, and turned embarrassment into a precious sense of pride in the struggle. One of her last projects was "Advice from the Dark Side," a column for *The Guardian*. In her final installment, she responds to the question, "I'm bipolar—how do you feel at peace with mental illness?" After a thoughtful, reassuring answer, she closes with, "You can let it all fall down and feel defeated and hopeless and that you're done. But you reached out to me—that took courage. Now build on that. Move through those feelings and meet me on the other side. As your bipolar sister, I'll be watching. Now get out there and show me and you what you can do."

Carrie narrated an audiobook version of every novel she wrote. The first thing I (and many other people alongside me on the public library wait list) did after her death was listen to them all, some for the first time. I was familiar with the content of *Wishful Drinking* from the HBO special, but it wasn't until I heard her read the book version in its entirety that I first heard the "Author's Note" at the end. And I cried because it was fifty-one seconds of the most accepting, supportive, legitimizing words I'd ever received in my life. "Now embedded like a rare insect in digital amber"[18] it exists for all of us to have and revisit forevermore.

> One of the things that baffles me (and there are quite a few) is how there can be so much lingering stigma with regards to mental illness, specifically bipolar disorder. In my opinion, living with manic depression takes a tremendous amount of balls. Not unlike a tour of Afghanistan (though the bombs and bullets, in this case, come from the inside). At times, being bipolar can be an all-consuming challenge, requiring a lot of stamina and even more courage, so if you're living with this illness and functioning at all, it's something to be proud of, not ashamed of. They should issue medals along with the steady stream of medication.[19]

While *Wishful Drinking* is a more enjoyable experience, *Shockaholic* is my favorite memoir. I find even the sound of her voice is at its most comforting to listen to. Far removed from the clear tone of her early novels yet

Fig. 10.2. Carrie Fisher attends a celebrity Q&A session at Fan Expo Vancouver in British Columbia (2015, photo by Phillip Chin/WireImage).

still years away from adenoidal, it is weary and husky. It captures her distinctive, hearty laugh with its blend of mischief and wisdom. You can even hear her smiling as she adlibs the line, "Say it again with me: shoe tycoon," or announces the chapter title "Oy! My Pa-pa." Written in her mid-fifties, after a tremendous weight gain as well as the death of her father, she shares with the listener, more than in any other creative work, scars earned from some of the most somber and grief-filled emotional journeys of her life.

She had discussed electroconvulsive therapy (ECT) before. The premise for both *Wishful Drinking* and *Shockaholic* is documenting her life in case she loses her memories, a side effect of the treatments. In *Wishful Drinking* the HBO special, she jokes about *One Flew Over the Cuckoo's Nest* (1975), remarking, "Wasn't I fantastic?" But in *Shockaholic* she is more serious about depictions of shock therapy in film, also citing *The Snake Pit* (1948), *Frances* (1982), and *The Changeling* (2008). As a film historian I've seen many more representations of mental illness acted out on-screen that are offensive to modern audiences. Frequently a combination of hysterical behaviors, they were intended to convey only a generalized state of "craziness" rather than realistic symptoms of specific diseases.

The bipolar life gets both easier and more difficult over time. You get better at predicting triggers and implementing self-care. After years of trial and error you discover which medications and dosages work best for you. But perspective always has and always will be a challenge capable of blindsiding you at any time. It often seems like you understand where you are only in retrospect. Carrie refers to this as being both "the archaeologist" and "the pit."[20] You can either keep constant watch over yourself or you can be yourself, but you can't do both at the same time. Often it seems like your life slips up while you're looking in the wrong direction. The "archaeologist" keeps watch over the terrain and is tasked with being the lookout for the clues things are slipping. Like too much sleep, too much spending, too much eating, or too many days in a row without bathing.

For most people, external events affect mood. For the bipolar, both the internal weather system *and* external events affect mood. No amount of planning can prepare for or diminish a response destined to be overpowering. No amount of logic or will can correct the faulty wiring.

From the time I was way too young to be pondering death, I've had a peculiar fear—suicide. This anxiety is the reason George Sanders's death has always especially haunted me. At age sixty-five the actor, singer-songwriter, composer, and author left the following note. "Dear World, I am leaving because I am bored. I feel I have lived long enough. I am leaving you with your worries in this sweet cesspool. Good luck." Reportedly, he had been anticipating this final act since his early thirties.

It is strange to fear a death within my control but it has always been with me. I both fear and respect that at any point Depression could overwhelm and distort my reality. The irreversible hopelessness that leads to suicide is an undeniably possible complication of the bipolar life. In *Shockaholic* Carrie calls this place "the suicidal ideation lounge."[21]

But now some of the greatest weapons I take with me into my future are Carrie's stories. Her gift for telling and her honesty revealed a last resort that I would never have known I had. ECT may in the coming decades turn out to be even more mainstream, safe, and successful. But she demystified the process and was willing to share her participation first. Now I can move through my life with a safety net made of peace of mind. As she said in *Wishful Drinking*, "I like to think of myself as a threshold guardian. There but for the sake of me, go *you!*"[22]

So, you see for me, it's not an exaggeration to say that someday Carrie Fisher may save my life.

In *Wishful Drinking* Carrie tells the story of her birth and of both her parents being in the delivery room. She compares Debbie's beauty to a Christmas morning.[23] When I heard that it made me smile because by then I too had associated Debbie with Christmas for years in my own way.

In the fall of 2006 I was enduring the last months of my first marriage. Steeped in anguish and alienated by my former love, the holidays approached and I was going to be alone for them. One of the small, happy distractions of that year for me had been Dick Powell. June Allyson had died in July and so I had spent some time studying both of their careers. Shortly before Christmas I stumbled upon *Susan Slept Here* (1954).

This movie is as charming as it is strange. Narrated by the Oscar statuette on the fireplace, Debbie is twenty-two playing seventeen while Powell is fifty playing thirty-five. It would be his last feature film as an actor. He would continue to direct and explore television until his death, the second day of 1963. Glenda Farrell, Anne Francis, Alvy Moore, and Maidie Norman round out the primary cast. It is a movie, in small part, about the movie industry, which is one of my favorite subgenres. Debbie plays a juvenile delinquent maturing from a teenager into a wife. She is vivacious and funny, silly but also earnest and likable. The unlikely pairing between her and Powell works because her transformation is believable.

Facing both divorce and my thirties, I needed something more than my childhood tradition of *Rudolph the Red-Nosed Reindeer* (1964). I fell in love with *Susan Slept Here* and watched it on Christmas Day for the next nine years. In December 2016, I was struggling to make it to Christmas break after a stressful year at work. When midway through the month I took a personal day, I broke tradition and watched it early to cheer myself up. I will always be grateful I did.

One of the main reasons I was so taken aback by the news of Carrie's death was because of Debbie's tweet on Christmas Day. It was as if she refused to allow sadness to creep in yet. "Carrie is in stable condition. If there is a change, we will share it. For all her fans & friends. I thank you for your prayers & good wishes." If Debbie knew that wasn't true, I thought a couple days later, Howard Strickling (head of MGM publicity) would have been proud. Christmas in these subsequent years is a little melancholier, and, at least for the time being, I am looking for another tradition that doesn't in any way remind me of Christmas *that* year. Not of the day itself when I thought with such blissful ignorance everything was going to be OK, or the following days when everything happened so quickly and suddenly, nothing was ever going to be the same again.

I was always aware of what *Star Wars* was. My neighbors loved it, my friends loved it—but the trilogy never appealed to me. The more I learned about film history, the less inclined I was to spend my time on cultural juggernauts. It seemed that everyone I knew had only heard of Carrie within the context of this franchise. I couldn't imagine a film role living up to how interesting her actual life was. I remembered there being years of hype around the prequels followed by a lot of disappointment. And the new installments didn't even have the original cast. Finally, when I was in my mid-thirties I watched the original trilogy in one day with a friend who had always loved them. Underwhelmed, I was at least glad to have finally seen them.

I would never have guessed, five years later, how grateful I would be for the global company of millions of grieving Leia fans.

Princess Leia symbolizes, among many things, strength and defiance. But having heard how the role transformed Carrie's life, it was difficult for me to see that character. I still can only see an insecure girl in an invisible catapult, unaware of the life challenges ahead. Unprepared at age nineteen to have "super-attenuated dialed-up sci-fi fame"[24] for a lifetime.

In *Bright Lights*, after a day of "celebrity lap danc[ing]," she explains, "They love her and I'm her custodian and I'm as close as you're gonna get. She's me and I'm her. I mean, they talk to me like I'm Princess Leia, who happens to have had all these difficult experiences to go through, and that's like me fighting for The Force."

In *Wishful Drinking* the HBO special, she jokes about the licensing of her image. She shares a selection of memorabilia that captures the ridiculous extent of *Star Wars'* merchandising. At the time of *Wishful Drinking* and *Shockaholic* her involvement was in the past.

Despite my disinterest in Episodes I–VI, news the original cast was returning for Episode VII intrigued me. I caught the *Good Morning America* episode a couple weeks before the premiere with Carrie (and Gary), enchanted to see her as eccentric and irreverent as ever. With *Star Wars* fans all around me eager to see it, we went to the theater within the first couple days it opened. I had heard the rumors that Harrison Ford wished to be written out and Mark Hamill would not be in it much. It was a film full of youthful characters and new storylines. But the audience's cheers came when the now-General Organa appeared. Later we would learn of the scrutiny she was under to lose and maintain her weight for the role.[25] Perhaps there were a couple injectables employed, intended to smooth a few years of hard-earned wrinkles. But finally, with a regal new hairstyle, she was both Leia and also the sum of a life and its maturity. She looked healthy and absolutely beautiful, with a poise that reminded me of Debbie but was 100 percent her own. OK *Star Wars*, I thought, you win. This is a Leia I can get behind. I'm just here for Space Mom . . . but I'll never leave her.

When I look back, *The Force Awakens* was such a lighthearted experience. (Had I been a Han fan it would not have been.) *The Last Jedi* would be much harder to wait for and sit through on account of the chronic lump in my throat. I found myself looking for General Organa merchandise. Wondering, was stricter control of her image part of her contract negotiation? Or doesn't the marketing department see value in producing ephemera for adults?

In the summer of 2018, director, writer, and producer J. J. Abrams announced, "We desperately loved Carrie Fisher. Finding a truly satisfying conclusion to the Skywalker saga without her eluded us."[26] After much speculation, footage shot for Episode VII was fashioned together to create a brief final appearance. The trailer for *Star Wars IX: The Rise of Skywalker* was released on October 21, 2019—what would have been Carrie's sixty-third birthday. The film was released in December 2019 with Carrie receiving top billing—the only film in the Skywalker Saga to give that honor to a woman.[27]

The *Star Wars* fan community has the venerable saying, "She'll always be royalty to me." Her final line in *The Last Jedi* is "We have everything we need." I hate that this moment means so much to me, manufactured as it is

Fig. 10.3. *Star Wars*: Journey to *The Last Jedi* #92 (2017). Topps® trading card used courtesy of The Topps Company, Inc.

for torrential sentimentality, but it does. It's a transcendent tribute. In those final words Leia and Carrie merge to do what they have always done, one last time—inspire us to be strong.

One year, one month, and one day after her death, Carrie won a Grammy for Best Spoken Word Album for *The Princess Diarist*. Immediately, I thought of the part in *Wishful Drinking* the HBO special, where she uses the line "Having waited my entire life to get an award for something . . ." as a segue into her mental health accolades. Other posthumous honors included an Emmy nomination for Outstanding Guest Actress in *Catastrophe*, and a Dorian Award for Wilde Wit of the Year, both in 2017.

But no addendum to her legacy thus far seems more poignant than the "love letter" her brother Todd wrote to her and their mother, called *My Girls*. It was not the first time Todd had wanted to write a book. Debbie had discouraged him in the past, worried Carrie would be threatened by another author in the family. While this was a terribly unfair veto, I can't help but be grateful that Todd added his voice when he did. Like the missing note of a three-part harmony, he opened up his life and heart in the tradition of his storytelling family. In honor of his profound losses he welcomed those of us who loved them from afar to join him. Finally we heard from the one person who knew how the public responded to and loved his girls. He graciously understood why we could still be so sad. The book's dedication reads, "To all of you who loved my girls as much as I did."[28]

First in the hold queue at my public library, I began listening to *My Girls* a few weeks after its June 5, 2018, release. Hour after delightful hour there were many topics to hear about from Todd's perspective and even more he shared for the first time about his own life. From Stanley the wandering alligator, to observing the technology of filmmaking change over the decades, to Todd's career, to his friends, relationships, and pets.

Suddenly, it seemed, I had caught up to the ending I knew had to eventually come. I was reluctant to relive those December days but figured if Todd had the courage to share it I could sit through it without losing my composure. I had driven to work that Friday morning sensing the ride back would be it. I met my fiancée for dinner but declined our evening plans and steeled myself for the drive home. It had been stormy on and off all day. The type of summer storm that makes the sky very dark in some places while staying sunny in others. I left the restaurant distracted and took a wrong turn it took me twenty minutes to correct, but then I was on my way.

And it was heartbreaking. Over a year and a half later I was finally learning how it all happened and what it was like to be there. I was speeding down the interstate in the sunny light rain, listening to Todd tell this tragic story, and I started crying like it was happening for the first time all over again. Then I came around a curve in the road where there is a valley. Starting from below my sight line and towering beside the interstate was the biggest and most vibrant rainbow I have ever seen in my life. The bands of each and every color were twice as wide and twice as rich as usual. Stunned, I was now speeding down the interstate in the sunny light rain, listening to Todd tell this tragic story, crying, and glancing repeatedly in awe at this wonder that defied my understanding of what a rainbow could be. I have no doubt other passengers on the road at that exact time remember it too—unless I hallucinated it, but I really don't think I did. (That's *not* part of my diagnosis.)[29] Soon after, I arrived home and sat in my car in the driveway until the book was done. Toward the very end Todd says, "Thank you for the joy, appreciation and love you so generously showed them. That inspired and propelled my girls throughout their lives. I can tell you firsthand, from the bottom of my heart, they felt exactly the same way about you." When it was over I felt catharsis.

Ever since that day my sense of loss over these two incredible women is eclipsed by the memory of that exquisite display of light. It is still difficult to not want their contributions to this world that has had to move on without them in it, but they leave tremendous legacies. For many they continue to permeate popular culture, for some their impact remains deeply personal and profoundly singular. These were very real people once and we can continue to love them now as abstractions. Powerful, inspirational, elegant, energetic, beautiful, and brilliant. Everything we ever had of them, we still do and always will.

In *Bright Lights*, we see Debbie struggling to sell an ensemble from her collection with particular sentimental value, right before the auction. As Carrie sits beside her sympathetically, Debbie explains, "I love having my ghosts and I love having my memories. It's like you have a friend forever. Makes me smile when I even just say their name."

Debbie Reynolds. Carrie Fisher. Their influence endures, extending across time to keep us fortified with life and joy whenever we need them. Like a rainbow squared.

Notes

1 The jacket is strikingly similar to if not the exact same one worn in "My Alleged Mother—An Exclusive Interview with Debbie Reynolds," where she speaks to being a concerned and supportive parent to a child living with bipolar. The footage is also reused in part in *Bright Lights: Starring Debbie Reynolds and Carrie Fisher.*

2 Carrie discusses these terms in *Wishful Drinking*. "Well if you have a life like mine, then these experiences gradually accumulate until you become known as '*a survivor*.' This is a term that I loathe. But, the thing is that when you are a survivor, which fine, I reluctantly agree that I am—and who over 40 isn't?—when you are a survivor, in order to be a *really* good one, you have to keep getting in trouble to show off your gift" (Carrie Fisher, *Wishful Drinking* [New York: Simon & Schuster Audio, 2009], 70).

Debbie's role in *The Unsinkable Molly Brown* (1964) cemented her persona of strength and resilience, and the title became synonymous with her for the rest of her life.

3 Wikipedia, "Xennials," https://en.wikipedia.org/wiki/Xennials.

4 Carrie Fisher, *Postcards from the Edge* (Beverly Hills: Phoenix Books, 1988), 108.

5 Fisher, *Wishful Drinking*, 5.

6 *Wishful Drinking*, 8.

7 Carrie Fisher, *Shockaholic* (Prince Frederick: Recorded Books, 2011), 70.

8 Fisher, *Shockaholic*, 66.

9 *Shockaholic*, 59.

10 Fisher, *Wishful Drinking*, 112.

11 Carrie Fisher, *Surrender the Pink* (Studio City: Dove Books on Tape, 1990), 13.

12 Carrie Fisher, *Delusions of Grandma* (New York: Simon & Schuster Audio, 1994), 19.

13 Wikipedia, "Cyclothymia," https://en.wikipedia.org/wiki/Cyclothymia.

14 In Kay Redfield Jamison, *Touched with Fire: Manic-Depressive Illness and the Artistic Temperament* (New York: Free Press Paperbacks, 1993), 34.

15 These terms are discussed in both *Wishful Drinking* and *Shockaholic*.

16 Fisher, *Wishful Drinking*, 21.

17 *Wishful Drinking*, 121.

18 Fisher, *Shockaholic*, 122. She used this phrase to describe a voice mail she revisited from her father after his death.

19 Fisher, *Wishful Drinking* ("Author's Note"), 159. It is also worth mentioning the journey of acceptance and support Debbie went on with Carrie. She spoke of the onset of Carrie's illness in *Unsinkable: A Memoir*. "I'd worked with the Thalians for years, raising millions of dollars for mental health treatment and research—it's ironic that this was my charity. But it didn't occur to me that my daughter might need professional help at that time" (Debbie Reynolds and Dorian Hannaway, *Unsinkable, a Memoir* [New York: Harper Audio, 2013], 131).

20 Fisher, *Shockaholic*, 17.

21 *Shockaholic*, 10.

22 Fisher, *Wishful Drinking*, 157.

23 *Wishful Drinking*, 30.

24 Fisher, *Shockaholic*, 99.

25 This is referenced in *The Princess Diarist* and shown in *Bright Lights: Starring Debbie Reynolds and Carrie Fisher*.

26 "Star Wars: Episode IX announces its cast—which includes Carrie Fisher," Vox.com.

27 *Star Wars: Episode IX—The Rise of Skywalker* (2019), IMDb Trivia.

28 Todd Fisher, *My Girls* (New York: Harper Collins, 2018), v.

29 This is a callback to *Wishful Drinking*, 127, when Carrie was remembering being given a list of other sufferers of bipolar in recent history. "Naturally, after this list I felt *invigorated!* . . . but then that *is* part of my diagnosis." She gives it an especially funny delivery in the audiobook.

Appendix 1:

What Would Carrie Fisher Do?

Lindsay van Ekelenburg

I t was a question I would often ask myself in times of personal struggle. In the fall of 2017, a year after Carrie's death, I found myself awake in bed in the wee hours, caught in such a moment. Unable to sleep and completely overwhelmed by a number of difficult decisions looming over me, I asked myself aloud, "What Would Carrie Fisher Do?" I had recently been laid off from my day job working at a local art college, without any certainty when or if I might return. Every day I dipped into my meager savings to pay my bills while my anxiety and depression crept in, wrapping their dark tendrils around me and weighing me down with whispers of my fears and doubts: "how long can you go on like this?" "if you were destined to be a successful artist you should have made it by now," and "maybe you should just give up on being an artist and settle for some sort of desk job."

All my life I have struggled with the demons of anxiety and depression—demons that could easily overwhelm and limit me. In times of struggle and uncertainty, they are louder and even harder to face down. One reason Carrie Fisher mattered so much to me was how well she articulated this experience of struggling with mental health, and how she showed us that these struggles do not need to define or control you.

So instead of giving up, I threw glitter on those dark demons, just like Space Mom taught me.

Four weeks into my unemployment, sitting in my bed at three in the morning, watching Carrie sit in her fantastically cluttered set on *Wishful Drinking* and talking so honestly about her life, I began sketching out a picture, a tribute, a portrait of this woman I adored. A woman who faced so much adversity, who struggled with mental health, with the hardships the world dealt her. A wonderful, real, flawed human continued to bring wonderful, visceral creations to the world, filled with compassion and wit. Carrie is a badass who always gave me great strength and comfort to face my demons and say, "Fuck off."

I painted *Blessed Rebel Queen* in an attempt to process the grief I still felt over her loss, to say thank you to her memory, and to express thanks for how she so frankly faced the world and talked about her struggles and reminded us over and over again that we had to love ourselves and keep trying.

When I finished the painting, I shared it on my Facebook page as usual. At the time, I had only just over one hundred followers, composed largely of friends and family. Something magical happened on that November evening: within seconds of posting I saw the number of likes jump to ten. Minutes later, fifty likes. In an hour the number was in the hundreds. I was completely overwhelmed watching the engagements rise in real time, not fully believing what I was seeing unfold. At seven hundred likes and shares, it was time for bed, and I slept half expecting to wake up and find that it had been a dream—nothing I had ever created had seven hundred likes! It felt preposterous.

The next morning, I was almost nervous to look at my phone. When I finally summoned the nerve to check on my Facebook, to my astonishment I was met with the news that my art page now had thousands of new followers and thousands of shares. Viral success is a very strange experience and one I was wholly unprepared for. Given the success of the piece, it is almost funny to look back on those few days. The truth is that I really never expected the portrait to take on its own life. It was a piece that I made for myself, an extremely personal expression of gratitude to a woman whose influence on my life was enormous and whose legacy was to empower women like myself, encourage us to not give up or give in to our darkness, to live and create beauty despite the weight of our struggles.

Years later, it still overwhelms me to think that so many people have found that my painting speaks to them, and that so many have been touched by its tribute to the memory and legacy of this incredible woman. It is an honor to know that so many have been inspired by this piece as I was inspired by Carrie's life, that they look at *Blessed Rebel Queen*, remember Space Mom, and feel comfort. I still receive so many beautiful messages from people who were touched by her, thanking me for this painting and wanting to share with me the way she touched their lives as her legacy touched mine. I am always overwhelmed and always so grateful.

Carrie Fisher's life affected so many people, but she quite literally gave me a new start to life. It was her legacy that encouraged me to summon the will to create this piece of art, and its unexpected, incredible success has given me a renewed enthusiasm and opened doors for me, helping me to move forward and chase this dream of being an artist.

The original painting holds a place of prestige in my studio space: in the center of everything the *Blessed Rebel Queen* watches over my work, flipping the bird as a reminder to my demons that they are not in control and they can shut up and take a back seat. It's time to live and move forward.

Appendix 2:
Carrie Fisher Media Work, Appearances, and Fanworks

Maghan Jackson

Filmography

Debbie Reynolds and the Sound of Children. Television Film. Directed by Marc Breaux. Written by Dorothy Kingsley. New York: NBC, November 6, 1969. (Girl Scout)

Shampoo. Film. Directed by Hal Ashby. Written by Robert Towne and Warren Beatty. Culver City: Columbia Pictures, 1975. (Lorna Karpf)

Star Wars: Episode IV—A New Hope. Film. Written and directed by George Lucas. Los Angeles: Twentieth Century Fox, 1977. (Princess Leia Organa)

Come Back, Little Sheba. Television Film. Directed by Silvio Narizzano. Written by William Inge. New York: NBC, December 31, 1977. (Marie)

Ringo. Television Film. Directed by Jeff Margolis. Written by Neal Israel and Pat Proft. New York: NBC, April 26, 1978.

Leave Yesterday Behind. Television Film. Directed by Richard Michaels. Written by Paul Harrison. Burbank: ABC, May 14, 1978. (Marnie Clarkson)

The Star Wars Holiday Special. Television Film. Directed by Steve Binder and David Acomba (uncredited). Written by Rod Warren et al. New York: CBS, November 17, 1978. (Princess Leia Organa)

Star Wars: Episode V—The Empire Strikes Back. Film. Directed by Irvin Kershner. Written by Leigh Brackett and Lawrence Kasdan. Los Angeles: Twentieth Century Fox, 1980. (Princess Leia Organa)

The Blues Brothers. Film. Directed by John Landis. Written by Dan Aykroyd and John Landis. Universal City: Universal Pictures, 1980. (Mystery Woman)

Under the Rainbow. Film. Directed by Steven Rash. Written by Fed Bauer et al. Burbank: Warner Bros. Studios, 1981. (Annie Clark)

Star Wars: Episode VI—Return of the Jedi. Film. Directed by Richard Marquand. Written by George Lucas and Lawrence Kasdan. Los Angeles: Twentieth Century Fox, 1983. (Princess Leia Organa)

Garbo Talks. Film. Directed by Sidney Lumet. Written by Larry Grusin. Beverly Hills: MGM/UA Entertainment, 1984. (Lisa Rolfe)

Frankenstein. Television Film. Directed by James Ormerod. Written by Victor Gialanella. New York: Showtime Networks, December 27, 1984. (Elizabeth)

The Man with One Red Shoe. Film. Directed by Stan Dragoti. Written by Robert Klane. Los Angeles: Twentieth Century Fox, 1985. (Paula)

From Here to Maternity. Television Film. Directed by Tom Schiller. Written by Maryedith Burrell. Distribution Unknown. 1985. (Veronica)

Hannah and Her Sisters. Film. Written and directed by Woody Allen. Los Angeles: Orion Pictures, 1986. (April)

Hollywood Vice Squad. Film. Directed by Penelope Spheeris. Written by James J. Docherty. Los Angeles: Concorde Pictures, 1986. (Betty Melton)

Liberty. Television Film. Directed by Richard C. Sarafian. Written by Pete Hamill. New York: NBC, June 23, 1986. (Emma Lazarus)

"Reckless Youth." *Amazon Women on the Moon*. Film. Directed by Joe Dante. Written by Michael Barrie and Jim Mulholland. Universal City: Universal Pictures, 1987. (Mary Brown)

The Time Guardian. Film. Directed by Brian Hannant. Written by John Baxter and Brian Hannant. Los Angeles: Hemdale Film Corporation, 1987. (Petra)

Appointment with Death. Film. Directed by Michael Winner. Written by Michael Winner et al. Los Angeles: Cannon Film Distributors, 1988. (Nadine Boynton)

The 'Burbs. Film. Directed by Joe Dante. Written by Dana Olsen. Universal City: Universal Pictures, 1989. (Carol Peterson)

Loverboy. Film. Directed by Joan Micklin Silver. Written by Robin Schiff. Culver City: TriStar Pictures, 1989. (Monica Delancy/Pizza Customer)

She's Back. Film. Directed by Tim Kincaid. Written by Buddy Giovinazzo. Los Angeles: Image Entertainment, 1989. (Beatrice)

When Harry Met Sally . . . Film. Directed by Rob Reiner. Written by Nora Ephron. Culver City: Columbia Pictures, 1989. (Marie)

Sibling Rivalry. Film. Directed by Carl Reiner. Written by Martha Goldhirsh. Culver City: Columbia Pictures, 1990. (Iris Turner-Hunter)

Sweet Revenge. Television Film. Directed by Charlotte Brandstrom. Written by Janet Brownell. Atlanta: TNT, July 9, 1990. (Linda)

Drop Dead Fred. Film. Directed by Ate de Jong. Written by Carlos Davis and Anthony Fingleton. Burbank: New Line Cinema, 1991. (Janie)

Soapdish. Film. Directed by Michael Hoffman. Written by Robert Harling and Andrew Bergman. Hollywood: Paramount Pictures, 1991. (Betsy Faye Sharon)

Hook. Film. Directed by Steven Spielberg. Written by Jim V. Hart and Malia Scotch Marmo. Culver City: TriStar Pictures, 1991. (Woman kissing on bridge—uncredited)

This Is My Life. Film. Directed by Nora Ephron. Written by Nora Ephron and Delia Ephron. Los Angeles: Twentieth Century Fox, 1992. (Claudia Curtis)

Present Tense, Past Perfect. Television Film. Directed by Richard Dreyfuss. Written by Richard Dreyfuss and Kristi Kane. New York: Showtime Networks, 1995. (Unnamed character)

Austin Powers: International Man of Mystery. Film. Directed by Jay Roach. Written by Mike Meyers. Burbank: New Line Cinema, 1997. (Therapist—uncredited)

Scream 3. Film. Directed by Wes Craven. Written by Ehren Kruger. New York: Dimension Films, 2000. (Bianca)

Lisa Picard Is Famous. Film. Directed by Griffin Dunne. Written by Nat DeWolf and Laura Kirk. Century City: First Look International, 2000. (Carrie Fisher—cameo)

Heartbreakers. Film. Directed by David Mirkin. Written by Robert Dunn et al. Beverly Hills: MGM/UA Entertainment, 2001. (Ms. Surpin)

Jay and Silent Bob Strike Back. Film. Written and directed by Kevin Smith. Los Angeles: Miramax, 2001. (Nun)

These Old Broads. Television Film. Directed by Matthew Diamond. Written by Carrie Fisher and Elaine Pope. Burbank: ABC, February 12, 2001. (Hooker)

A Midsummer Night's Rave. Film. Directed by Gil Cates Jr. Written by Robert Raymond. Los Angeles: Velocity Home Entertainment, 2002. (Mia's Mom)

Charlie's Angels: Full Throttle. Film. Directed by McG. Written by John August et al. Culver City: Sony Pictures, 2003. (Mother Superior)

Wonderland. Film. Directed by James Cox. Written by James Cox et al. Santa Monica: Lionsgate, 2003. (Sally Hansen)

Stateside. Film. Directed by Reverge Anselmo. Written by Reverge Anselmo. Culver City: Samuel Goldwyn Films, 2004. (Mrs. Dubois)

Undiscovered. Film. Directed by Meiert Avis. Written by John Galt. Santa Monica: Lionsgate, 2005. (Carrie)

Romancing the Bride. Television Film. Directed by Kris Isacsson. Written by Kris Isacsson. New York: Oxygen Media, December 3, 2005. (Edwina)

Friendly Fire. Film/Album. Directed by Michele Civetta. Written by Sean Lennon and Michele Civetta. Los Angeles: Capitol Records, 2006. (Chanteuse)

Suffering Man's Charity. Film. Directed by Alan Cumming. Written by Thomas Gallagher. Los Angeles: Genius, 2007. (Reporter)

Cougar Club. Film. Directed by Christopher Duddy. Written by Cris Mancusco. Universal City: Vivendi Entertainment, 2008. (Glady Goodbey)

The Women. Film. Written and directed by Diane English. Burbank: Warner Bros. Pictures, 2008. (Bailey Smith)

White Lightnin'. Film. Directed by Dominic Murphy. Written by Eddy Moretti and Shane Smith. Toronto: Momentum Pictures, 2009. (Cilla)

Fanboys. Film. Directed by Kyle Newman. Written by Ernest Cline and Adam F. Goldberg. Universal City: Vivendi Entertainment, 2009. (Doctor)

Sorority Row. Film. Directed by Stewart Hendler. Written by Josh Stolberg and Pete Goldfinger. Universal City: Summit Entertainment, 2009. (Mrs. Crenshaw)

Wright vs. Wrong. Television Film. Directed by Andy Fickman. Written by Stephnie Weir. Burbank: ABC, 2010. (Joan Harrington)

It's Christmas, Carol! Television Film. Directed by Michael M. Scott. Written by William Penick and Christopher Sey. Studio City: Hallmark Channel, November 18, 2012. (Eve)

Maps to the Stars. Film. Directed by David Cronenberg. Written by Bruce Wagner. Universal City: Focus Features, 2014. (Carrie Fisher—cameo)

Star Wars: Episode VII—The Force Awakens. Film. Directed by J. J. Abrams. Written by Lawrence Kasdan et al. Burbank: Walt Disney Studios Motion Pictures, 2015. (General Leia Organa)

Star Wars: Episode VII—The Last Jedi. Film. Written and directed by Rian Johnson. Burbank: Walt Disney Studios Motion Pictures, 2017. (General Leia Organa)

Wonderwell. Film. Directed by Vlad Marsavin. Written by William Brookfield. Distribution TBD. (Hazel)

Television Appearances

Captain Kangaroo. "Episode dated December 1, 1977." Written by Bob Keeshan et al. CBS, December 1, 1977. (Herself—Guest)

Saturday Night Live. "The Rolling Stones." Episode 4.1. Directed by Dave Wilson et al. Written by Dan Aykroyd et al. NBC, October 7, 1978. (Herself— Uncredited)

———. "Carrie Fisher/The Blues Brothers." Episode 4.6. Directed by Dave Wilson et al. Written by Dan Aykroyd et al. NBC, November 18, 1978. (Herself—Host)

———. "Paul Simon, James Taylor & David Sanborn." Episode 5.14. Directed by Dave Wilson. Written by Dan Aykroyd et al. NBC, March 15, 1980. (Leprechaun—Uncredited)

Laverne and Shirley. "The Playboy Show." Episode 8.5. Directed by Michael McKean. Written by Ed Solomon. ABC, November 9, 1982. (Cathy)

Faerie Tale Theatre. "Thumbelina." Episode 3.4. Directed by Michael Lindsay-Hogg. Written by Maryedith Burrell. Showtime, June 11, 1984. (Thumbelina)

The Magical World of Disney. "Sunday Drive." Episode 31.9. Directed by Mark Cullingham. Written by Larry Brand. ABC, November 30, 1986. (Franny Jessup)

Amazing Stories. "Gershwin's Trunk." Episode 2.17. Directed by Paul Bartel. Written by John Meyer and Paul Bartel. NBC, March 13, 1987. (Laurie McNamara—Uncredited)

Trying Times. "Hunger Chic." Episode 2.1. Directed by Buck Henry. Written by George C. Wolfe. PBS, October 12, 1989. (Enid)

Ellen. Episode 3.9. "The Movie Show." Directed by Robby Benson. Written by Tracy Newman and Jonathan Stark. ABC, November 22, 1995. (Herself)

Gun. "The Hole." Episode 1.5. Directed by Ted Demme. Written by James Steven Sadwith. ABC, May 24, 1997. (Nancy)

It's Like, You Know. "Arthur 2: On the Rocks." Episode 2.5. Directed by John Fortenberry. Written by Richard Doctorow. ABC, October 19, 1999. (Carrie Fisher)

Sex and the City. "Sex and Another City." Episode 3.14. Directed by John David Coles. Written by Jenny Bicks. HBO, September 17, 2000. (Carrie Fisher)

A Nero Wolfe Mystery. "Motherhunt: Part 1." Episode 2.6. Directed by Alan Smithee. Written by Sharon Elizabeth Doyle. A&E Networks, May 12, 2002. (Ellen Tenzer)

———. "Motherhunt: Part 2." Episode 2.7. Directed by Alan Smithee. Written by Sharon Elizabeth Doyle. A&E Networks, May 19, 2002. (Ellen Tenzer)

Good Morning, Miami. "A Kiss before Lying." Episode 2.7. Directed by Steve Zuckerman. Written by Bill Prady. NBC, November 18, 2003. (Judy Silver)

Jack and Bobby. "The First Lady." Episode 1.5. Directed by David Petrarca. Written by Jonathan Lisco. The WB Television Network, October 10, 2004. (Madison Skutcher)

Smallville. "Thirst." Episode 5.5. Directed by Paul Shapiro. Written by Steven S. DeKnight. The WB Television Network, October 27, 2005. (Pauline Kahn)

Weeds. "The Brick Dance." Episode 3.3. Directed by Lev L. Spiro. Written by Roberto Benabib et al. Showtime, August 27, 2007. (Arlene Cutter)

Side Order of Life. "Funeral for a Phone." Episode 1.13. Directed by Ron Lagomarsino. Written by Margaret Nagle. Warner Horizon Television, October 7, 2007. (Dr. Gilbert)

30 Rock. "Rosemary's Baby." Episode 2.4. Directed by Michael Engler. Written by Jack Burditt. NBC, October 25, 2007. (Rosemary Howard)

Entourage. "Tequila and Coke." Episode 7.7. Directed by David Nutter. Written by Doug Ellin and Ally Musika. HBO, August 15, 2010. (Anna Fowler)

The Big Bang Theory. "The Convention Conundrum." Episode 7.14. Directed by Mark Cendrowski. Written by Steven Molaro et al. CBS, January 30, 2014. (Carrie Fisher)

Legit. "Licked." Episode 2.9. Directed by Peter O'Fallon. Written by Peter O'Fallon et al. FX Network, April 24, 2014. (Angela McKinnon)

Girlfriends' Guide to Divorce. "Rule #23: Never Lie to the Kids." Episode 1.1. Directed by Adam Brooks. Written by Marti Noxon. Bravo, December 2, 2014. (Cat)

——. "Rule #25: Beware the Second Chance." Episode 2.6. Directed by J. Miller Tobin. Written by Ilene Rosenzweig. Bravo, January 5, 2016.

The Keith Lemon Sketch Show. "Episode #1.1." Episode 1.1. Directed by Jamie Deeks et al. Written by Leigh Francis et al. ITV2, February 5, 2015. (Princess Leia)

——. "Episode #1.3." Episode 1.3. Directed by Jamie Deeks et al. Written by Leigh Francis et al. ITV2, February 19, 2015. (Princess Leia)

Catastrophe. "Episode #1.2." Episode 1.2. Directed by Ben Taylor. Written by Rob Delaney and Sharon Horgan. Channel 4, June 19, 2015. (Mia)

——. "Episode #1.5." Episode 1.5. Directed by Ben Taylor. Written by Rob Delaney and Sharon Horgan. Channel 4, June 19, 2015. (Mia)

——. "Episode #2.1." Episode 2.1. Directed by Ben Taylor. Written by Rob Delaney and Sharon Horgan. Channel 4, April 8, 2016. (Mia)

——. "Episode #2.6." Episode 2.6. Directed by Ben Taylor. Written by Rob Delaney and Sharon Horgan. Channel 4, April 8, 2016. (Mia)

———. "Episode #3.6." Episode 3.6. Directed by Ben Taylor. Written by Rob Delaney and Sharon Horgan. Channel 4, April 28, 2017. (Mia)

Voice Work

Happily Ever After. Television Movie. Directed by Bill Melendez. Written by Bill Scott. Arlington: Public Broadcasting System, 1985. (Alice Conway—Voice)

Two Daddies? Television Movie. Directed by Bill Melendez. Written by Ron Friedman et al. Arlington: Public Broadcasting System, 1989. (Alice Conway—Voice)

Frasier. "She's the Boss." 3.1. Directed by Philip Charles MacKenzie. Written by Chuck Ranberg and Anne Flett-Giordano. NBC, September 19, 1995. (Phyllis—Voice)

Dr. Katz, Professional Therapist. "Thanksgiving." 5.18. Written by Carl W. Adams et al. Comedy Central, November 23, 1998. (Roz Katz—Voice)

Family Guy. "Jungle Love." Episode 4.13. Directed by Seth Kearsley and Peter Shin. Written by Mark Hentemann et al. Fox Network, September 25, 2005. (Angela—Voice)

———. "The Courtship of Stewie's Father." Episode 4.16. Directed by Kurt Dumas et al. Written by Kirker Butler. Fox Network, November 20, 2005. (Angela)

———. "Hell Comes to Quahog." Episode 5.3. Directed by Dan Povenmire et al. Written by Kirker Butler. Fox Network, September 24, 2006. (Angela)

———. "Whistle While Your Wife Works." Episode 5.5. Directed by Greg Colton et al. Written by Steve Callaghan. Fox Network, November 12, 2006. (Angela)

———. "It Takes a Village Idiot, and I Married One." Episode 5.17. Directed by Zac Moncrief et al. Written by Alex Borstein. Fox Network, May 13, 2007. (Angela)

———. "Padre de Familia." Episode 6.6. Directed by Pete Michels et al. Written by Kirker Butler. Fox Network, November 18, 2007. (Angela)

———. "Tales of a Third Grade Nothing." Episode 7.6. Directed by Jerry Langford et al. Written by Alex Carter. Fox Network, November 16, 2008. (Angela)

———. "Peter-assment." Episode 8.14. Directed by Julius Wu et al. Written by Chris Sheridan. Fox Network, March 21, 2010. (Angela)

———. "Baby, You Knock Me Out." Episode 9.5. Directed by Julius Wu et al. Written by Alex Carter. Fox Network, November 14, 2010. (Angela)

———. "Road to the North Pole." Episode 9.7. Directed by Greg Colton et al. Written by Chris Sheridan and Danny Smith. Fox Network, December 12, 2010. (Angela)

———. "Friends of Peter G." Episode 9.10. Directed by John Holmquist et al. Written by Brian Scully. Fox Network, February 13, 2011. (Angela)

———. "Episode VI: It's a Trap." Episode 9.18. Directed by Peter Shin et al. Written by Cherry Chevapravatdumrong and David A. Goodman. Fox Network, May 22, 2011. (Angela as Mon Mothma)

———. "Trading Places." Episode 9.13. Directed by Joseph Lee et al. Written by Steve Callaghan. Fox Network, March 20, 2011. (Angela)

———. "The Blind Side." Episode 10.11. Directed by Bob Bowen et al. Written by Cherry Chevapravatdumrong. Fox Network, January 15, 2012. (Angela)

———. "Vestigial Peter." Episode 12.2. Directed by Julius Wu et al. Written by Brian Scully. Fox Network, October 6, 2013. (Angela)

———. "Into Harmony's Way." Episode 12.7. Directed by Brian Iles et al. Written by Julius Sharpe. Fox Network, December 8, 2013. (Angela)

———. "Peter Problems." Episode 12.9. Directed by Bob Bowen et al. Written by Teresa Hsiao. Fox Network, January 5, 2014. (Angela)

———. "Mom's the Word." Episode 12.12. Directed by John Holmquist et al. Written by Ted Jessup. Fox Network, March 9, 2014. (Angela)

———. "Secondhand Spoke." Episode 12.15. Directed by Julius Wu et al. Written by Dave Ihenfeld and David Wright. Fox Network, March 30, 2014. (Angela)

———. "The Most Interesting Man in the World." Episode 12.17. Directed by Joseph Lee et al. Written by Tom Devanney. April 13, 2014. (Angela)

———. "Candy, Quahog Marshmallow." Episode 14.10. Directed by Joseph Lee et al. Written by Cherry Chevapravatdumrong. Fox Network, January 3, 2016. (Angela)

———. "Carter and Tricia." Episode 15.8. Directed by Mike Kim et al. Written by Patrick Meighan. Fox Network, December 4, 2016. (Angela)

———. "Peter's Lost Youth." Episode 15.17. Directed by Julius Wu et al. Written by Danny Smith. Fox Network, March 26, 2017. (Angela)

———. "Three Directors." Episode 16.5. Directed by Joe Vaux et al. Written by Travis Bowe. Fox Network, November 5, 2017. (Angela)

———. "Don't Be a Dickens at Christmas." Episode 16.9. Directed by Jerry Langford et al. Written by Danny Smith. Fox Network, December 10, 2017. (Angela)

Odd Job Jack. "The Beauty Beast." Episode 4.6. Directed by Adrian Carter. Written by Jeremy Diamond and Tim Polley. CTV, August 26, 2007. (Dr. Finch—Voice)

Robot Chicken. "Star Wars: Episode II." Television Short. Directed by Seth Green. Written by Douglas Goldstein et al. Adult Swim, November 16, 2008. (Princess Leia Organa / Mon Mothma / Krayt Dragon's Mother—Voice)

A Child's Garden of Poetry. Television Movie. Directed by Amy Schatz. HBO,
    April 28, 2011. (Herself—Voice)

Dishonored. Video Game. Directed by Raphael Colantonio and Harvey Smith.
    Written by Terri Brosius et al. Rockville: Bethesda Softworks, 2012. (Alternate
    Street Speaker—Voice)

Family Guy: The Quest for Stuff. Video Game. Written by Steve Callaghan et al. Los
    Angeles: Fox Digital Entertainment, 2014. (Angela—Voice)

Lego Star Wars: The Force Awakens. Video Game. Directed by Hez Chorba et al.
    Written by Graham Goring. Burbank: Warner Bros. Interactive Entertainment,
    2016. (Leia Organa—Voice)

Appearances as Herself

The Mike Douglas Show. Variety Show. Episode 16.208. Westinghouse Broadcast-
    ing, July 20, 1977. (Herself—Guest)

Spécial Cinéma. Talk Show. Written by Christian Defaye and Christian Zeender.
    Radio Télévision Suisse, September 20, 1977. (Herself—Guest)

Today. Talk Show. NBC, July 8, 1977. (Herself—Guest)

———. NBC, July 11, 1977. (Herself—Guest)

———. NBC, January 26, 2012. (Herself—Guest Coanchor)

———. NBC, December 14, 2015. (Herself—Guest)

———. NBC, November 21, 2016. (Herself—Guest)

Dinah! Daytime Talk Show. NBC, July 13, 1977. (Herself—Guest)

———. NBC, October 10, 1977. (Herself—Guest)

Revista de Cine. Talk Show. Directed by Alfonso Eduardo. TVE, October 17, 1977.
    (Herself—Guest)

The 20th Annual Grammy Awards. Television Special. Directed by Marty
    Pasetta. Written by Bob Arnott. CBS, February 23, 1978. (Herself)

Mr. Mike's Mondo Video. Television Special. Directed by Michael O'Donoghue.
    Written by Michael O'Donoghue et al. New Line Cinema, September 21, 1979.
    (Herself)

The New Show. Sketch Comedy Show. Episode 1.2. Directed by Heino Ripp. Writ-
    ten by Valri Bromfield et al. NBC, January 13, 1984. (Herself—Guest)

Late Night with David Letterman. Late Night Talk Show. NBC, May 30, 1983.
    (Herself—Guest)

———. NBC, August 27, 1987. (Herself—Guest)

———. NBC, December 13, 1988. (Herself—Guest)

———. NBC, September 6, 1990. (Herself—Guest)

The Tonight Show with Johnny Carson. Late Night Talk Show. Episode 22.100. NBC, July 29, 1983. (Herself—Guest)

———. Episode #23.153. NBC, October 16, 1984. (Herself—Guest)

———. Episode #25.36. NBC, March 3, 1986. (Herself—Guest)

———. Episode #26.16. NBC, January 29, 1987. (Herself—Guest)

———. Episode #26.121. NBC, September 11, 1987. (Herself—Guest)

George Burns Comedy Week. Episode 1.5. "The Couch." Directed by Steve Martin. Written by Pamela Pettler and Ed Scharlach. CBS, October 16, 1985. (Herself)

The Film Society of Lincoln Center Gala Tribute to Alec Guinness. Television Special. NBC, April 28, 1987. (Herself—Speaker)

Paul Reiser: Out on a Whim. Television Special. Directed by Carl Gottlieb. Written by Paul Reiser, Peter Farrelly, Bennett Yellin. HBO, May 12, 1987. (Herself)

Hour Magazine. Talk Show. CBS, September 7, 1987. (Herself—Guest)

The Last Resort with Jonathan Ross. Talk Show. Episode 2.5. Written by Lise Mayer. Channel X, October 16, 1987. (Herself—Guest)

The 3rd Annual Mr. Abbot Awards. Television Special. NBC, November 16, 1987. (Herself)

Good Morning America. ABC, April 15, 1988. (Herself—Guest)

———. ABC, December 4, 2015. (Herself—Guest)

The 61st Annual Academy Awards. Television Special. Directed by Jeff Margolis. ABC, March 29, 1989. (Herself—Presenter)

The American Cinematheque Honors Ron Howard. Television Special. The American Cinematheque, March 24, 1990. (Herself)

Movie Memories with Debbie Reynolds. Film Retrospective Series. Directed by Todd Fisher. AMC, 1991. (Herself)

Showbiz Today. News. HLN, September 13, 1991. (Herself)

———. HLN, April 5, 1994. (Herself)

———. HLN, December 2, 1996. (Herself)

The Movie Awards. Television Special. Directed by Marty Pasetta. La Quinta: Pasetta Productions, 1991. (Herself—Presenter)

Saturday Night Clive. Talk Show. Episode #4.3. BBC, October 5, 1991. (Herself—Guest)

The Late Show with David Letterman. Talk Show. CBS, April 5, 1994. (Herself—Guest)

———. Episode #17.51. CBS, November 24, 2009. (Herself—Guest)

Late Night with Conan O'Brien. Talk Show. Episode #1.144. Directed by Dana
    Calderwood and J. J. Sedelmaier. Written by Robert Smigel et al. NBC, April 7,
    1994. (Herself—Guest)

———. Episode #17.27. Directed by Alan Kartun. Written by Mike Sweeney
    et al. NBC, February 17, 2009. (Herself—Guest)

———. Episode #17.31. Directed by Alan Kartun. Written by Mike Sweeney et al.
    NBC, February 18, 2009. (Herself—Guest)

The Tonight Show with Jay Leno. Talk Show. Episode #3.62. NBC, April 12, 1994.
    (Herself—Guest)

———. Episode #5.8. NBC, January 10, 1997. (Herself—Guest)

———. Episode #6.112. NBC, June 24, 1998. (Herself—Guest)

Clive Anderson Talks Back. Talk Show. Episode #9.12. Channel 4, December 2,
    1994. (Herself—Guest)

The Annual Artist Rights Foundation Honors Steven Spielberg. Television
    Special. Directed by Peter R. J. Deyell. NBC, April 28, 1995. (Herself)

Dennis Miller Live. Talk Show. Episode #2.25. "The O. J. Simpson Trial."
    Directed by Debbie Palacio. Written by Jeff Cesario et al. HBO, June 30, 1995.
    (Herself)

The Little Picture Show. Talk Show. Directed by Rufus Roubiceck. ITV, Novem-
    ber 2, 1995. (Herself—Guest)

Very Important Pennis. Comedy Special. "Very Important Pennis: Part 2."
    Written by Anthony Hines and Paul Kaye. BBC, August 16, 1996. (Herself)

Very Important Pennis: Uncut. Video Release. 1996. (Herself)

The 3rd Annual Women in Hollywood Awards. Television Special. NBC, Decem-
    ber 2, 1996. (Herself)

Comic Relief's American Comedy Festival. Television Special. Directed by Walter C.
    Miller. Written by John Davies. ABC, 1996. (Herself)

The 11th Annual American Comedy Awards. Television Special. NBC, February 17,
    1997. (Herself—Presenter)

The Rosie O'Donnell Show. Talk Show. Warner Bros. Television, February 20, 1997.
    (Herself—Guest)

The 69th Annual Academy Awards. Television Special. Directed by Louis J. Horvitz
    and Shanda Sawyer. ABC, March 24, 1997. (Herself)

Ruby. Talk Show. Episode #1.4. BBC Two, May 19, 1997. (Herself—Guest)

———. Episode #1.5. BBC Two, May 20, 1997. (Herself—Guest)

———. Episode #1.6. BBC Two, May 21, 1997. (Herself—Guest)

———. Episode #2.6. BBC Two, July 15, 1998. (Herself—Guest)

———. Episode #2.7. BBC Two, July 20, 1998. (Herself—Guest)

———. Episode #2.12. BBC Two, July 29, 1998. (Herself—Guest)

———. Episode #3.2. BBC Two, September 14, 1999. (Herself—Guest)

1997 MTV Movie Awards. Television Special. Directed by Bruce Gowers and Troy Miller. Written by Gary Campbell and Will Forte. MTV, June 10, 1997. (Presenter—Lifetime Achievement Award)

So Graham Norton. Talk Show. Episode #3.4. Directed by Steve Smith. Written by Kevin Anderson et al. Channel 4, December 10, 1999. (Herself—Guest)

———. Episode #4.8. Channel 4, December 22, 2000. (Herself—Guest)

The Best of So Graham Norton. Compilation. 2004. (Herself—Guest)

AFI Life Achievement Award: A Tribute to Harrison Ford. Television Special. Directed by Bruce Gowers. Written by Buz Kohan and George Schlatter. CBS, 2000. (Herself—Presenter)

AFI's 100 Years . . . 100 Passions: America's Greatest Love Stories. Television Special. Directed by Gary Smith. Written by Bob Gazzale. CBS, June 11, 2002. (Herself)

Dinner for Five. Talk Show. Episode #2.4. IFC, February 10, 2003. (Herself—Special Guest)

———. Episode #3.8. IFC, May 28, 2004. (Herself—Special Guest)

Celebrity Poker Showdown. Television Series. "Tournament 1, Game 5." Bravo, January 6, 2004. (Herself—Player)

The O'Reilly Factor. Talk Show. Fox News, January 22, 2004. (Herself—Guest)

Today with Des and Mel. Talk Show. ITV, February 19, 2004. (Herself—Guest)

T4. Talk Show. Channel 4, February 20, 2004. (Herself—Guest)

AFI Life Achievement Award: A Tribute to Meryl Streep. Television Special. Directed by Louis J. Horvitz. Written by Bob Gazzale. CBS, June 21, 2004. (Herself)

Conversations from the Edge with Carrie Fisher. Talk Show. "Lisa Kudrow." Oxygen, August 18, 2002. (Herself—Host)

———. "Diane Sawyer." Oxygen, September 8, 2002. (Herself—Host)

———. "Debbie Reynolds." Oxygen, May 11, 2003. (Herself—Host)

———. "Sharon Stone." Oxygen, July 22, 2004. (Herself—Host)

GMTV. Talk Show. ITV, September 17, 2004. (Herself—Guest)

The Aristocrats (documentary). Directed by Penn Jillette and Paul Provenza. 2005. (Herself)

The Tony Danza Show. Talk Show. Episode #1.78. NBC, January 11, 2005. (Herself—Guest)

The Early Show. Talk Show. CBS, January 11, 2005. (Herself—Guest)

Tavis Smiley. Talk Show. Directed by Jonathan X. PBS, March 9, 2005. (Herself—Guest)

AFI Life Achievement Award: A Tribute to George Lucas. Television Special. Directed by Louis J. Horvitz. Written by Bob Gazzale. CBS, June 20, 2005. (Herself—Presenter)

The Late Show with Craig Ferguson. Talk Show. Episode #1.140. Directed by Brian McAloon. Written by Hugh Fink et al. CBS, August 25, 2005. (Herself—Guest)

———. Episode #2.124. CBS, April 11, 2006. (Herself—Guest)

———. Episode #3.32. CBS, October 31, 2006. (Herself—Guest)

———. Episode #4.75. CBS, May 22, 2007. (Herself—Guest)

———. Episode #5.69. CBS, December 12, 2008. (Herself—Guest)

———. Episode #6.4. CBS, September 3, 2009. (Herself—Guest)

———. Episode #6.95. CBS, February 9, 2010. (Herself—Guest)

———. Episode #6.199. CBS, July 28, 2010. (Herself—Guest)

———. Episode #7.64. CBS, December 7, 2010. (Herself—Guest)

———. Episode #7.166. CBS, May 20, 2011. (Herself—Guest)

———. Episode #8.96. CBS, January 3, 2012. (Herself—Guest)

———. Episode #8.240. CBS, May 31, 2012. (Herself—Guest)

———. Episode #9.10. CBS, January 18, 2013. (Herself—Guest)

———. Episode #11.64. CBS, December 8, 2014. (Herself—Guest)

The Ellen DeGeneres Show. Talk Show. Written by Karen Anderson et al. NBC, December 2, 2005. (Herself—Guest)

———. Episode #13.68. Directed by Suzanne Luna and Liz Patrick. Written by Alison Balian et al. NBC, December 14, 2015. (Herself—Guest)

———. Episode #13.72. Directed by Suzanne Luna and Liz Patrick. Written by Alison Balian et al. NBC, December 18, 2015. (Herself—Guest)

———. Episode #14.59. Directed by Suzanne Luna and Liz Patrick. Written by Alison Balian et al. NBC, November 29, 2016. (Herself—Guest)

Richard and Judy. Talk Show. Channel 4, June 20, 2006. (Herself—Guest)

The Megan Mullally Show. Talk Show. Episode #1.54. Written by Wendy Molyneux et al. NBC, December 1, 2006. (Herself—Guest)

On the Lot. Television Show. Episode #1.3. "Box Office Performance Show #1." Written by Dan O'Keefe. Fox, May 28, 2007. (Herself—Judge)

Episode #1.4. "Box Office Results #1." Written by Dan O'Keefe. Fox, May 29, 2007. (Herself—Judge)

———. Episode #1.5. "15 Directors Compete." Directed by Michael Simon. Written by Dan O'Keefe and Hilary Weisman Graham. Fox, June 5, 2007. (Herself—Judge)

———. Episode #1.6. "14 Directors Compete." Directed by Michael Simon. Written by Dan O'Keefe and Dan Perry. Fox, June 12, 2007. (Herself—Judge)

———. Episode #1.7. "14 Cut to 13 & 13 Directors Compete." Written by Dan O'Keefe. Fox, June 19, 2007. (Herself—Judge)

———. Episode #1.8. "13 Cut to 12 & 12 Directors Compete." Written by Dan O'Keefe. Fox, June 26, 2007. (Herself—Judge)

———. Episode #1.9. "12 Cut to 11 & 11 Directors Compete." Written by Dan O'Keefe. Fox, July 3, 2007. (Herself—Judge)

———. Episode #1.10. "11 Cut to 10 & 10 Directors Compete." Written by Dan O'Keefe. Fox, July 9, 2007. (Herself—Judge)

———. Episode #1.11. "10 Cut to 8 & 8 Directors Compete." Written by Dan O'Keefe. Fox, July 17, 2007. (Herself—Judge)

———. Episode #1.12. "8 Cut to 6 & 6 Directors Compete." Written by Dan O'Keefe. Fox, July 24, 2007. (Herself—Judge)

———. Episode #1.13. "6 Cut to 5 & 5 Directors Compete." Written by Dan O'Keefe. Fox, July 31, 2007. (Herself—Judge)

Deal or No Deal. Television Show. Episode #3.60. NBC, April 28, 2008. (Herself)

The View. Talk Show. ABC, December 12, 2008. (Herself—Guest)

The Bonnie Hunt Show. Talk Show. Written by Ellie Barancik et al. Warner Bros. Television, January 7, 2009. (Herself—Guest)

The 63rd Annual Tony Awards. Television Special. Directed by Glenn Weiss. Written by Dave Boone et al. CBS, June 7, 2009. (Herself)

Charlie Rose. Talk Show. PBS, October 28, 2009. (Herself—Guest)

Late Night with Jimmy Fallon. Talk Show. NBC, October 29, 2009. (Herself—Guest)

Shrink Rap. Talk Show. Episode #2.8. More4, January 20, 2010. (Herself—Guest)

Good News Week. Game Show. Episode #9.31. Directed by Martin Coombes. Written by Mat Blackwell et al. Australian Broadcasting Corporation, October 18, 2010. (Herself—Guest)

The 7PM Project. Talk Show. Episode #1.313. Written by Gerard McCulloch. Network Ten Australia, October 21, 2010. (Herself—Guest)

A Quiet Word With . . . Talk Show. "Carrie Fisher." Directed by Gary McCaffrie. Written by Tony Martin. Australian Broadcasting Corporation, November 9, 2010. (Herself—Guest)

The Oprah Winfrey Show. Talk Show. "Living Legend Debbie Reynolds and Her Daughter Icon Carrie Fisher." CBS, February 15, 2011. (Herself—Guest)

Spoilers with Kevin Smith. Talk Show. Episode #1.1. "Girls Just Wanna Have Guns." Directed by Joey Figueroa and Zak Knutson. Hulu, June 4, 2012. (Herself—Guest)

The Comedy Central Roast of Roseanne Barr. Television Special. Directed by Joel Gallen. Written by Ben Hoffman et al. Comedy Central, August 12, 2012. (Herself—Roaster)

Indie Cinema Showcase. Talk Show. "Star Wars Celebration VI Special." Directed by Gerald J. Godbout III. Written by Gerald J. Godbout III and Jennifer Vargas. September 2, 2012. (Herself)

The Talk. Talk Show. Directed by Gene Bernard. CBS, November 13, 2012. (Herself—Guest)

Just for Laughs: All Access. Talk Show. Episode #5.4. Directed by Shelagh O'Brien. CTV, 2012. (Herself—Host)

The 40th Annual Daytime Emmy Awards. Television Special. Directed by Mark Lucas. ABC, June 16, 2013. (Herself—Presenter)

Words with Warwick. Talk Show. Episode #1.6. "Carrie Fisher." The Star Wars Corporation, July 31, 2013. (Herself/Princess Leia Organa)

QI. Game Show. Episode #12.12. "No-L." Directed by Ian Lorimer. Written by John Lloyd et al. BBC, December 25, 2014. (Herself—Guest)

The 21st Annual Screen Actors Guild Awards. Television Special. Directed by Alan Carter. Written by Dave Boone. TNT, January 25, 2015. (Herself—Presenter)

Star Wars Celebration. Television Mini-Series. Episode #1.1. "Day 1." Written by Scott Bromley. The Star Wars Corporation, April 16, 2015. (Herself—Guest)

Jimmy Kimmel Live! Talk Show. Episode #13.158. "The Cast of Star Wars: The Force Awakens." Directed by Zack Bornstein. Written by Danny Ricker et al. November 23, 2015. (Herself—Guest)

Crackanory. Television Series. Episode #3.1. "Uncivil War and Dread and Breakfast." Directed by Richard Pengelley. Written by Nico Tatarowicz. UKTV, December 7, 2015. (Herself—Storyteller)

Star Wars: The Force Awakens World Premiere Red Carpet. Television Special. Written by Scott Bromley. The Star Wars Corporation, December 14, 2015. (Herself)

The Tonight Show Starring Jimmy Fallon. Talk Show. Episode #3.65. "Mark Wahlberg/Bill Burr/Sheryl Crow." NBC, December 15, 2015. (Herself—Uncredited)

Entertainment Tonight. News. Episode #34.180. ABC, May 16, 2014. (Herself)

———. ABC, December 7, 2015. (Herself)

———. ABC, December 15, 2015. (Herself)

BuzzFeed Video. Online Content. "Star Wars Cast Members Do Star Wars Impersonations." BuzzFeed, December 15, 2015. (Herself)

Conan. Talk Show. Episode #6.20. "The Cast of Star Wars: The Force Awakens." Directed by Allan Kartun. Written by Matt O'Brien et al. TBS, December 17, 2015. (Herself—Guest)

Extra. News. Episode #22.66. Directed by Rob Dorn and Sean Olson. Warner Bros. Television, December 7, 2015. (Herself)

———. Episode #22.75. Warner Bros. Television, December 18, 2015. (Herself)

Access Hollywood. News. NBC, December 11, 2015. (Herself)

———. NBC, December 21, 2015. (Herself)

The Graham Norton Show. Talk Show. Episode #18.12. "David Beckham/Carrie Fisher/Daisy Ridley/John Boyega/Kylie Minogue." Directed by Steve Smith. Written by Rob Colley. BBC, December 18, 2015. (Herself—Guest)

———. Episode #20.10. "Carrie Fisher/Grayson Perry/Sandi Toksvig/Nadiya Hussain/Busted." Directed by Steve Smith. Written by Rob Colley and Christine Rose. BBC, December 17, 2016. (Herself—Guest)

The 38th Annual Kennedy Center Honors. Television Special. Directed by Glenn Weiss. Written by Dave Boone. CBS, December 29, 2015. (Herself—Presenter)

The Insider. News. Episode #12.77. Directed by Earnest Winborne and Ryan Neary. Bravo, December 11, 2015. (Herself)

———. Episode #12.93. Bravo, December 30, 2015. (Herself)

The EE British Academy Film Awards. Television Special. BBC, February 14, 2016. (Herself—Presenter)

Live! With Kelly. Talk Show. Episode #28.63. "Carrie Fisher/Toy Guy Chris Byrne." ABC, December 3, 2015. (Herself—Guest)

———. Episode #28.123. "LIVE's Pre-Oscar Celebration 2016." ABC, February 26, 2016. (Herself—Guest)

The Last Leg. Talk Show. Episode #5.3. Channel 4, August 15, 2014. (Herself—Guest)

———. Episode #9.4. Channel 4, July 1, 2015. (Herself—Guest)

The Late Show with Stephen Colbert. Talk Show. Episode #2.48. "Michael Weatherly/Carrie Fisher/The Pretenders." Written by Michael Pielocik. CBS, November 21, 2016. (Herself—Guest)

8 Out of 10 Cats. Game Show. Episode #20.7. Written by Lou Sanders. E4, December 21, 2016. (Herself—Guest)

Documentary and Archival Footage

The Making of Star Wars. Directed by Robert Guenette. Los Angeles: 20th Century Fox, 1977. (Herself)

The Making of The Empire Strikes Back. Directed by Michael Parbot. Paris: Sygma Television, 1980. (Herself)

Classic Creatures: Return of the Jedi. Directed by Robert Guenette. San Francisco: LucasFilm, 1983. (Host and Narrator)

From Star Wars to Jedi: The Making of a Saga. Directed by Richard Schickel. San Francisco: LucasFilm, 1983. (Herself)

American Masters: George Lucas; Heroes, Myths, and Magic. Directed by Jane Paley and Larry Price. London: Eagle Rock Entertainment, 1993. (Herself)

Science Fiction: A Journey into the Unknown. Directed by Scott Goldstein and Judy Korin. Los Angeles, Fox Broadcasting Company, 1994. (Herself)

Carrie on Hollywood: Live and Love in La-La Land. No director listed. British Broadcasting Corporation, 1995. (Herself)

Bright Lights: Starring Carrie Fisher and Debbie Reynolds. Directed by Alexis Bloom and Fisher Stevens, HBO, 2017. (Herself)

Bibliography of Written Works

Fisher, Carrie. *Postcards from the Edge*. Novel. New York: Simon & Schuster, 1987.

Fisher, Carrie. *Surrender the Pink*. Novel. New York: Simon & Schuster, 1990.

Fisher, Carrie. *Postcards from the Edge*. Screenplay. Directed by Mike Nichols. Sony, 1990.

Fisher, Carrie. *Delusions of Grandma*. Novel. New York: Simon & Schuster, 1993.

Fisher, Carrie. *Carrie Fisher: The Hollywood Family*. Documentary. A&E, 1995.

Fisher, Carrie. *Carrie on Hollywood*. Documentary. Directed by Rhonda Evans. BBC, 1995.

Fisher, Carrie. *The 69th Annual Academy Awards*. Special Material: Telecast. Directed by Louis J. Horvitz. ABC, March 24, 1997.

Fisher, Carrie. *Roseanne*. "Arsenic and Old Mom." Teleplay. Directed by Mark K. Samuels. ABC, May 13, 1997.

Fisher, Carrie. "Star Wars Taught Me Everything." *Newsweek*. Essay. New York: Newsweek, May 1999.

Fisher, Carrie, and Jonathan Hensleigh. "Demons of Deception." *The Adventures of Young Indiana Jones*. Teleplay. Directed by René Manzor and Nicolas Roeg. ABC, October 9, 1999.

Fisher, Carrie, and Elaine Pope. *These Old Broads*. Screenplay. Burbank: ABC, 2001.

Fisher, Carrie. *The 74th Annual Academy Awards*. Special Material: Telecast. Directed by Louis J. Horvitz. ABC, March 24, 2002.

Fisher, Carrie. *The Best Awful*. Novel. New York: Simon & Schuster, 2004.

Fisher, Carrie. *The 79th Annual Academy Awards*. Special Material: Telecast. Directed by Louis J. Horvitz. ABC, February 25, 2007.

Fisher, Carrie, and Joshua Ravetch. *Wishful Drinking*. Memoir. New York: Simon & Schuster, 2008.

Fisher, Carrie, and Joshua Ravetch. *Carrie Fisher: Wishful Drinking*. Documentary. Directed by Fenton Bailey and Randy Barbato. HBO, December 12, 2010.

Fisher, Carrie. *Shockaholic*. Memoir. New York: Simon & Schuster, 2011.

Fisher, Carrie. *The Princess Diarist*. Memoir. New York: Simon & Schuster, 2016.

Notable Carrie/Leia Fanworks

Video and Music

Ophelian, Annalise. *Looking for Leia*. Docuseries. 2019.
    Web Site: www.lookingforleia.com.
Leia's Lair. YouTube Channel. 2018.
    Channel: www.youtube.com/channel/UCHz6YNoL7Ke9CiIl2NS-1IA.
Palette-Swap Ninja. *Princess Leia's Stolen Death Star Plans*. FLAC Album. 2017.
    Album Download: www.paletteswapninja.com/music.
    Video Series: http://bit.ly/starwarsbeatles.
A Tribute to Carrie Fisher. Video. 2017.
    Video: www.youtube.com/watch?v=sE99le5FBrY.

Podcasts

Fandom Podcast Network, "FPN Classic: A Tribute to Carrie Fisher." 2018.
    Site: https://fpnet.podbean.com/e/fpnet-classic-a-tribute-to-carrie-fisher.
The Story Geeks, "Star Wars: LEIA ORGANA—from Princess to General." 2018.

Site: https://thestorygeeks.org/2018/09/18/star-wars-leia-organa-from-princess
-to-general.

The Story Geeks, "Celebrating Leia: Happy Birthday, Carrie Fisher!" 2019.
Site: https://thestorygeeks.org/2019/10/21/digging-into-leia-happy-birthday
-carrie-fisher.

Fan Groups

Carrie Fisher's Official Page, https://carriefisher.com.

Carrie Fisher Fanpop, www.fanpop.com/clubs/carrie-fisher.
Archive of Carrie Fisher images, fan tributes, and videos.

The Galactic Fempire, www.facebook.com/groups/TheGalacticFempire.
Feminist, female only *Star Wars* fan group.

Bun Squad,www.facebook.com/groups/118413528803579/.
Leia specific cosplay group.

Fandom Documentary Films

The Stars of Star Wars: Interviews from the Cast. Directed by Kent Hagan, Passport
Video, 93 min. 2001.

The People vs. George Lucas. Directed by Alexandre O. Philippe, Exhibit A Pictures, 93 min. 2010.

Jedi Junkies: The Force Is Strong with Them. Directed by Mark Edlitz, Docudrama,
73 min. 2013.

Plastic Galaxies: The Story of Star Wars Toys. Directed by Brian Stillman, X-Ray
Films, 70 min. 2014.

Works Cited

ABC News. "PrimeTime: Carrie Fisher Interview." *ABC News*, December 21, 2000. https://abcnews.go.com/Primetime/story?id=132315&page=1.

Abramovitch, Seth. "Carrie Fisher Comes Full Circle." *Gawker*, December 10, 2008. https://gawker.com/5106681/carrie-fisher-comes-full-circle.

Adams, Marjory. "Author Susann Has 'Em Guessing on 'Dolls' Stars." *Boston Globe*, May 10, 1966, 21.

Advertisement: *Postcards from the Edge*. *New York Times Book Review*. June 12, 1988, 39. ProQuest Historical Newspapers.

Almasy, Steve. "Debbie Reynolds Dies One Day after Daughter Carrie Fisher Passes." *CNN*. Last modified December 28, 2016. www.cnn.com/2016/12/28/entertainment/debbie-reynolds-hospitalized/index.html.

Andrejevic, Mark. *Infoglut: How Too Much Information Is Changing the Way We Think and Know*. New York: Routledge, 2013.

Andress, Jamal. "The Empire Strikes It Rich: How 'Star Wars' Built a Franchise Dynasty." *Newsy.com*. Last modified December 11, 2017. www.newsy.com/stories/how-much-is-star-wars-actually-worth/.

Anger, Kenneth. *Hollywood Babylon*. New York: Simon & Schuster, 1975. First published 1959 as *Hollywood Babylone*.

Appointment with Death. Directed by Michael Winner. Cannon Group, 1988.

Assmann, Jan. "Communicative and Cultural Memory." In *Cultural Memory Studies: An International and Interdisciplinary Handbook*, edited by Astrid Erll, Ansgar Nünning, and Sara B. Young. Berlin: de Gruyter, 2008.

Associated Press. "Next 'Star Wars' Film to Use Unreleased Carrie Fisher Footage." *Nation World*. Last updated July 27, 2018. www.wkyc.com/article/news/nation-world/next-star-wars-film-to-use-unreleased-carrie-fisher-footage/507-578084422.

"August 29, 1954." *What's My Line?*, 1954. Directed by Franklin Heller. New York: CBS.

Bacon-Smith, Camille. *Enterprising Women: Television Fandom and the Creation of Popular Myth*. Philadelphia: University of Pennsylvania Press, 1992.

Bainbridge, Jason. "Fully Articulated: The Rise of the Action Figure and the Changing Face of 'Children's' Entertainment." *Continuum: Journal of Media and Cultural Studies* 24, no. 6 (2010).

Banner, Lois. *In Full Flower: Aging Women, Power, and Sexuality* (New York: Alfred A. Knopf, 1992), 15.

Barcella, Laura. "How Carrie Fisher Championed Mental Health." *Rolling Stone*, December 28, 2016. www.rollingstone.com/culture/culture-news/how-carrie-fisher-championed-mental-health-115009/.

Barounis, Cynthia. "Witches, Terrorists, and the Biopolitics of Camp." *GLQ: A Journal of Lesbian and Gay Studies* 24, no. 2/3 (2018): 213–38.

Bazin, Victoria, and Rosie White. "Generations: Women, Age, and Difference." *Studies in the Literary Imagination* 39, no. 2 (Fall 2006): i–ix.

Beauchamp, Cari. "The Girl with the Golden Wardrobe." *Wall Street Journal*. Last modified May 26, 2011. www.wsj.com/articles/SB10001424052748703730804576321351713438800.

Beech, Peter. "Sci fi—It's Not Just for Boys." *The Guardian*. Last modified May 16, 2009. www.theguardian.com/commentisfree/2009/may/16/science-fiction-men-women.

Behind the Candelabra. Directed by Steven Soderbergh. HBO Home Entertainment, 2013.

Bell, Gabriel. "A Year after Carrie Fisher's Death, #CarrieOnForever Unites a Grieving Galaxy." *Salon*, December 27, 2017. www.salon.com/2017/12/27/carrieonforever-hashtag-carrie-fisher-death/.

Bell, Sue. "The Force Awakens, but What Happened to Carrie Fisher's Face?" *midlifexpress*, December 23, 2015. http://midlifexpress.com/the-force-awakens-but-what-happened-to-carrie-fishers-face/.

Bennetts, Leslie. "Carrie on Baggage." *Vanity Fair*, November 2009. www.vanityfair.com/news/2009/11/carrie-fisher-200911.

Biggar, Trisha. *Dressing a Galaxy: The Costumes of Star Wars*. New York: Insight Editions, 2005.

Bingen, Steven. *MGM Hollywood's Greatest Backlot*. Foreword by Debbie Reynolds. Santa Monica, CA: Santa Monica Press, 2010.

Bjorkman, Carol. "Features: Carol." *Women's Wear Daily*, March 28, 1966, 8.

Blackwell, Jeffrey. "Carrie Fisher of 'Star Wars' Fame Continues the Battle," *Harvard Gazette*, April 2016, https://news.harvard.edu/gazette/story/2016/04/carrie-fisher-of-star-wars-fame-continues-the-battle.

The Blues Brothers. Directed by John Landis. Universal Pictures Home Entertainment, 1980.

Booth, John. *Collect All 21!: Memoirs of a Star Wars Geek—The First 30 Years*. Milton: Lightning Source UK, 2008.

Booth, Paul. "Disney's Princess Leia." In *Disney's Star Wars: Forces of Production, Promotion, and Reception*, edited by William Proctor and Richard McCulloch. Iowa City: University of Iowa Press, 2019.

Boudewyns, Vanessa, Itai Himelboim, Derek L. Hansen, and Brian G. Southwell. "Stigma's Effect on Social Interaction and Social Media Activity." *Journal of Health Communication* 20, no. 11 (2015): 1337–45.

Bowles Eagle, Ryan. "Loitering, Lingering, Hashtagging: Women Reclaiming Public Space via #BoardTheBus, #StopStreetHarrassement, and the #EverydaySexism Project." *Feminist Media Studies* 15, no. 2 (2015): 350–53.

bp Magazine. "bp Magazine's Tribute to Carrie Fisher." *bp Magazine*, December 29, 2016. www.bphope.com/hope-harmony-headlines-bp-magazines-tribute-to -carrie-fisher/.

Breznican, Anthony. "Kathleen Kennedy Says *Star Wars: Episode IX* 'Started Over' after Carrie Fisher's Death." *Entertainment Weekly*, April 14, 2017. https://ew .com/movies/2017/04/14/kathleen-kennedy-episode-ix-carrie-fisher-death/.

Breznican, Anthony, Twitter/@Breznican: "Carrie Fisher Isn't Gone. She Was Alive and Well at the #WomensMarch." January 21, 2017.

Bright Lights: Starring Carrie Fisher and Debbie Reynolds. Directed by Alexis Bloom and Fisher Stevens. Home Box Office, 2016.

Brooker, Will. *Using the Force: Creativity, Community, and Star Wars Fans*. New York: Continuum, 2002.

Brough, Melissa M., and Sangita Shresthova. "Fandom Meets Activism: Rethinking Civic and Political Participation." *Transformative Works and Cultures* 10 (March 30, 2011). http://journal.transformativeworks.org/index.php/twc/ article/view/303.

Bruin-Molé, Megen de. "'Does It Come with a Spear?' Commodity Activism, Plastic Representation, and Transmedia Story Strategies in Disney's Star Wars: Forces of Destiny." *Film Criticism* 42, no. 2 (2018).

———. "Space Bitches, Witches, and Kick-Ass Princesses: Star Wars and Popular Feminism." In *Star Wars and the History of Transmedia Storytelling*, edited by Sean Guynes and Dan Hassler-Forest. Amsterdam: Amsterdam University Press, 2017.

Bryant, Jacob. "Carrie Fisher's 'Star Wars' Advice to Daisy Ridley: 'Don't Be a Slave Like I Was.'" *Variety*, October 30, 2015. http://variety.com/2015/film/news/star -wars-carrie-fisher-daisy-ridley-sexist-costumes-1201630611/.

The 'Burbs. Directed by Joe Dante. Universal Pictures Home Entertainment, 1989.

Burleson, Ryan, and Tara Parker-Pope. "Fans Tweet about Mental Illness to Honor Carrie Fisher." *New York Times*, December 27, 2016. www.nytimes.com/2016/12/27/arts/carrie-fisher-bipolar-disorder.html?_r=0.

Cagle, Jess, and Julie Jordan. "Carrie Fisher Died of Sleep Apnea and Used Drugs, Report Reveals—as Daughter Billie Releases Emotional Statement." *People*, June 16, 2017. https://people.com/movies/carrie-fisher-cause-of-death/.

Call, Deborah. *The Art of Star Wars: The Empire Strikes Back*. New York: Del Rey, 1994.

Carey, Benedict. "Carrie Fisher Put Pen and Voice in Service of 'Bipolar Pride.'" *New York Times*, December 28, 2016. www.nytimes.com/2016/12/28/health/carrie-fisher-bipolar-disorder.html.

"Carrie Fisher Answers the Proust Questionnaire." *Vanity Fair*. Last updated April 1, 2001. www.vanityfair.com/culture/2001/04/carrie-fisher-answers-the-proust-questionnaire.

"Carrie Fisher—Anorexia Fears over *Star Wars* Pressure." *National Enquirer*, May 17, 2016. www.nationalenquirer.com/photos/carrie-fisher-star-wars-weight-loss-studio-pressure/.

"Carrie Fisher's Dog Gary Makes an Awesome Action Figure." *Revenge of the 5th* (blog), December 12, 2015. www.revengeofthe5th.net/2015/12/carrie-fishers-dog-gary-makes-awesome.html.

"Carrie Fisher Draws From Her Personal Journals in *The Princess Diarist*." *All Things Considered*. NPR, November 22, 2016. www.npr.org/2016/11/22/503052653/carrie-fisher-draws-from-her-personal-journals-in-the-princess-diarist.

"Carrie Fisher/John Waters/Rue McClanahan/F Castelluccio." *Celebrity Ghost Stories*, 2019. Directed by Seth Jarrett. Biography Channel.

Carrie Fisher: Wishful Drinking. Directed by Fenton Bailey and Randy Barbato. HBO Documentary, 2010.

Carrie Fisher: Wishful Drinking Special Features "My Alleged Mother—An Exclusive Interview with Debbie Reynolds," Directed by Fenton Bailey and Randy Barbato. HBO Documentary, 2010.

Carucci, John. "Celebrities Highlight Mental Health Issues." *U.S. News and World Report*, May 17, 2018. www.usnews.com/news/healthiest-communities/articles/2018-05-17/celebrities-bring-awareness-to-mental-health-issues.

The Catered Affair. Directed by Richard Brooks. Metro-Goldwyn-Mayer, 1956.

Cawelti, John. "The Evolution of Social Melodrama." In *Imitations of Life*, edited by Marcia Landy. Detroit: Wayne State University Press, 1991.

Charlie's Angels: Full Throttle. Directed by McG. Sony Pictures Home Entertainment, 2003.

Chaudoir, Stephenie R., Valerie A. Earnshaw, and Stephanie Andel. " 'Discredited' versus 'Discreditable': Understanding How Shared and Unique Stigma Mechanisms Affect Psychological and Physical Health Disparities." *Basic and Applied Social Psychology* 35, no. 1 (2013): 75–87.

Chenoweth, Erica, and Jeremy Pressman. "Estimated Women's March Attendance and Visualization." January 22, 2017. https://geographer.carto.com/viz/ a229d5d2-e04a-11e6-9c98-0e98b61680bf/embed_map.

Chichizola, Corey. "Why Carrie Fisher Was Mentioned By Green Book's Producers." *CinemaBlend.* Last modified February 25, 2019. www.cinemablend .com/news/2467411/why-carrie-fisher-was-mentioned-by-green-books -producers.

Child, Ben. "Carrie Fisher: I Felt Pressured to Lose Weight for *Star Wars: The Force Awakens.*" *The Guardian.* Last modified December 1, 2015. www .theguardian.com/culture/2015/dec/01/carrie-fisher-weight-loss-star-wars-the -force-awakens.

Citter, Victoria. "Thank You to Carrie Fisher, Who Gave Me Courage to Fight Bipolar Disorder." *The Mighty,* February 7, 2017. https://themighty.com/2017/ 02/carrie-fisher-bipolar-disorder-thank-you/.

Cleto, Fabio. "Introduction: Queering the Camp." In *Camp: Queer Aesthetics and the Performing Subject,* 1–43. Edinburgh: Edinburgh University Press, 1999.

Cohan, Steven. *Incongruous Entertainment: Camp, Cultural Value, and the MGM Musical.* Durham, NC: Duke University Press, 2005.

———. " 'This Industry Lives on Gossip and Scandal': Female Star Narratives and the Marilyn Monroe Biopic." *Celebrity Studies* 8, no. 4 (2017): 527–43.

Cohen, Jonathan. "Mediated Relationships and Media Effects: Parasocial Interaction and Identification." In *The Sage Handbook of Media Processes and Effects,* edited by Robin L. Nabi and Mary B. Oliver, 223–36. Thousand Oaks, CA: Sage, 2009.

The Congress. Film. Directed by Ari Folman. Drafthouse Films, Austin, Texas, 2013.

"Convention Conundrum." *The Big Bang Theory.* Directed by Mark Cendrowski, 2014. Burbank, CA: CBS.

Coombe, Rosemary. "The Celebrity Image and Cultural Identity: Publicity Rights and the Subaltern Politics of Gender." *Discourse* 14, no. 3 (1992): 59–88.

Corkins, Matthew. "Princess Leia Poster: Legal Issues Won't Keep This Artist Out of the Rebellion." *New York Observer*. Last modified February 17, 2017. https:// observer.com/2017/02/princess-leia-poster-legal-issues-wont-keep-this-artist -out-of-the-rebellion.

Corrigan, Patrick W., and Kristin A. Kosyluk. "Mental Illness Stigma: Types, Constructs, and Vehicles for Change." In *The Stigma of Disease and Disability: Understanding Causes and Overcoming Injustices*, edited by Patrick W. Corrigan, 35–56. Washington, DC: American Psychological Association, 2014.

Corrigan, Patrick W., Kristin A. Kosyluk, and Nicolas Rüsch. "Reducing Self-Stigma by Coming Out Proud." *American Journal of Public Health* 103, no. 5 (2013): 794–800.

Corrigan, Patrick W., and Deepa Rao. "On the Self-Stigma of Mental Illness: Stages, Disclosure, and Strategies for Change." *Canadian Journal of Psychiatry* 57, no. 8 (2012): 464–69.

Cram, Peter, A. Mark Fendrick, John Inadomi, Mark E. Cowen, Daniel Carpenter, and Sandeep Vijan. "The Impact of a Celebrity Promotional Campaign on the Use of Colon Cancer Screening: The Katie Couric Effect." *Archives of Internal Medicine* 163, no. 13 (2003): 1601–5.

Darrow, Barb. "More Than 1 in 100 of All Americans Were at Women's March Events." *Fortune*, January 23, 2017.

Davis, Jason, and Larry Pakowski. "The Influence of The Force." In *Fan Phenomena: Star Wars*, edited by Mika Elovaara, 98–107. Bristol: Intellect, 2013.

Day, Kathleen. "Looking for Leia? May the Force Be with You." *Washington Post*. Last modified March 15, 1997. www.washingtonpost.com/wp-dyn/articles/ A99038-1997Mar15.html.

"Debbie Reynolds and Carrie Fisher." *Intimate Portraits*, 1994. Lifetime Television.

De Kosnik, Abigail. "Memory, Archive, and History in Political Fan Fiction." In *Fandom: Identities and Communities in a Mediated World*, 2nd ed., edited by Jonathan Gray, Cornel Sandvoss, and C. Lee Harrington. New York: New York University Press, 2017.

"Demons and Spacesuits and Slippers, Oh My." *Hollywood Treasure*. Produced by Joe Maddalena. 2011. Syfy.

D'Enbeau, Suzy, and Patrice M. Buzzanell. "The Erotic Heroine and the Politics of Gender at Work: A Feminist Reading of *Mad Men*'s Joan Harris." In *Heroines of Film and Television: Portrayals in Popular Culture*, edited by Norma Jones, Maja Bajac-Carter, and Bob Batchelor, 3–16. Lanham, MD: Rowman and Littlefield, 2014.

Desjardins, Mary R., 2015. *Recycled Stars: Female Film Stardom in the Age of Television and Video*. Durham, NC: Duke University Press.

Delaney, Rob. "I Revered Carrie Fisher Until I Met Her, Then I Loved Her." *The Guardian*, December 28, 2016.

Dicker, Rachel. "Carrie Fisher's Struggle with Bipolar Disorder Inspired Many." *U.S. News and World Report*, December 28, 2016. www.usnews.com/news/articles/2016-12-28/carrie-fishers-struggle-with-bipolar-disorder-inspired-many.

Divorce American Style. Directed by Bud Yorkin. Columbia TriStar, 1967.

Drunk 3PO. "Star Wars Toys Not Selling. No One Is Buying." YouTube video. 8:50. January 14, 2019. www.youtube.com/watch?v=Ex7ojOsCfk4.

Dominguez, Diana. "Feminism and the Force: Empowerment and Disillusionment in a Galaxy, Far, Far Away." In *Culture, Identities, and Technology in the Star Wars Films: Essays on the Two Trilogies*, edited by Carol Silvio and Tony M. Vinci, 109–33. Jefferson, NC: McFarland, 2007.

Dorfman, Lori, and Ingrid Daffner Krasnow. "Public Health and Media Advocacy." *Annual Review of Public Health* 35 (2014): 293–306.

Duke, Patty, and Kenneth Turan. *Call Me Anna: The Autobiography of Patty Duke*. New York: Bantam Books, 1988.

Dupere, Katie. "These Simple Badges Are Helping Social Media Users Talk about Mental Illness." *Mashable*, January 6, 2017. https://mashable.com/2017/01/06/mental-illness-badges-endthestigma/.

Dyer, Richard. "*A Star Is Born* and the Construction of Authenticity." In *Stardom: Industry of Desire*, edited by Christine Gledhill, 132–40. London: Routledge, 1991.

———. *Heavenly Bodies: Film Stars and Society*. London: British Film Institute/Macmillan Education, 1986.

———. *Stars*. London: Palgrave Macmillan, 1998.

Ebert, Roger. "Postcards from the Edge Movie Review," Roger Ebert. September 12, 1990. www.rogerebert.com/reviews/postcards-from-the-edge-1990.

Ellie Ann, Twitter/@EllieAnnesWords: "An Older Man Handed A—— His Lightsaber and Said, 'Take this.' She Is glowing. Pass On Your Light to the Next Gen." January 21, 2017.

"Episode 163—Carrie Fisher Remembered." *Now, This Is Podcasting!* (podcast audio), December 29, 2016. www.podbean.com/media/share/dir-9hsdm-3354e7a?utm_campaign=w_share_ep&utm_medium=dlink&utm_source=w_share.

"Episode #2.4." *Dinner for Five*. Hosted by Jon Favreau. 2003. IFC (Independent Film Channel).

"Episode #3.6." *Catastrophe*. Directed by Ben Taylor, 2017. Amazon Instant Video.

"Episode #4.6." *Catastrophe*. Directed by Jim O'Hanlon, 2019. Amazon Instant Video.

"Episode 41: So Long Princess." *Toy Run: The Star Wars Action Figure Cast* (podcast), January 6, 2017. https://open.spotify.com/episode/3ekqPzPnuj5yltAJBmxvP8?si=uV0GVJRxRHiAALoireLYWg.

"Episode dated 4 December 2015." *Good Morning America*. Produced by Michael Corn, 2015. ABC.

Evans-Lacko, Sara, Elizabeth Corker, Paul Williams, Claire Henderson, and Graham Thornicroft. "Effect of the Time to Change Anti-stigma Campaign on Trends in Mental-Illness-Related Public Stigma among the English Population in 2003–13: An Analysis of Survey Data." *Lancet Psychiatry* 1, no. 2 (2014): 121–28.

Fahrenthold, David A. "Trump Recorded Having Extremely Lewd Conversation about Women in 2005." *Washington Post*, October 18, 2016.

Fairclough, Kirsty. "Nothing Less Than Perfect: Female Celebrity, Ageing, and Hyper-scrutiny in the Gossip Industry." In *Gender, Race and Class in the Media*, edited by Gail Dines, Jean M. Humez, Bill Yousman, and Lori Bindig Yousman, 265–71. London: Sage, 2017.

Fear and Loathing in Las Vegas. Directed by Terry Gilliam. Criterion Collection, 1998.

Feil, Ken. "'Fearless Vulgarity': Camp Love as Queer Love for Jackie Susann and *Valley of the Dolls*." In *Queer Love in Film and Television*, edited by Pamela Demory and Christopher Pullen, 141–51. London: Palgrave Macmillan, 2013.

———. "Scandal, Critical Gossip, and Queer Failure: Jacqueline Susann, *Valley of the Dolls*, and Star Biography." *Celebrity Studies*, 2017. DOI: 10.1080/19392397.2017.1370829.

Finch, Mark. "Sex and Address in Dynasty." *Screen* 27, no. 6 (November–December 1986): 24–42.

Fisher, Carrie. "Advice from the Dark Side." *The Guardian*. Last modified November 30, 2016. www.theguardian.com/lifeandstyle/series/advice-from-the-dark-side.

———. "Ask Carrie Fisher: I'm Bipolar—How Do You Feel at Peace with Mental Illness?" *The Guardian*, November 30, 2016. www.theguardian.com/lifeandstyle/2016/nov/30/carrie-fisher-advice-column-mental-illness-bipolar-disorder.

———. "Carrie Fisher in 1999: '*Star Wars* Taught Me Everything.'" *Newsweek*, December 27, 2016. www.newsweek.com/carrie-fisher-star-wars-essay-167072.

———. "Carrie Fisher on How George Lucas Stole Her Identity." *Newsweek*, December 27, 2016. www.newsweek.com/carrie-fisher-george-lucas-star-wars-archive-interview-67321.

———. *The Best Awful*. New York: Simon & Schuster, 2004.

———. *The Best Awful*. New York: Simon & Schuster Audio, 2004.

———. "Character Study: Carrie Fisher Bids Farewell to Princess Leia." *BulletMedia*. Last modified January 4, 2013. http://bullettmedia.com/article/character-study-carrie-fisher-makes-peace-with-princess-leia/ (URL inactive).

———. *Delusions of Grandma*. New York: Simon & Schuster, 1994.

———. *Delusions of Grandma*. New York: Simon & Schuster Audio, 1994.

———. Interview by Terry Gross. "Carrie Fisher Opens Up about *Star Wars*, The Gold Bikini, and Her On-Set Affair." *Fresh Air*, National Public Radio, November 28, 2016.

———. *The Princess Diarist*. New York: Blue Rider Press, 2016.

———. *The Princess Diarist*. New York: Penguin Audio, 2016.

———. *Postcards from the Edge*. Beverly Hills: Phoenix Books, 1988.

———. *Shockaholic*. New York: Simon & Schuster, 2011.

———. *Shockaholic*. Prince Frederick: Recorded Books, 2011.

———. *Surrender the Pink*. New York: Simon & Schuster, 1990.

———. *Surrender the Pink*. Studio City: Dove Books on Tape, 1990.

———. Twitter/@carrieffisher: "Please stop debating about whetherOR not [I]aged well.unfortunately it hurts all3 of my feelings.My BODY hasnt aged as well as I have.Blow us." December 28, 2015. Tweet.

———. Twitter/@carrieffisher: "Trump speaking his mind isn't refreshing, it's appalling. Coca Cola is refreshing . . ." November 6, 2016.

———. Twitter post. December 21, 2016. https://twitter.com/carrieffisher/status/811620111752663040.

———. *Wishful Drinking*. New York: Simon & Schuster, 2008.

———. *Wishful Drinking*. New York: Simon & Schuster Audio, 2008.

Fisher, Joely. *Growing Up Fisher: Musings, Memories, and Misadventures*. New York: William Morrow, 2017.

Fisher, Todd. *My Girls*. New York: Harper Collins, 2018.

Fleming, Mike, Jr. "*Star Wars* Legacy II: An Architect of Hollywood's Greatest Deal Recalls How George Lucas Won Sequel Rights." *Deadline.com*. Last

modified December 18, 2015. http://deadline.com/2015/12/star-wars-franchise
-george-lucas-historic-rights-deal-tom-pollock-1201669419/.

Flinn, Caryl. "The Deaths of Camp." In *Camp: Queer Aesthetics and the Performing Subject*, 433–57. Edinburgh: Edinburgh University Press, 1999.

Fogel, Jennifer. "The Force Is Now Female: The Gendered Marketing of *Star Wars*." In *Beyond Princess Culture: Gender and Children's Marketing*, edited by Katherine Foss, 117–34. New York: Peter Lang, 2019.

Francis, Diane B., Elise M. Stevens, Seth M. Noar, and Laura Widman. "Public Reactions to and Impact of Celebrity Health Announcements: Understanding the Charlie Sheen Effect," *Howard Journal of Communications* 30, no. 5 (2019): 479–94.

Freeman, Hadley. "*Star Wars'* Mark Hamill: 'I said to Carrie Fisher: I'm a good kisser—next, we're making out like teenagers!'" *The Guardian*, December 15, 2017. www.theguardian.com/film/2017/dec/14/star-wars-the-last-jedi-mark -hamill-carrie-fisher-good-kisser.

Freud, Sigmund. "Humor." *International Journal of Psychoanalysis* 9 (1928): 1–6.

Gal, Noam, Limor Shifman, and Zohar Kampf. "'It Gets Better': Internet Memes and the Construction of Collective Identity." *New Media and Society* 18, no. 8 (2015): 1698–714. https://doi.org/10.1177/1461444814568784.

Galloway, Alexander. *The Interface Effect*. Cambridge: Polity Press, 2012.

Garbo Talks. Directed by Sidney Lumet. Metro-Goldwyn-Mayer, 1984.

Gardner, Eriq. "'Back to the Future II' from a Legal Perspective: Unintentionally Visionary." *Hollywood Reporter*, October 21, 2015. www.hollywoodreporter .com/thr-esq/back-future-ii-a-legal-833705.

Geek+Gamers. "Star Wars—Nobody Wants Toys from The Last Jedi." YouTube video. 6:52. February 6, 2018. www.youtube.com/watch?v=P5Rbvow-03Y &t=53s.

Gekoski, Anna, and Steve Broome. *What's Normal Anyway? Celebrities' Own Stories of Mental Illness*. London: Constable, 2014.

Gelder, Ken. *Popular Fiction: The Logics and Practices of a Literary Field*. New York: Routledge, 2004.

Geraghty, Lincoln. *Cult Collectors: Nostalgia, Fandom, and Collecting Popular Culture*. New York: Routledge, 2014.

Giles, Howard, Richard Y. Bourhis, Nicholas J. Gadfield, Graham J. Davies, and Ann P. Davies. "Cognitive Aspects of Humour in Social Interaction: A Model and Some Linguistic Data." In *Humour and Laughter: Theory, Research, and*

Applications, edited by Anthony J. Chapman and Hugh C. Foot, 139–54. London: Wiley, 1976.

Gledhill, Christine. "The Signs of Melodrama." In *Home Is Where the Heart Is*, edited by Christine Gledhill, 207–29. London: British Film Institute, 1987.

Goffman, Erving. *Stigma: Notes on the Management of Spoiled Identity*. New York: Simon & Schuster, 1963.

Gray, Jonathan. *Show Sold Separately: Promos, Spoilers, and other Media Paratexts*. New York: New York University Press, 2010.

Greene, Andy. "The Last Word: Carrie Fisher on LSD, Death, and Sex with Han Solo." *Rolling Stone*, November 28, 2016. www.rollingstone.com/movies/movie -features/the-last-word-carrie-fisher-on-lsd-death-and-sex-with-han-solo -117225/.

Griffin, Kathy. *Kathy Griffin's Celebrity Run-Ins: My A–Z Index*. New York: Flatiron Books, 2016.

GROBI.TV. "Wir waren wieder in der Filmfigurenausstellung in Mönchengladbach." YouTube video. 12:27. December 30, 2015. www.youtube.com/watch?v= UySJSMqjz48&t=1s.

Halberstam, J. *The Queer Art of Failure*. Durham, NC: Duke University Press, 2011.

Halloweentown. Directed by Duwayne Dunham. Disney Channel, 1998.

Halloweentown II: Kalabar's Revenge. Directed by Mary Lambert. Disney Channel, 2001.

Hamill, Mark, Twitter/@HamillHimself: "I know where she stood. You know where she stood. Such an honor to see her standing with you today." January 21, 2017.

Hannah and Her Sisters. Directed by Woody Allen. MGM Home Entertainment, 1986.

Hart, Danielle. "'A War for a Better Tomorrow': *Ms. Marvel* Fanworks as Protest against the 2017 Immigration Ban." Fandom and Activism Panel at the Fan Studies Network North America Conference, DePaul University, Chicago, IL, October 25, 2018.

Harwell, Drew. "Fake-Porn Videos Are Being Weaponized to Harass and Humiliate Women: 'Everybody Is a Potential Target.'" *Washington Post*, December 30, 2018. www.washingtonpost.com/technology/2018/12/30/fake-porn-videos-are -being-weaponized-harass-humiliate-women-everybody-is-potential-target/ ?utm_term=.3dd39bfa3737.

Hastie, Amelie. *Cupboards of Curiosity: Women, Recollection, and Film History.* Durham, NC: Duke University Press, 2007.

Hather, Michelle. "If My Life Wasn't Funny It Would Only Be True." *Good Housekeeping UK*, January 2016, 18–22.

Hawke, Lisa D., Erin E. Michalak, Victoria Maxwell, and Sagar V. Parikh. "Reducing Stigma toward People with Bipolar Disorder: Impact of a Filmed Theatrical Intervention Based on a Personal Narrative." *International Journal of Social Psychiatry* 60, no. 8 (2014): 741–50.

Henderson, Claire, Sara Evans-Lacko, and Graham Thornicroft. "Mental Illness Stigma, Help Seeking, and Public Health Programs." *American Journal of Public Health* 103, no. 5 (2013): 777–80.

Henke, Richard. "*Imitation of Life*: Imitation World of Vaudeville." *Jump Cut*, no. 39 (June 1994): 31–39. July 7, 2011. www.ejumpcut.org/archive/onlinessays/JC39folder/imitationLife.html.

Hiatt, Brian. "Carrie Fisher on *The Force Awakens*: 'I've Always Been in *Star Wars.*'" December 9, 2015. www.rollingstone.com/movies/movie-features/carrie-fisher-on-the-force-awakens-ive-always-been-in-star-wars-55662/.

Hidalgo, Pablo. *Star Wars Propaganda: A History of Persuasive Art in the Galaxy.* New York: Harper, 2016.

Hirst, David L. *Comedy of Manners.* London: Methuen, 1979.

Hoffner, Cynthia A. "Responses to Carrie Fisher's Personal Disclosures about Mental Health: Identification, Humor, and Perceived Influence on Public Stigma." Presented at the International Communication Association conference, Prague, Czech Republic, May 24–29, 2018.

———. "Sharing on Social Network Sites Following Carrie Fisher's Death: Responses to Her Mental Health Advocacy." *Health Communication* 35, no. 12 (2020): 1475–86.

Hoffner, Cynthia A., and Elizabeth L. Cohen. "Mental Health–Related Outcomes of Robin Williams' Death: The Role of Parasocial Relations and Media Coverage in Stigma, Outreach, and Help-Seeking." *Health Communication* 33, no. 12 (2018): 1573–82.

———. "Portrayal of Mental Illness on the TV Series *Monk*: Presumed Influence and Consequences of Exposure." *Health Communication* 30, no. 10 (2015): 1046–54.

———. "Responses to Obsessive Compulsive Disorder on *Monk* among Series Fans: Parasocial Relations, Presumed Media Influence, and Behavioral Outcomes." *Journal of Broadcasting and Electronic Media* 56, no. 4 (2012): 650–68.

Hollows, Joanne. "The Masculinity of Cult." In *Defining Cult Movies*, edited by Mark Jancovich et al., 35–53. Manchester: Manchester University Press, 2003.

Hollywood: The Dream Factory. Written by Irwin Rosten. Culver City, CA: Turner Classic Movies, 1972.

Hollywood Vice Squad. Directed by Penelope Spheeris. Cinema Group, 1986.

hooks, bell. "The Oppositional Gaze." In *Black Looks: Race and Representation*, 115–31. Boston: South End, 1992.

Horton, Donald, and R. Richard Wohl. "Mass Communication and Para-social Interaction: Observations on Intimacy at a Distance." *Psychiatry* 19, no. 3 (1956): 215–29.

Howard, Adam. "Carrie Fisher Was a Feminist Force to Be Reckoned With." *NBC News*. Last modified December 27, 2016. www.nbcnews.com/news/us-news/carrie-fisher-was-feminist-force-be-reckoned-n700531.

Howard, Jacqueline. "Carrie Fisher Was a Champion for Mental Health, Too." *CNN*, December 27, 2016. www.cnn.com/2016/12/27/health/mental-health -carrie-fisher/index.html.

Howley, Kevin. "'I Have a Drone': Internet Memes and the Politics of Culture." *Interactions: Studies in Communication and Culture* 7, no. 2 (2016): 155–75.

How Sweet It Is! Directed by Jerry Paris. Warner Archive Collection, 1968.

How the West Was Won. Directed by John Ford. Metro-Goldwyn-Mayer, 1962.

Hufbauer, Benjamin. "The Politics behind the Original 'Star Wars.'" *Los Angeles Review of Books*, December 21, 2015.

Ilic, Marie, Jost Reinecke, Gerd Bohner, Hans-Onno Röttgers, Thomas Beblo, Martin Driessen, Ulrich Frommberger and Patrick William Corrigan. "Protecting Self-Esteem from Stigma: A Test of Different Strategies for Coping with the Stigma of Mental Illness." *International Journal of Social Psychiatry* 58, no. 3 (2012): 246–57.

Independent.co.uk. "Rogue One's CGI Princess Leia: The sands of time are so cruel you can't even do motion capture for your younger self." Accessed December 16, 2018. www.independent.co.uk/arts-entertainment/films/news/rogue-one-cgi-princess-leia-organa-actress-carrie-fisher-ingvild-deila-motion -capture-new-star-wars-a7484161.html.

In & Out. Directed by Frank Oz. Paramount Home Entertainment, 1997.

Internet Movie Database, "Carrie Fisher (I)." www.imdb.com/name/nm0000402/ ?ref_=fn_al_nm_1.

Internet Movie Database, "Debbie Reynolds (I)." www.imdb.com/name/nm0001666/?ref_=fn_al_nm_1.

Intimate Portrait: Debbie Reynolds and Carrie Fisher. Directed by Bob Jaffe. Lifetime, 2011.

It's Christmas, Carol! Directed by Michael Scott. Hallmark Channel, 2012.

Ivie, Devon. "Harrison Ford, Mark Hamill, and Other Celebrities Mourn the Death of Carrie Fisher." *Vulture*, December 27, 2016. www.vulture.com/2016/12/celebrities-react-to-carrie-fishers-death.html.

Jain, Parul, Uma Shankar Pandey, and Enakshi Roy. "Perceived Efficacy and Intentions Regarding Seeking Mental Healthcare: Impact of Deepika Padukone, A Bollywood Celebrity's Public Announcement of Struggle with Depression." *Journal of Health Communication* 22, no. 8 (2017): 713–20.

Jamison, Kay Redfield. *Touched by Fire: Manic-Depressive Illness and the Artistic Temperament*. New York: Free Press Paperbacks, 1994.

Jacqueline Susann and Valley of the Dolls. US Dirs. Alan Foshko and Sherry W. Arden, 1967.

Jay and Silent Bob Strike Back. Directed by Kevin Smith. Lionsgate Home Entertainment, 2001.

Jenkins, Henry. "Fandom, Participatory Culture, and Web 2.0." *Confessions of an Aca-Fan*, January 9, 2010.

———. Foreword to *The Routledge Companion to Transmedia Studies*, edited by Matthew Freeman and Renira Rampazzo Gambarato. New York: Routledge, 2019.

———. *Textual Poachers: Television Fans and Participatory Culture*. New York: Routledge, 1992.

Jermyn, Deborah. "'Get a life, ladies. Your old one is not coming back': Ageing, Ageism and the Lifespan of Female Celebrity." *Celebrity Studies* 3, no. 1 (2012): 3.

Johnson, Derek. "'May the Force Be with Katie': Pink Media Franchising and the Postfeminist Politics of HerUniverse." *Feminist Media Studies* 14, no. 6 (February 28, 2014): 895–900.

Johnson, Elizabeth. "Carrie Fisher Talks about Mental Illness and Career." *Herald-Tribune*, April 20, 2013. http://health.heraldtribune.com/2013/04/20/14065/.

"JotW—Carrie Fisher Tribute & Bloodline Recap." *TumblingSaber—A Star Wars Podcast* (podcast audio), December 29, 2016. https://tumblingsaber.podbean.com/e/jotw-carrie-fisher-tribute-bloodline-recap.

Jowett, Lorna. "Rey, Mary Sue, and Phasma Too: Feminism and Fan Responses to *The Force Awakens* Merchandise." In *Disney's Star Wars: Forces of Production,*

Promotion, and Reception, edited by William Proctor and Richard McCulloch. Iowa City: University of Iowa Press, 2019.

Kaplan, E. Ann. 2003. "Wicked Old Ladies from Europe: Jeanne Moreau and Marlene Dietrich on the Screen and Live." In *Bad: Infamy, Darkness, Evil, and Slime on Screen*, edited by Murray Pomerance. Albany: State University of New York Press.

Karbo, Karen. *In Praise of Difficult Women: Life Lessons from 29 Heroines Who Dared to Break the Rules*. Washington, DC: National Geographic, 2018.

"Karl and Amy enjoy Christmas 1983." *I Grew Up Star Wars* (blog). Accessed October 23, 2019. http://igrewupstarwars.com/karl-and-amy-enjoy-christmas -1983/.

"Karl and Amy share a Moment—1983." *I Grew Up Star Wars* (blog). Accessed October 23, 2019. http://igrewupstarwars.com/karl-and-amy-share-a -moment-1983/.

Kean, Hilda. Introduction to *The Public History Reader*, edited by Hilda Kean and Paul Martin. New York: Routledge, 2013.

Keck, William. "Scandal's History for 'These Old Broads.'" *Los Angeles Times*, February 12, 2001, F1.

Keepers of the Frame. Directed by Mark McLaughlin. Mount Pilot Productions, 1999.

Keidl, Philipp Dominik. "Behind-the-(Museum)Scenes: Fan-Curated Exhibitions as Tourist Attractions." In *The Routledge Companion to Media and Tourism*, edited by Maria Månsson, Anne Buchmann, Cecilia Cassinger, and Lena Eskilsson. New York: Routledge, forthcoming.

———. "Between Textuality and Materiality: Fandom and the Mediation of Action Figures." *Film Criticism* 42, no. 2 (2018).

———. "Plastic Heritage: Fans and the Making of History." PhD diss., Concordia University, 2018.

Kennedy, Lauren P. "20 Questions for Carrie Fisher." *WebMD*, 2010. www .webmd.com/mental-health/addiction/features/questions-for-carrie -fisher#1.

Khatchatourian, Maane. "'Hunger Games: Mockingjay' Director Didn't Use CGI for Philip Seymour Hoffman Scenes." *Variety*, November 15, 2014. https:// variety.com/2014/film/news/hunger-games-mockingjay-director-didnt-use-cgi -for-philip-seymour-hoffman-scenes-1201357509/.

Knowles, Claire. "Working Girls: Femininity and Entrapment in *Peyton Place* and *Valley of the Dolls*." *Women: A Cultural Review* 27, no. 1 (2016): 62–78.

Krishna, Rachael. "11 Heartbreaking Cartoons in Memory of Carrie Fisher." *Buzz-FeedNews*, December 28, 2016. www.buzzfeednews.com/article/krishrach/11-heartbreaking-cartoons-in-memory-of-carrie-fisher.

Kyriazis, Stefan. "Star Wars: Carrie Fisher's Death 'TOTALLY Changed Episode 9' WHAT Was the Original Plot?" *Express*, May 5, 2017. www.express.co.uk/entertainment/films/800801/Star-Wars-8-Carrie-Fisher-death-Episode-9-Leia-plan-Lucasfilm-Kathleen-Kennedy.

"The Last Jedi: De-Feminized Fanedit (aka The Chauvinist Cut)." Archive.org video. 46:22. January 14, 2018. https://archive.org/details/thepiratebay-19660049_201809.

Latham, Sean. *The Art of Scandal: Modernism, Libel Law, and the Roman à Clef.* New York: Oxford University Press, 2009.

Laurens, Rhett H. "Year of the Living Dead: California Breathes New Life into Celebrity Public Rights." *Hastings Communications and Entertainment Law Journal* 24, no. 1 (2001): 109–48.

Lawler, Opheli Garcia. "There Will Not Be a Prince Hologram at the Super Bowl." *Fader*, February 4, 2018. www.thefader.com/2018/02/04/there-will-not-be-a-prince-hologram-at-the-super-bowl.

Leonard, Elizabeth. "Carrie Fisher's Bipolar Crisis: 'I Was Trying to Survive.'" *People*, March 25, 2013. https://people.com/archive/carrie-fishers-bipolar-crisis-i-was-trying-to-survive-vol-79-no-12/.

Limon, John. *Stand-up Comedy in Theory, or, Abjection in America.* Durham, NC: Duke University Press, 2000.

Linfield, Susan. "First It Was Drugs, and Now It's Mother." *New York Times*, September 2, 1990, H15.

Link, Bruce G., and Jo C. Phelan. "Labeling and Stigma." In *Handbook of the Sociology of Mental Health*, edited by Carol S. Aneshensel, Jo C. Phelan, and Alex Bierman, 524–41. New York: Springer, 2013.

"Living Legend Debbie Reynolds and Her Daughter Icon Carrie Fisher." *The Oprah Winfrey Show*. Produced by Neil Coleman. 2011.

Loew, William. "Irony in the Text or Insincerity in the Writer?" In *Text and Technology*, edited by M. Baker, G. Francis, and T. Togini-Bonelli, 157–76. Amsterdam: John Benjamins, 1993.

Lowry, Brian. "The Carrie Fisher Question: Why 'Star Wars' Should Have Recast Princess Leia." *CNN*. Last updated December 20, 2019. www.cnn.com/2019/12/20/entertainment/carrie-fisher-star-wars/?hpt=ob_blogfooterold.

Lusinski, Natalia. "15 Carrie Fisher Memes and Tributes to Share When You Just Miss Her Too Much." *Bustle*, December 27, 2016. www.bustle.com/p/15 -carrie-fisher-memes-tributes-to-share-when-you-just-miss-her-too-much -26461.

Ma, Lybi. "Interview: The Fisher Queen." *Psychology Today* (November/December 2001): 32+.

Macnicol, Glynnis. "In Defense of Princess Leia and 'Star Wars' Feminism." *Elle*. Last modified August 14, 2015. www.elle.com/culture/career-politics/a29876/ in-defense-of-princess-leia-and-star-wars-feminism/.

Maier, Julia A., Douglas A. Gentile, David L. Vogel, and Scott A. Kaplan. "Media Influences on Self-Stigma of Seeking Psychological Services: The Importance of Media Portrayals and Person Perception." *Psychology of Popular Media Culture* 3, no. 4 (2014): 239–56.

Manovich, Lev. *Software Takes Command*. New York: Bloomsbury, 2013.

Map to the Stars. Directed by David Cronenberg. Focus World, 2014.

Marcus, Mary B. "Carrie Fisher's Honesty about Bipolar Disorder, Addiction Helped Fight Stigma." *CBS News*, December 28, 2016. www.cbsnews.com/ news/carrie-fisher-bipolar-disorder-addiction-mental-health-stigma/.

Marshall, Barbara L., and Momin Rahman. "Celebrity, Ageing, and the Construction of 'Third Age' Identities." *International Journal of Cultural Studies* 18, no. 6 (2014): 577–93.

Marshall, Kelli. "Fred Astaire for Dirt Devil." *Critical Commons*. Accessed December 12, 2018. www.criticalcommons.org/Members/kellimarshall/clips/Astaire _DirtDevil2.mp4/view.

Marshall, P. David. *Celebrity and Power: Fame in Contemporary Culture*. Minneapolis: University of Minnesota Press, 1997.

Martin, Gary. " 'Women's Place Is in the Home'—the Meaning and Origin of This Phrase." Phrasefinder. Accessed March 18, 2017. https://phrases.org.uk/ meanings/womans-place-is-in-the-home.html.

Massachusetts Psychiatric Society. "APA Annual Meeting 2010 Convocation Speaker Carrie Fisher." *Massachusetts Psychiatric Society Bulletin*, April 2010.

"Matt Takes Aim at Star Wars Fun! 1978." *I Grew Up Star Wars* (blog). Accessed October 23, 2019. http://igrewupstarwars.com/matt-takes-aim-at-star-wars -fun-1978/.

Mayne, Judith. *Cinema and Spectatorship*. Routledge: New York, 1993.

———. "Lesbian Looks: Dorothy Arzner and Female Authorship." In *How Do I Look?: Queer Film and Video*, edited by Bad Object-Choices, 103–35. Seattle: Bay Press, 1991.

McCoy, Lauren. "Literary Gossip: Caroline Lamb's *Glenarvon* and the Roman à Clef." *Eighteenth-Century Fiction* 27, no. 1 (Fall 2014): 127–50.

McGinty, Emma E., Alene Kennedy-Hendricks, Seema Choksy, and Colleen L. Barry. "Trends in News Media Coverage of Mental Illness in the United States: 1995–2014." *Health Affairs* 35, no. 6 (2016): 1121–29.

McKeever, Robert. "Vicarious Experience: Experimentally Testing the Effects of Empathy for Media Characters with Severe Depression and the Intervening Role of Perceived Similarity." *Health Communication* 30, no. 11 (2015): 1122–34.

McLendon, Winzola. "Behind the Glamor of Show Business." *Washington Post*, February 22, 1966, B5.

McNally, Victoria. "Why 2016 Is the Year We Need to Stop Pretending Women Aren't Geeks." *MTV.com*. Last modified December 22, 2015. www.mtv.com/news/2683640/geek-media-numbers-breakdown/.

Meisenbach, Rebecca J. "Stigma Management Communication: A Theory and Agenda for Applied Research on How Individuals Manage Moments of Stigmatized Identity." *Journal of Applied Communication Research* 38, no. 3 (2010): 268–92.

MGM: When the Lion Roars. Directed by Frank Martin. Warner Archive Collection, 1992.

Miller, Matt. "'Star Wars' Is Not Anti-Trump, But It Is Anti-Fascism." *Esquire*, December 12, 2016.

"Mission and Vision." Women's March on Washington. Accessed March 18, 2017. https://womensmarch.com/mission-and-principles.

Mizejewski, Linda. "Feminism, Postfeminism, Liz Lemonism: Comedy and Gender Politics on 30 Rock." *Genders* 55 (2012).

———. *Pretty/Funny: Women Comedians and Body Politics*. Austin: University of Texas Press, 2014.

Moore, Trent. "Here's What Rogue One's Princess Leia Looked Like without the CGI." *Syfy Wire*, April 3, 2017. www.syfy.com/syfywire/heres-what-rogue-ones-princess-leia-looked-without-cgi.

Mother. Directed by Albert Brooks. Paramount Home Entertainment, 1996.

Moyer-Gusé, Emily, Chad Mahood, and Sarah Brookes. "Entertainment-Education in the Context of Humor: Effects on Safer Sex Intentions and Risk Perceptions." *Health Communication* 26, no. 8 (2011): 765–74.

Mulvey, Laura. "Visual Pleasure and Narrative Cinema." In *Film Theory and Criticism: Introductory Readings*, edited by Leo Braudy and Marshall Cohen. New York: Oxford University Press, 1999.

Murthi, Vikram. "Carrie Fisher's Honesty with Mental Illness Inspired '#InHonorOfCarrie' Social Media Movement." *IndieWire*, December 28, 2016. www.indiewire.com/2016/12/carrie-fisher-dead-mental-illness-honesty-social -media-movement-1201763248/.

My Star Wars Story (blog). Accessed August 29, 2018. http://mystarwarsstory .com/.

Myers, Maddy. "In Memoriam: We Already Miss Carrie Fisher So Much." *The Mary Sue*. December 27, 2016. www.themarysue.com/carrie-fisher-in -memoriam/.

Myrick, Jessica Gall. "Public Perceptions of Celebrity Cancer Deaths: How Identification and Emotions Shape Cancer Stigma and Behavioral Intentions." *Health Communication* 32, no. 11 (2017): 1385–95.

Nabi, Robin L., Jiyeon So, and Abby Prestin. "Media-Based Emotional Coping: Examining the Emotional Benefits and Pitfalls of Media Consumption." In *The Routledge Handbook of Emotions and Mass Media*, edited by Katrin Doveling, Christian V. Scheve, and Elly A. Konijn, 116–33. New York: Routledge, 2010.

National Alliance on Mental Illness. "Bipolar Disorder." *National Alliance on Mental Illness*, 2017. www.nami.org/learn-more/mental-health-conditions/bipolar -disorder.

———. "NAMI Honors Hollywood Actors for Confronting Mental Illness in Drama and Real Life," *National Alliance on Mental Illness*, June 14, 2001. www .nami.org/Press-Media/Press-Releases/2001/NAMI-Honors-Hollywood-Actors -for-Confronting-Menta.

Nguyen, Hanh. " 'Catastrophe': Rob Delaney and Sharon Horgan on Depicting a Type of Alcoholism Rarely Seen on TV." *IndieWire* May 5, 2017.

Noar, Seth M., Jessica Fitts Willoughby, Jessica Gall Myrick, and Jennifer Brown. "Public Figure Announcements about Cancer and Opportunities for Cancer Communication: A Review and Research Agenda." *Health Communication* 29, no. 5 (2014): 445–61.

Pacitti, Tony. *My Best Friend Is a Wookiee: A Memoir*. Avon, MA: Adams Media, 2010.

Park, Sejung, and Cynthia A. Hoffner. "Tweeting about Mental Health to Honor Carrie Fisher: How #InHonorOfCarrie Reinforced the Social Influence of

Celebrity Advocacy." *Computers in Human Behavior* 110, article 106353 (2020): 1–11.

Parker, Ryan. "R. Lee Ermey and John Wayne Shared Screen Time Together—Kind Of." *Hollywood Reporter*, April 15, 2018. www.hollywoodreporter.com/heat-vision/r-lee-ermey-john-wayne-shared-screen-time-together-kind-1102876.

Partington, Alan. "Phrasal Irony: Its Form, Function, and Exploitation." *Journal of Pragmatics* 43 (2011): 1786–800.

Paul, Pritha. "Helen Mirren Opens Up about Sexy Bikini Photo, Says She Tried to Look Good for the Paparazzi by 'Sucking In' Her Tummy." *Meaww*. September 13, 2019. https://meaww.com/helen-mirren-opens-up-about-viral-bikini-picture-from-2008-made-her-a-sex-icon-overnight.

Paz, Myke Dela. " '6' Custom Star Wars the Black Series Princess Leia Action Figures." YouTube video. 0:50. February 22, 2017. www.youtube.com/watch?v=S9PRHBl1BR4.

Pearson, Jennifer. " 'I will not apologize for how I look': *Star Wars* Star Daisy Ridley Hits Back at Body Shamer Who Ridiculed Her Online for Not Having Curves Like a 'Real Woman.' " *Daily Mail*. Last modified March 9, 2016. www.dailymail.co.uk/tvshowbiz/article-3484676/Daisy-Ridley-hits-body-shamers-complained-s-skinny.html.

Perez, Nistasha. "The Resistance Is Fannish." Fandom and Activism Panel at the Fan Studies Network North America Conference, DePaul University, Chicago, IL, October 25, 2018.

Pirkis, Jane, R. Warwick Blood, Catherine Francis, and Kerry McCallum. "On-screen Portrayals of Mental Illness: Extent, Nature, and Impacts." *Journal of Health Communication* 11, no. 5 (2006): 523–41.

Postcards from the Edge. Directed by Mike Nichols. Mill Creek Entertainment, 1990.

Prince. "Prince 1998 Guitar World Interview." *Music Interview Archive*. Accessed December 7, 2018. https://sites.google.com/site/themusicinterviewarchive/prince/prince-1998-guitar-world-interview.

Private Screenings. Directed by Tony Barbon. Turner Classic Movies, 2002.

Reagle, Joseph. "Geek Policing: Fake Geek Girls and Contested Attention." *International Journal of Communication* 9 (2015): 2862–80.

Reynolds, Debbie. "Carrie is in stable condition. If there is a change, we will share it. For all her fans & friends. I thank you for your prayers & good wishes." Twitter. @DebbieReynolds1, December 25, 2016. https://twitter.com/DebbieReynolds1/status/813112672002723841.

Reynolds, Debbie, and Dorian Hannaway. *Unsinkable, a Memoir*. New York: Harper Audio, 2013.

Robert D. Comment on "Princess Leia." *Sideshow.com*. December 31, 2016. www .sideshow.com/collectibles/star-wars-princess-leia-hot-toys-902490.

Robertson, Pamela. *Guilty Pleasures: Feminist Camp from Mae West to Madonna*. Durham, NC: Duke University Press, 1996.

Robinson, Joanna. "How Carrie Fisher Became the Surprising Face of the Rebellion against Trump." *Vanity Fair*. Last modified January 23, 2017. www .vanityfair.com/style/2017/01/carrie-fisher-todd-fisher-womens-march-donald -trump.

Rojek, Chris. *Celebrity*. London: Reaktion Books, 2001.

"Rosemary's Baby." *30 Rock*. Directed by Michael Engler. NBC, 2007.

Rothman, Michael, and Clayton Sandell. "Carrie Fisher's Reaction to Her Latest 'Star Wars' Cameo." *ABC News*, January 5, 2017. https://abcnews.go.com/ Entertainment/carrie-fishers-reaction-latest-star-wars-cameo/story?id= 44571752.

Rowe, Cami. *The Politics of Protest and U.S. Foreign Policy*. New York: Routledge, 2013.

Rowe, Kathleen. "Comedy, Melodrama, and Gender: Theorizing the Genres of Laughter." In *Classical Hollywood Comedy*, edited by Kristine Brunovska Karnick and Henry Jenkins, 39–59. New York: Routledge, 1995.

Ruelle, Ron. "Life, Death, and the Price of Princess Leia Action Figures." *hobbybd. com* (blog). December 30, 2016. https://blog.hobbydb.com/2016/12/30/life -death-and-the-price-of-princess-leia-action-figures/.

Rüsch, Nicolas, Matthias C. Angermeyer, and Patrick W. Corrigan. "Mental Illness Stigma: Concepts, Consequences, and Initiatives to Reduce Stigma." *European Psychiatry* 20, no. 8 (2005): 529–39.

Sadowsky, Jonathan. "Electroconvulsive Therapy: A History of Controversy, but Also of Help." *The Conversation*, January 12, 2017. www.scientificamerican .com/article/electroconvulsive-therapy-a-history-of-controversy-but-also-of -help/.

Salvato, Nick. "The Age of Gossipdom." *Modern Drama* 53, no. 3 (Fall 2010): 289–96.

Salvatore, Ron. "Princess Leia Organa Large Size Action Figure." *The Star Wars Collectors Archive* (blog). http://theswca.com/index.php?action=disp_item& item_id=39543.

Samuel, Raphael. *Theatres of Memory*. London: Verso, 1994.

"Sandcrawler #13: A New Year and Goodbye to a Princess." *A Star Wars Collector's Show* (podcast audio), January 8, 2017. https://sandcrawlerpodcast.libsyn.com/page/4/size/25.

Santo, Avi. "Fans and Merchandise." In *The Routledge Companion to Media Fandom*, edited by Melissa A. Click and Suzanne Scott. New York: Routledge, 2018.

Schiappa, Edward, Peter B. Gregg, and Dean E. Hewes. "The Parasocial Contact Hypothesis." *Communication Monographs* 72, no. 1 (2005): 92–115.

Schulman, Michael. "Postscript: Carrie Fisher, 1956–2016." *New Yorker*, December 28, 2016.

Scott, Jason. "*Star Wars* as a Character-Oriented Franchise." In *Fan Phenomena: Star Wars*, edited by Mika Elovaara, 10–19. Bristol: Intellect, 2013.

Scott, Sharon M. *Toys and American Culture: An Encyclopedia*, 2–6. Santa Barbara, CA: Greenwood, 2010.

Scott, Suzanne. *Fake Geek Fan Girls: Fandom, Gender, and the Convergence Culture Industry*. New York: New York University Press, 2019.

———. "#Wheresrey?: Toys, Spoilers, and the Gender Politics of Franchise Paratexts." *Critical Studies in Media Communication* 34, no. 2 (2017).

Seaman, Barbara. *Lovely Me: The Life of Jacqueline Susann*. New York: Seven Stories Press, 1996.

"Season 1, Episode 4—Star Wars." *The Sifl and Olly Show*. Directed by Matt Crocco and Liam Lynch. MTV, 1998.

Seltzer, Sarah. "Carrie Fisher Slams Critics of Her Appearance in 'The Force Awakens.'" *Flavorwire*. Last modified December 30, 2015. http://flavorwire.com/553819/carrie-fisher-slams-critics-of-her-appearance-in-the-force-awakens.

Setoodeh, Ramin. "Carrie Fisher on How George Lucas Stole Her Identity." *Newsweek*. Last modified December 27, 2016. www.newsweek.com/carrie-fisher-george-lucas-star-wars-archive-interview-67321.

Shaken Not Nerd. "Remembering Carrie Fisher-Princess Leia Hot Toy Review." YouTube video. 9:57. January 10, 2017. www.youtube.com/watch?v=awxYOYREjC8&t=132s.

Shapiro, Emily. "Carrie Fisher Was a Mental Health Advocate Inspired by Her Own Struggles." *ABC News*, December 27, 2016. https://abcnews.go.com/Entertainment/carrie-fisher-mental-health-advocate-inspired-struggles/story?id=44418344.

Shifman, Limor. *Memes in Digital Culture*. Cambridge, MA: MIT Press, 2013.

Singin' in the Rain. Directed by Stanley Donen. Metro-Goldwyn-Mayer, 1952.

Slaughter, Adele. "Carrie Fisher 'Strikes Back' at Mental Illness." *USA Today*, May 29, 2002. http://usatoday30.usatoday.com/news/health/spotlight/2002/05/29-fisher.htm.

Smith, Kyle. "If Carrie Fisher Doesn't Like Being Judged on Looks, She Should Quit Acting." *New York Post*, December 30, 2015. http://nypost.com/2015/12/30/if-carrie-fisher-doesnt-like-being-judged-on-looks-she-should-quit-acting/.

Smith, Rachel A. "Language of the Lost: An Explication of Stigma Communication." *Communication Theory* 17, no. 4 (2007): 462–85.

Smith, Rachel. "Media Depictions of Health Topics: Challenge and Stigma Formats." *Journal of Health Communication* 12, no. 3 (2007): 233–49.

"Sonnet 29 (Carrie Fisher, recitation)." *Take All My Loves*. Rufus Wainwright. Berlin: Deutsche Grammophon, 2016.

Sontag, Susan. *Against Interpretation and Other Essays*. New York: Farrar, Straus and Giroux, 1966.

Spacks, Patricia Meyer. *Gossip*. New York: Albert A. Knopf, 1985.

Staba, David. "Hollywood Kid Carrie Fisher and Her Best Awful." *bp Magazine*, November 7, 2004. www.bphope.com/hollywood-kid-carrie-fisher-and-her-best-awful/.

Staiger, Janet. *Interpreting Films*. Princeton, NJ: Princeton University Press, 1992.

———. "*Les Belles Dames sans Merci*, Femmes Fatales, Vampires, Vamps, and Gold Diggers: The Transformation and Narrative Value of Aggressive Fallen Women." In *Reclaiming the Archive: Feminism and Film History*, edited by Vicki Callahan, 32–57. Detroit: Wayne State University Press, 2010. ProQuest Ebook Central, http://ebookcentral.proquest.com/lib/emerson/detail.action?docID=3416553. Created from Emerson on 2017-09-03 18:42:50.

StarWars.com. "A Statement Regarding New Rumors." Accessed December 17, 2018. www.starwars.com/news/a-statement-regarding-new-rumors.

"Star Wars Collector Podcast#13: Remembering Royalty." *The Star Wars Collector* (podcast audio), December 30, 2016. www.thestarwarscollector.com/?m=201612.

Star Wars: Episode VII—The Force Awakens. Directed by J. J. Abrams. Walt Disney Studios Home Entertainment, 2015.

Star Wars: Episode VIII—The Last Jedi. Directed by Rian Johnson. Walt Disney Studios Home Entertainment, 2017.

Star Wars: Episode IX—The Rise of Skywalker. Directed by J. J. Abrams. Walt Disney Studios Home Entertainment, 2019.

Stephen Fry: The Secret Life of the Manic Depressive. Directed by Ross Wilson. London: IWC Media, 2006.

Stever, Gayle. "Parasocial Theory: Concepts and Measures." In *International Encyclopedia of Media Effects*, edited by Patrick Rössler, Cynthia A. Hoffner, and Liesbet van Zoonen, 1457–68. Boston: Wiley-Blackwell, 2017.

Stewart, David. "'Bolshevik Marketing'—The Rhetoric of Ideas." YouTube video (5:03). February 4, 2018. www.youtube.com/watch?v=be4VNXKVKUA &t=2s.

———. "Star Wars Toys Don't Sell—Bolshevik Marketing and Marketing in Reverse." YouTube video. 16: 28. January 29, 2018. www.youtube.com/watch?v =8Zd6ljuRikY&t=5s.

Substance Abuse and Mental Health Services Administration (SAMHSA). "SAMHSA to Recognize Behavioral Health Champions at 2017 Voice Awards," SAMHSA, August 16, 2017. https://www.samhsa.gov/newsroom/press -announcements/201708161145

Susan Slept Here. Directed by Frank Tashlin. Warner Archive Collection, 1954.

Susann, Jacqueline. *Dolores.* New York: William Morrow, 2010.

———. *Every Night, Josephine.* New York: Penguin, 2004.

———. *The Love Machine.* New York: Grove Press, 1997.

———. *Once Is Not Enough.* New York: Grove Press, 1997.

———. *Valley of the Dolls.* New York: Grove Press, 1997.

Sweet Revenge. Directed by Charlotte Brandstrom. TNT, 1990.

Sydell, Laura. "In the Future Movie Stars May Be Performing Even after They're Dead." *NPR*, March 5, 2018. www.npr.org/sections/alltechconsidered/2018/03/ 05/590238807/in-the-future-movie-stars-may-be-performing-even-after-their -dead.

Tab Hunter Confidential. Directed by Jeffrey Schwarz. Film Collaborative, 2015.

Tal-Or, Nurit, and Yael Papirman. "The Fundamental Attribution Error in Attributing Fictional Figures' Characteristics to the Actors." *Media Psychology* 9, no. 2 (2007): 331–45.

Taylor, Chris. *How Star Wars Conquered the Universe.* New York: Basic Books, 2014.

Thalmann, Daniel, and Nadia Magnenat Thalmann. *Rendez-vous in Montreal.* Filmed 1987. YouTube video. Posted August 5, 2015. www.youtube.com/watch ?v=vuvvv7Bie4U.

That's Entertainment! Directed by Jack Haley Jr. MGM/UA Home Entertainment, 1974.

"There Goes the Bride: Part 2." *The Golden Girls*. Directed by Matthew Diamond, 1991. Los Angeles, CA: Hallmark Channel.

These Amazing Shadows. Directed by Paul Mariano and Kurt Norton. PBS Home Video, 2011.

These Old Broads. Directed by Matthew Diamond. Sony Pictures Home Entertainment, 2001.

Tinkcom, Matthew. *Working Like a Homosexual: Camp, Capital, Cinema*. Durham, NC: Duke University Press, 2002.

Titelman, Carol. *The Art of Return of the Jedi*. New York: Ballantine, 1983.

Tortajada, Iolanda, Frederik Dhaenens, and Cilia Willem. "Gendered Ageing Bodies in Popular Media Culture." *Feminist Media Studies* 8, no. 1 (2018): 2.

Travis, Erika. "From Bikinis to Blasters: The Role of Gender in the *Star Wars* Community." In *Fan Phenomena: Star Wars*, edited by Mika Elovaara, 48–58. Bristol: Intellect, 2013.

Unbox Boys. "Carrie Fisher 'Princess Leia' Toy Tribute." YouTube video. 1:15. December 23, 2016. www.youtube.com/watch?v=lYd9O3IjeTQ.

Unsinkable Molly Brown. Directed by Charles Walters. Metro-Goldwyn-Mayer, 1964.

"Vader and the Rest of the Lineup." *I Grew Up Star Wars* (blog). Accessed October 23, 2019. http://igrewupstarwars.com/vader-and-the-rest-of-the-lineup-1982/.

Valley of the Dolls. 1967. Directed by Mark Robson. DVD. Fox, 2006.

Van den Bulck, Hilde. "Growing Old in Celebrity Culture." In *Aging, Media, and Culture*, edited by C. Lee Harrington, Denise D. Bielby, and Anthony R. Bardo, 71 (Lanham, MD: Lexington Books, 2014).

VanDerWerff, Emily. "Star Wars: Episode IX Announces Its Cast—Which Includes Carrie Fisher." *Vox*. Last updated July 27, 2018. www.vox.com/culture/2018/7/27/17623418/star-wars-episode-ix-cast-carrie-fisher-mark-hamill-billy-dee-williams.

Van Ekelenburg, Lindsay. Twitter post. December 27, 2018. https://twitter.com/LindsayvanekArt/status/1078405595911340038.

Van Someren, Anna. "On Chuck and Carrot Mobs: Mapping the Connections between Participatory Culture and Public Participation." *Confessions of an Aca-Fan*. January 16, 2009.

Vermaak, Janelle. "Fan Gifting and Merchandise Collecting Practices within the Alien Film Franchise." Fan Practices and Labor Panel at the Fan Studies Network North America Conference, DePaul University, Chicago, IL, October 26, 2018.

Vogel, David L., Douglas A. Gentile, and Scott A. Kaplan. "The Influence of Television on Willingness to Seek Therapy." *Journal of Clinical Psychology* 64, no. 3 (2008): 276–95.

Warner, Brian. "How One Brilliant Decision in 1973 Made George Lucas a Multi-Billionaire Today." *Celebrity Net Worth*. Last modified December 14, 2015. www.celebritynetworth.com/articles/entertainment-articles/how-one-genius -decision-made-george-lucas-a-billionaire/.

Warner, Jamie. "Political Culture Jamming: The Dissident Humor of *The Daily Show with Jon Stewart*." *Popular Communication* 5, no. 1 (2007): 17–26.

Weaver, Hilary. "Debbie Reynolds Protected and Preserved Hollywood's Most Precious Relics." *Vanity Fair*. Last modified December 29, 2016. www.vanityfair .com/style/2016/12/debbie-reynolds-protected-and-preserved-hollywoods -most-precious-relics.

———. "How Debbie Reynolds's Beloved Hollywood Memorabilia Could Be Saved." *Vanity Fair*. Last modified April 6, 2017. www.vanityfair.com/style/ 2017/04/debbie-reynolds-memorabilia-preserved.

Webb, Glenn. "Star Wars Black Series 2 Princess Leia 6 Inch Action Figure Review." YouTube video, November 11, 2013. 3:11. www.youtube.com/watch?v =a6xh5iCcBUo&t=26s.

Weinraub, Bernard. "For 4 Superstars, Art Is Now Imitating Life." *New York Times*, October 12, 2000, E1, E5.

Whalen, Andrew. " 'Star Wars: Episode IX': Every Detail about Carrie Fisher's Return as General Leia Organa." *Newsweek*. Last modified July 30, 2018. www.newsweek.com/star-wars-episode-9-ix-cast-carrie-fisher-leia-organa-jj -abrams-force-awakens-1048987.

Whelehan, Imelda. *The Feminist Bestseller: From* Sex and the Single Girl *to* Sex and the City. New York: Palgrave Macmillan, 2005.

Wikipedia. "George Sanders." https://en.wikipedia.org/wiki/George_Sanders.

———. "The Thalians." https://en.wikipedia.org/wiki/The_Thalians.

Williams, Mary Elizabeth. "*Star Wars* Lets Princess Leia Age Realistically: Is This an Alternate Hollywood Universe?" *Salon*. Last modified October 20, 2015. https://www.salon.com/2015/10/20/star_wars_lets_princess_leia_age _realistically_is_this_an_alternate_hollywood_universe.

Williams, Rebecca. "Introduction: Starting at the End." In *Everybody Hurts: Transitions, Endings, and Resurrections in Fan Cultures*, edited by Rebecca Williams, 1–16. Iowa City: University of Iowa Press, 2018.

Winick, Erin. "Actors Are Digitally Preserving Themselves to Continue Their Careers beyond the Grave." *MIT Technology Review*, October 16. 2018. www.technologyreview.com/s/612291/actors-are-digitally-preserving-themselves-to-continue-their-careers-beyond-the-grave/.

Woerner, Meredith. "Carrie Fisher Thinks Slave Leia Bikini Haters Are Asinine." *Los Angeles Times*. Last modified December 17, 2015. www.latimes.com/entertainment/herocomplex/la-et-hc-star-wars-carrie-fisher-20151216-story.html.

———. "Remembering Carrie Fisher: Actress, Writer, Icon." *Baltimore Sun*. Last modified December 27, 2016. www.baltimoresun.com/sdhoy-remembering-carrie-fisher-actress-writer-icon-20161229-story.html.

Women. Directed by Diane English. New Line Home Video, 2008.

Wong, Norman C. H., Kathryn L. Lookadoo, and Gwendelyn S. Nisbett. "'I'm Demi and I Have Bipolar Disorder': Effect of Parasocial Contact on Reducing Stigma toward People with Bipolar Disorder." *Communication Studies* 68, no. 3 (2017): 314–33.

Worland, Justin. "Carrie Fisher Didn't Just Break Boundaries Onscreen. She also Fought the Stigma of Mental Illness." *Time*, December 27, 2016. http://time.com/4618486/carrie-fisher-dead-mental-health-legacy/.

WorldClassBullshitters. "The Cheapest Star Wars Toys Ever." YouTube video. 10:46. April 25, 2018. www.youtube.com/watch?v=sMcZZrRlFhA.

———. "The New Star Wars Toys Are Practically Free." YouTube video. 12:51. April 18, 2018. www.youtube.com/watch?v=S5nbbU7dHuM.

———. "The $1 Star Wars Toys." YouTube video. 12:17. January 21, 2018. www.youtube.com/watch?v=JcHBUqpxOMg.

———. "Star Wars Toys and Hasbro Layoffs." YouTube video 16:22. October 20, 2018. www.youtube.com/watch?v=zdf5WQdBSIg.

———. "Who Buys Star Wars Toys? No One . . ." YouTube video. 15:23. January 15, 2018. www.youtube.com/watch?v=RFqsiuPxfn8.

World Health Organization. "Mental Health Policy and Service Guidance Package: Advocacy for Mental Health." World Health Organization, 2003. www.who.int/mental_health/policy/services/1_advocacy_WEB_07.pdf?ua=1.

Yagoda, Maria. "Inside Carrie Fisher's Revolutionary Openness about Her Mental Illness: 'She Changed the World.'" *People*, December 28, 2016. http://people.com/celebrity/impact-carrie-fisher-mental-illness/.

Yahr, Emily. "Carrie Fisher, the Inspiring Mental Health Advocate: 'I Am Mentally Ill . . . I Am Not Ashamed of That.'" *Washington Post*, December 27, 2016. www.washingtonpost.com/news/arts-and-entertainment/wp/2016/12/27/carrie-fisher-the-inspiring-mental-health-advocate-i-am-mentally-ill-i-am-not-ashamed-of-that/.

Zacharek, Stephanie. "*The Force Awakens* Is Everything You Could Hope for in a *Star Wars* Movie—and Less." *Time*, December 16, 2015. https://time.com/4150168/review-star-wars-the-force-awakens.

Zachary, Brandon. "JJ Abrams: Carrie Fisher Is 'Very Much Alive with Us' in Rise of Skywalker." *CBR.com*. Last updated December 15, 2019. www.cbr.com/jj-abrams-carrie-fisher-is-very-much-alive-with-us-in-rise-of-skywalker/amp/.

Zapata, Kimberly. "Remembering Carrie Fisher & Her Contributions to Mental Health." *Greater Than Illness*, December 27, 2019. https://greaterthanillness.com/2019/12/27/remembering-carrie-fisher-her-contributions-to-mental-health/.

Zuckerman, Esther. " 'The Nerds Are Also Here': Talking With the Women Who Marched with Princess Leia." *AV Club*. Last updated January 24, 2017. https://film.avclub.com/the-nerds-are-also-here-talking-to-the-women-who-mar-1798256791.

Contributors

Ken Feil is an Assistant Professor in Emerson College's Visual and Media Arts Department. Recipient of a 2016/2017 National Endowment for the Humanities "Enduring Questions" grant, he is the author of *Rowan and Martin's Laugh-In* (2014) and *Dying for a Laugh: Disaster Movies and the Camp Imagination* (2005) in addition to articles for *Reading the Bromance* (2014) and the journal *Celebrity Studies*. His book on the queer, feminist comedy of Jacqueline Susann is forthcoming from Wayne State University Press.

Jennifer M. Fogel is an Associate Professor of Broadcasting and Mass Communication at SUNY-Oswego. Her research examines contemporary popular culture, particularly the way that gender is represented on television. Her previous work has analyzed the gendered marketing of *Star Wars* toys, cognitive dissonance in fandom, and articulations of family life in recent television series.

Cynthia A. Hoffner is a professor in the Department of Communication, Georgia State University. Her research focuses on media psychology, specifically psychological aspects of media uses and effects. Her recent work explores issues related to media and mental health, use of new media technologies for emotion regulation, the role of emotion in media selection and response, and parasocial relationships with media figures.

Maghan Jackson is a PhD candidate and Distinguished University Fellow in the Department of Women's, Gender, and Sexuality Studies at the Ohio State University. Her current work considers queer utopian temporalities in speculative fiction and secondary fan production, and her interest in fan practices encompasses properties from Sherlock Holmes to the Marvel Cinematic Universe to (of course) *Star Wars*.

Philipp Dominik Keidl is a postdoctoral fellow in the Graduate Research Training Program "Configurations of Film" at Goethe University Frankfurt. He holds a master's degree in Preservation and Presentation of the

Moving Image from the University of Amsterdam and a PhD in Film and Moving Image Studies from Concordia University in Montreal. His research concentrates on fandom, media and material culture, and moving image preservation and exhibition.

Andrew Kemp-Wilcox is a PhD candidate at Georgia State University specializing in studies in video games, film, and new media, with particular interest in audience engagement, digital adaptation, and new modes of narrative. Andrew has worked professionally in media creation as a screenwriter and content creator as well as a video game writer, designer, and producer.

Slade Kinnecott is a pseudonym, but the person behind her has been a film historian for thirty years, specializing in film preservation and media archiving for twenty. She has worked primarily on movie sets, in university archives, and for museums. She has lived in several of the United States and countless mental ones. She currently lives on her nonnative coast with her husband and emotional support reptile, doing the best she can to pass as a functional adult—and at times even perhaps a successful and wise one.

Linda Mizejewski is a Distinguished Arts and Sciences Professor of Women's, Gender, and Sexuality Studies at the Ohio State University. She is the author of five monographs on women in film and popular culture, including *Pretty/Funny: Women Comedians and Body Politics* (2014). With Victoria Sturtevant, she is the coeditor of the anthology *Hysterical! Women in American Comedy* (2017), which won the Susan Koppelman Prize from the Popular Culture Association.

Sejung Park is an assistant professor in the Division of Global and Interdisciplinary Studies, Pukyong National University. Her research focuses on the role of new digital technologies in health communication, public diplomacy, and social network analysis. Her recent work examines public engagement in issues on social media, health and environmental communication using new media and its influence on public perceptions and behaviors, and crisis communication.

Lindsay van Ekelenburg is an artist and illustrator based in Hamilton, Ontario, specializing in watercolor and ink. Her work *Our Heavenly Mother* graces the cover of this anthology and her piece *Blessed Rebel Queen* inspired its title. Most of her pieces are heavily inspired by women and nature, and her gentle and organic use of her preferred mediums capture the delicate grace of her subject matter. Lindsay has also done illustration and design work for many small businesses and NGOs in Ontario. Find out more about Lindsay and her work at her website, https://www.lindsayvanek.com or contact her directly at lindsayvanek.art@gmail.com regarding commissions.

Kristen Anderson Wagner is the author of *Comic Venus: Women and Comedy in American Silent Film* (2017). Her work on the intersections of gender and genre has been published in *Hysterical! Women in American Comedy* (2014), *Not So Silent: Women in Cinema before Sound* (2010), *The Blackwell Companion to Film Comedy* (2012), and the journals *Feminist Media Histories* and *Velvet Light Trap*. She works as an adjunct professor in Northern California and lives with a child who refuses to watch *Star Wars*.

Tanya D. Zuk is a Moving Image Studies PhD candidate at Georgia State University in the School of Film, Media, and Theater. Her work has been published in the *Journal of Religion and Popular Culture* and the *Journal of Transformative Works and Culture*. With a background in television, audience reception, and LGBTQ+ studies, her current research focuses on new media, minority self-representation, and collaborative authorship between indie creatives and audience-participants.

Index

Italicized page numbers indicate photographs.